The Heart Burns
Even Though The Rain Falls

BLEACH THE
58 FIRE

Shonen Jump Manga

ALL STARS★ AND

山本元柳斎重國
ヤマモトゲンリュウサイシゲクニ

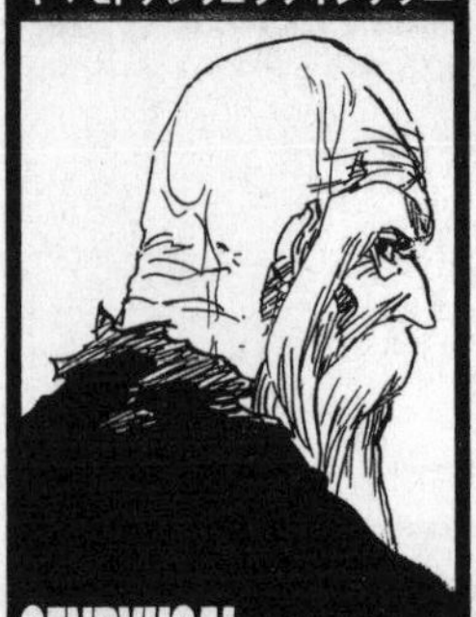

GENRYUSAI SHIGEKUNI YAMAMOTO

黒崎一護
クロサキイチゴ

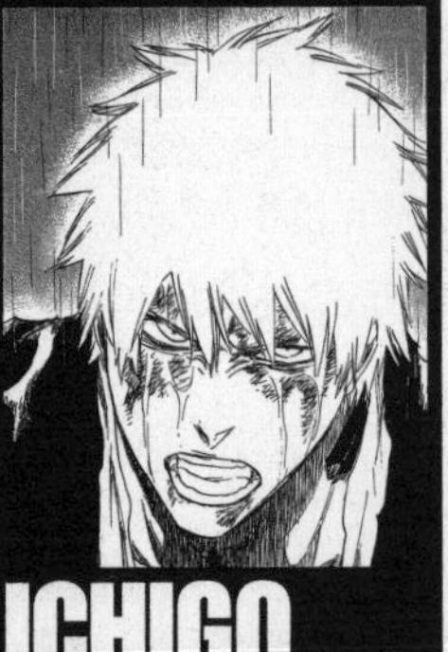

ICHIGO KUROSAKI

plot

Ichigo Kurosaki meets Soul Reaper Rukia Kuchiki and ends up helping her eradicate Hollows. After developing his powers as a Soul Reaper, Ichigo enters battle against Aizen and his dark ambitions! Ichigo finally defeats Aizen in exchange for his powers as a Soul Reaper.

With the battle over, Ichigo regains his normal life. But his tranquil days end when he meets Ginjo, who offers to help Ichigo get his powers back. But it was all a plot by Ginjo to steal Ichigo's new powers! Ginjo, who was the first ever Deputy Soul Reaper, then reveals to Ichigo the truth behind the deputy badge. However, even after learning of the Soul Society's plans for him, Ichigo chooses to continue protecting his friends and defeats Ginjo.

Suddenly, a group calling itself the Vandenreich launches a full-on invasion of the Soul Society. Facing off against the Vandenreich's king, Yhwach, Yamamoto unleashes his bankai and cuts through his foe. But as Yhwach lies dying, he utters a mysterious apology...

BLEACH
VOL. 58: THE FIRE
SHONEN JUMP Manga Edition

STORY AND ART BY
TITE KUBO

Translation/Joe Yamazaki
Touch-up Art & Lettering/Mark McMurray
Design/Kam Li
Editor/Alexis Kirsch

Printed in the U.S.A.

Published by VIZ Media, LLC
P.O. Box 77010
San Francisco, CA 94107

10 9 8 7 6 5 4 3 2 1
First printing, October 2013

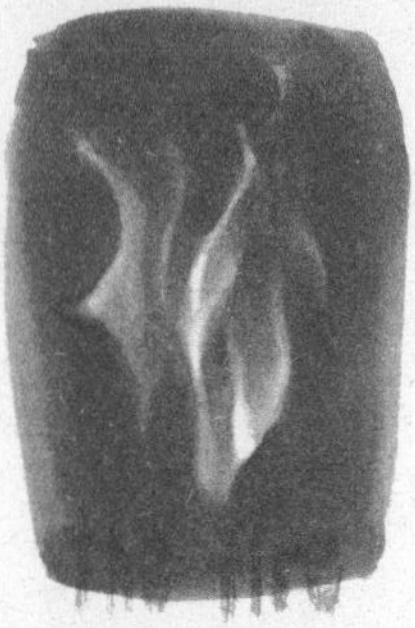

I've been catching bad colds every year lately, and it's taking even longer to recover. I've always been prone to sickness, and it's really starting to affect me. I hope I can finish the series before totally collapsing!

-Tite Kubo

Bleach is author Tite Kubo's second title. Kubo made his debut with *ZOMBIEPOWDER.*, a four-volume series for *Weekly Shonen Jump*. To date, *Bleach* has been translated into numerous languages and has also inspired an animated TV series that began airing in the U.S. in 2006. Beginning its serialization in 2001, *Bleach* is still a mainstay in the pages of *Weekly Shonen Jump*. In 2005, *Bleach* was awarded the prestigious Shogakukan Manga Award in the *shonen* (boys) category.

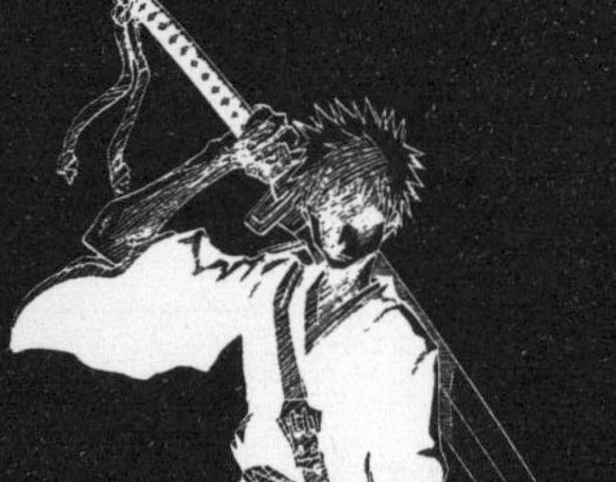

BLEACH

HASCHWALTH

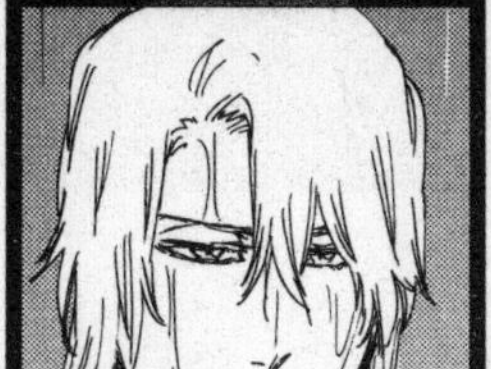

ハッシュヴァルト

YHWACH

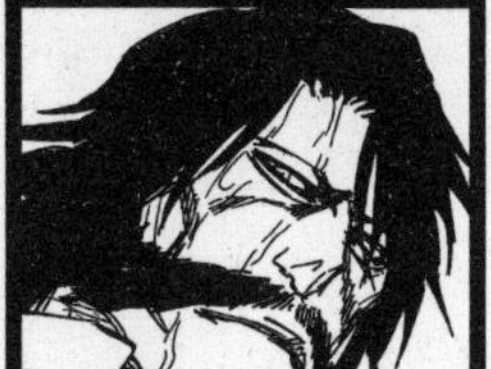

ユーハバッハ

STORIES

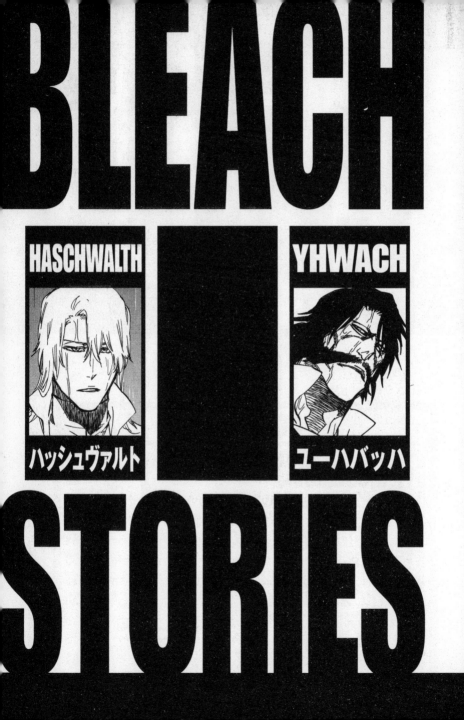

BLEACH 58

THE FIRE

CONTENTS

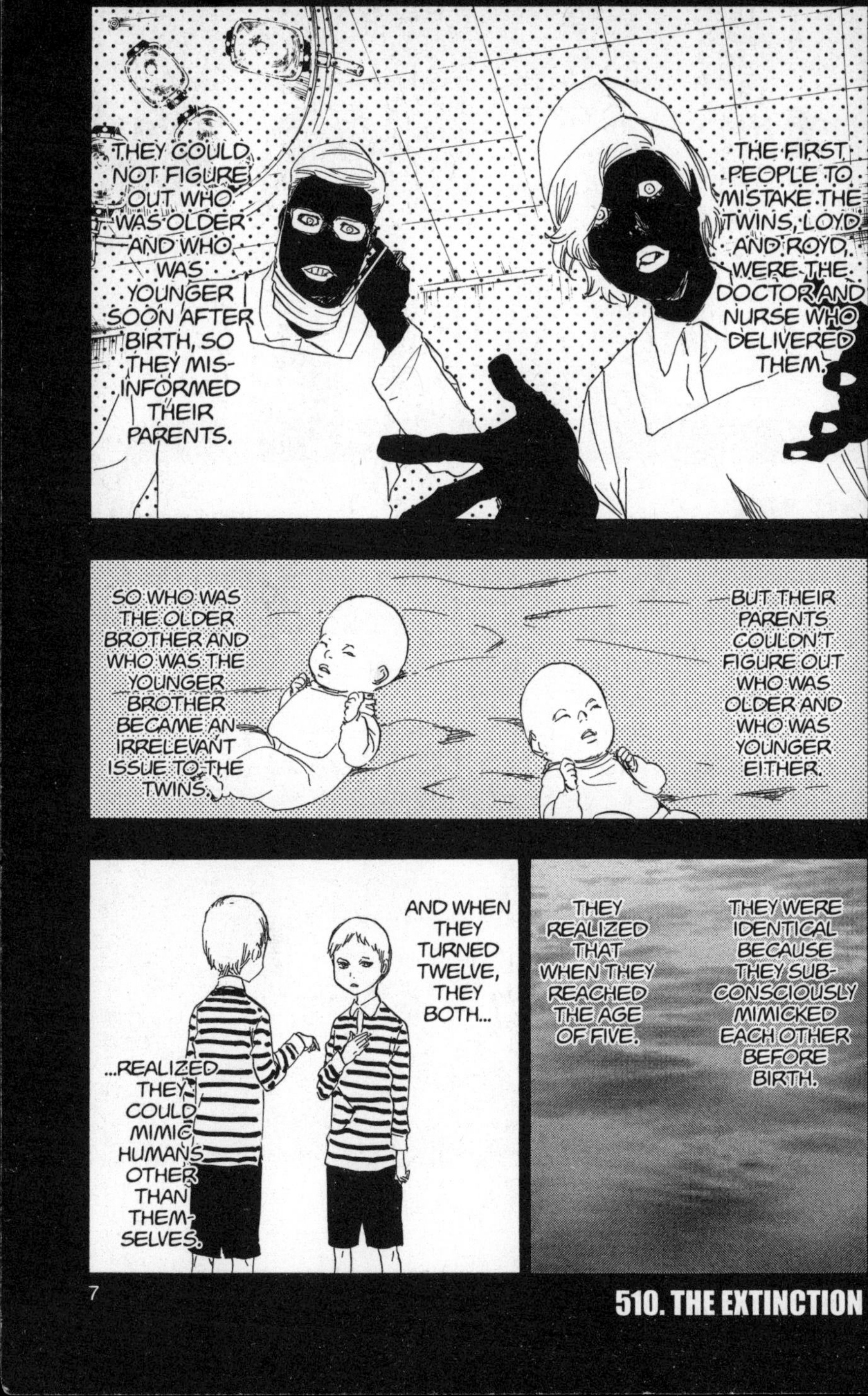
THE FIRST PEOPLE TO MISTAKE THE TWINS, LOYD AND ROYD, WERE THE DOCTOR AND NURSE WHO DELIVERED THEM.
THEY COULD NOT FIGURE OUT WHO WAS OLDER AND WHO WAS YOUNGER SOON AFTER BIRTH, SO THEY MIS-INFORMED THEIR PARENTS.
BUT THEIR PARENTS COULDN'T FIGURE OUT WHO WAS OLDER AND WHO WAS YOUNGER EITHER.
SO WHO WAS THE OLDER BROTHER AND WHO WAS THE YOUNGER BROTHER BECAME AN IRRELEVANT ISSUE TO THE TWINS.
THEY WERE IDENTICAL BECAUSE THEY SUB-CONSCIOUSLY MIMICKED EACH OTHER BEFORE BIRTH.
THEY REALIZED THAT WHEN THEY REACHED THE AGE OF FIVE.
AND WHEN THEY TURNED TWELVE, THEY BOTH...
...REALIZED THEY COULD MIMIC HUMANS OTHER THAN THEM-SELVES.

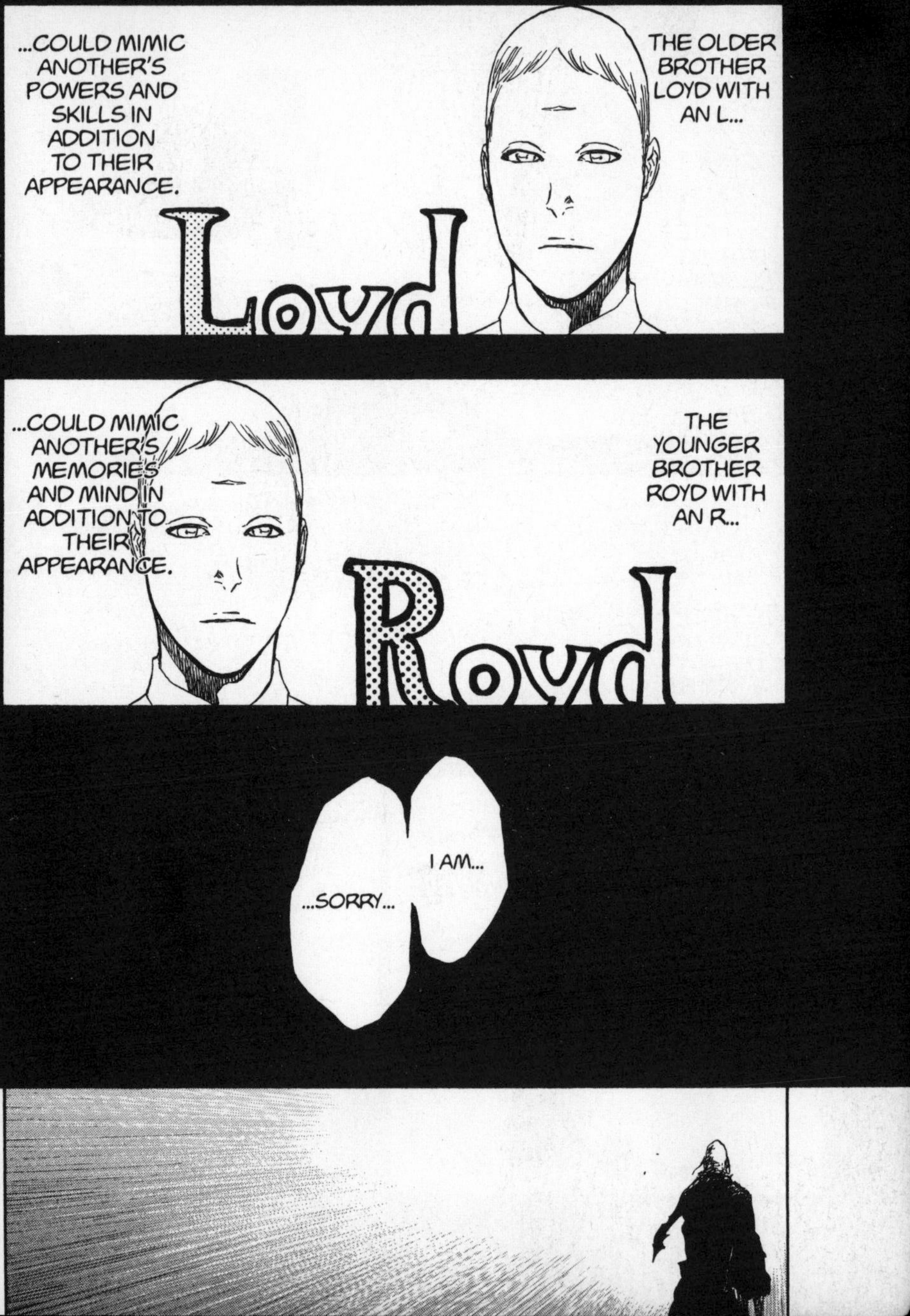
THE OLDER BROTHER LOYD WITH AN L...
...COULD MIMIC ANOTHER'S POWERS AND SKILLS IN ADDITION TO THEIR APPEARANCE.
Loyd
THE YOUNGER BROTHER ROYD WITH AN R...
...COULD MIMIC ANOTHER'S MEMORIES AND MIND IN ADDITION TO THEIR APPEARANCE.
Royd
I AM...
...SORRY...

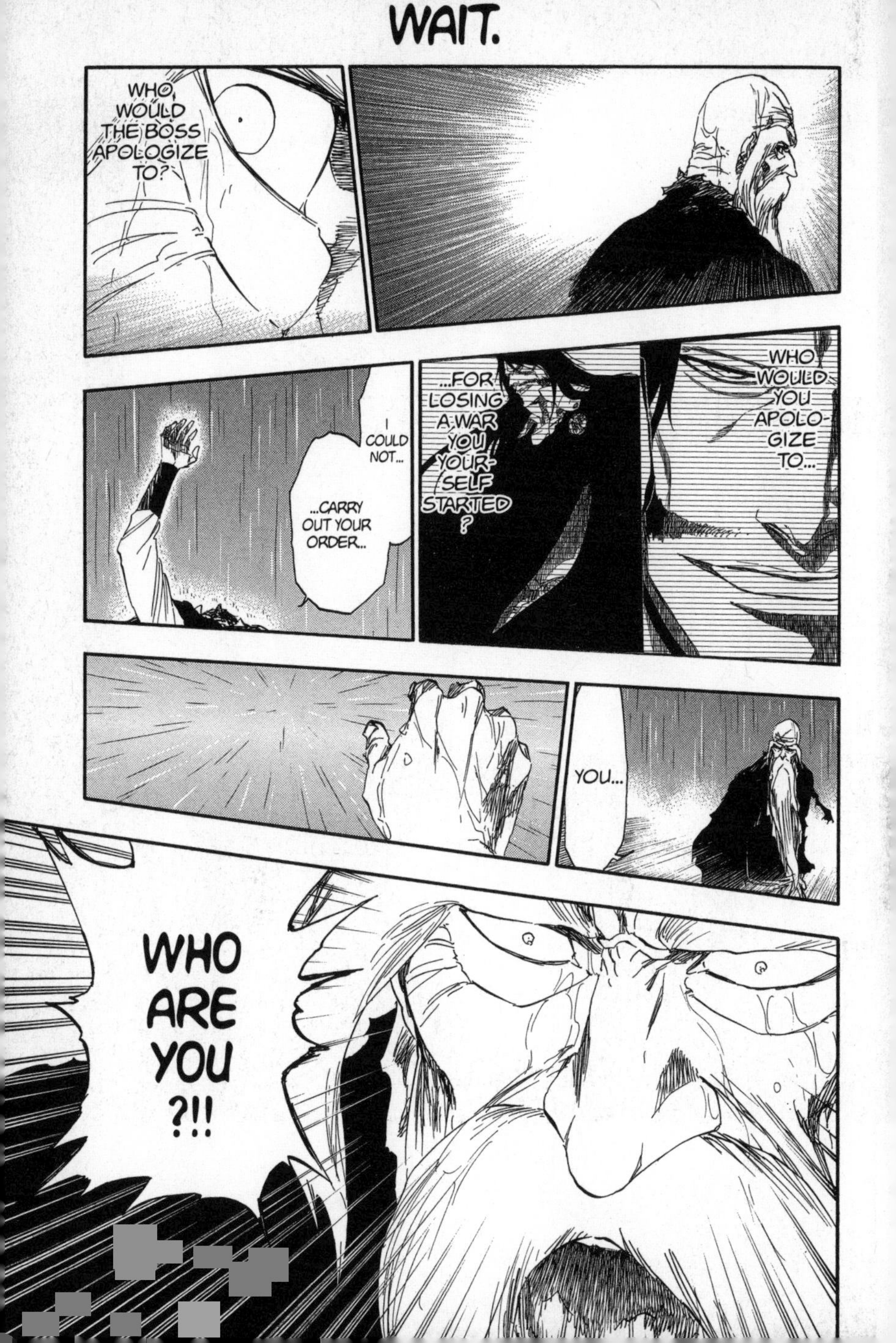
WAIT.
WHO WOULD THE BOSS APOLOGIZE TO?
WHO WOULD YOU APOLOGIZE TO...
...FOR LOSING A WAR YOU YOURSELF STARTED?
I COULD NOT...
...CARRY OUT YOUR ORDER...
YOU...
WHO ARE YOU ?!!

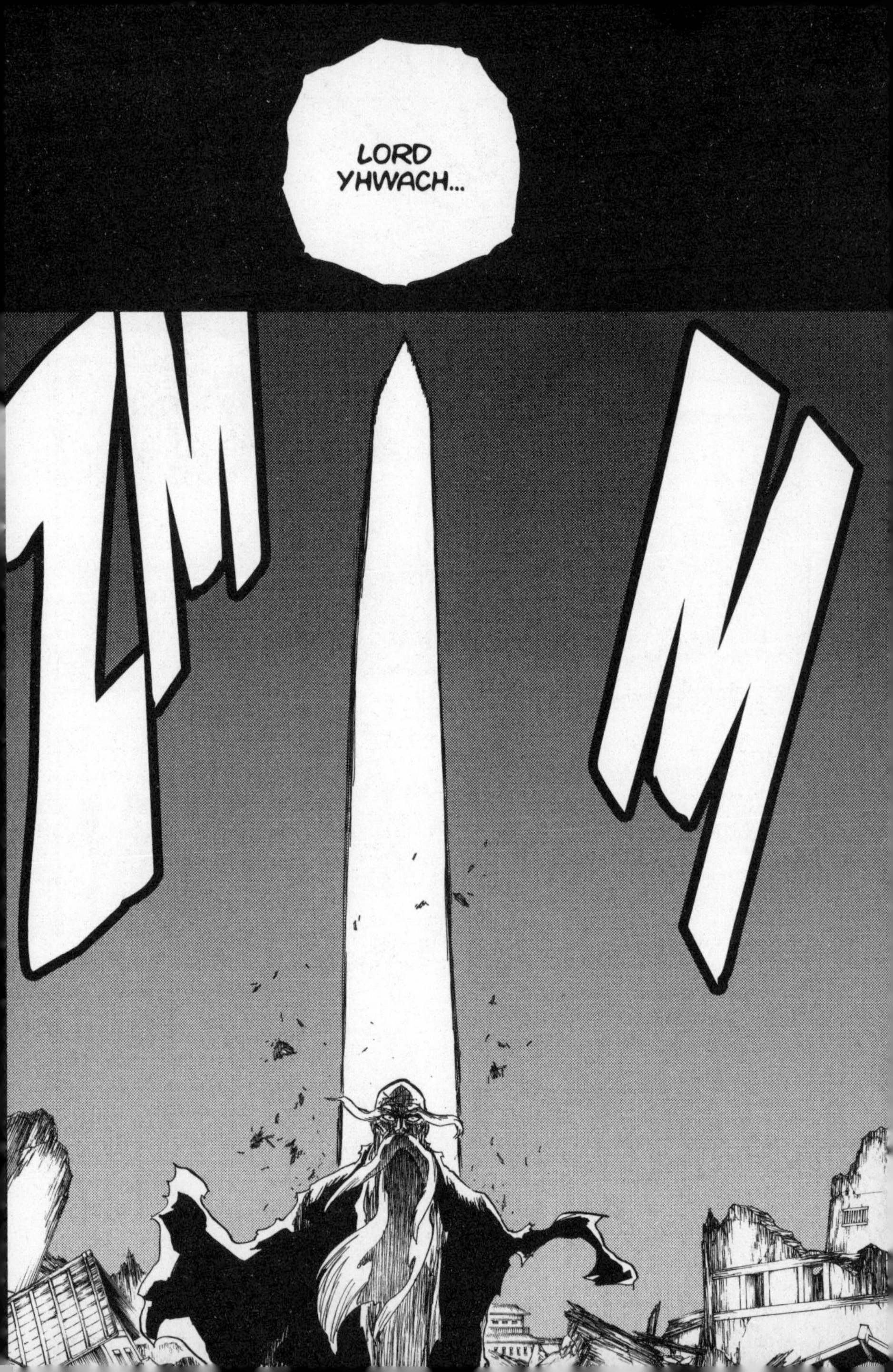
LORD YHWACH...
ZMM

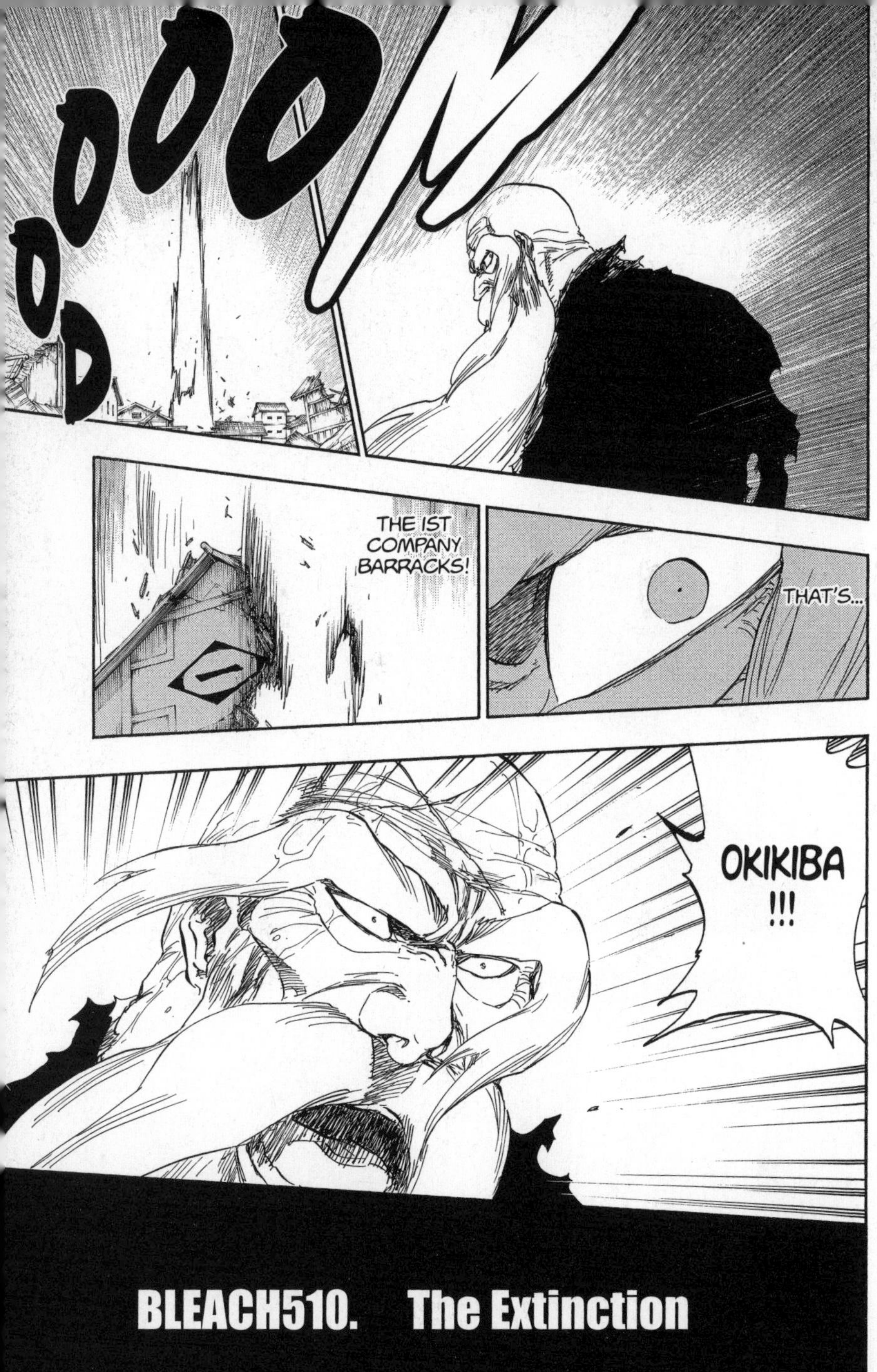
DOOOOOOM
THAT'S...
THE 1ST COMPANY BARRACKS!
OKIKIBA!!!

BLEACH510. The Extinction

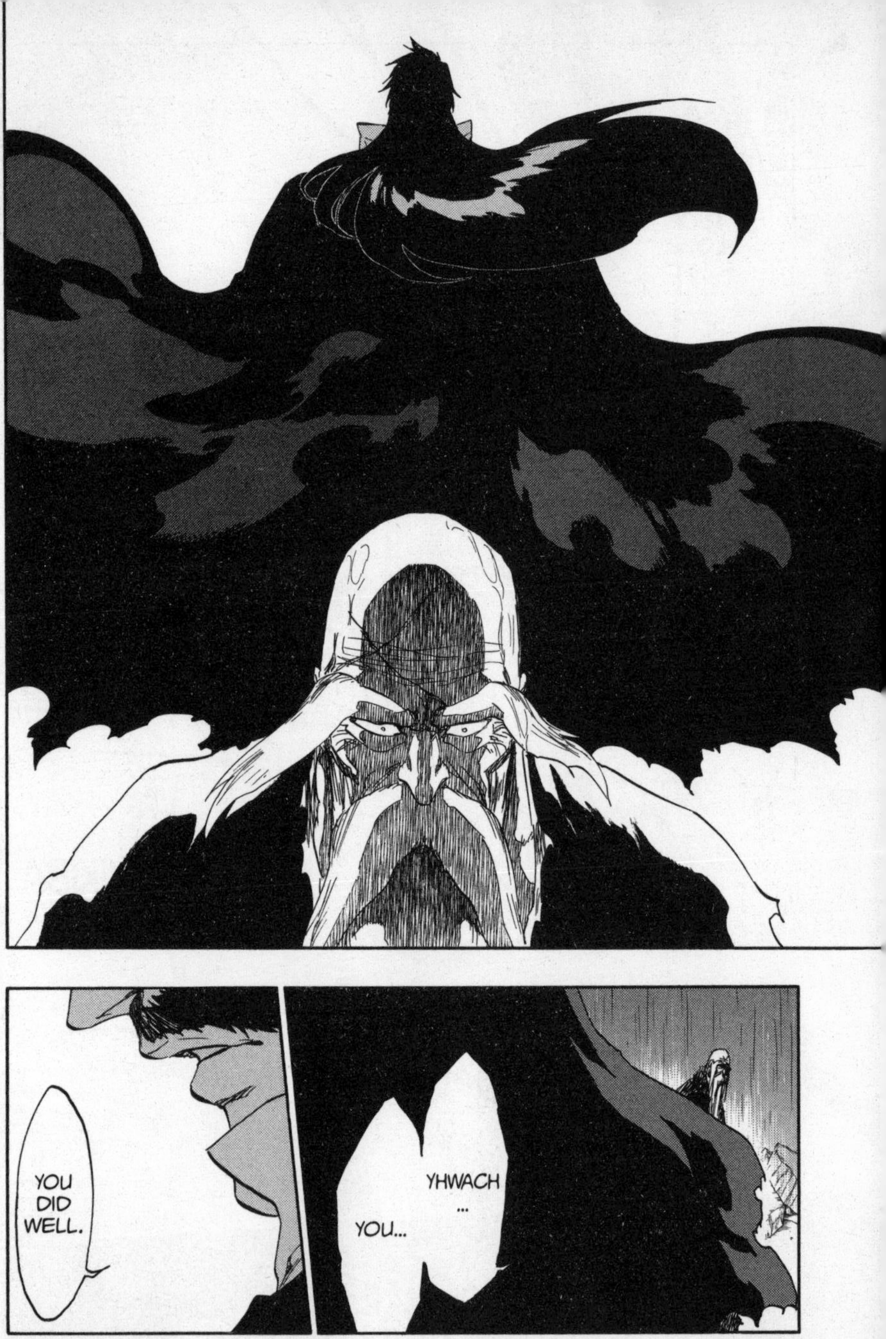
YHWACH...
YOU...
YOU DID WELL.

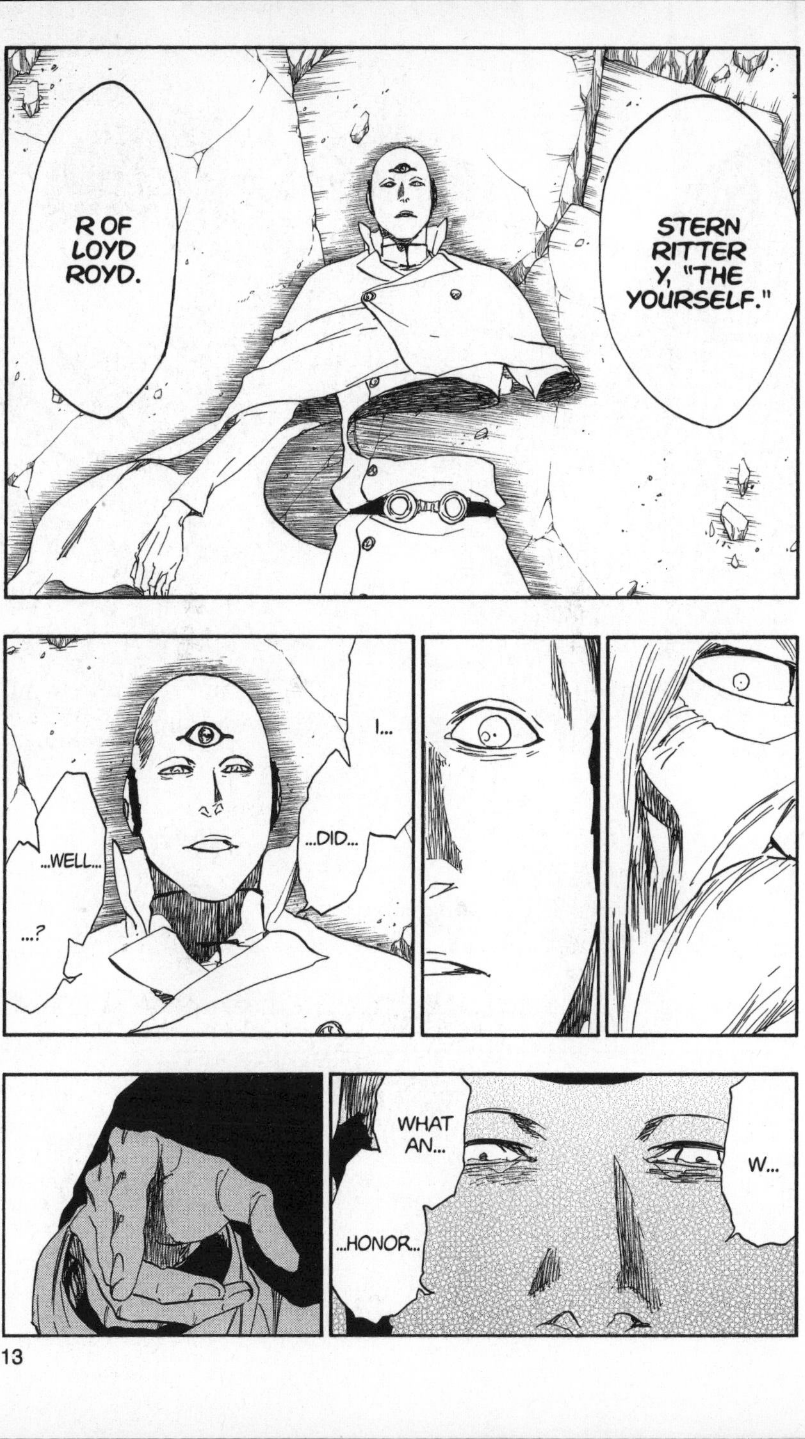
STERN RITTER Y, "THE YOURSELF."
R OF LOYD ROYD.
I...
...DID...
...WELL...
...?
W...
WHAT AN...
...HONOR...

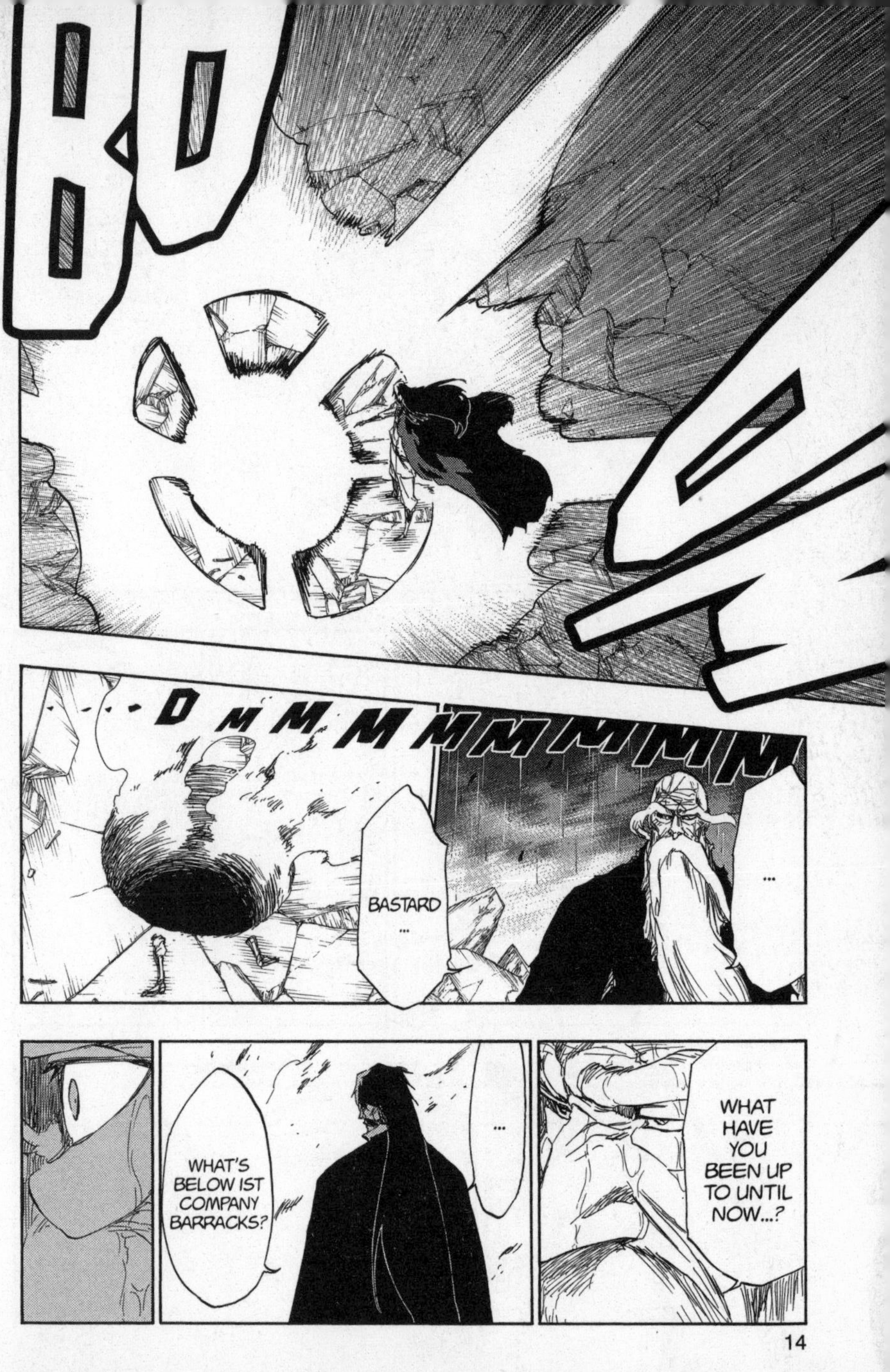

...DMMMMMMMMMM
...
BASTARD ...
WHAT HAVE YOU BEEN UP TO UNTIL NOW...?
...
WHAT'S BELOW IST COMPANY BARRACKS?

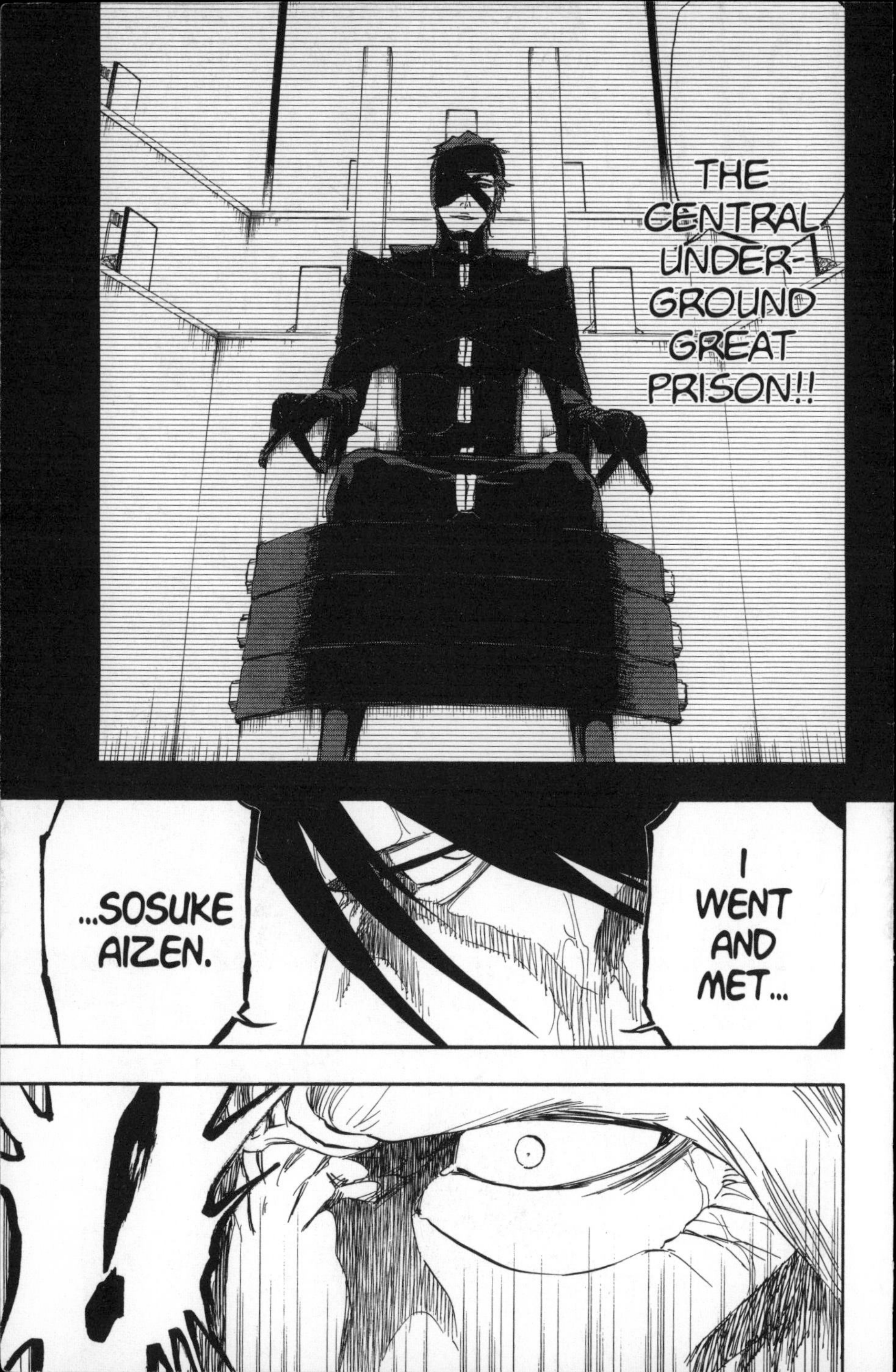
THE CENTRAL UNDER-GROUND GREAT PRISON!!
I WENT AND MET...
...SOSUKE AIZEN.

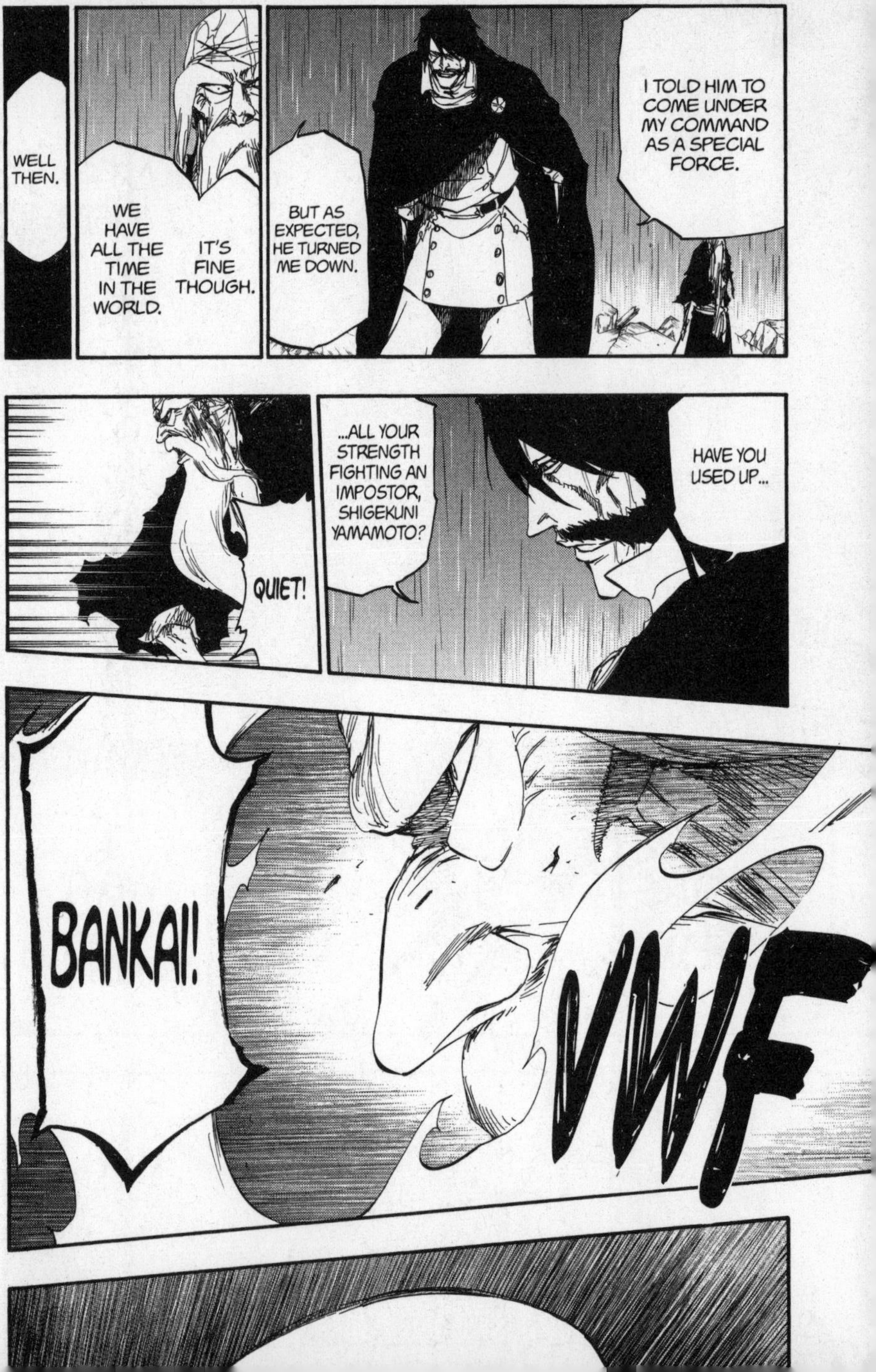

I TOLD HIM TO COME UNDER MY COMMAND AS A SPECIAL FORCE.
BUT AS EXPECTED, HE TURNED ME DOWN.
IT'S FINE THOUGH.
WE HAVE ALL THE TIME IN THE WORLD.
WELL THEN.
HAVE YOU USED UP...
...ALL YOUR STRENGTH FIGHTING AN IMPOSTOR, SHIGEKUNI YAMAMOTO?
QUIET!
VWF
BANKAI!

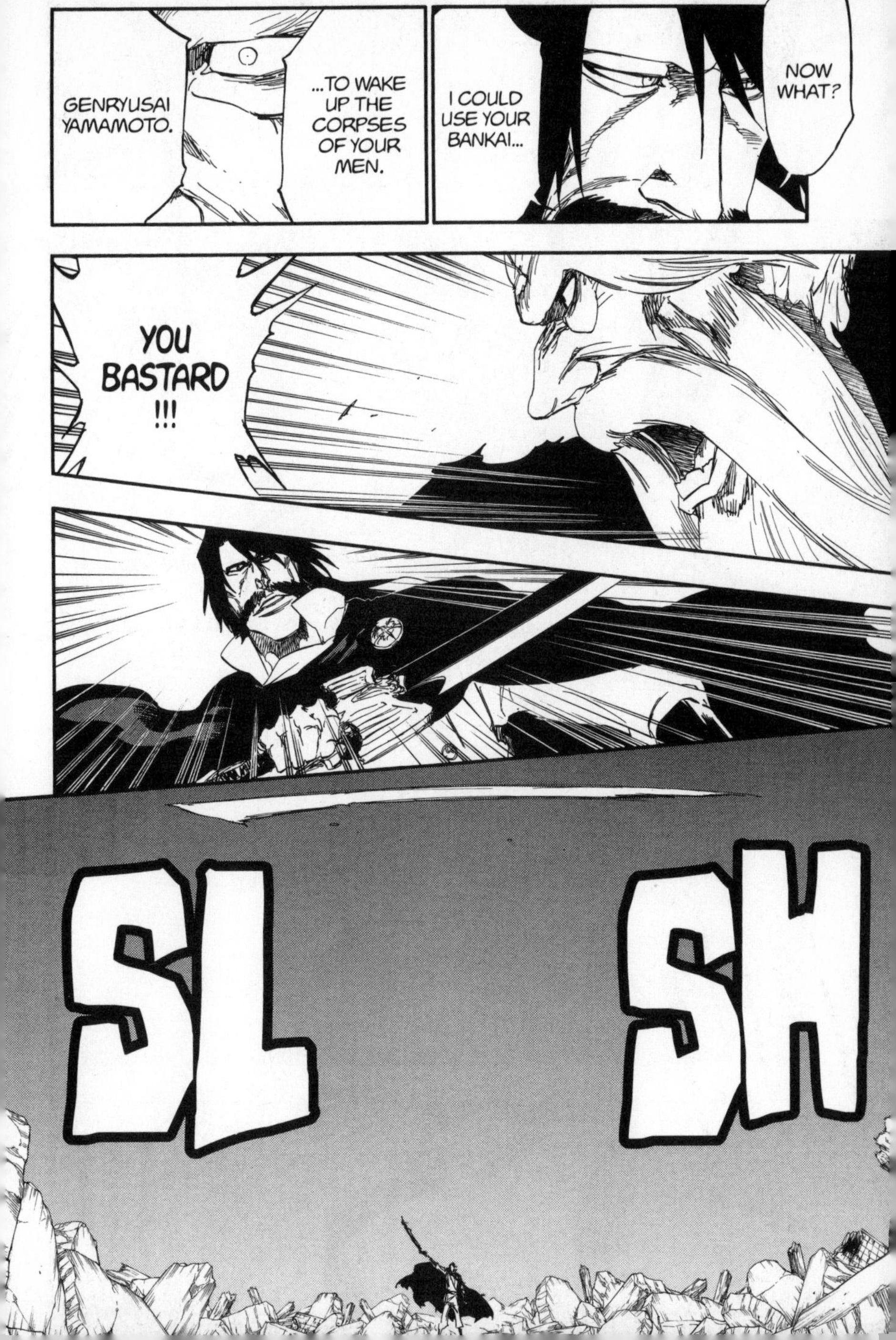
NOW WHAT?
I COULD USE YOUR BANKAI...
...TO WAKE UP THE CORPSES OF YOUR MEN.
GENRYUSAI YAMAMOTO.
YOU BASTARD !!!
SL SH

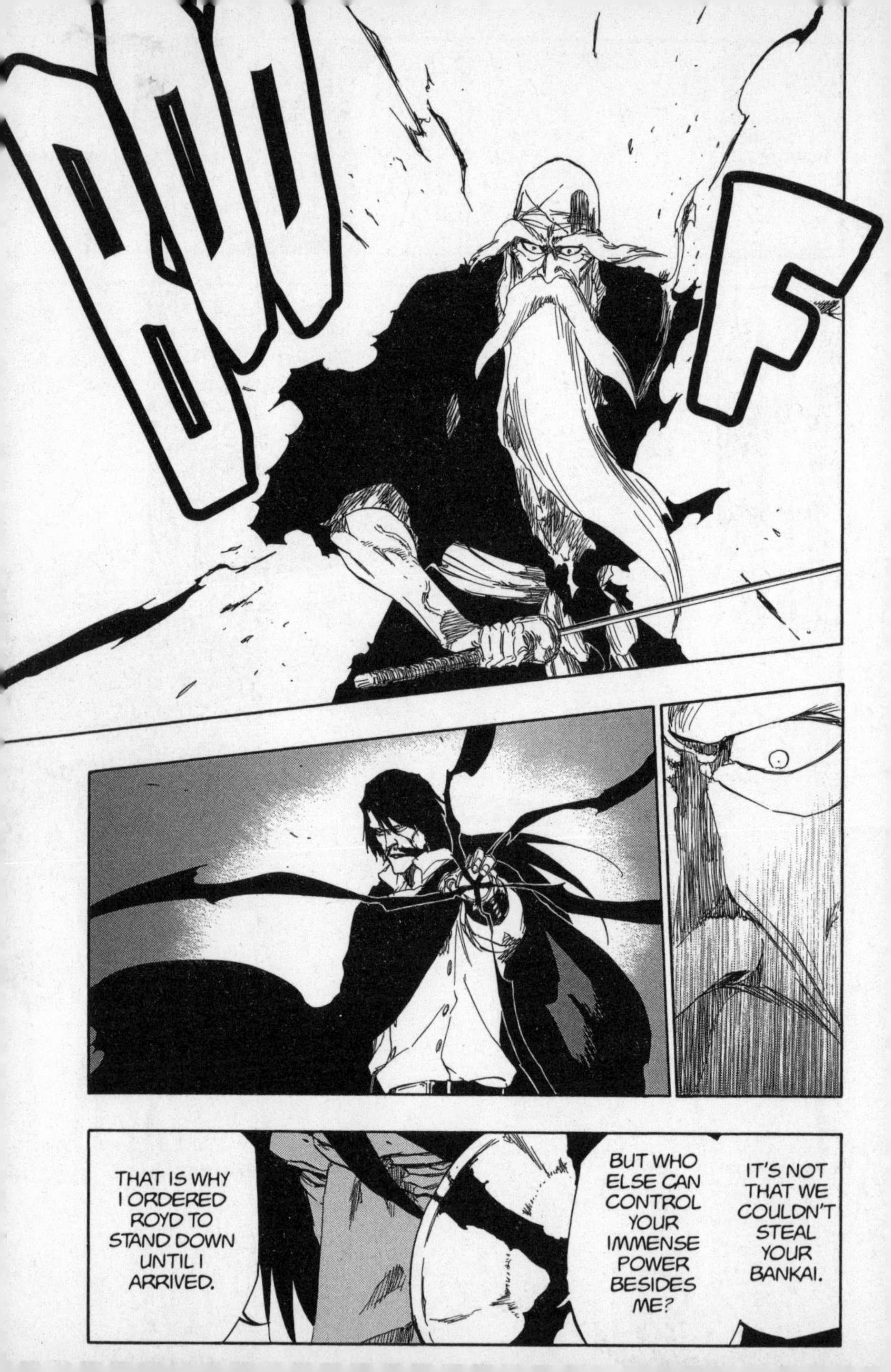
BOOF
IT'S NOT THAT WE COULDN'T STEAL YOUR BANKAI.
BUT WHO ELSE CAN CONTROL YOUR IMMENSE POWER BESIDES ME?
THAT IS WHY I ORDERED ROYD TO STAND DOWN UNTIL I ARRIVED.

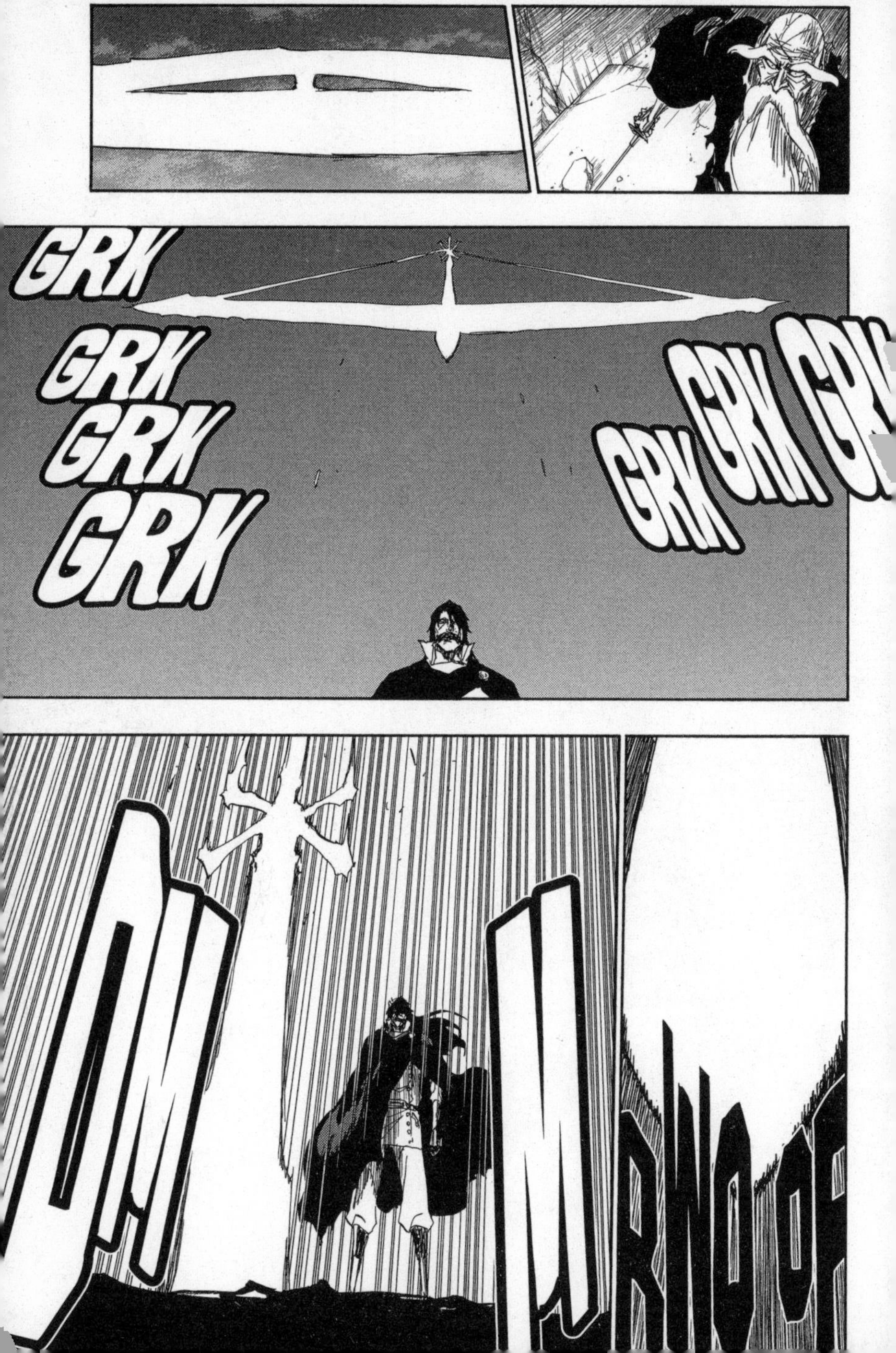
GRK GRK GRK
GRK
GRK
GRK
GRK

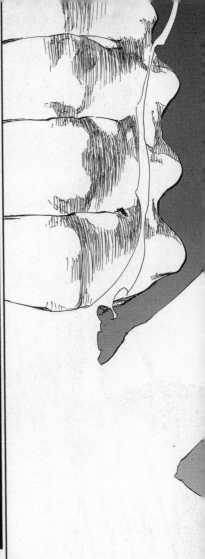
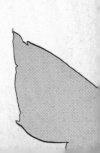

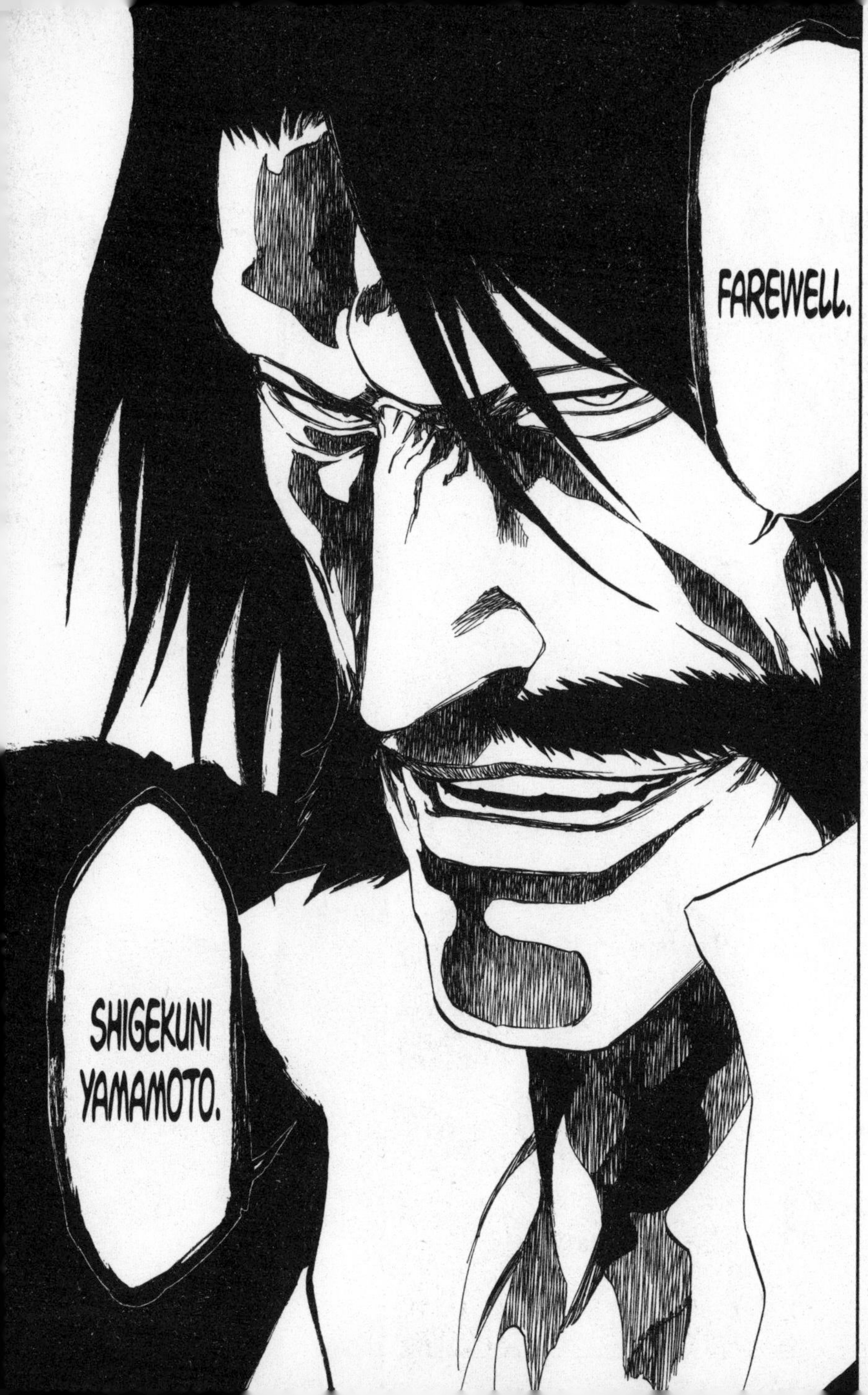
FAREWELL.
SHIGEKUNI YAMAMOTO.

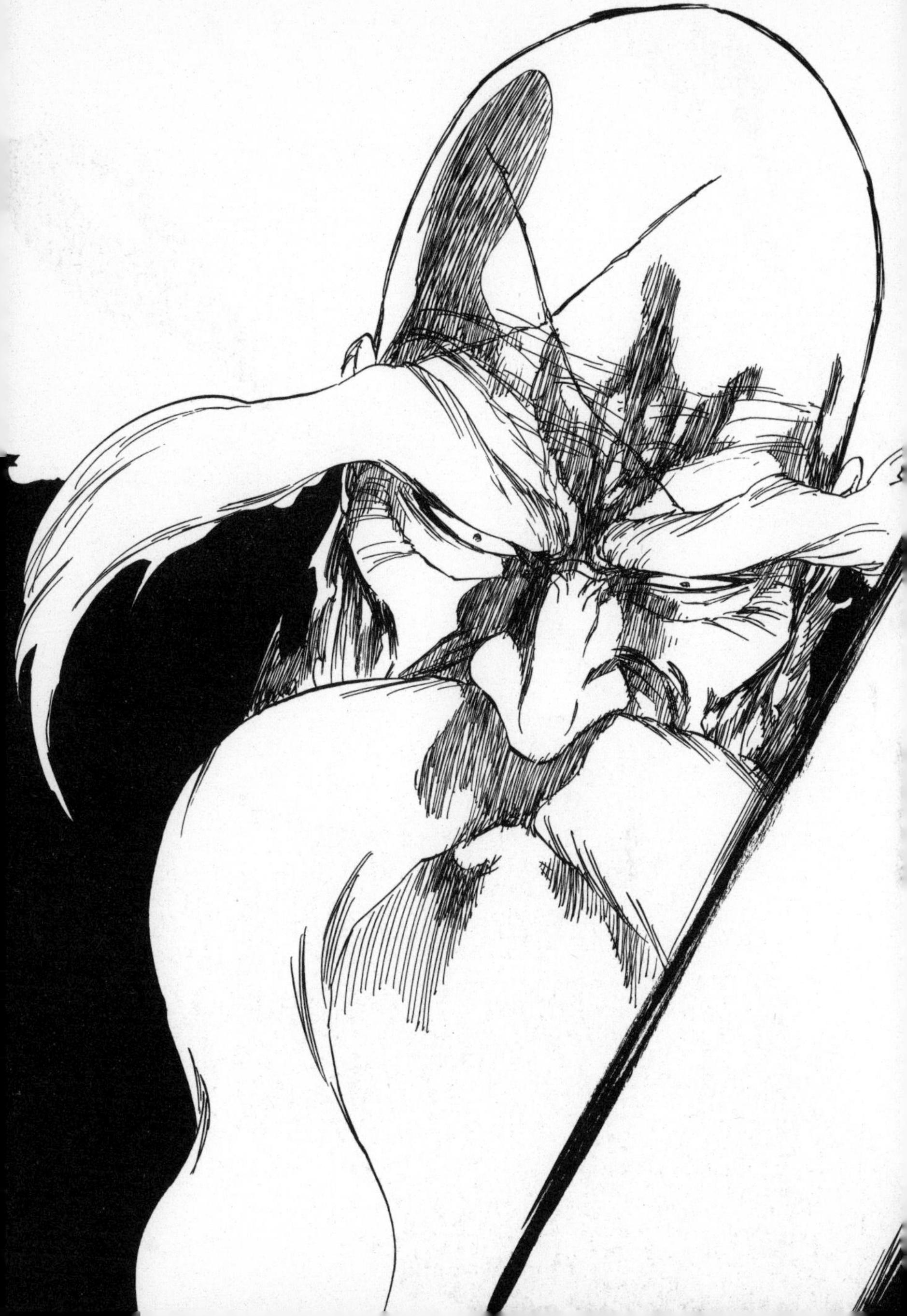

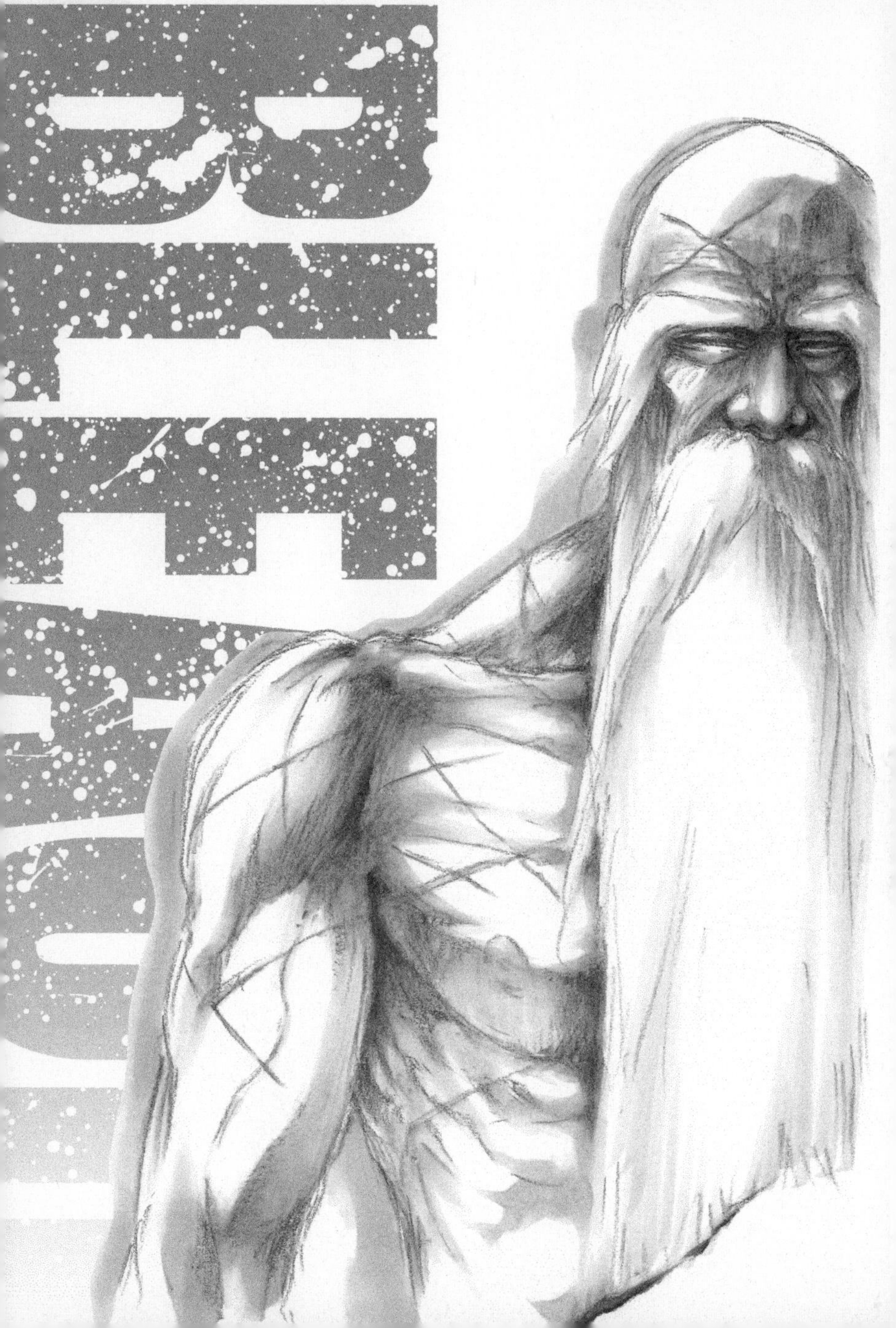

BLEACH
ブリーチ

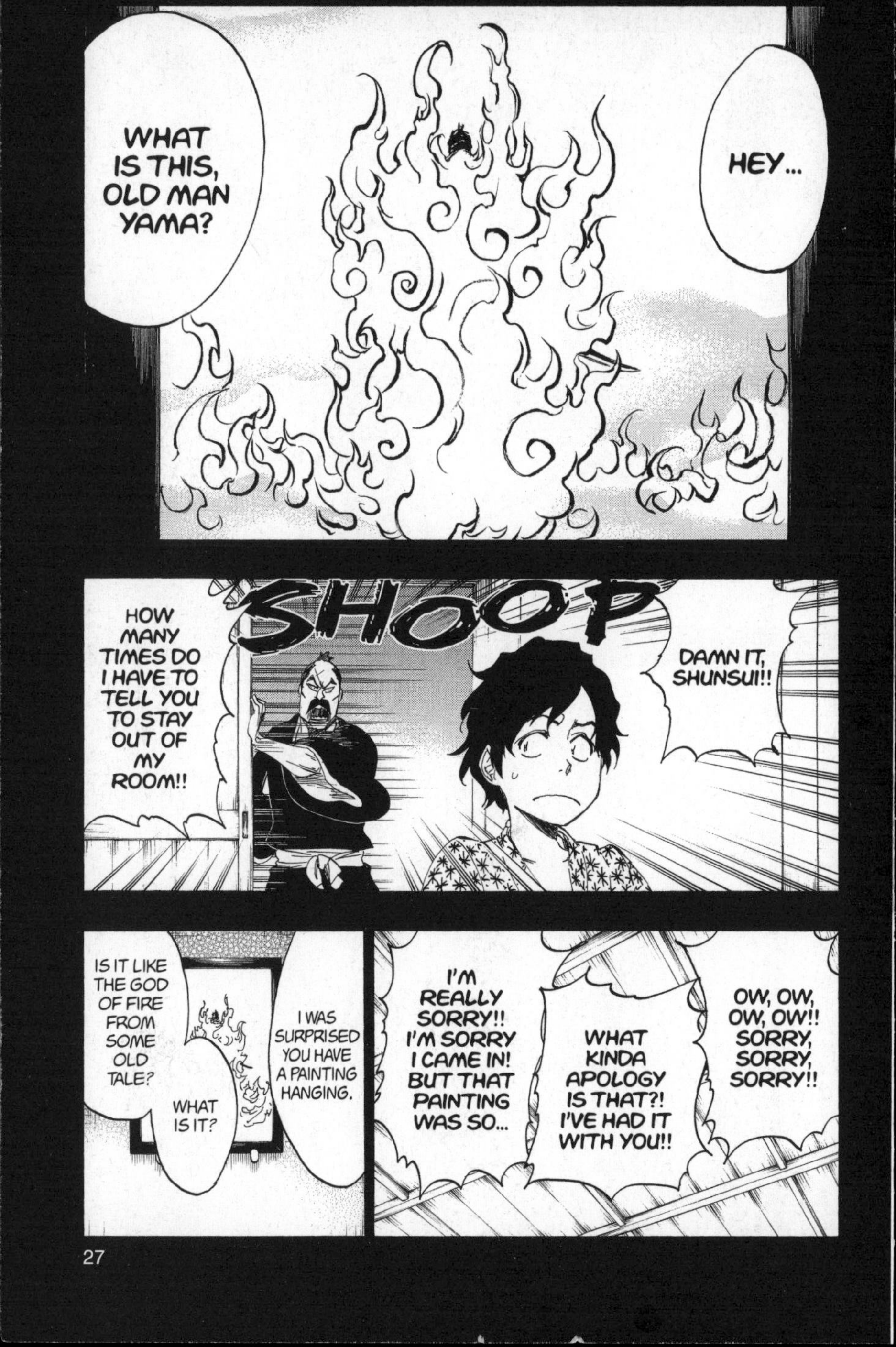
HEY...
WHAT IS THIS, OLD MAN YAMA?
SHOOP
DAMN IT, SHUNSUI!!
HOW MANY TIMES DO I HAVE TO TELL YOU TO STAY OUT OF MY ROOM!!
OW, OW, OW, OW!! SORRY, SORRY, SORRY!!
WHAT KINDA APOLOGY IS THAT?! I'VE HAD IT WITH YOU!!
I'M REALLY SORRY!! I'M SORRY I CAME IN! BUT THAT PAINTING WAS SO...
I WAS SURPRISED YOU HAVE A PAINTING HANGING.
IS IT LIKE THE GOD OF FIRE FROM SOME OLD TALE?
WHAT IS IT?

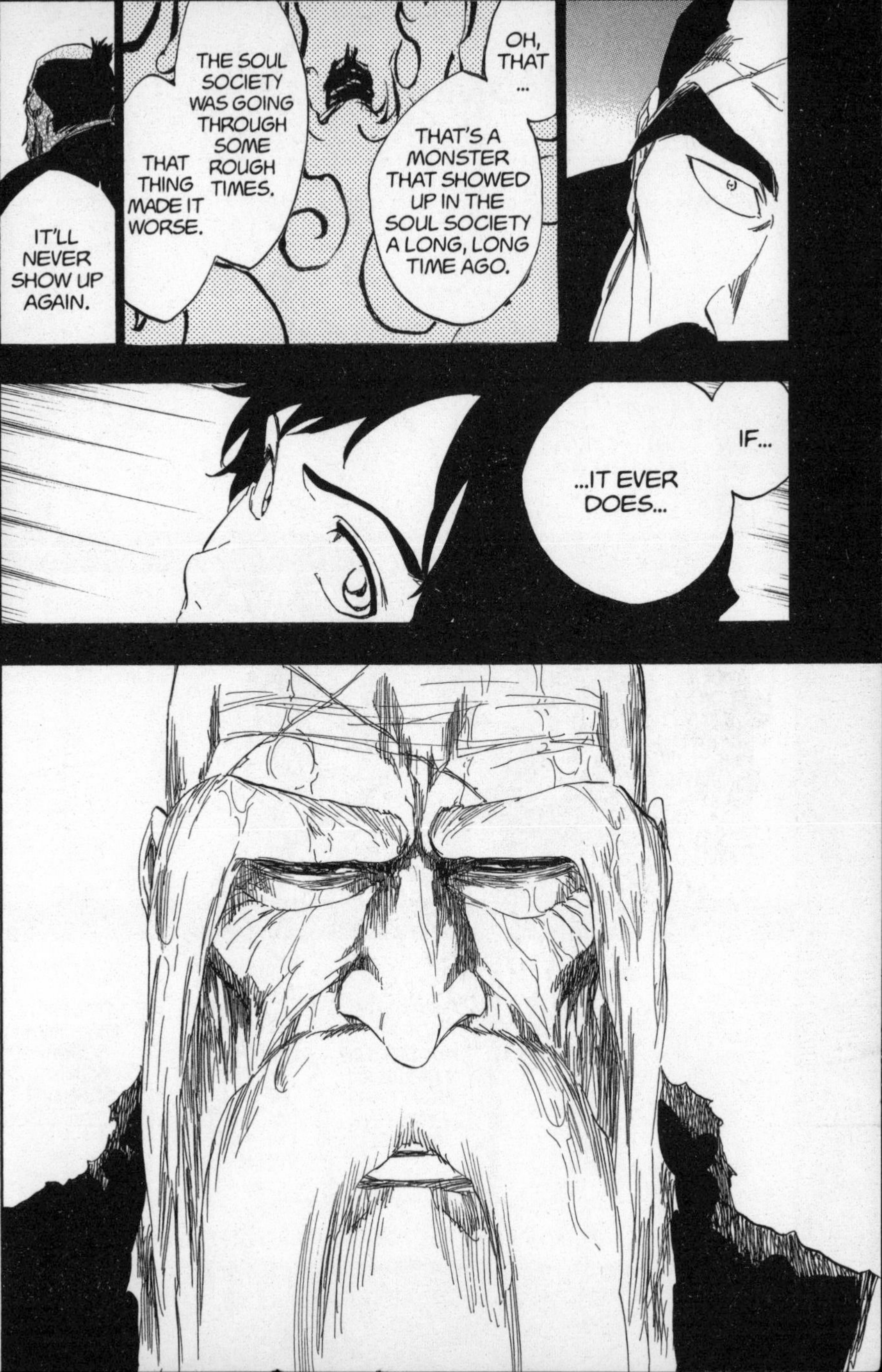
OH, THAT ...
THAT'S A MONSTER THAT SHOWED UP IN THE SOUL SOCIETY A LONG, LONG TIME AGO.
THE SOUL SOCIETY WAS GOING THROUGH SOME ROUGH TIMES.
THAT THING MADE IT WORSE.
IT'LL NEVER SHOW UP AGAIN.
IF...
...IT EVER DOES...

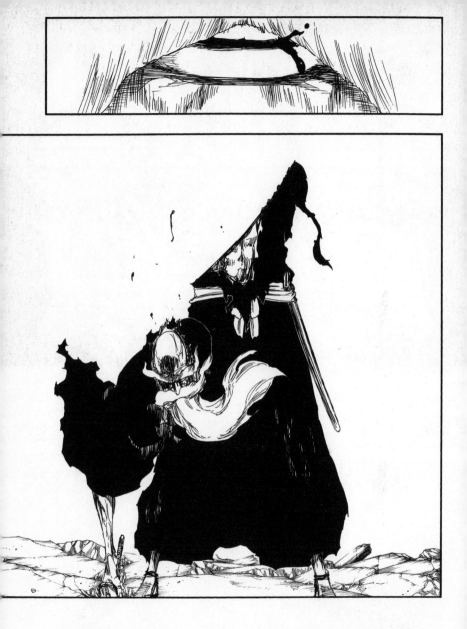

...I'LL PROBABLY NEVER BE BACK HERE AGAIN.

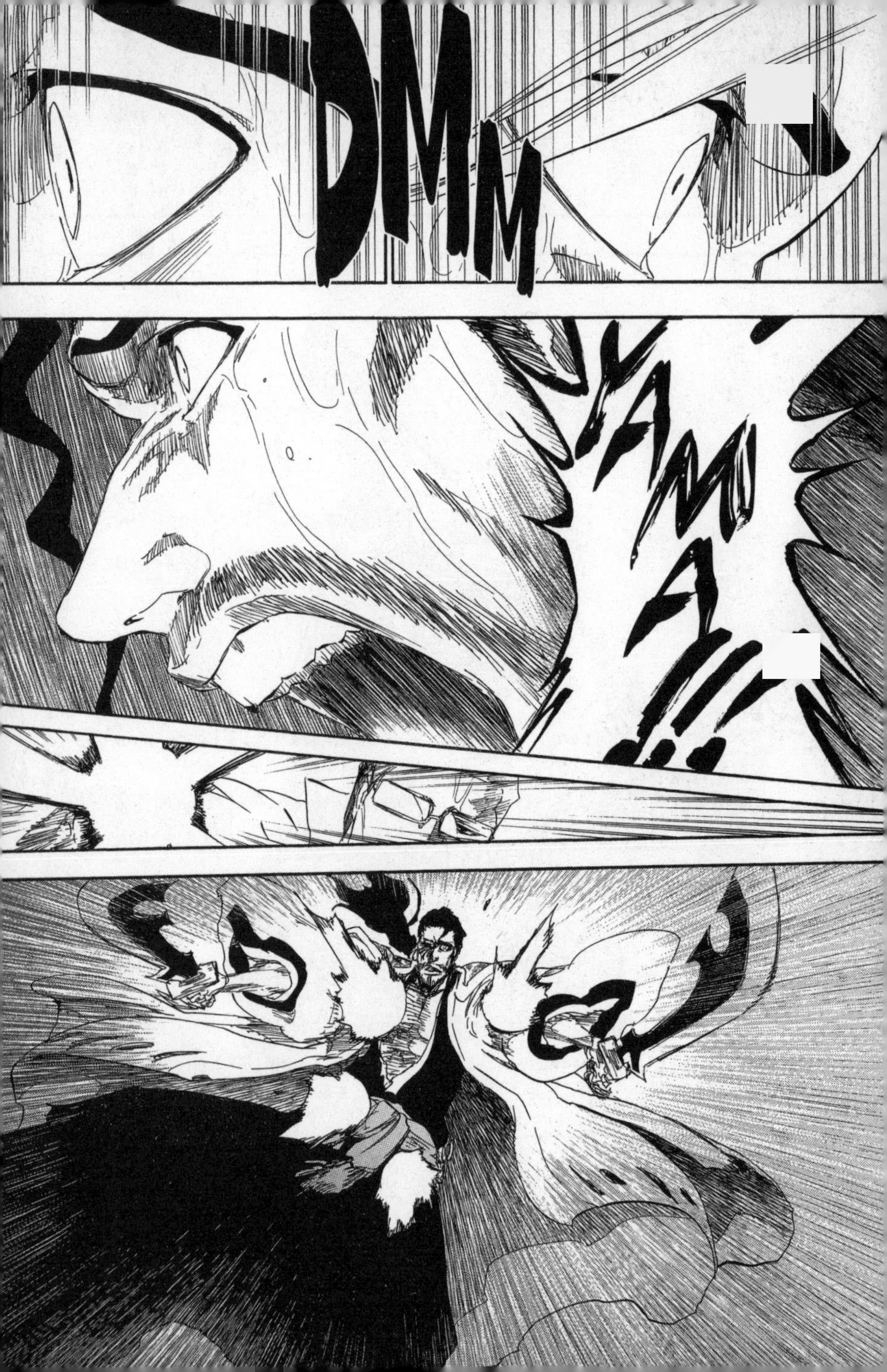
DMM

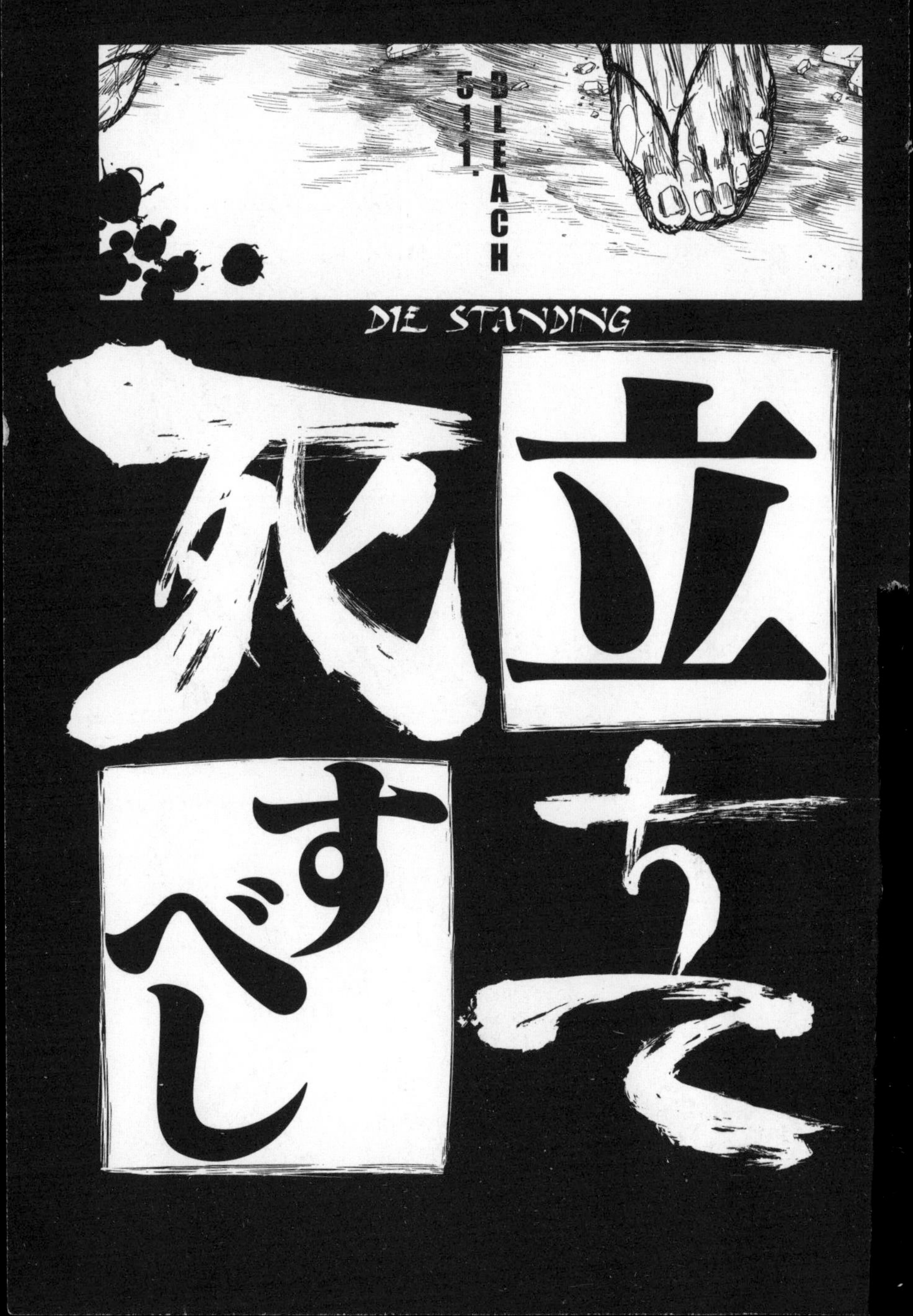
BLEACH
511.
DIE STANDING
立って死すべし

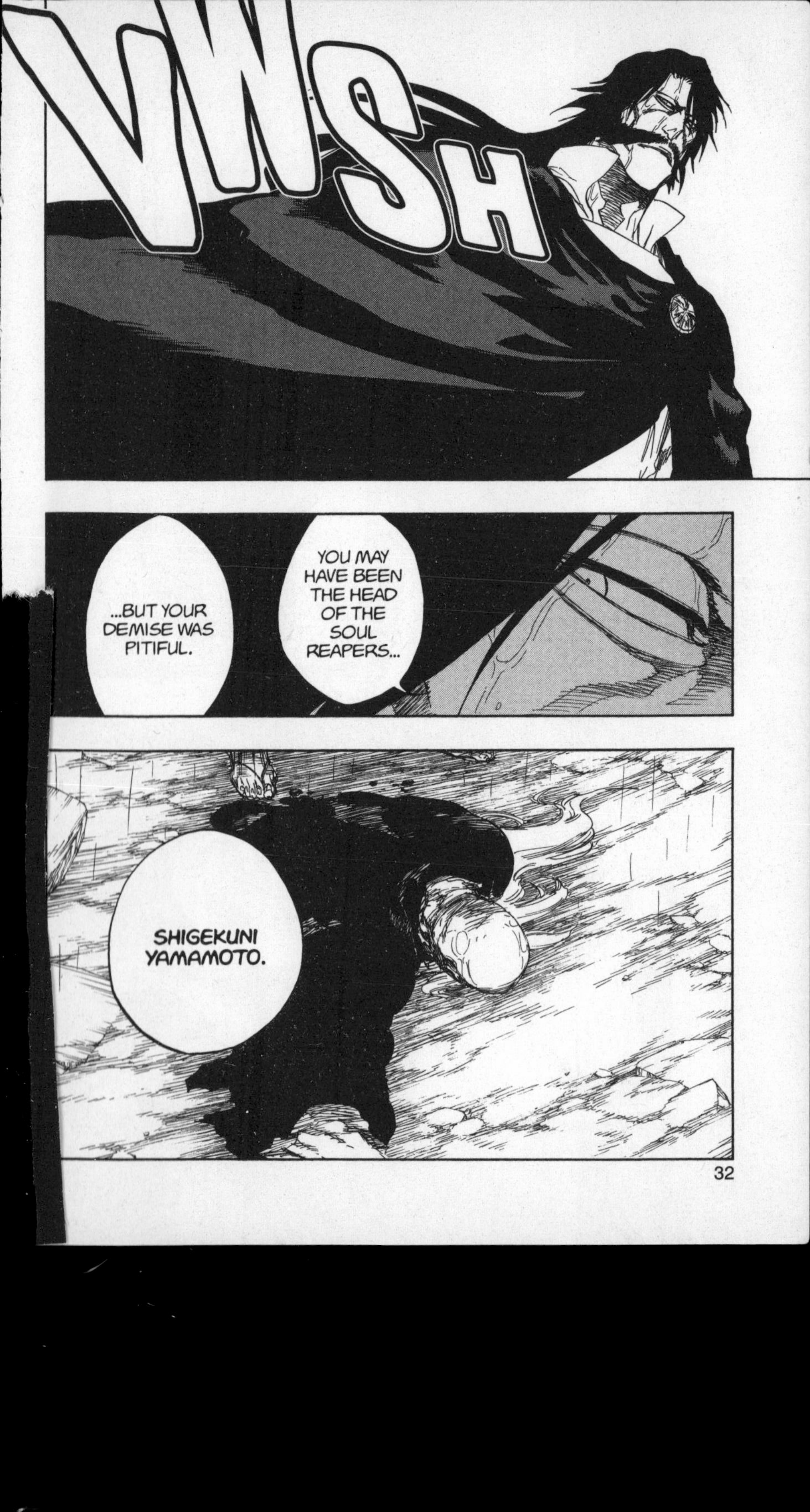
VWSH
YOU MAY HAVE BEEN THE HEAD OF THE SOUL REAPERS...
...BUT YOUR DEMISE WAS PITIFUL.
SHIGEKUNI YAMAMOTO.

READ THIS WAY

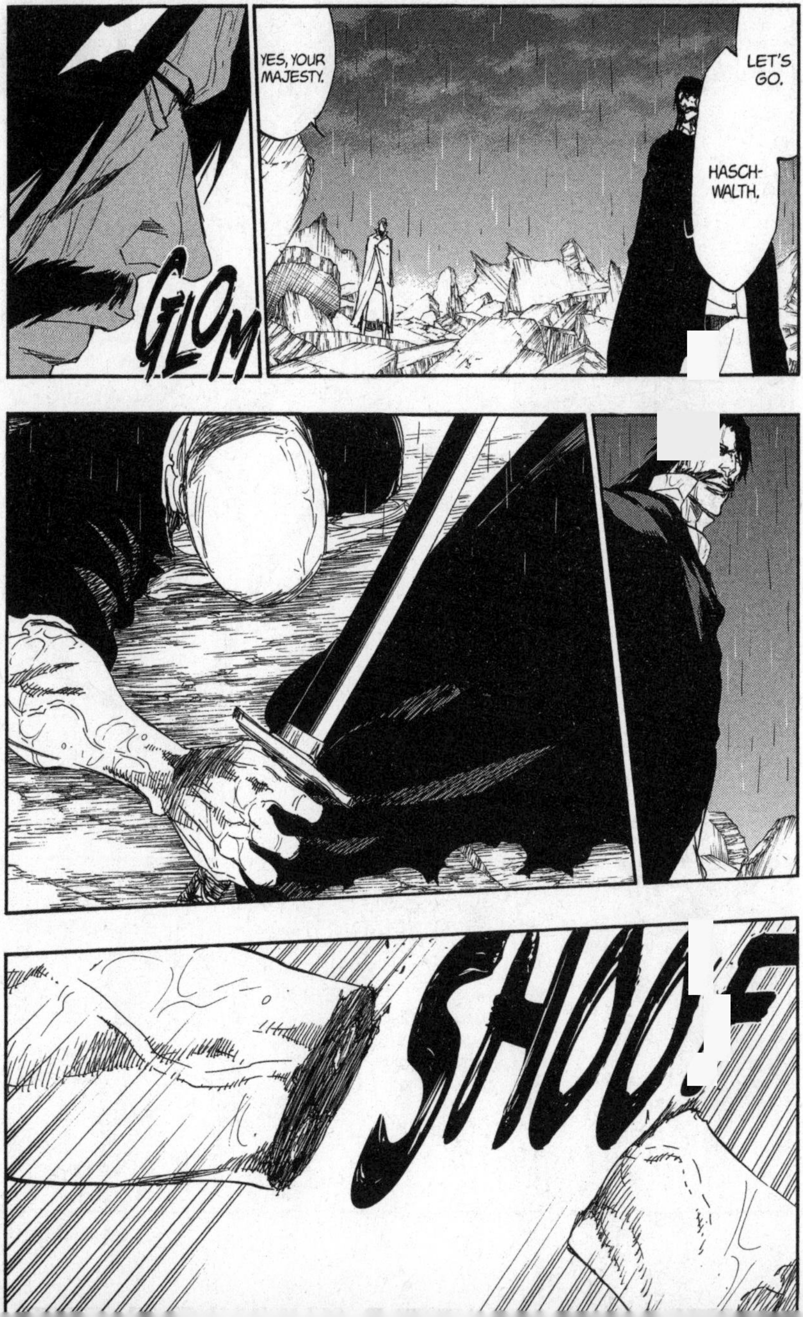
LET'S GO.
HASCH-WALTH.
YES, YOUR MAJESTY.
GLOM
SHOO

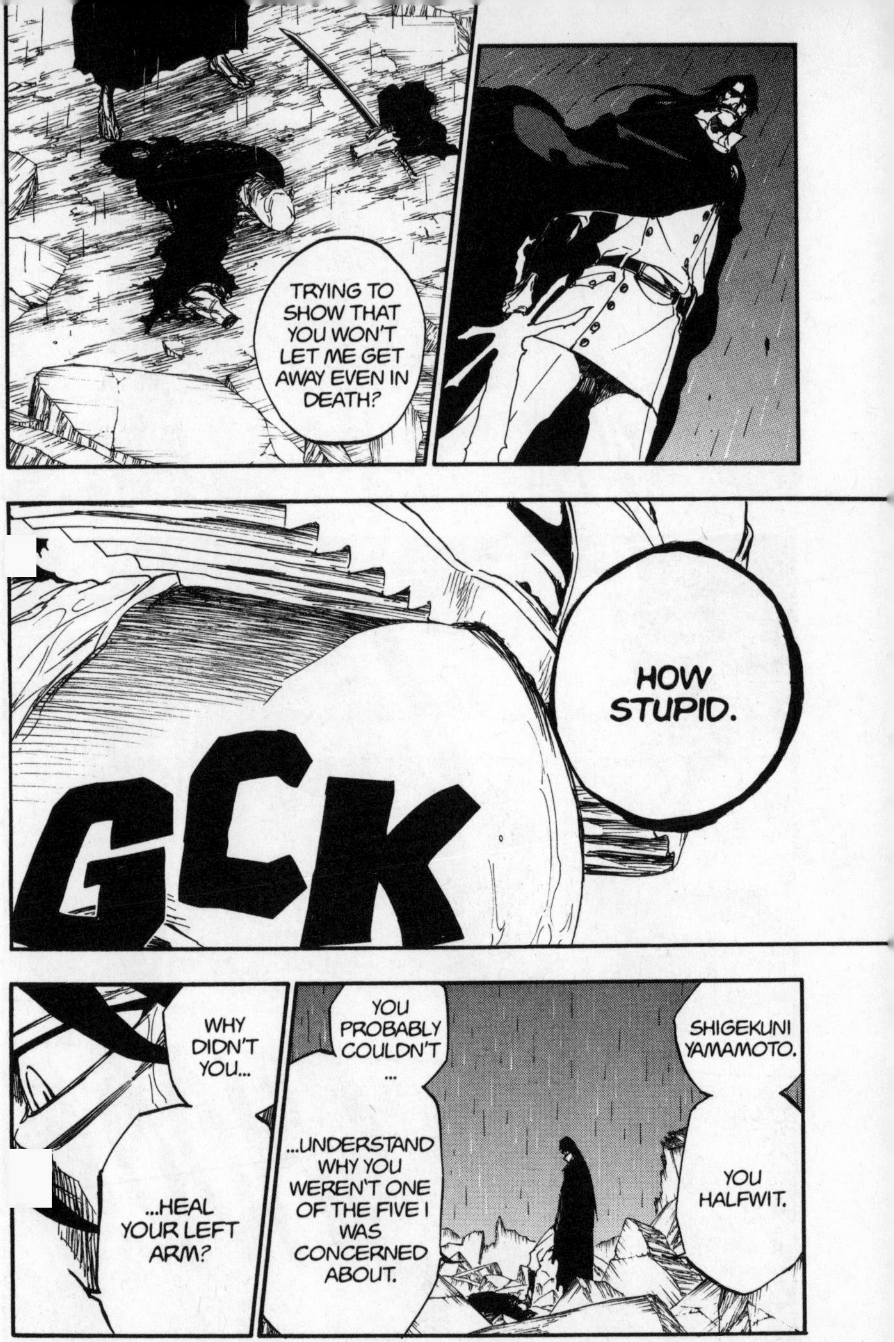
TRYING TO SHOW THAT YOU WON'T LET ME GET AWAY EVEN IN DEATH?
HOW STUPID.
GCK
SHIGEKUNI YAMAMOTO.
YOU HALFWIT.
YOU PROBABLY COULDN'T ...
...UNDERSTAND WHY YOU WEREN'T ONE OF THE FIVE I WAS CONCERNED ABOUT.
WHY DIDN'T YOU...
...HEAL YOUR LEFT ARM?

READ THIS WAY

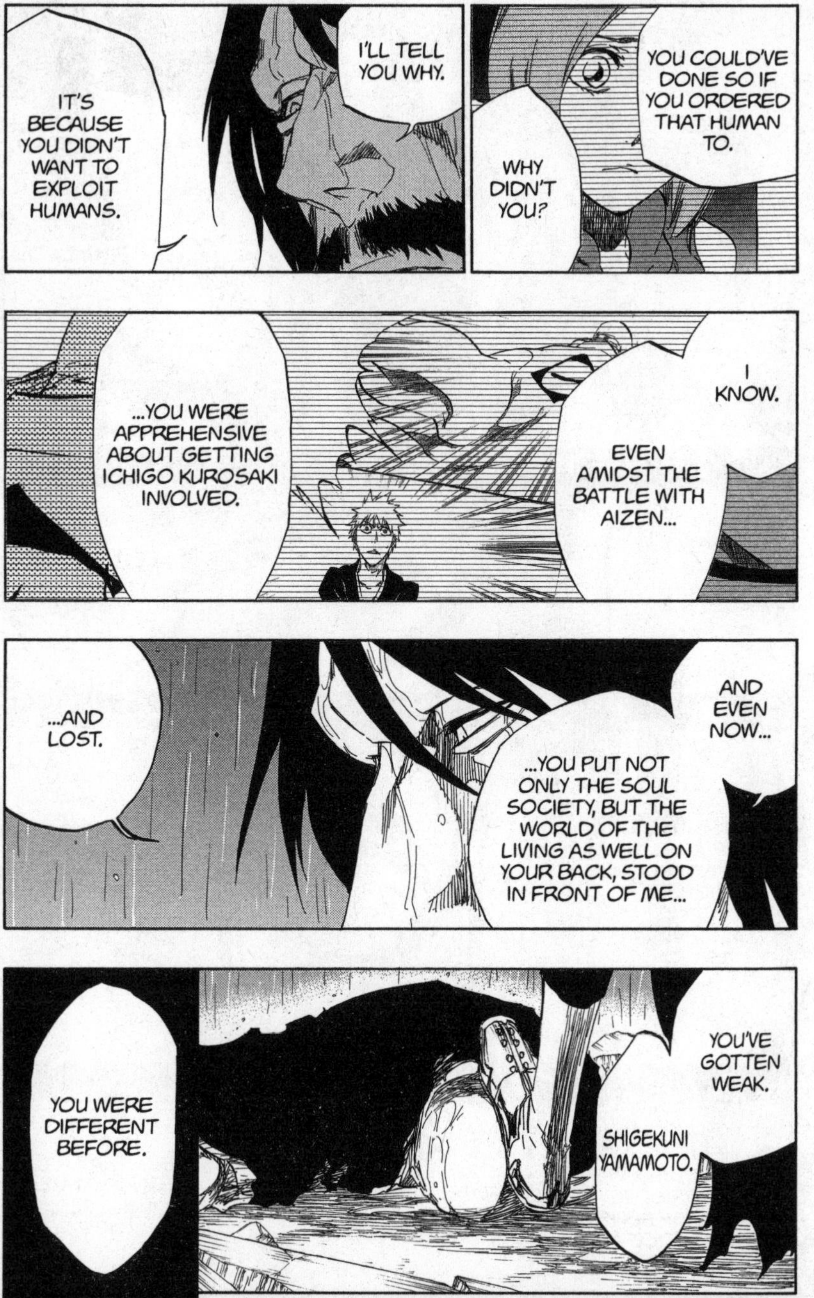

YOU COULD'VE DONE SO IF YOU ORDERED THAT HUMAN TO.
WHY DIDN'T YOU?
I'LL TELL YOU WHY.
IT'S BECAUSE YOU DIDN'T WANT TO EXPLOIT HUMANS.
I KNOW.
EVEN AMIDST THE BATTLE WITH AIZEN...
...YOU WERE APPREHENSIVE ABOUT GETTING ICHIGO KUROSAKI INVOLVED.
AND EVEN NOW...
...YOU PUT NOT ONLY THE SOUL SOCIETY, BUT THE WORLD OF THE LIVING AS WELL ON YOUR BACK, STOOD IN FRONT OF ME...
...AND LOST.
YOU'VE GOTTEN WEAK.
SHIGEKUNI YAMAMOTO.
YOU WERE DIFFERENT BEFORE.

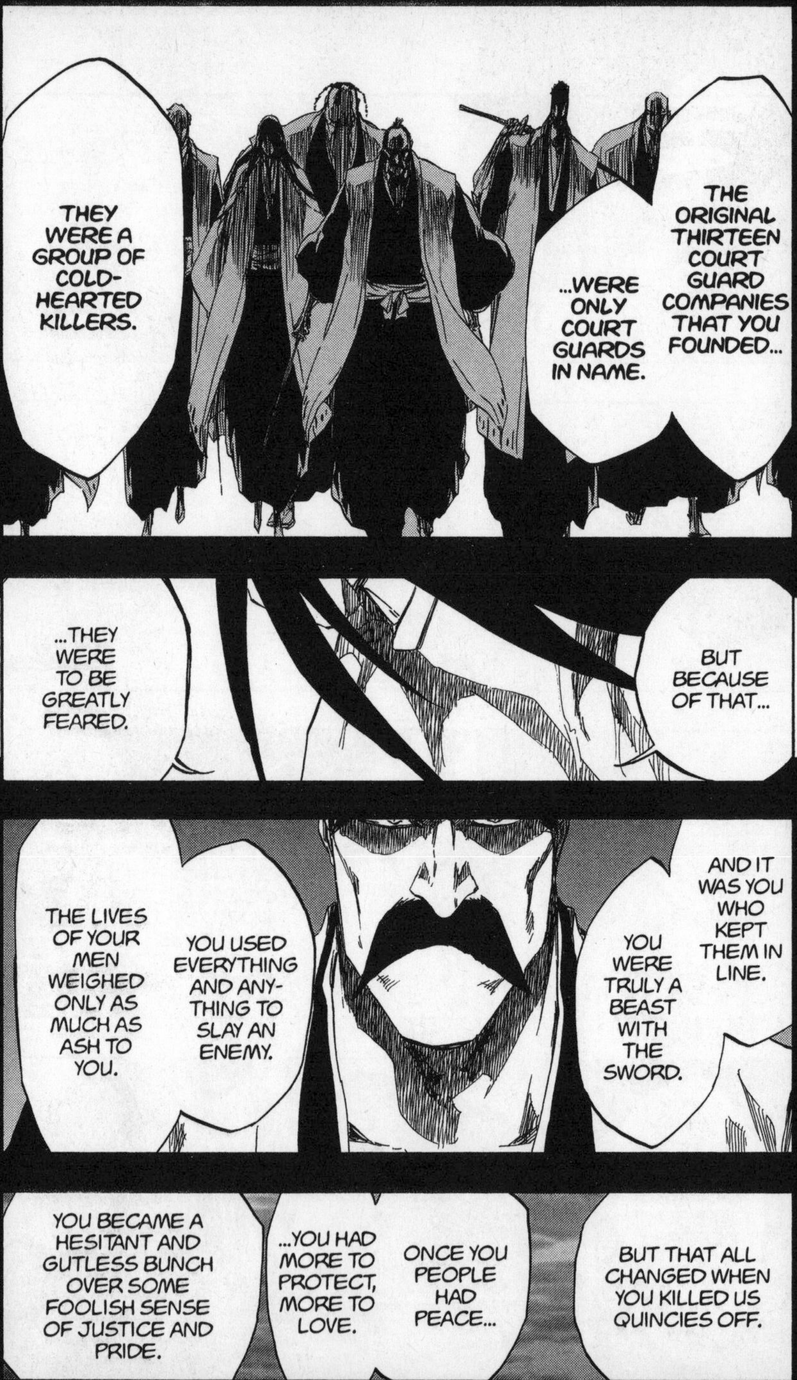
THE ORIGINAL THIRTEEN COURT GUARD COMPANIES THAT YOU FOUNDED...
...WERE ONLY COURT GUARDS IN NAME.
THEY WERE A GROUP OF COLD-HEARTED KILLERS.
BUT BECAUSE OF THAT...
...THEY WERE TO BE GREATLY FEARED.
AND IT WAS YOU WHO KEPT THEM IN LINE.
YOU WERE TRULY A BEAST WITH THE SWORD.
YOU USED EVERYTHING AND ANYTHING TO SLAY AN ENEMY.
THE LIVES OF YOUR MEN WEIGHED ONLY AS MUCH AS ASH TO YOU.
BUT THAT ALL CHANGED WHEN YOU KILLED US QUINCIES OFF.
ONCE YOU PEOPLE HAD PEACE...
...YOU HAD MORE TO PROTECT, MORE TO LOVE.
YOU BECAME A HESITANT AND GUTLESS BUNCH OVER SOME FOOLISH SENSE OF JUSTICE AND PRIDE.

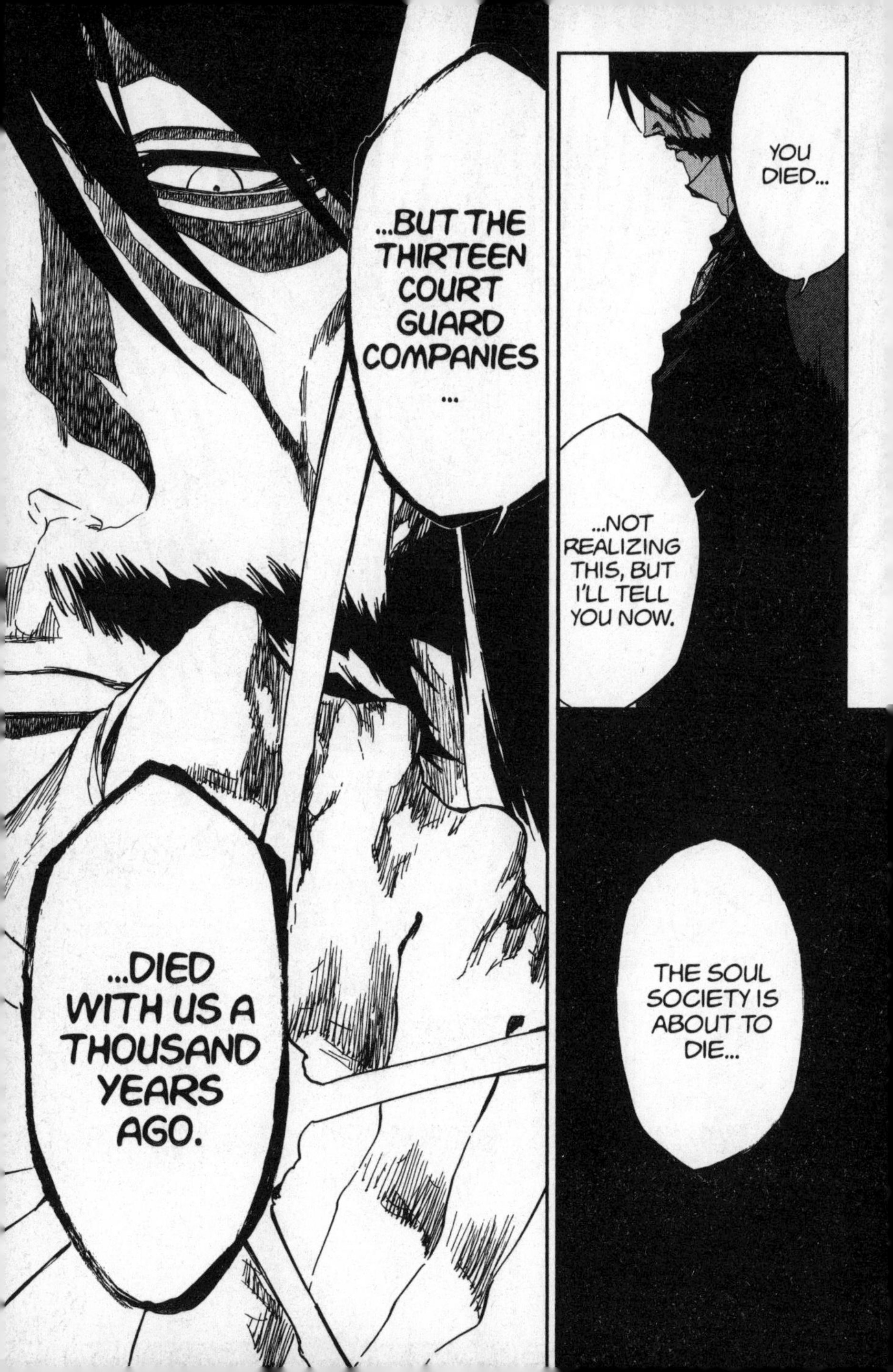
YOU DIED...
...NOT REALIZING THIS, BUT I'LL TELL YOU NOW.
THE SOUL SOCIETY IS ABOUT TO DIE...
...BUT THE THIRTEEN COURT GUARD COMPANIES ...
...DIED WITH US A THOUSAND YEARS AGO.

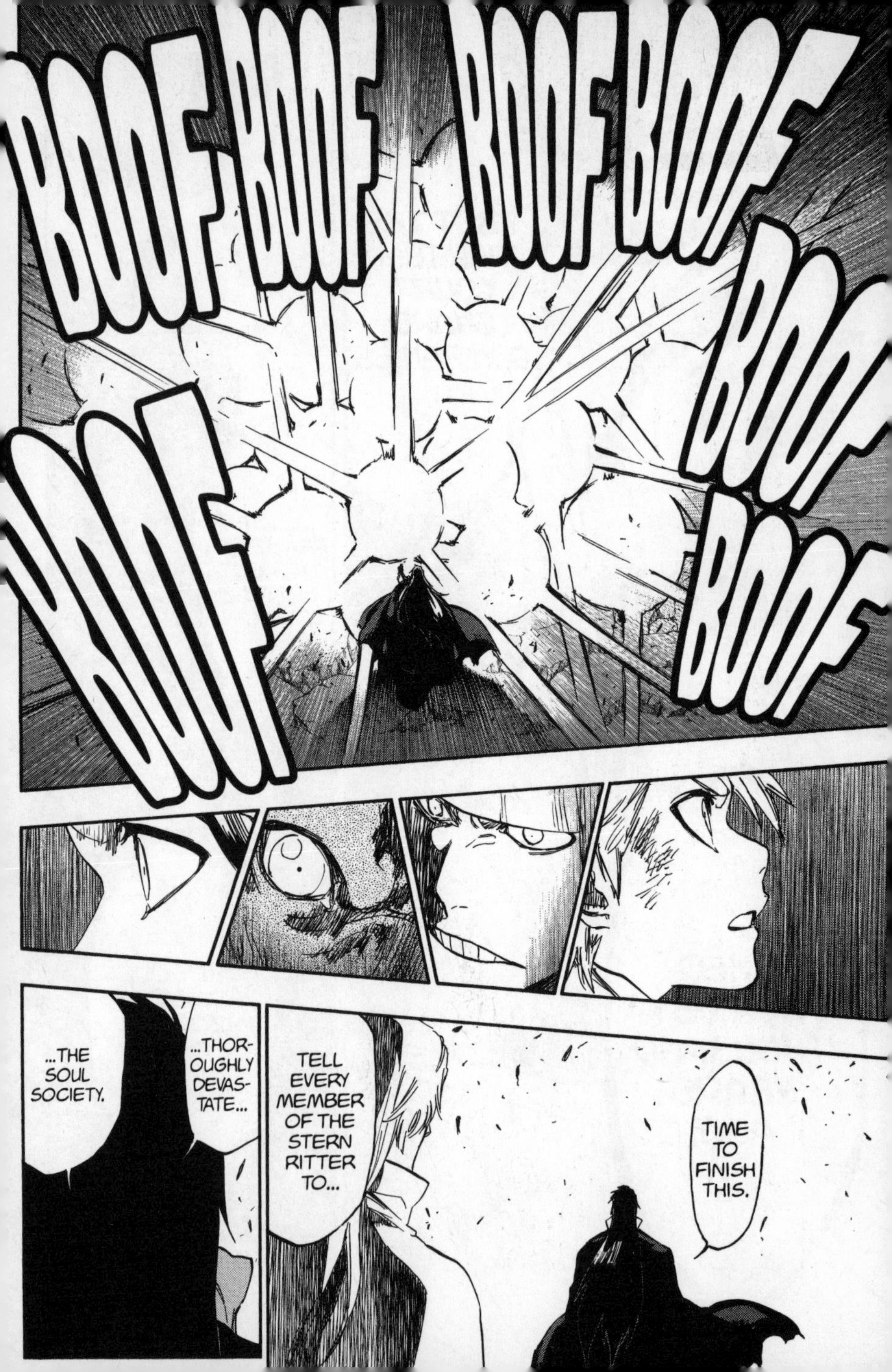
BOOF BOOF
BOOF BOOF
BOOF BOOF
BOOF
TIME TO FINISH THIS.
TELL EVERY MEMBER OF THE STERN RITTER TO...
...THOROUGHLY DEVASTATE...
...THE SOUL SOCIETY.

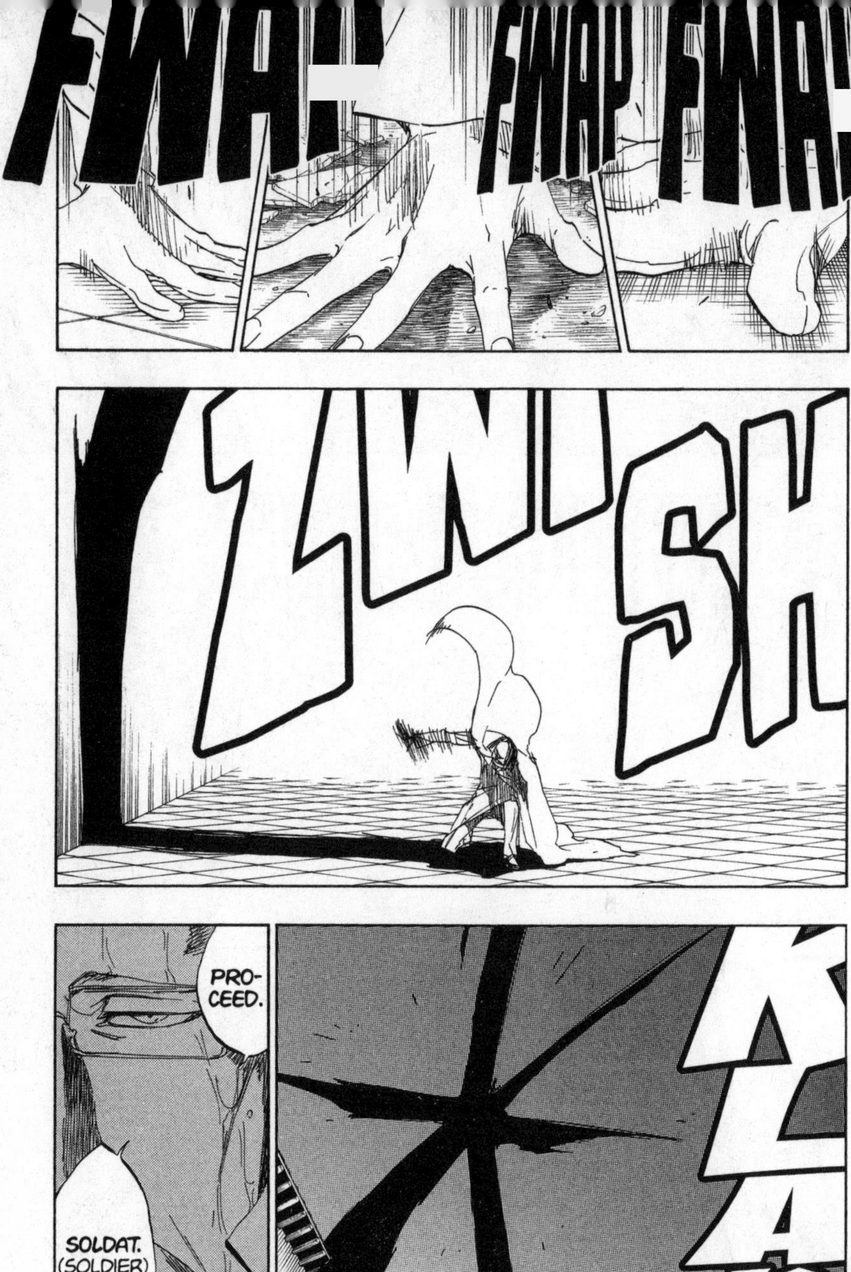
PRO-
CEED.
SOLDAT.
(SOLDIER)

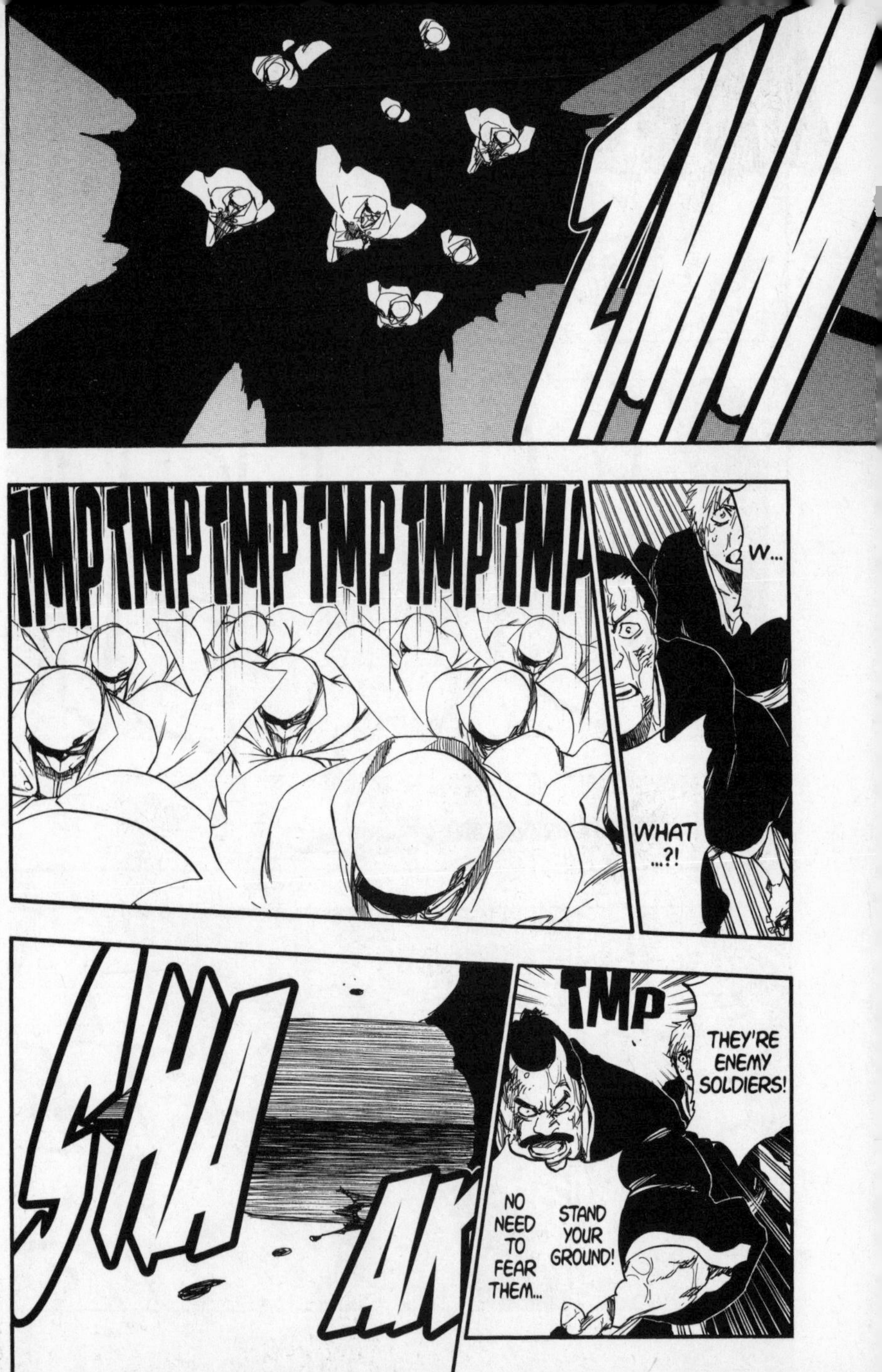
W...
WHAT ...?!
TMP TMP TMP TMP TMP TMP
TMP
THEY'RE ENEMY SOLDIERS!
STAND YOUR GROUND!
NO NEED TO FEAR THEM...
SHAAK

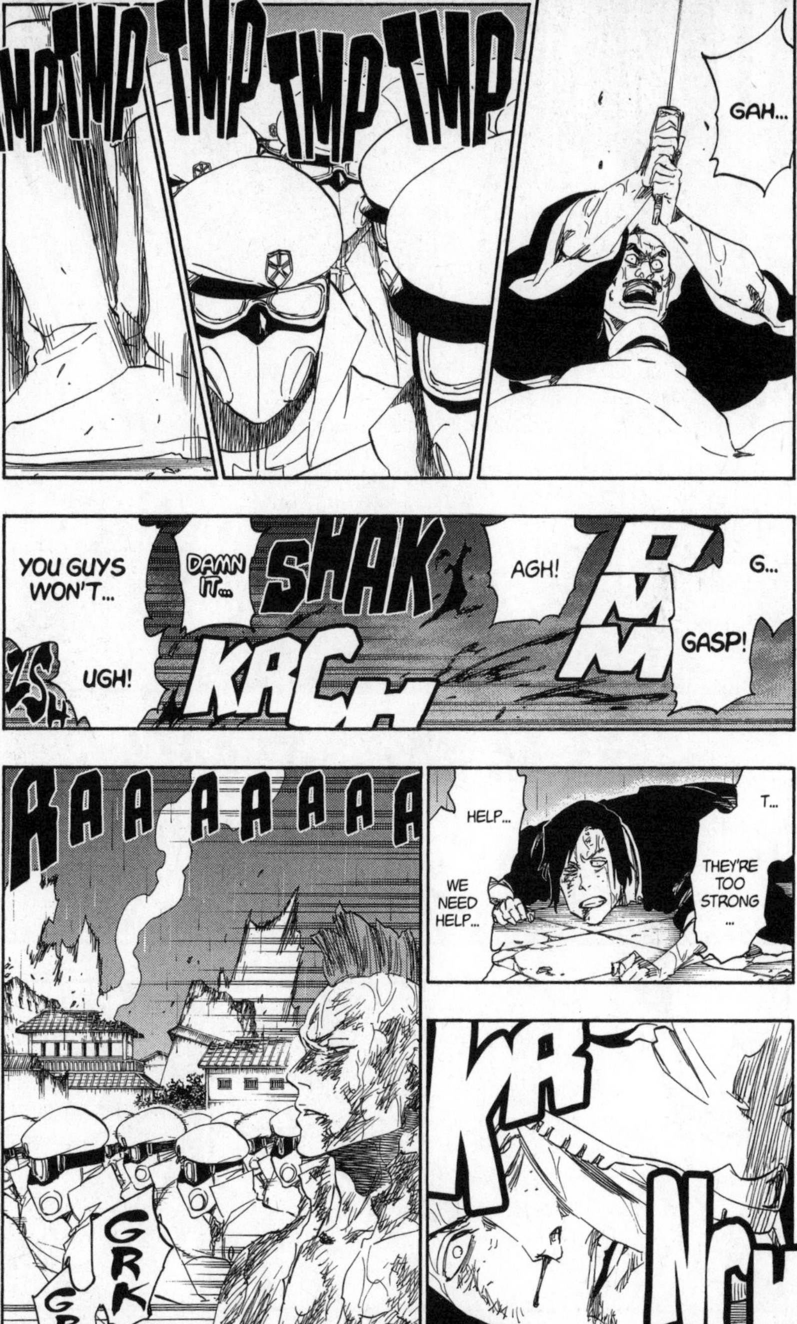
GAH...
TMP TMP TMP TMP TMP TMP
G...
GASP!
AGH!
SHAK
KRCH
DAMN IT...
YOU GUYS WON'T...
UGH!
T...
THEY'RE TOO STRONG ...
HELP...
WE NEED HELP...
KR
NCH
RAAAAAAAA
GRK
GRK
GRK

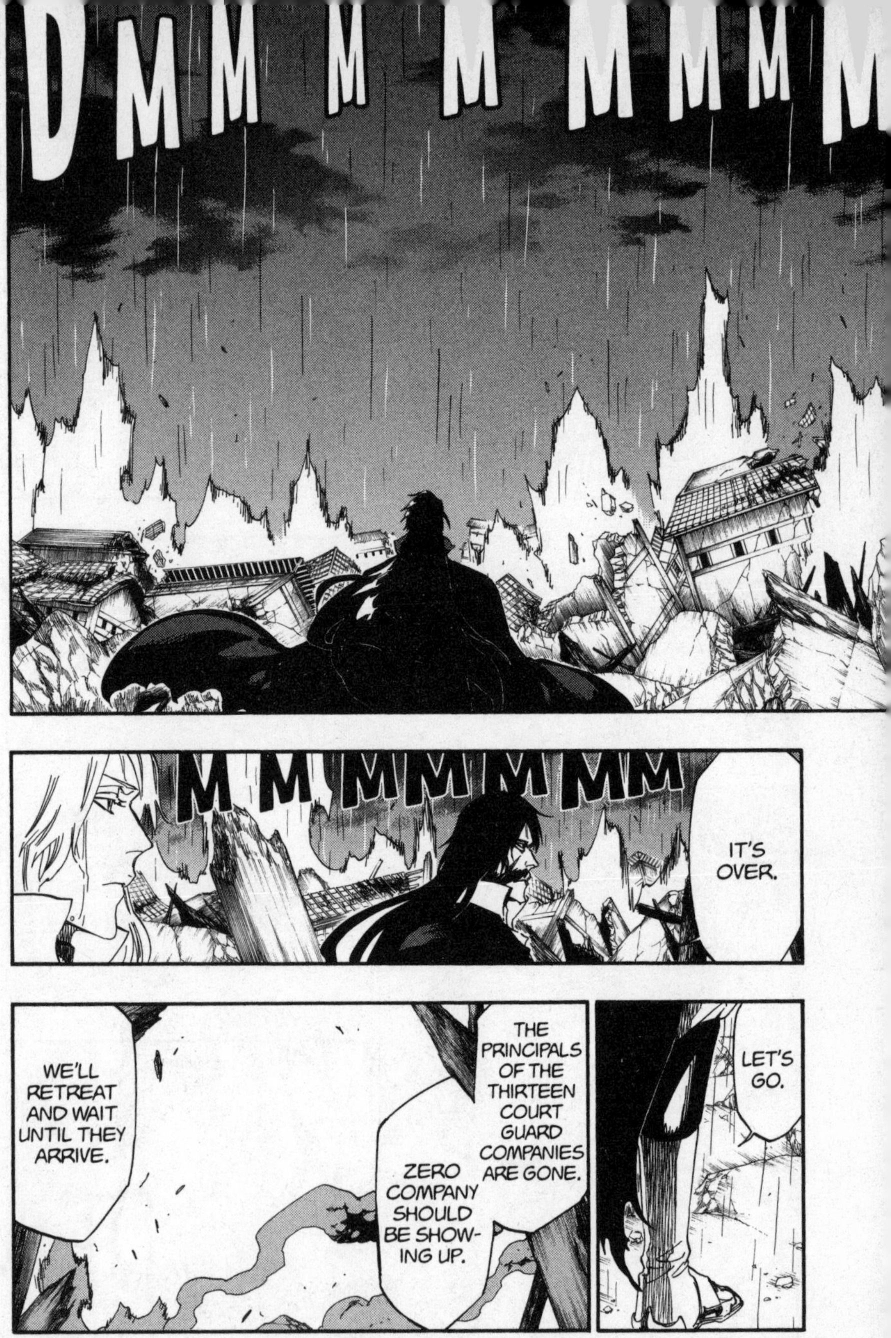
DMMMMMMMMM
MMMMMMMM
IT'S OVER.
LET'S GO.
THE PRINCIPALS OF THE THIRTEEN COURT GUARD COMPANIES ARE GONE.
ZERO COMPANY SHOULD BE SHOWING UP.
WE'LL RETREAT AND WAIT UNTIL THEY ARRIVE.

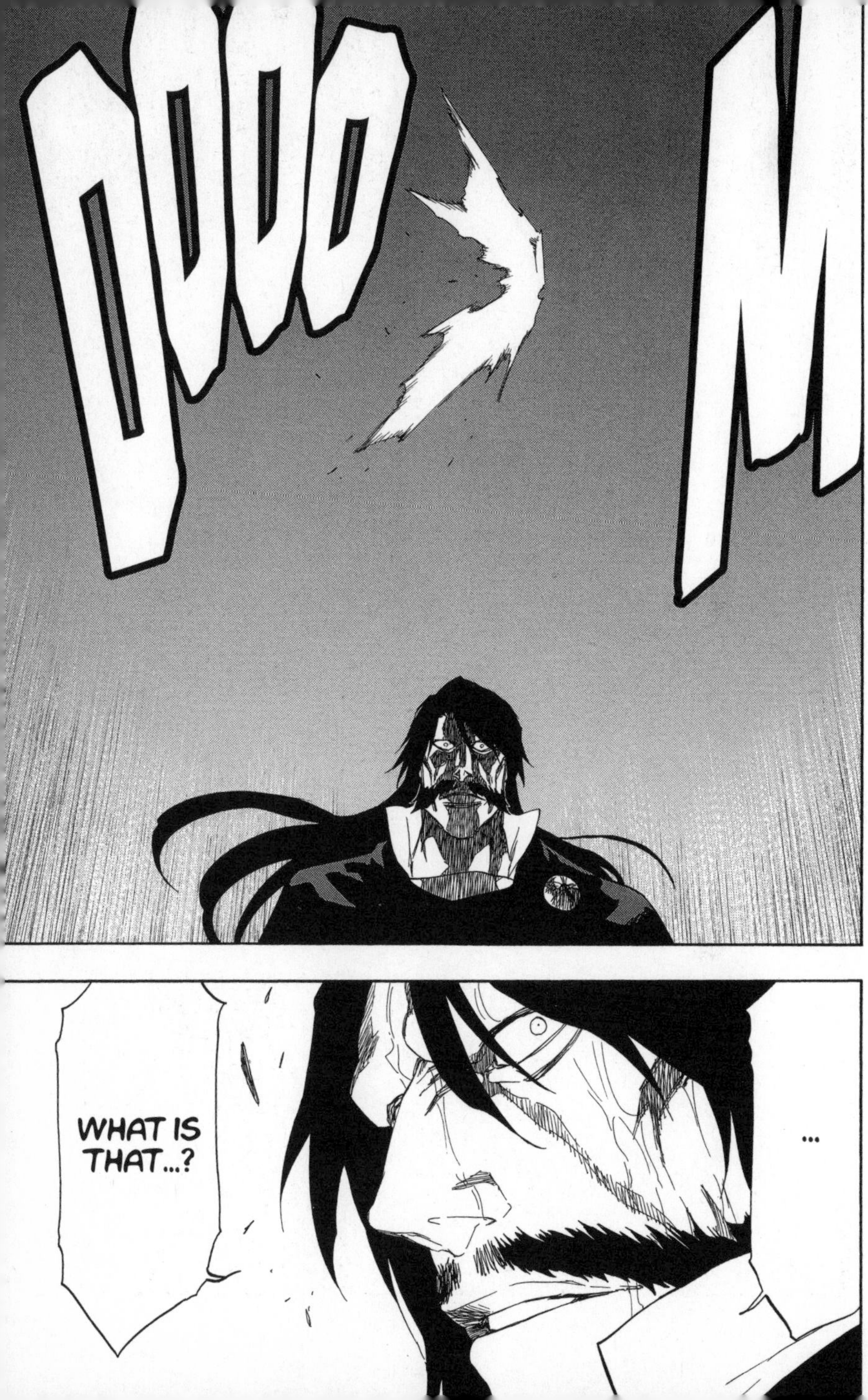
...
WHAT IS THAT...?

512. THE STAND ABLAZE

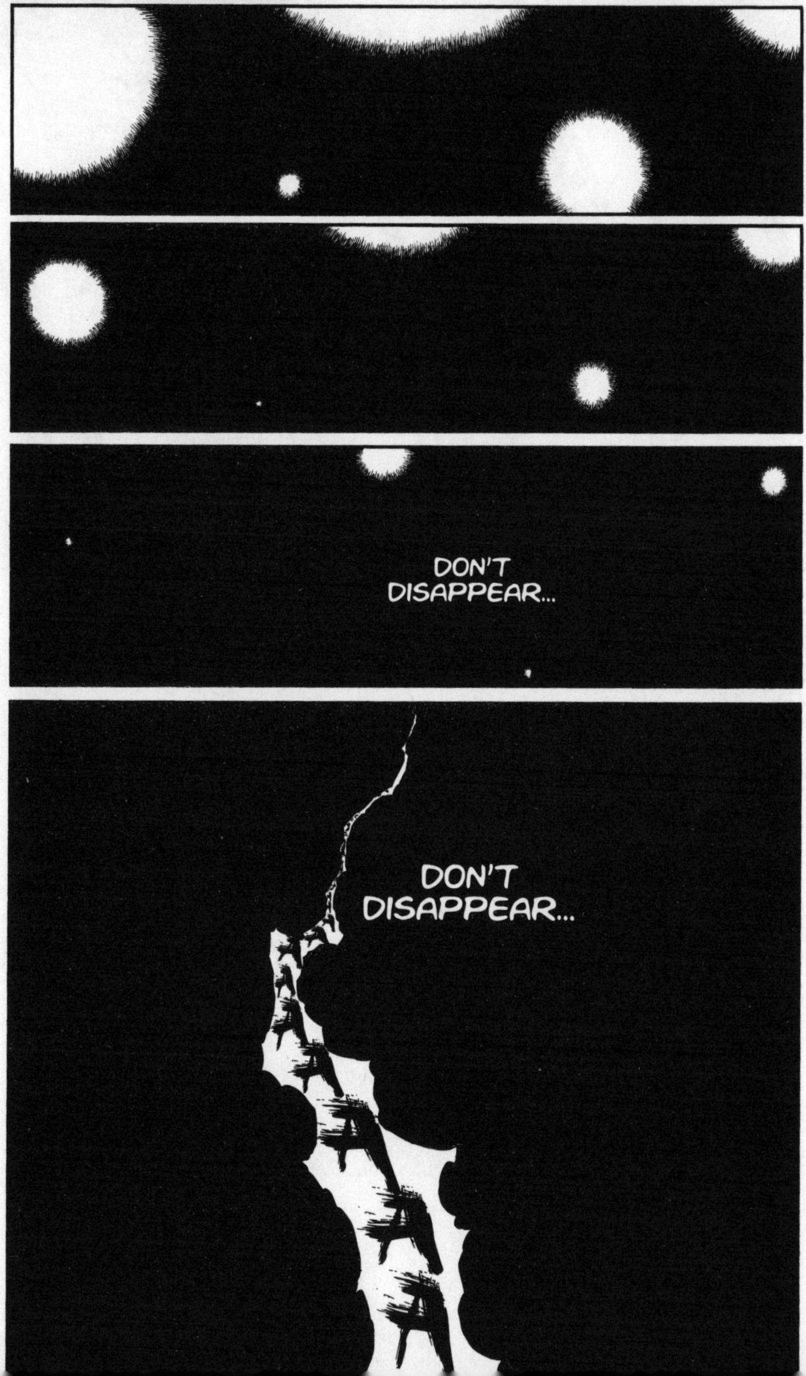
DON'T DISAPPEAR...
DON'T DISAPPEAR...

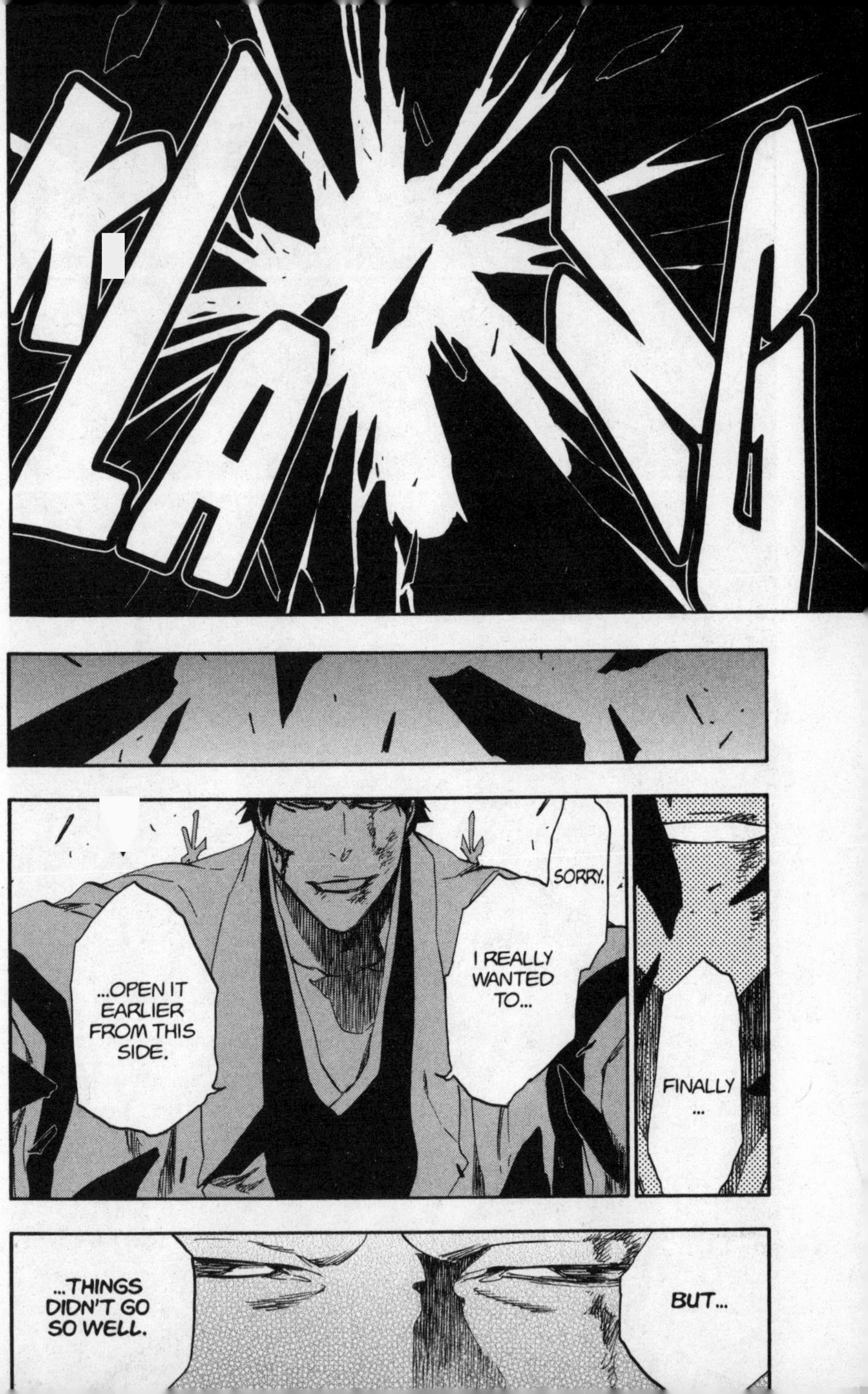
KLANG
FINALLY ...
SORRY.
I REALLY WANTED TO...
...OPEN IT EARLIER FROM THIS SIDE.
BUT...
...THINGS DIDN'T GO SO WELL.

READ THIS WAY

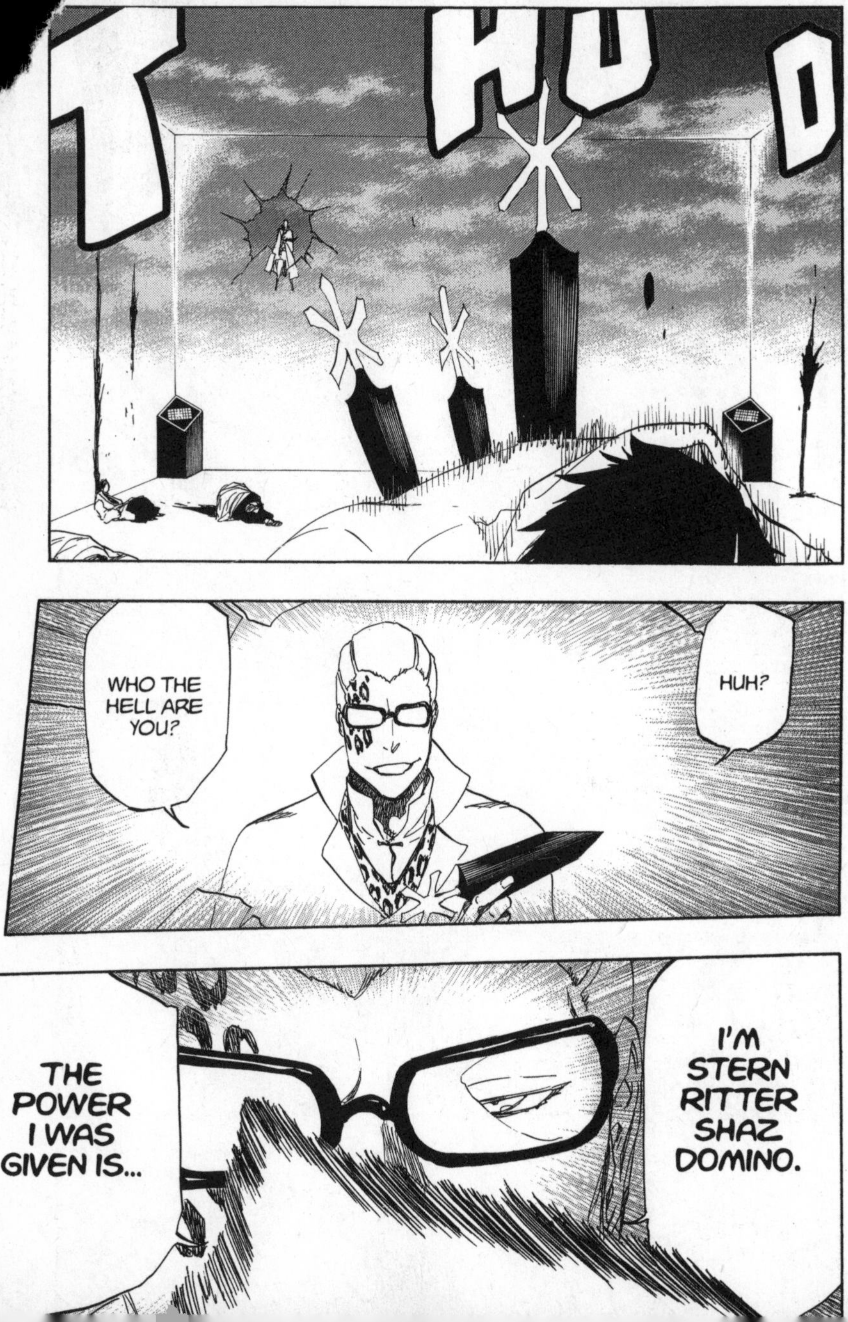
THUD
HUH?
WHO THE HELL ARE YOU?
I'M STERN RITTER SHAZ DOMINO.
THE POWER I WAS GIVEN IS...

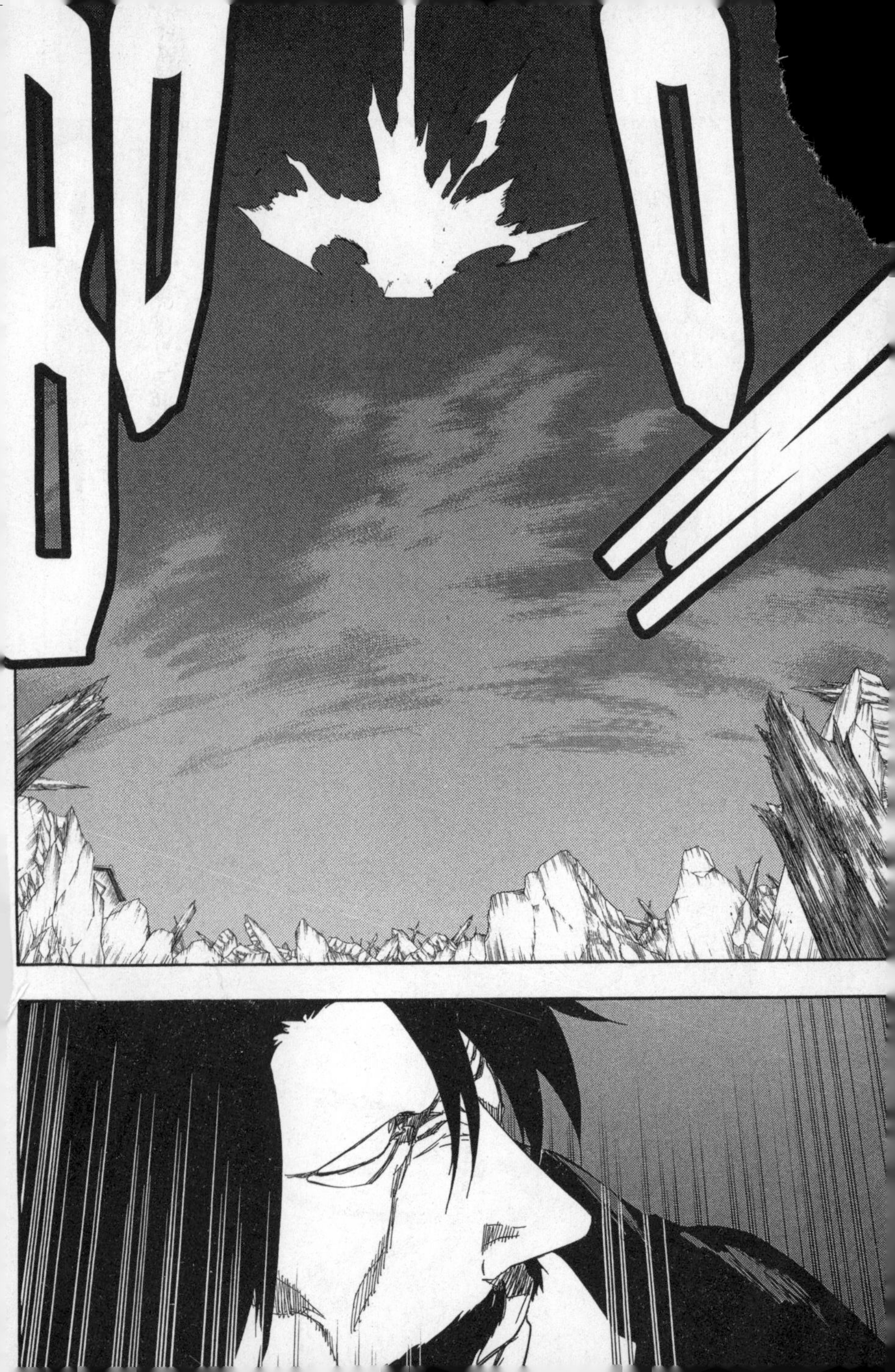
BOOM

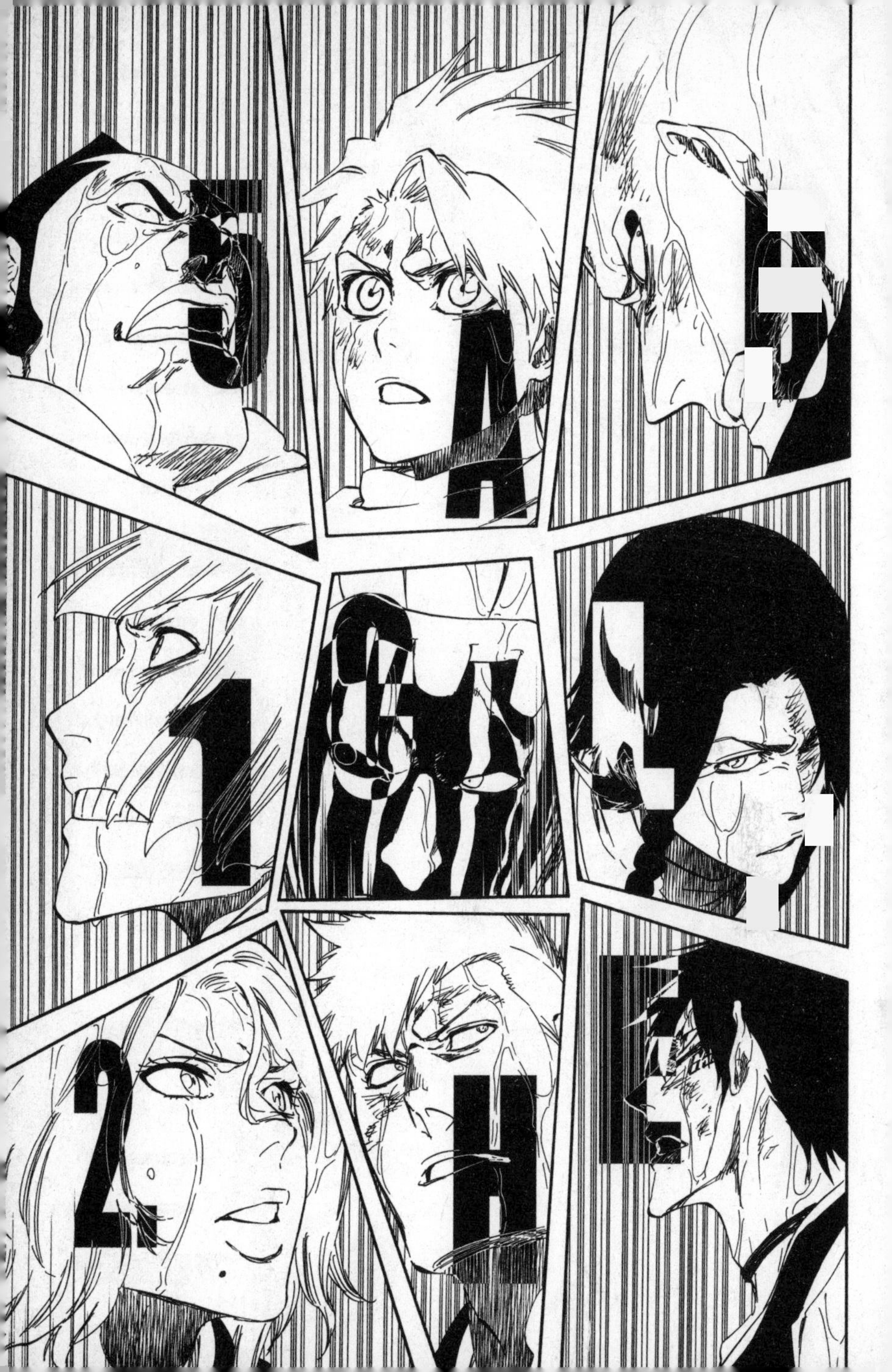

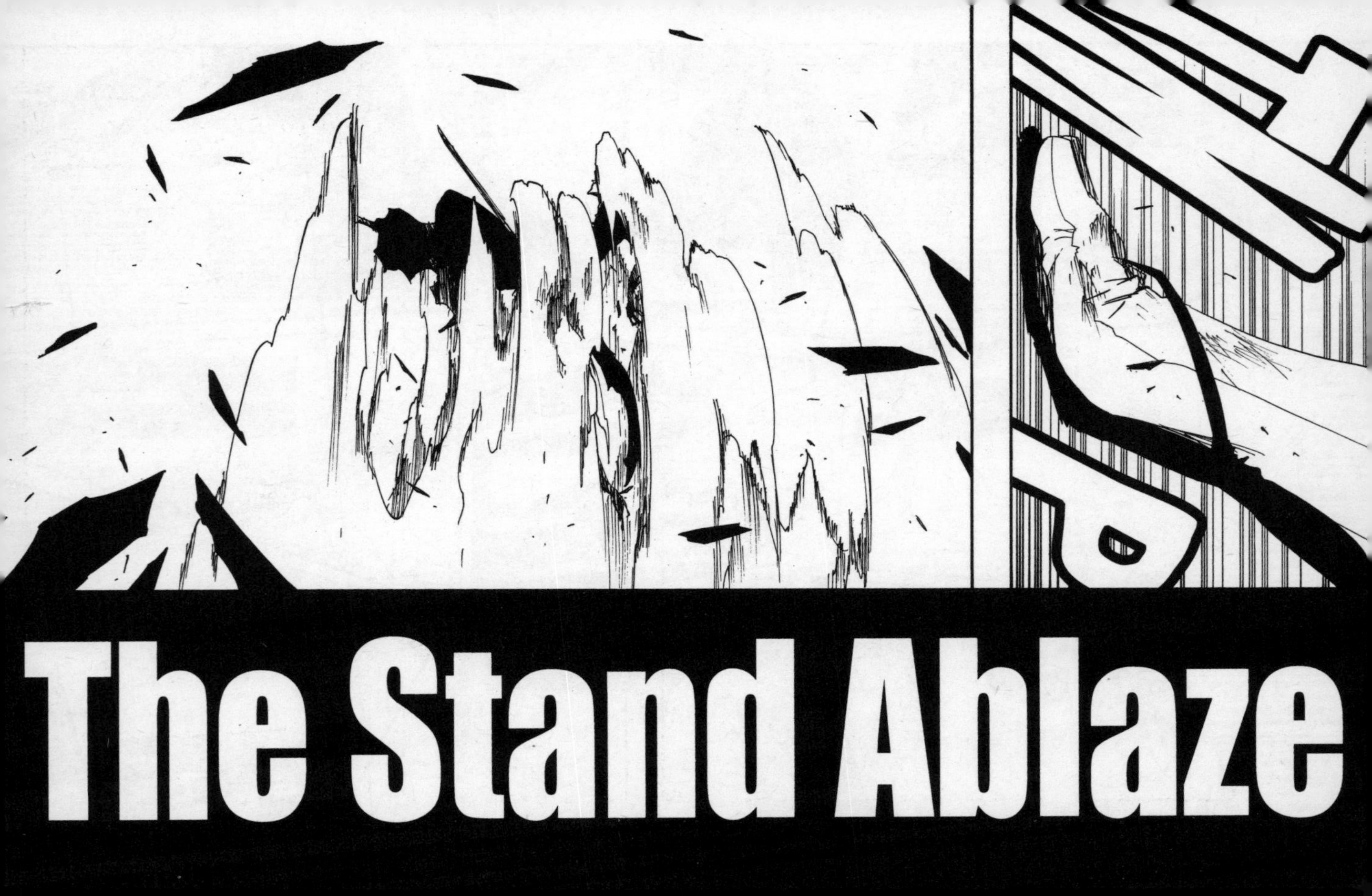

The Stand Ablaze

READ THIS WAY

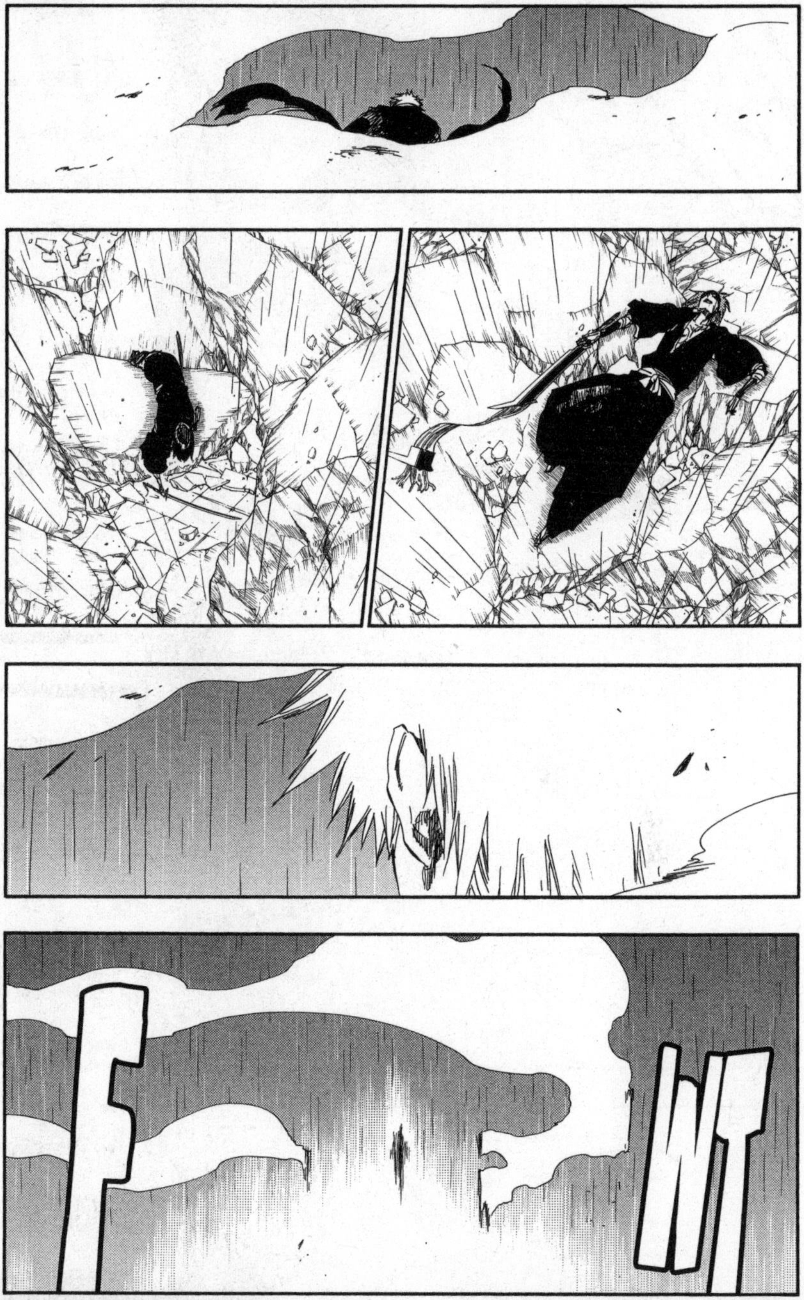
FNT

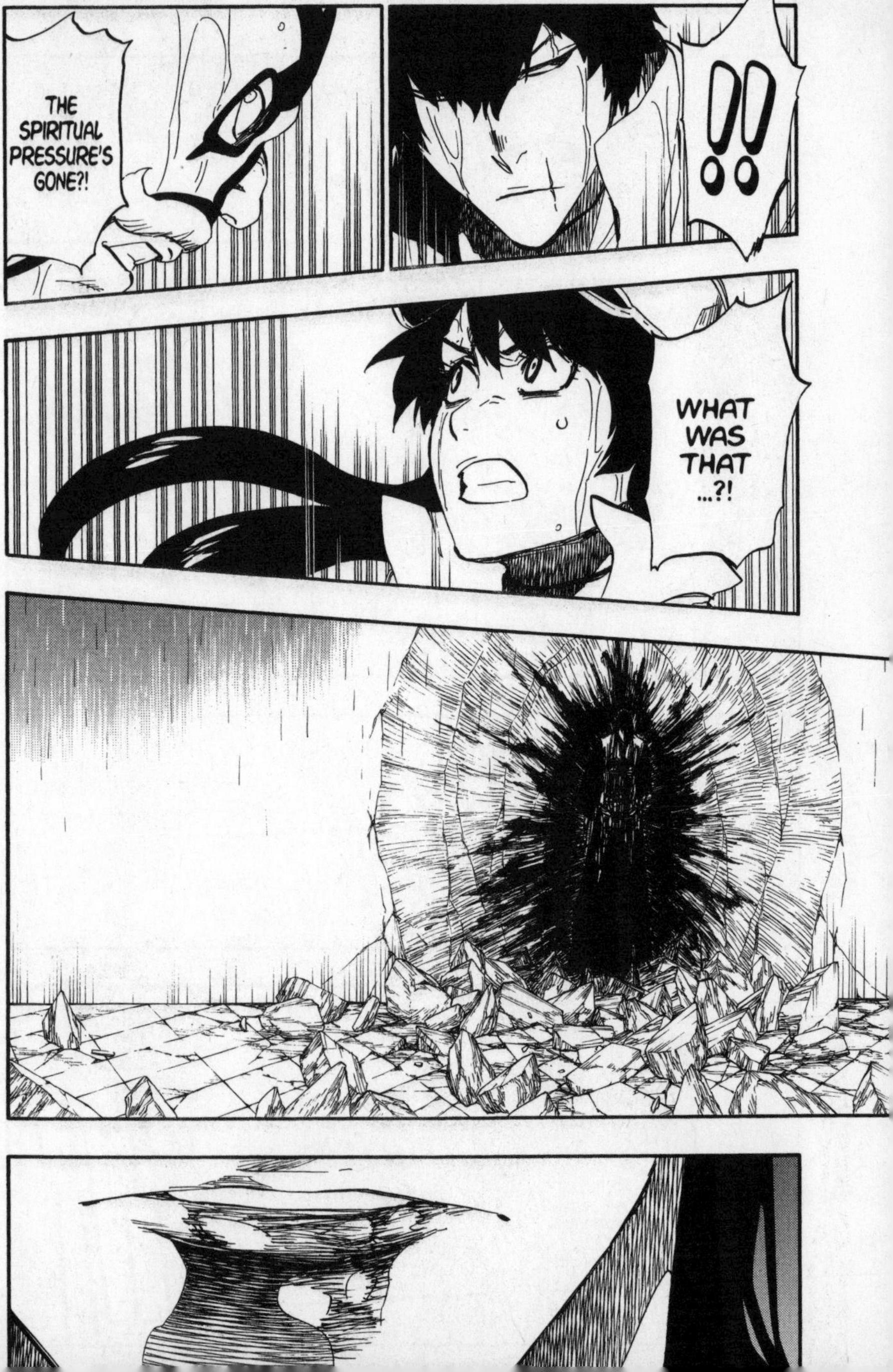
!!
THE SPIRITUAL PRESSURE'S GONE?!
WHAT WAS THAT ...?!

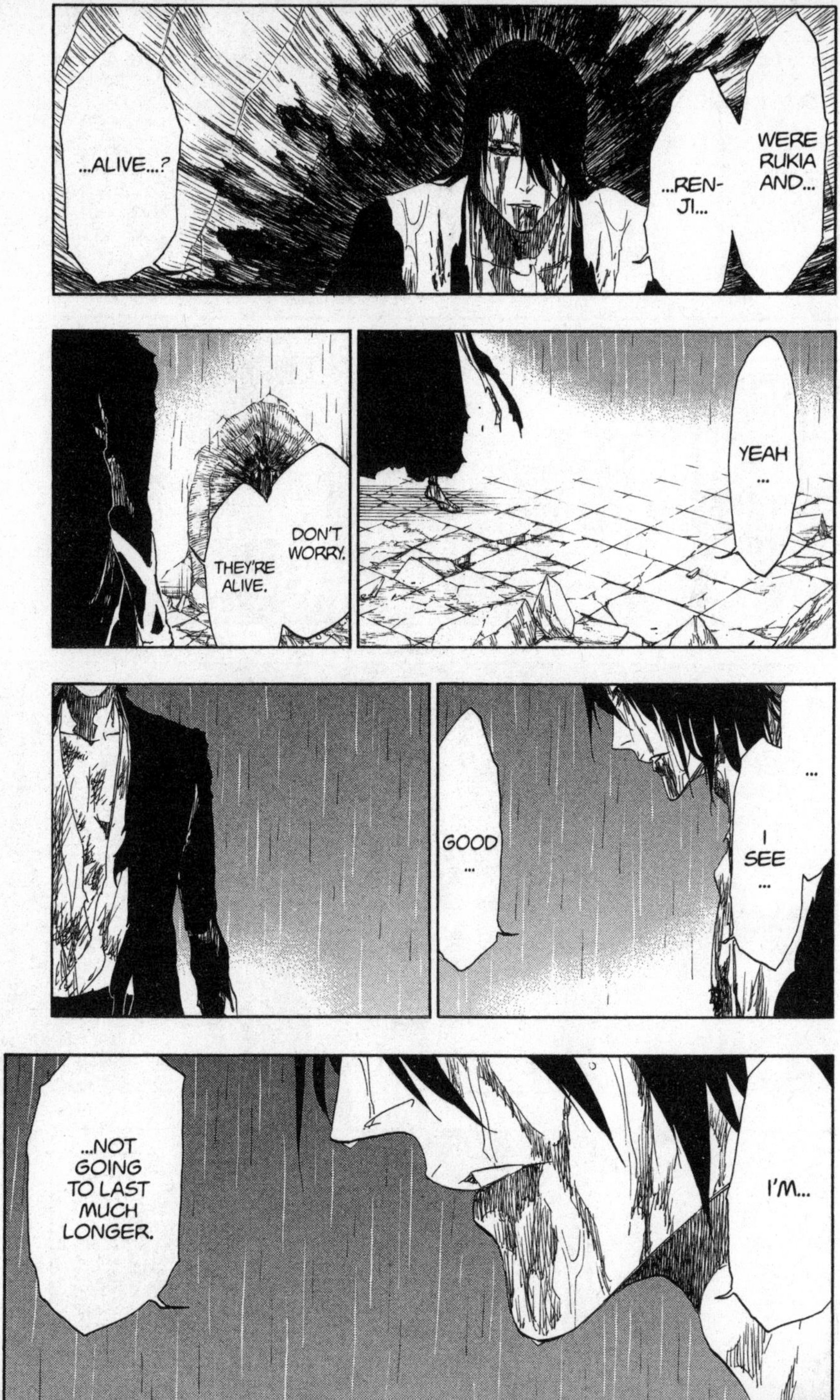
WERE RUKIA AND...
...REN-JI...
...ALIVE...?
YEAH ...
DON'T WORRY.
THEY'RE ALIVE.
... I SEE ...
GOOD ...
I'M...
...NOT GOING TO LAST MUCH LONGER.

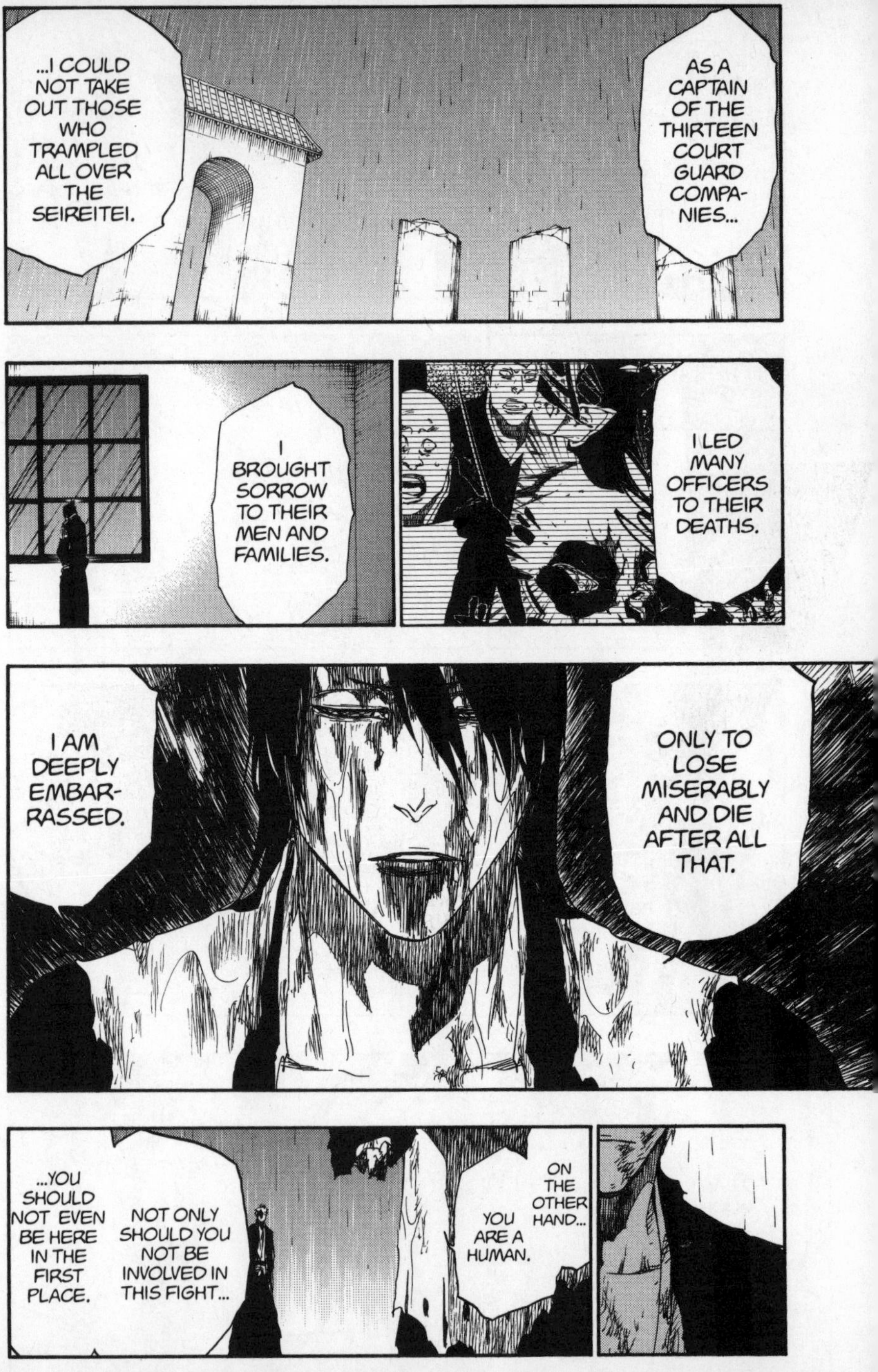
AS A CAPTAIN OF THE THIRTEEN COURT GUARD COMPANIES...
...I COULD NOT TAKE OUT THOSE WHO TRAMPLED ALL OVER THE SEIREITEI.
I LED MANY OFFICERS TO THEIR DEATHS.
I BROUGHT SORROW TO THEIR MEN AND FAMILIES.
ONLY TO LOSE MISERABLY AND DIE AFTER ALL THAT.
I AM DEEPLY EMBARRASSED.
ON THE OTHER HAND...
YOU ARE A HUMAN.
NOT ONLY SHOULD YOU NOT BE INVOLVED IN THIS FIGHT...
...YOU SHOULD NOT EVEN BE HERE IN THE FIRST PLACE.

READ THIS WAY

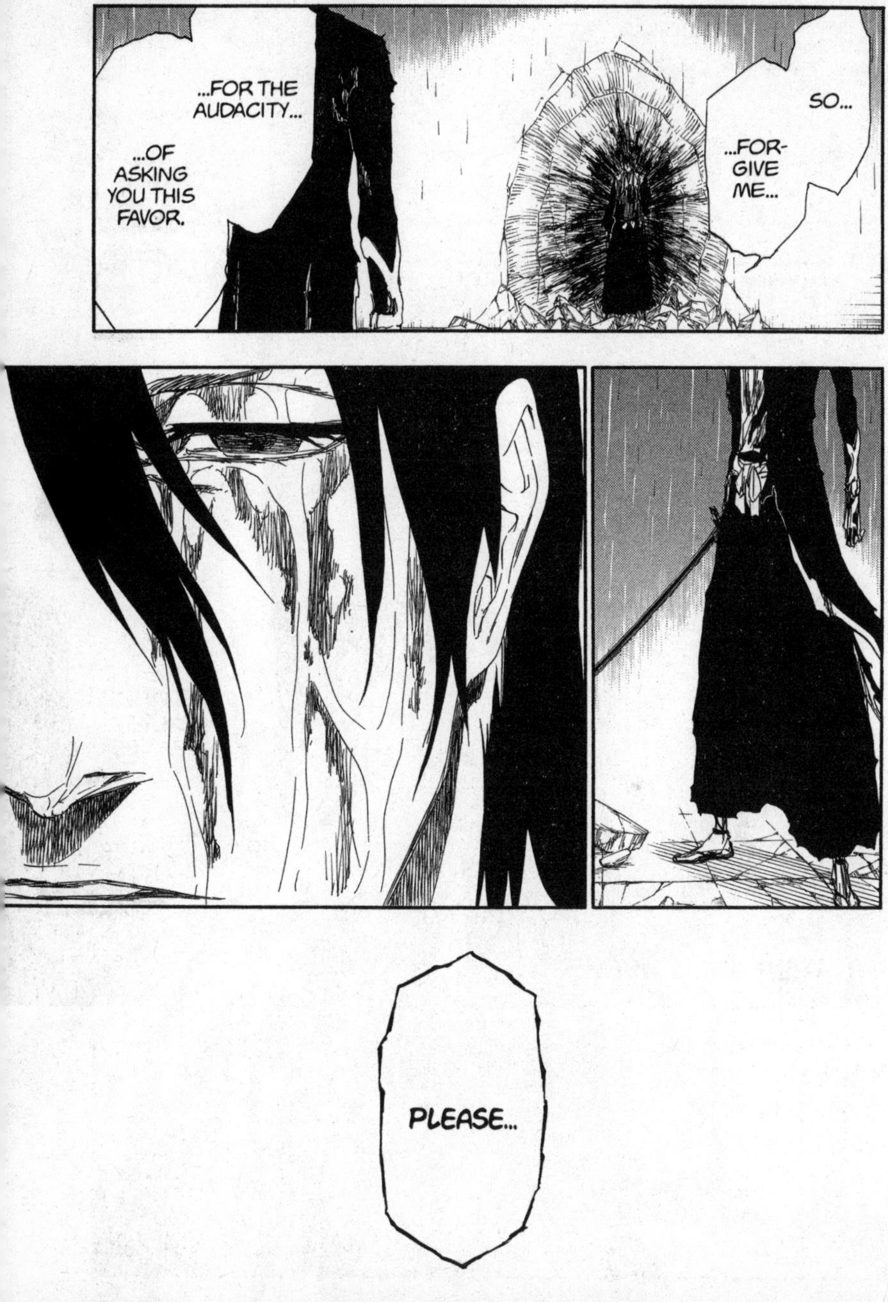
SO...
...FOR-GIVE ME...
...FOR THE AUDACITY...
...OF ASKING YOU THIS FAVOR.
PLEASE...

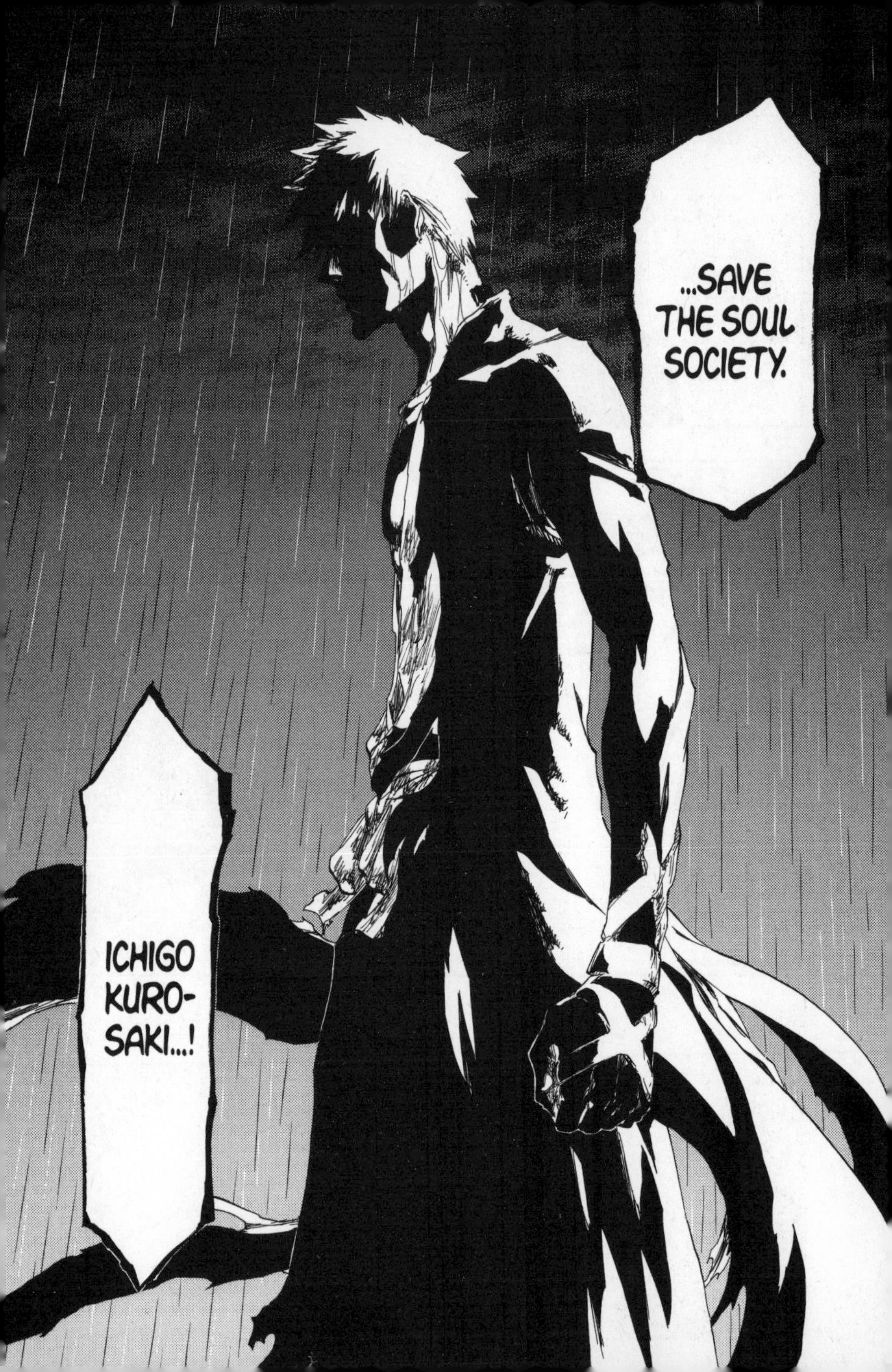
...SAVE THE SOUL SOCIETY.
ICHIGO KURO-SAKI...!

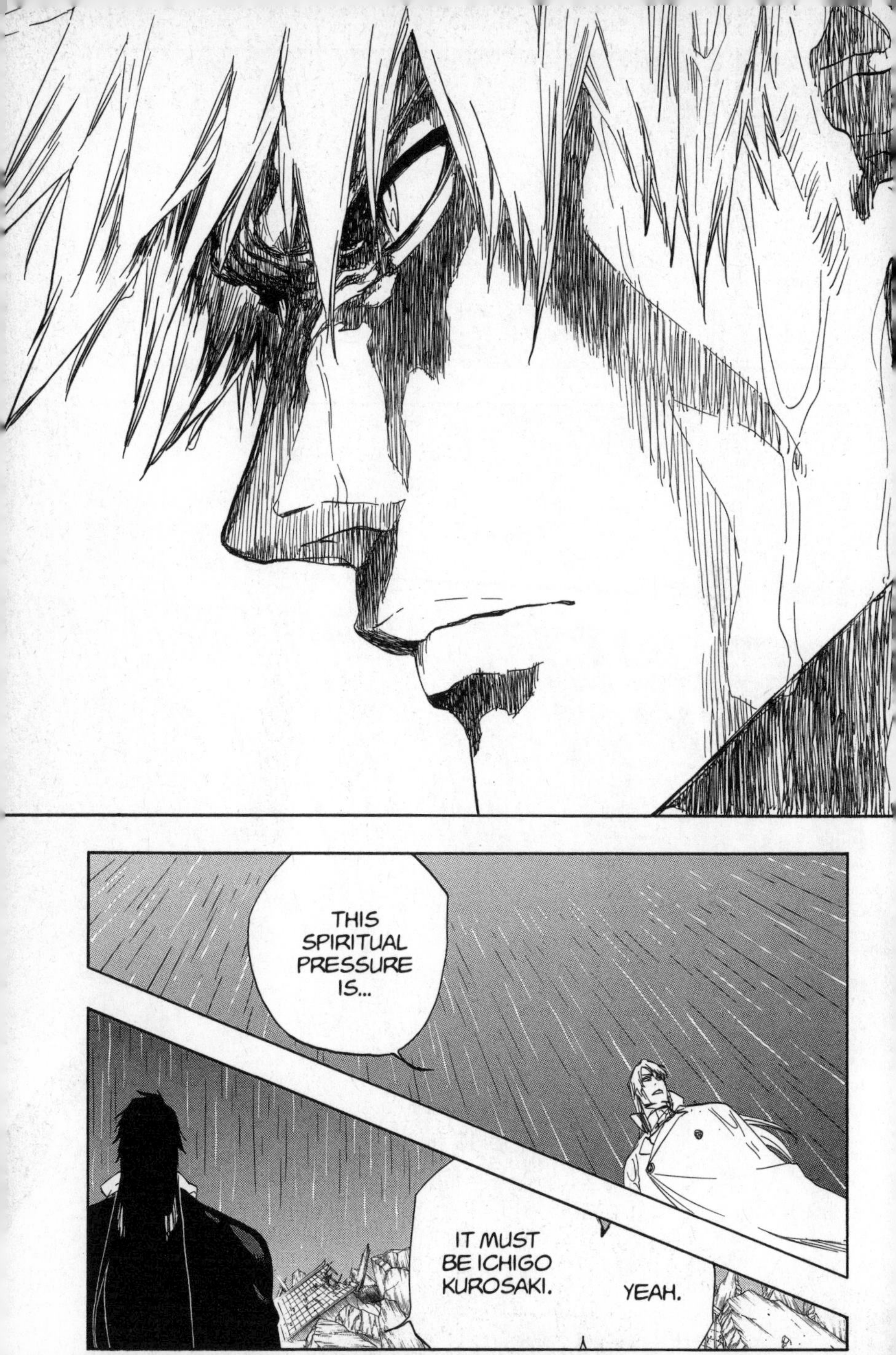
THIS SPIRITUAL PRESSURE IS...
IT MUST BE ICHIGO KUROSAKI.
YEAH.

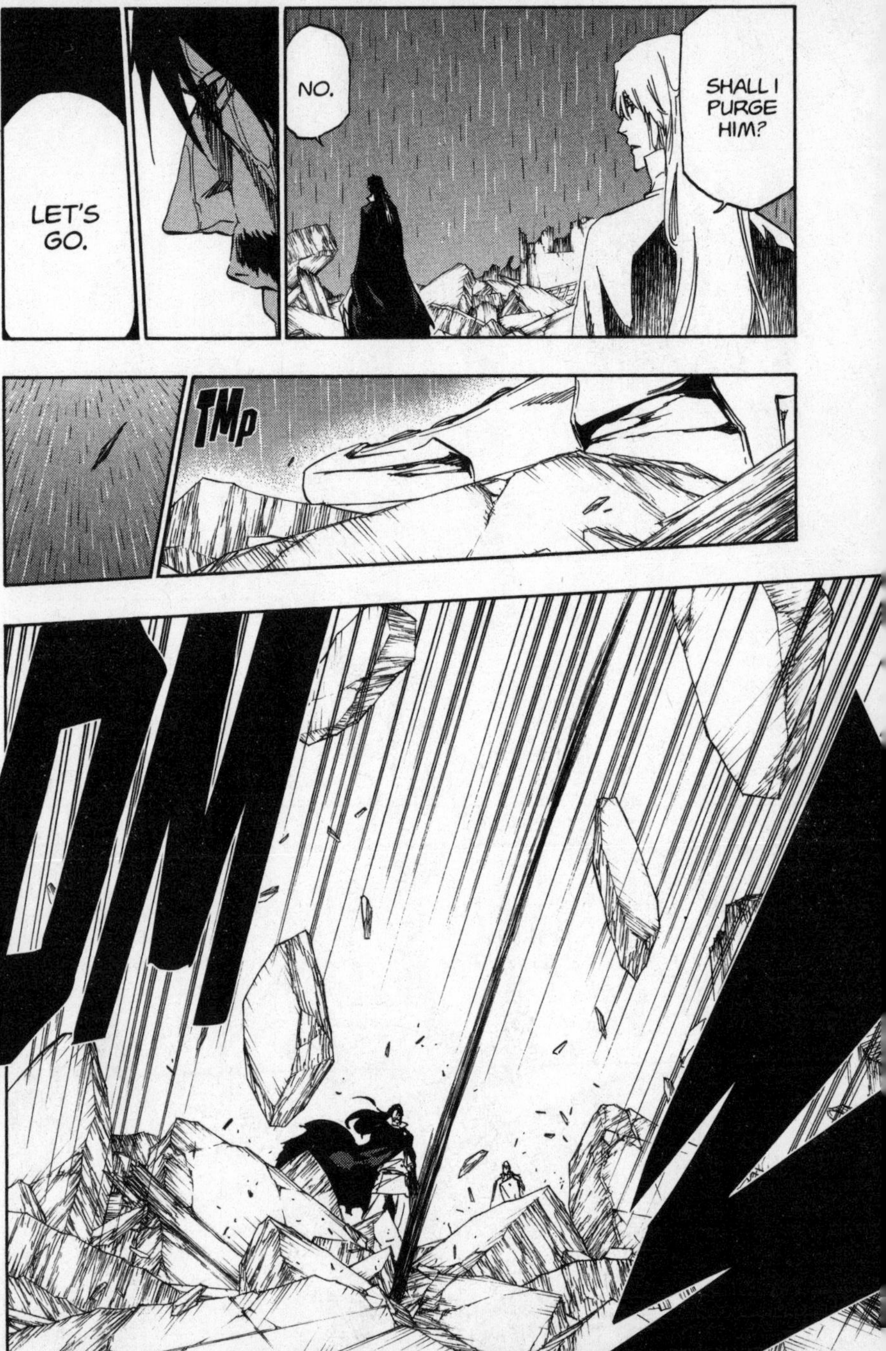
SHALL I PURGE HIM?
NO.
LET'S GO.
TMP

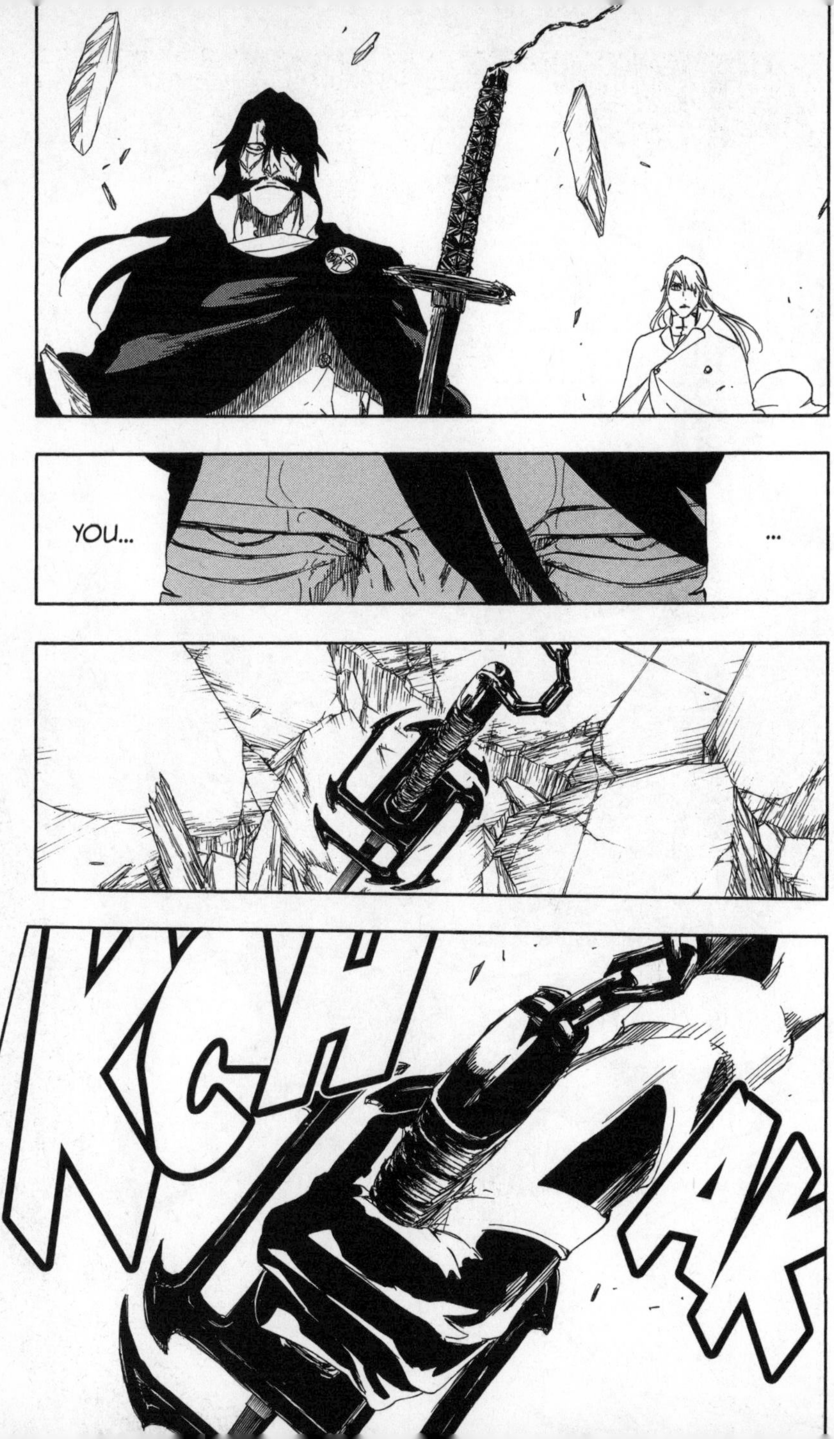
...
YOU...
KCHAK

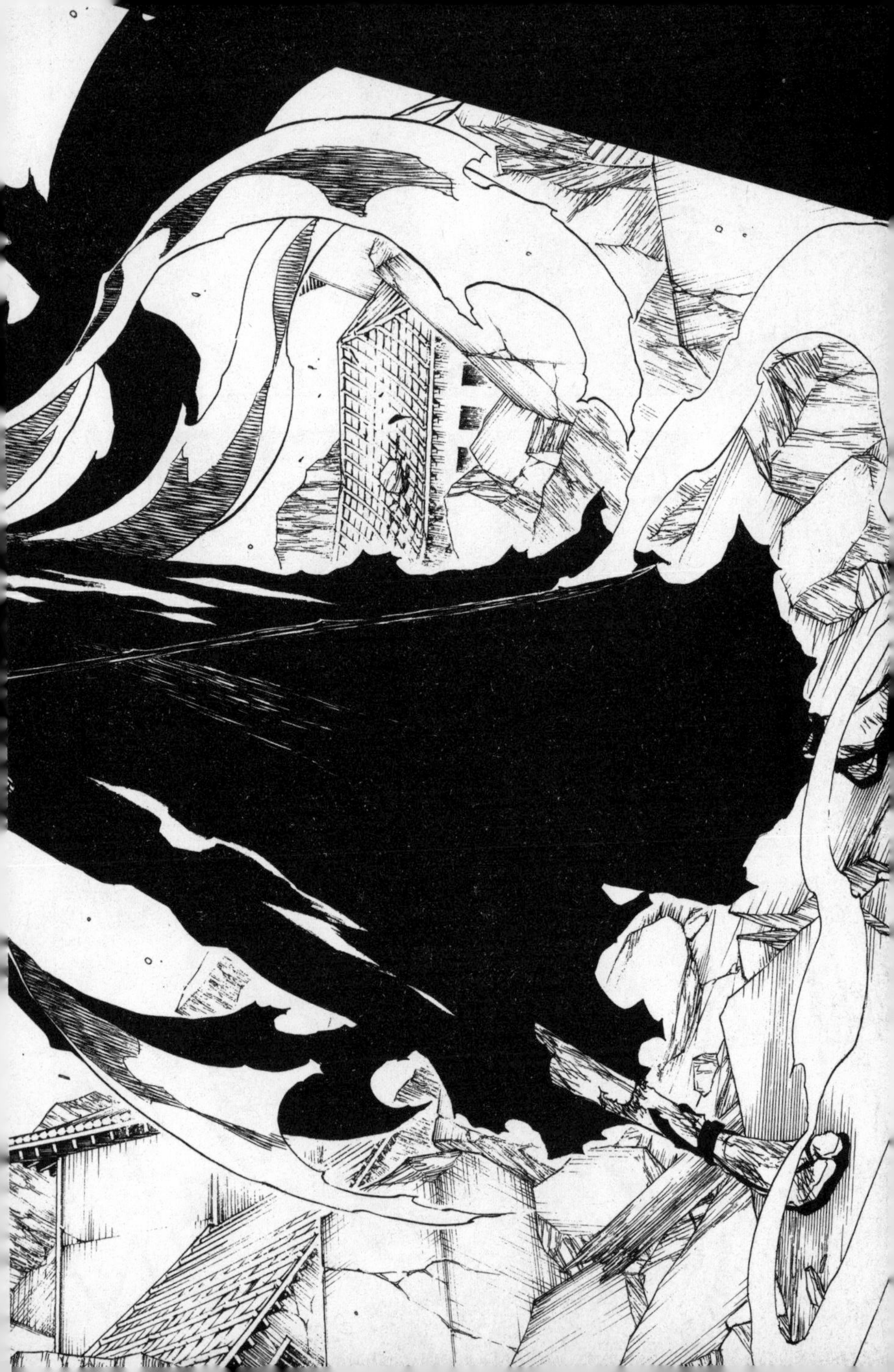

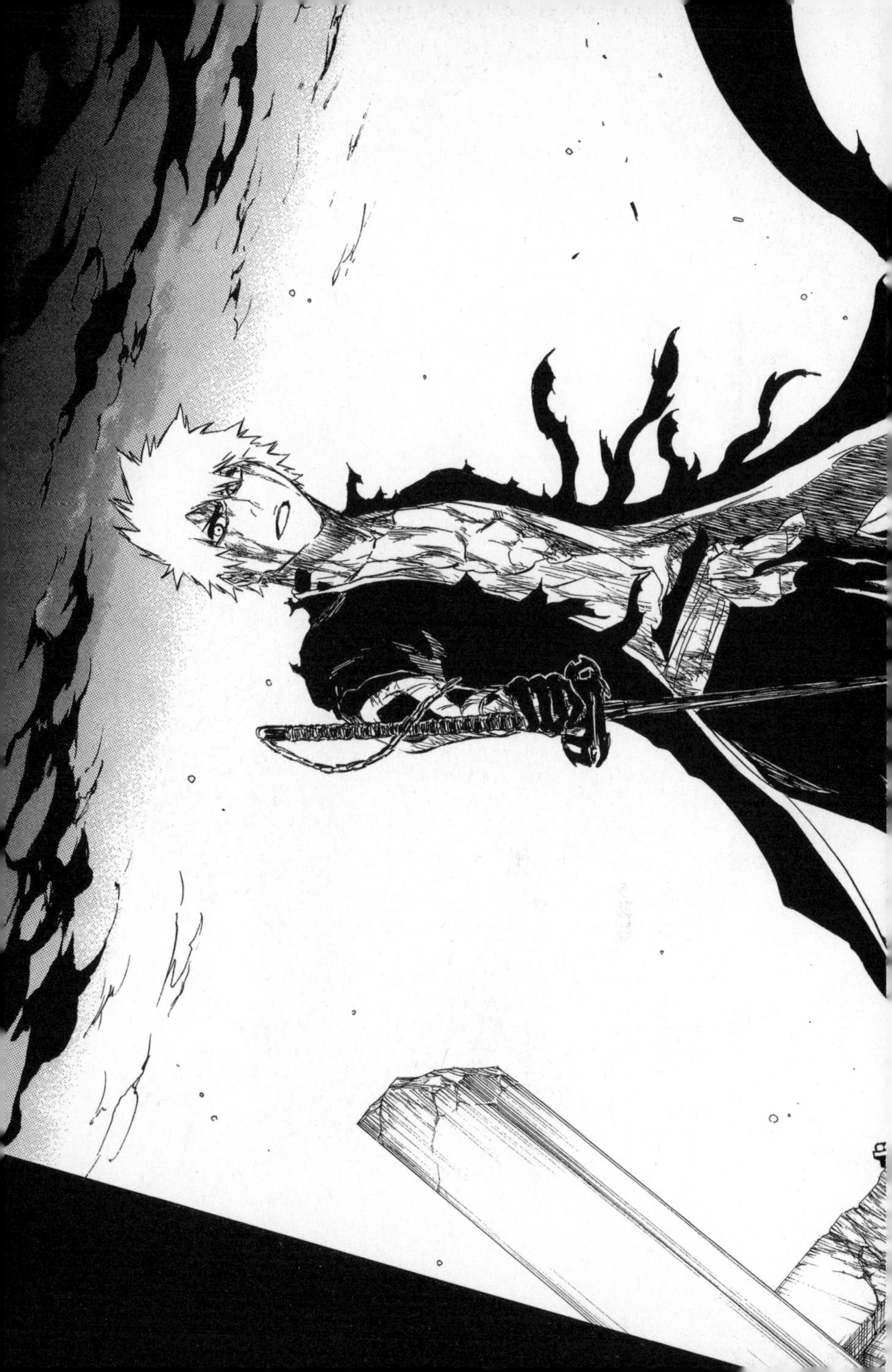

513. THE DARK MOON STROKE

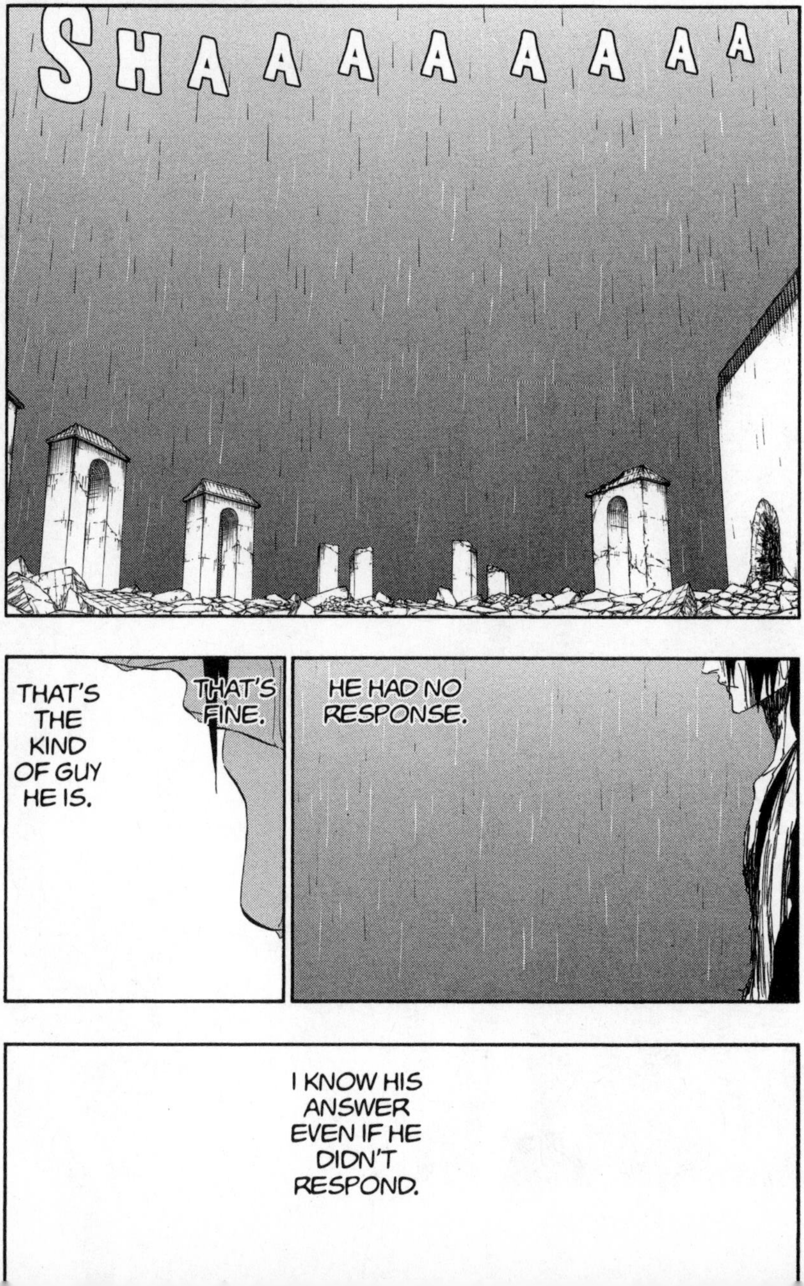
SHAAAAAAAAA
HE HAD NO RESPONSE.
THAT'S FINE.
THAT'S THE KIND OF GUY HE IS.
I KNOW HIS ANSWER EVEN IF HE DIDN'T RESPOND.

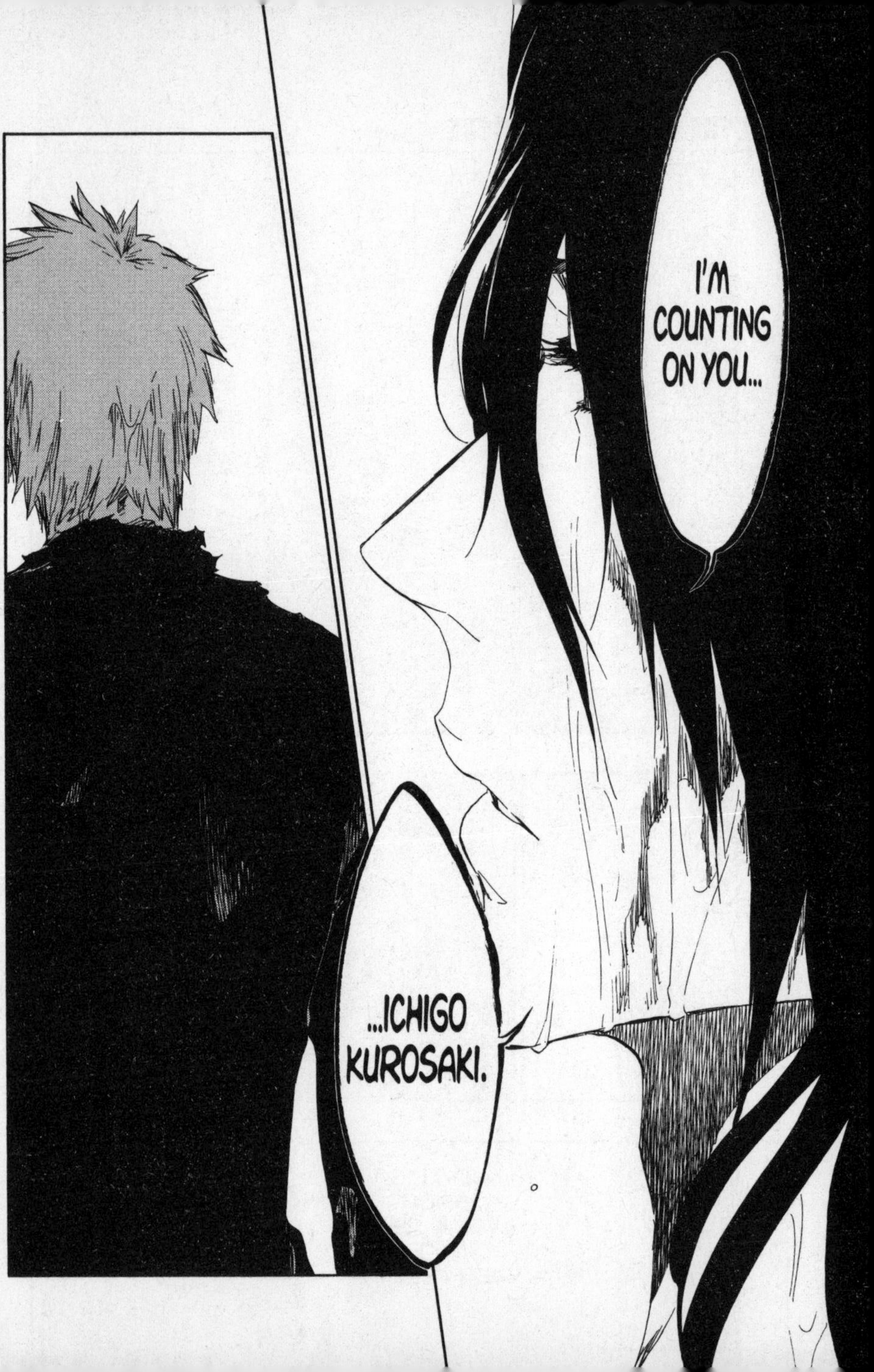
I'M COUNTING ON YOU...
...ICHIGO KUROSAKI.

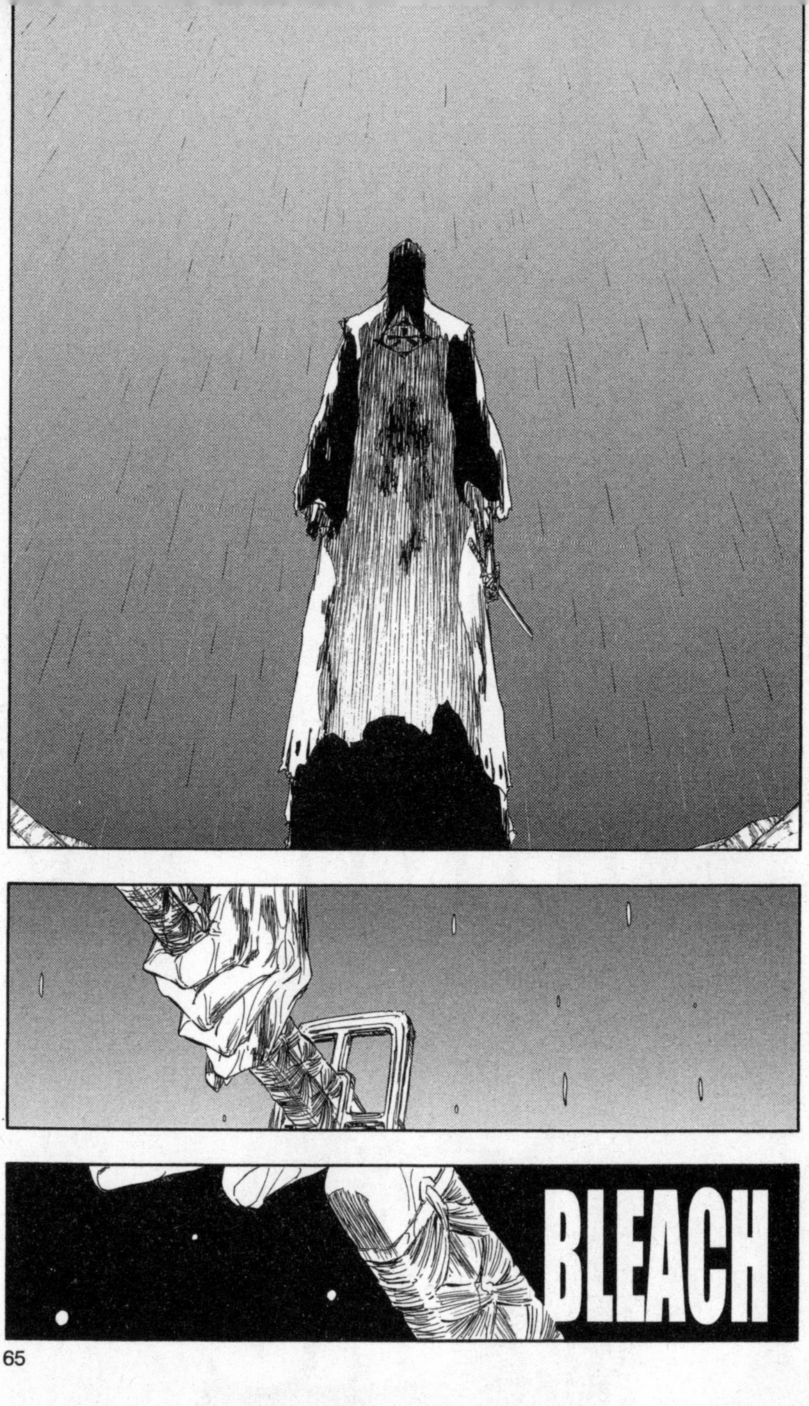
BLEACH

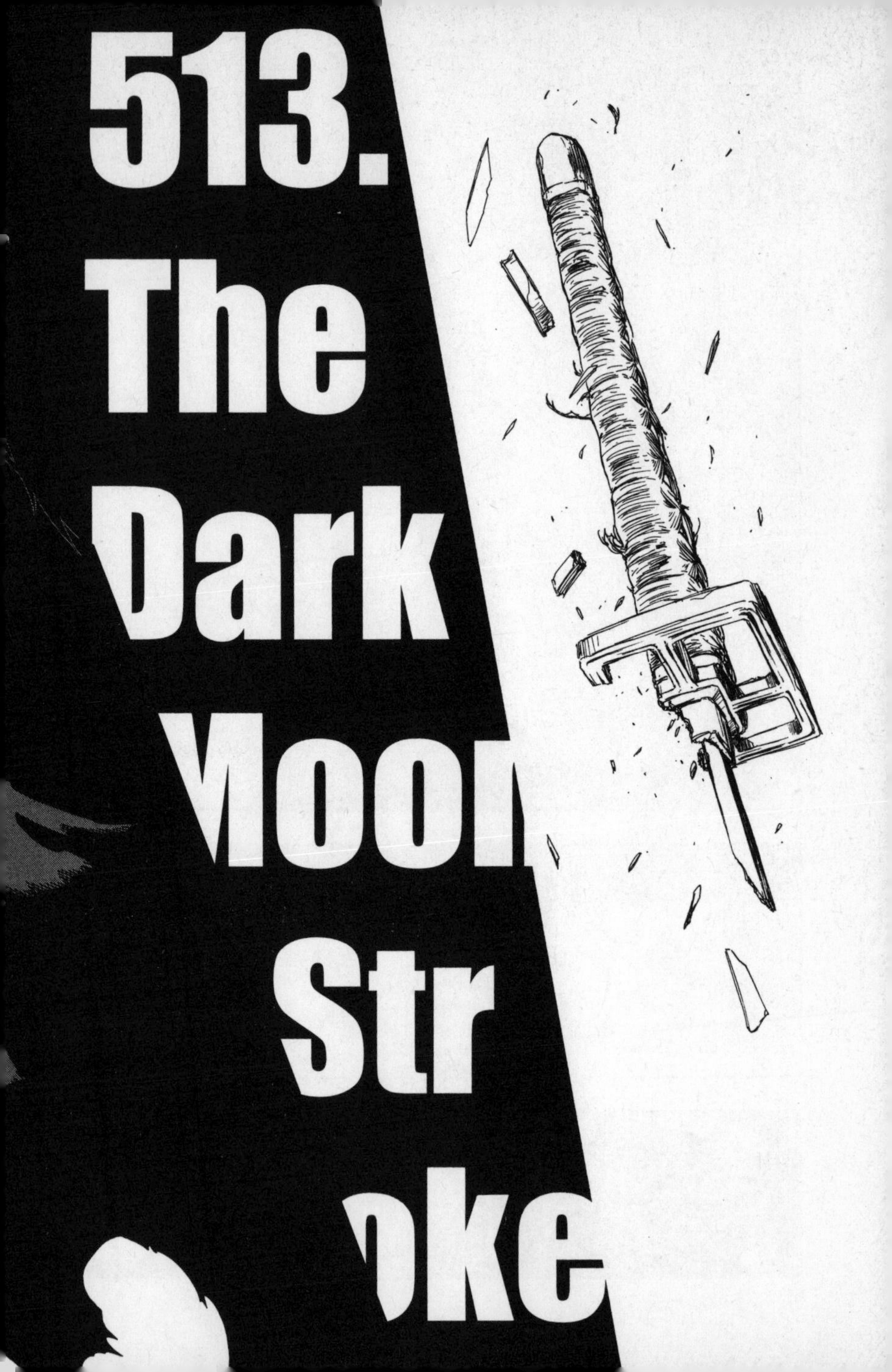
513. The Dark Moon Stroke

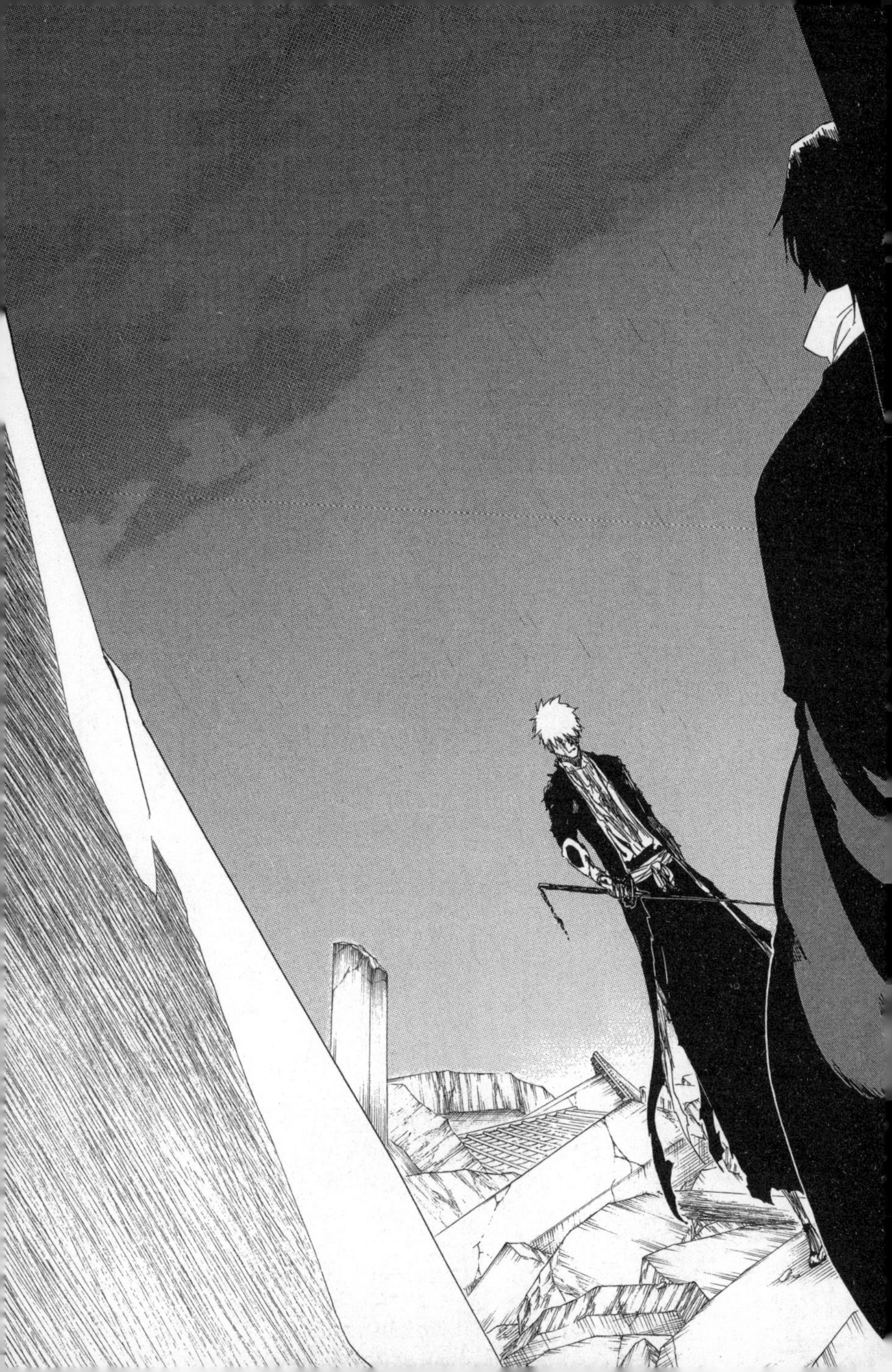

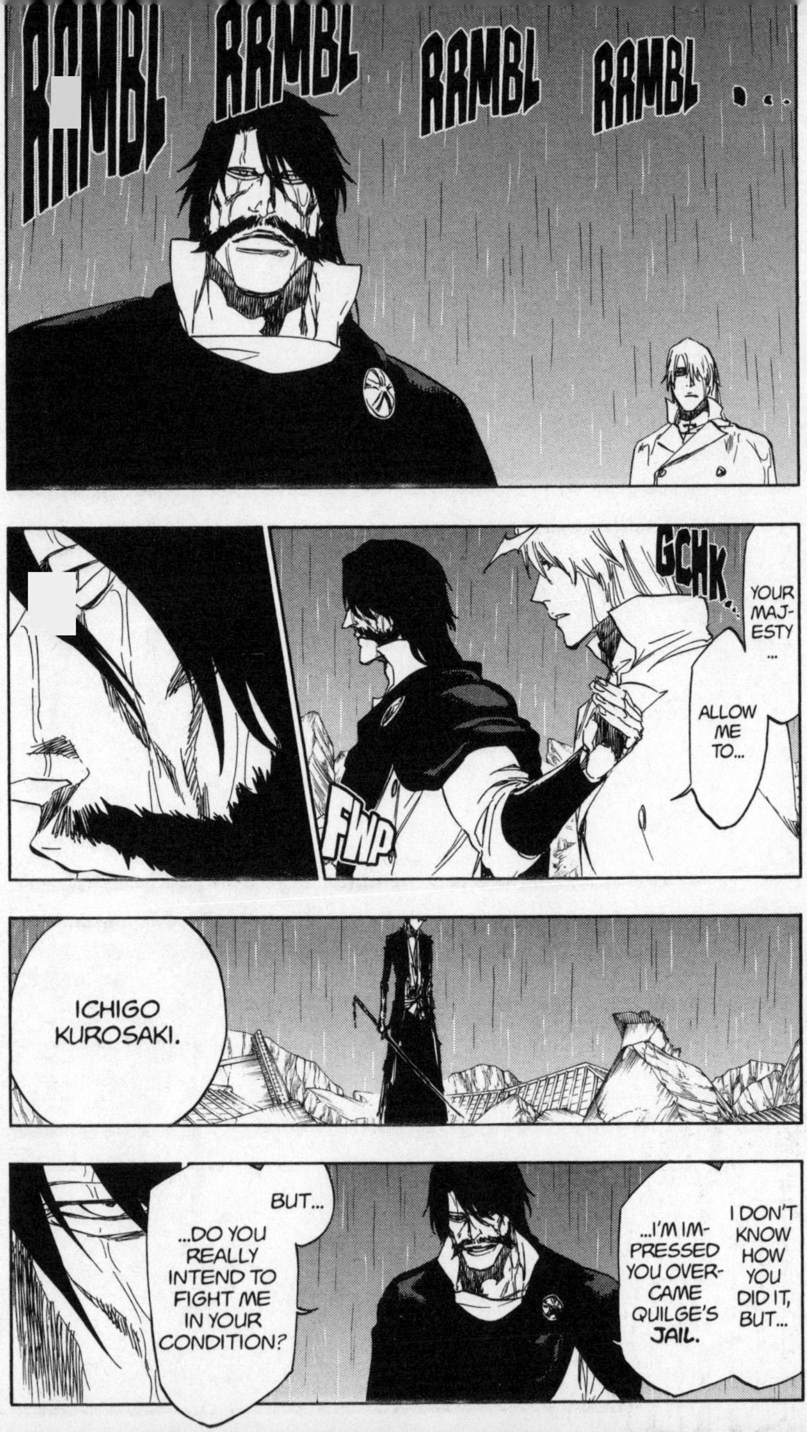
RRMBL RRMBL RRMBL RRMBL . . .
GCHK . .
YOUR MAJ-ESTY ...
ALLOW ME TO...
FWP
ICHIGO KUROSAKI.
I DON'T KNOW HOW YOU DID IT, BUT...
...I'M IM-PRESSED YOU OVER-CAME QUILGE'S **JAIL.**
BUT...
...DO YOU REALLY INTEND TO FIGHT ME IN YOUR CONDITION?

READ THIS WAY

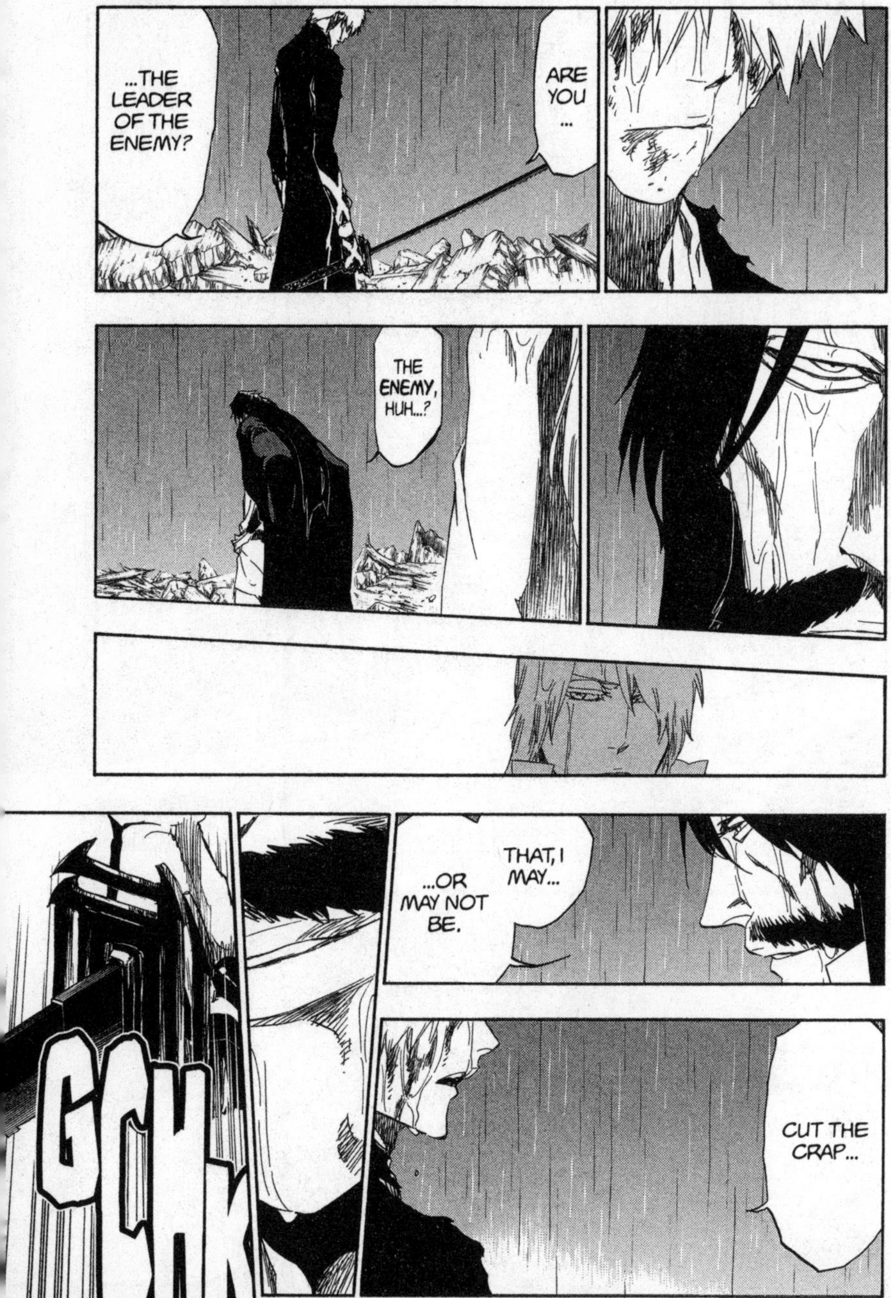
ARE YOU ...
...THE LEADER OF THE ENEMY?
THE ENEMY, HUH...?
THAT, I MAY...
...OR MAY NOT BE.
CUT THE CRAP...
GCHK

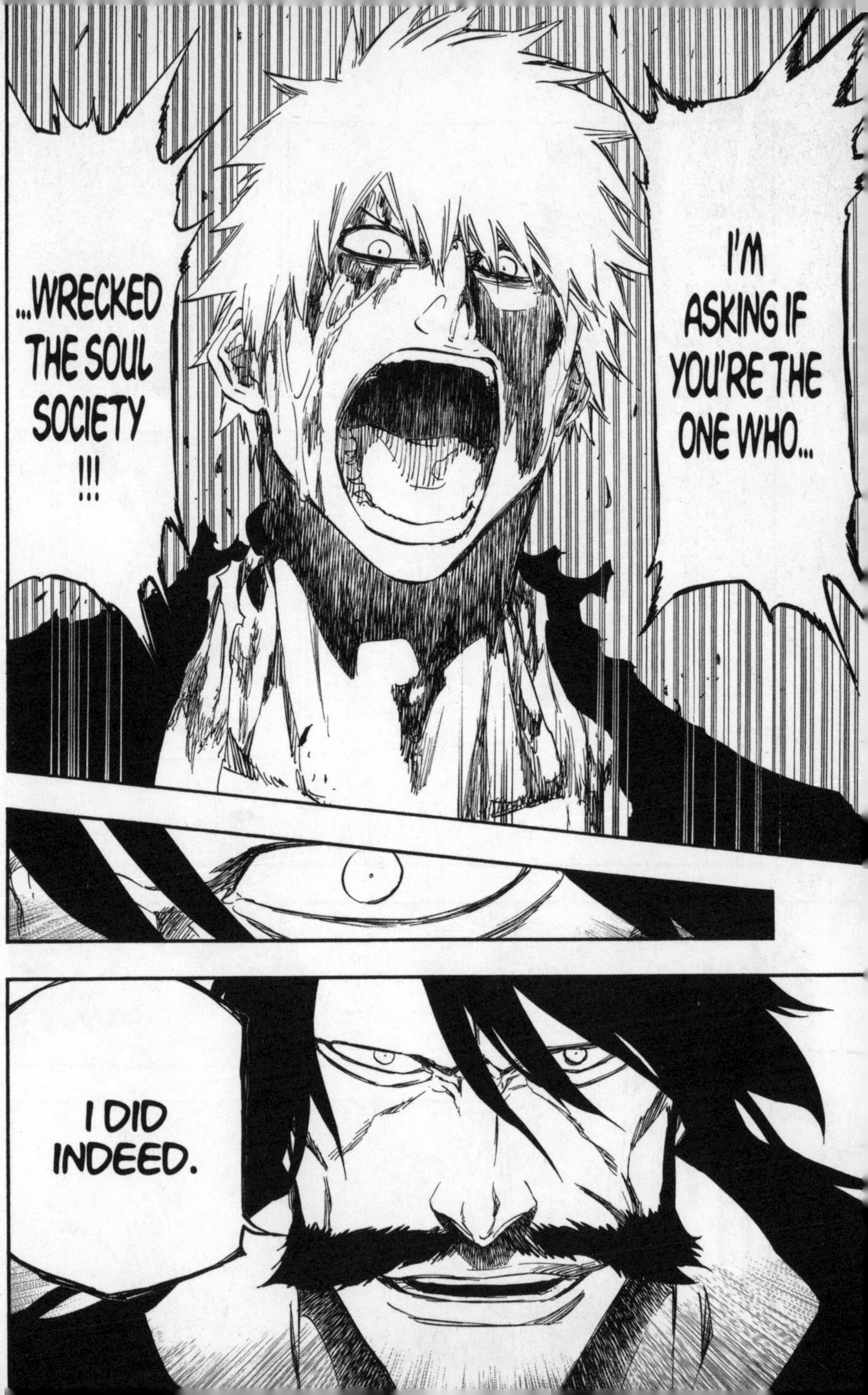
I'M ASKING IF YOU'RE THE ONE WHO...
...WRECKED THE SOUL SOCIETY !!!
I DID INDEED.

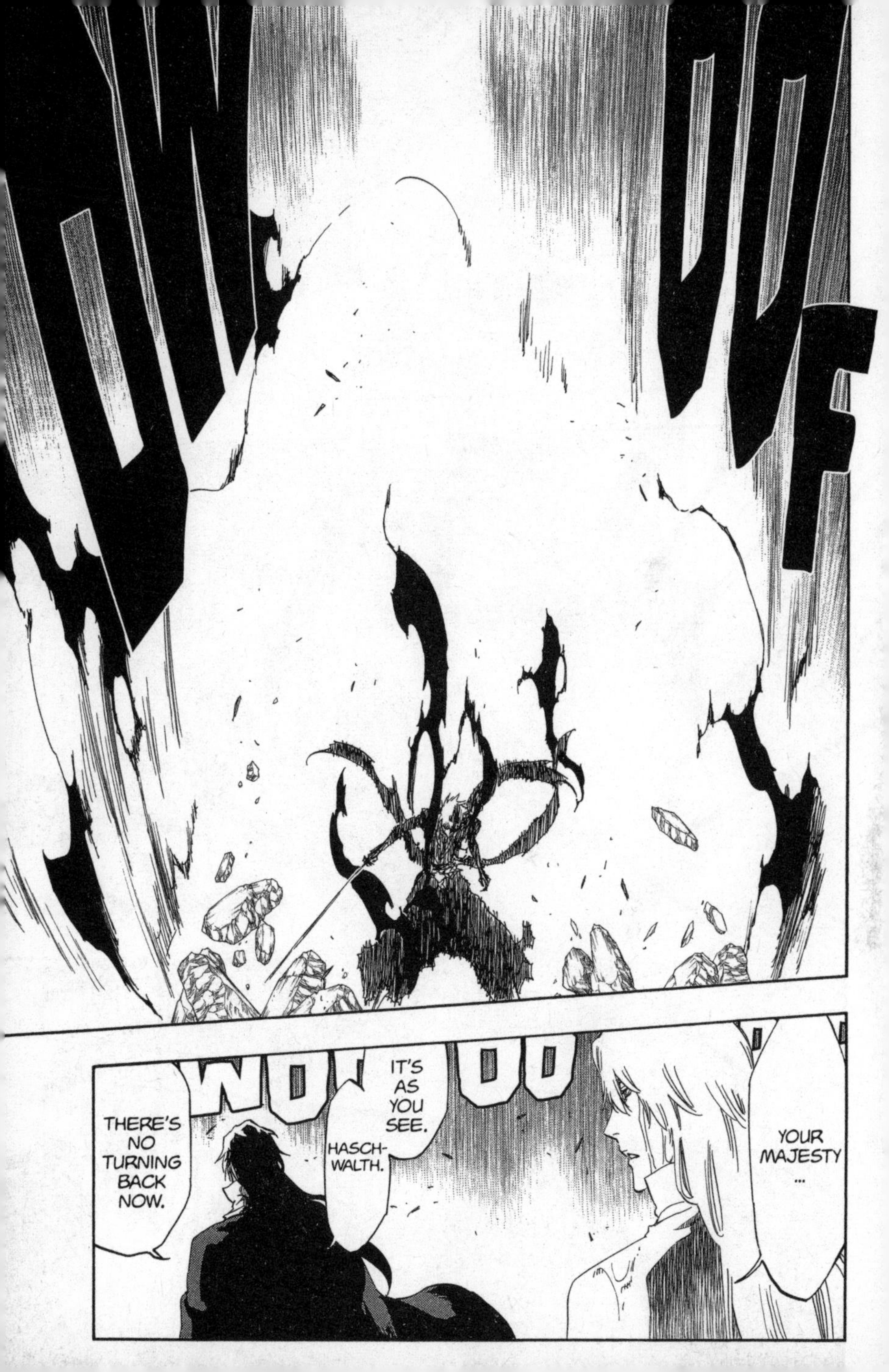
YOUR MAJESTY ...
IT'S AS YOU SEE.
HASCH-WALTH.
THERE'S NO TURNING BACK NOW.

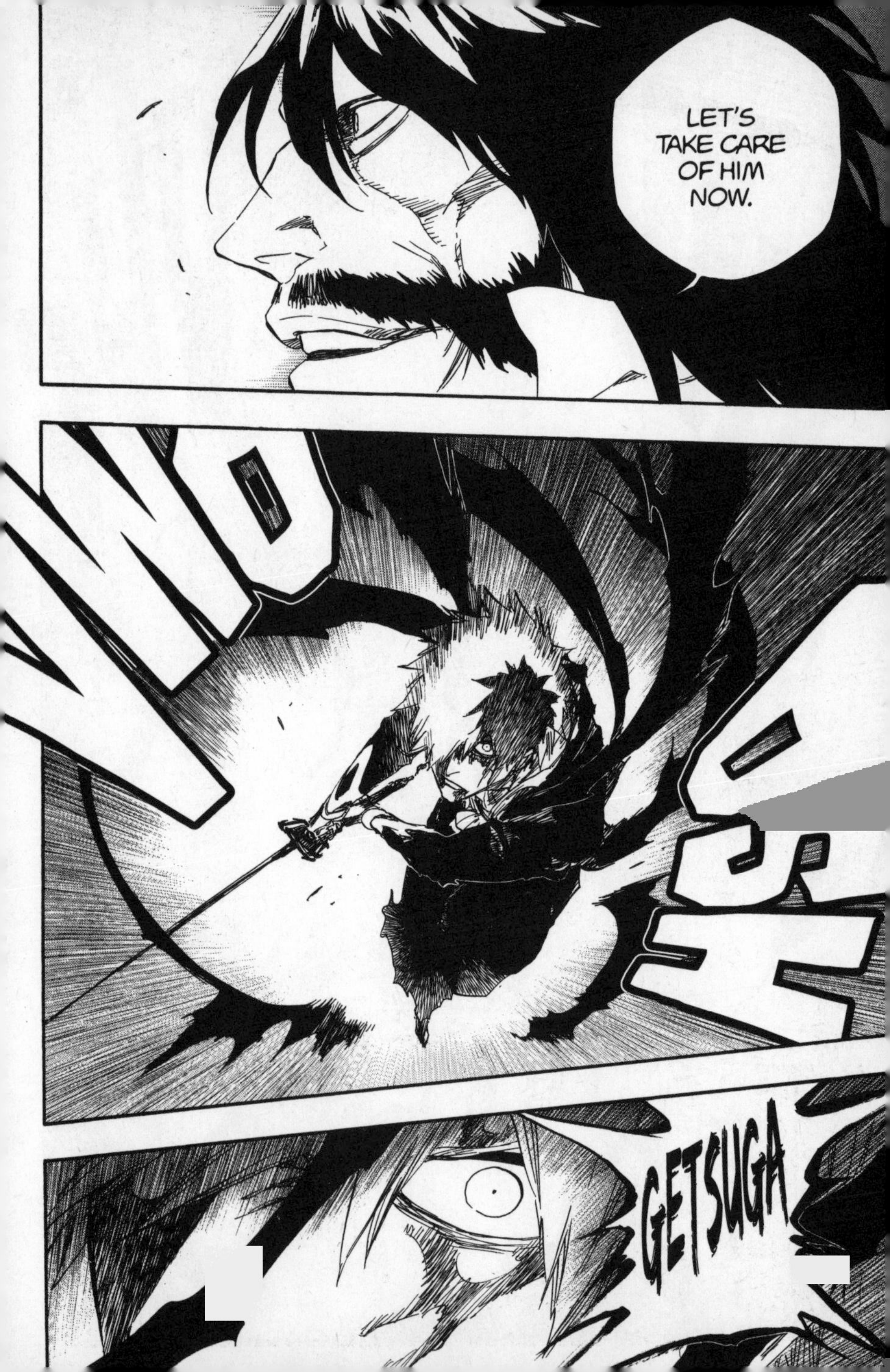
LET'S TAKE CARE OF HIM NOW.
GETSUGA

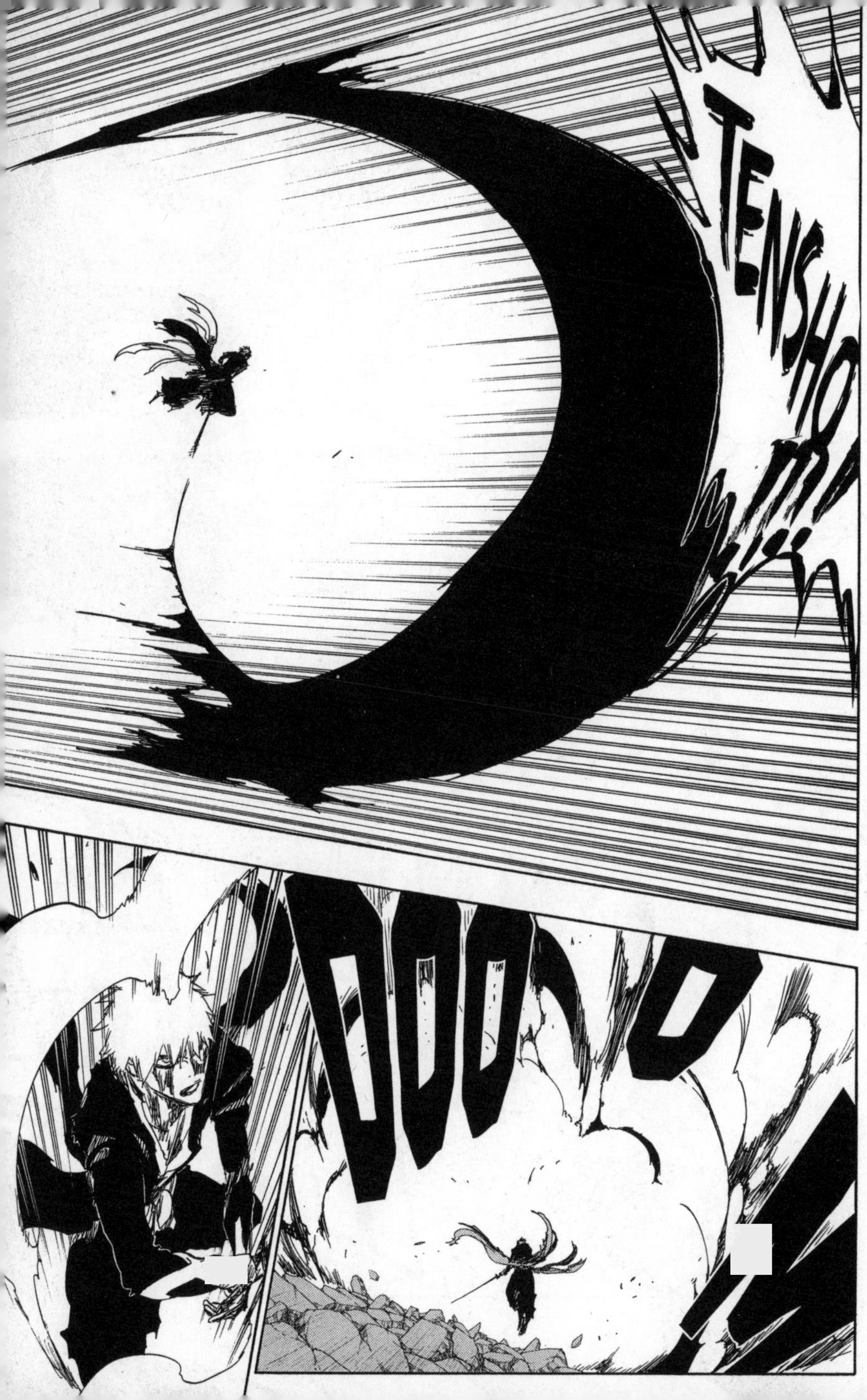
TENSHO

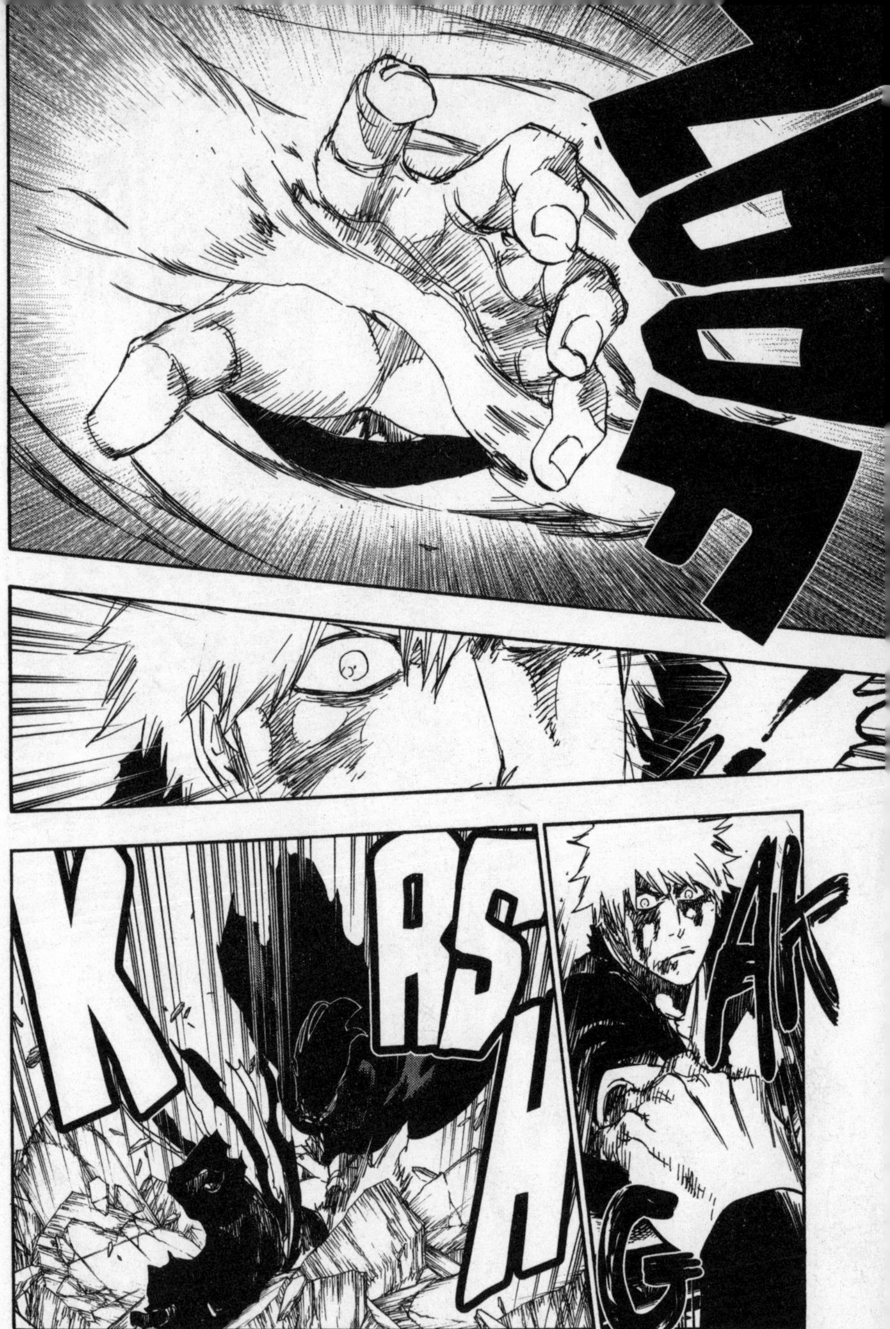
KRASH

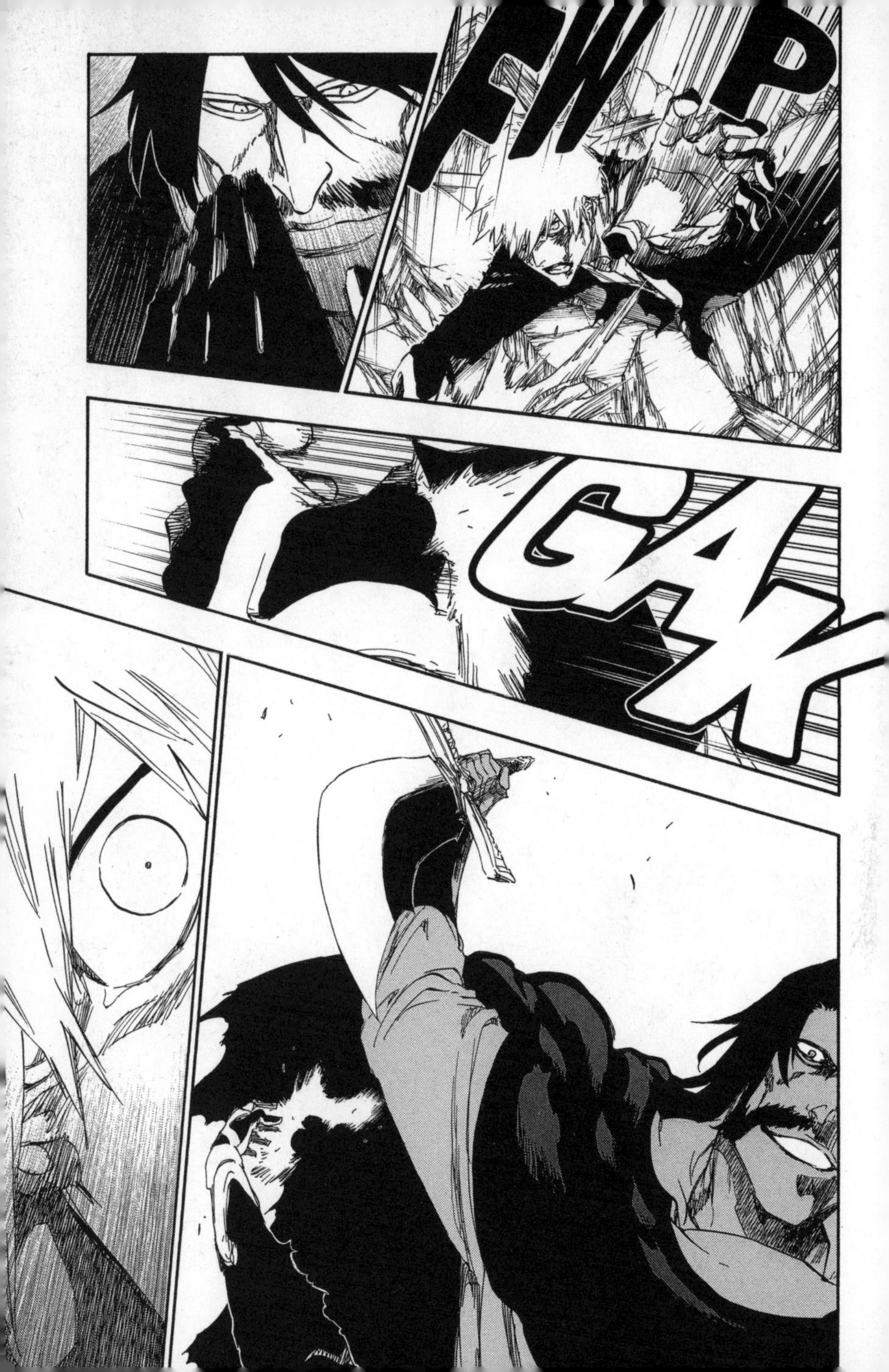
FWIP
GAK

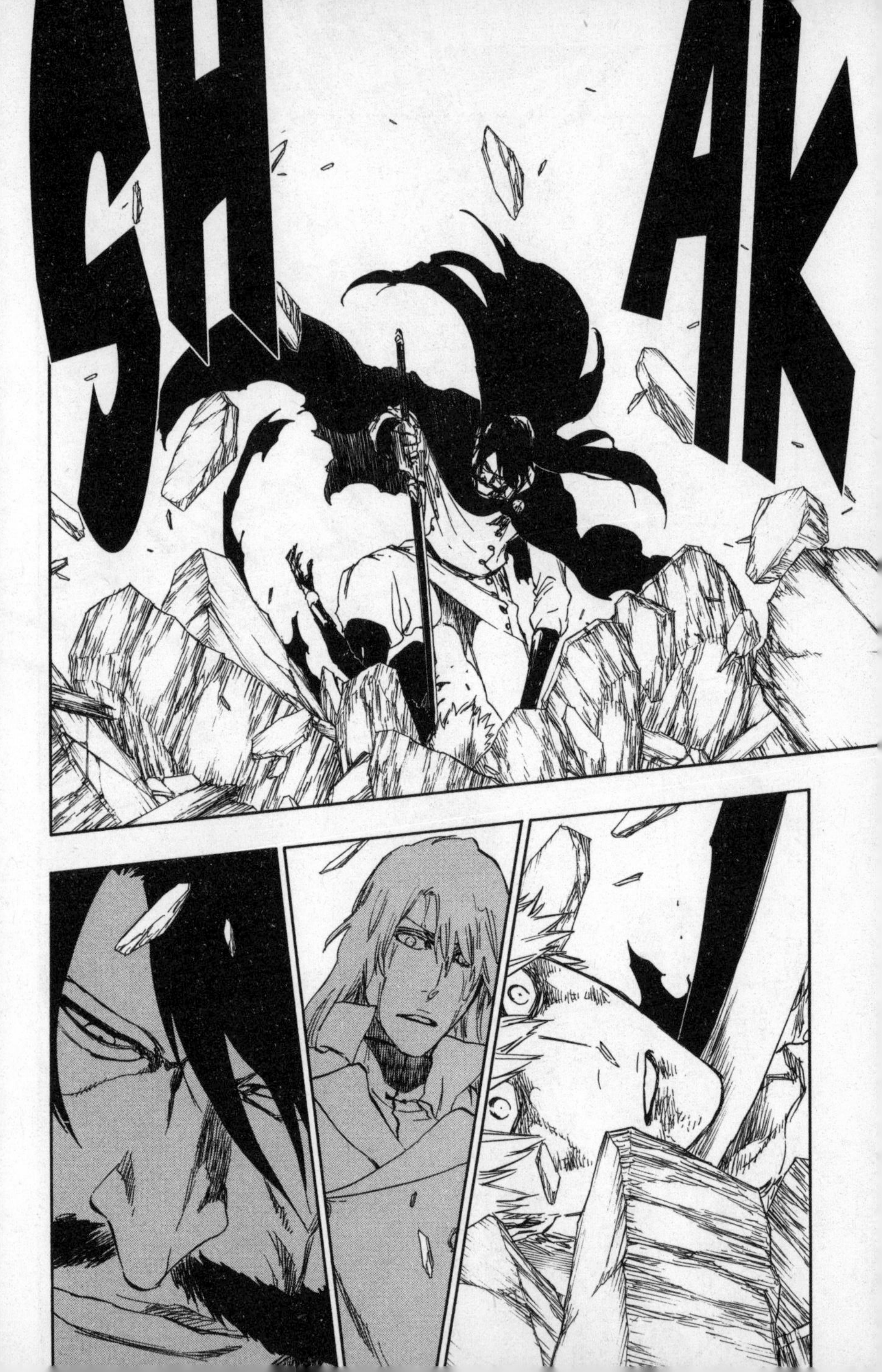
SHAK

READ THIS WAY

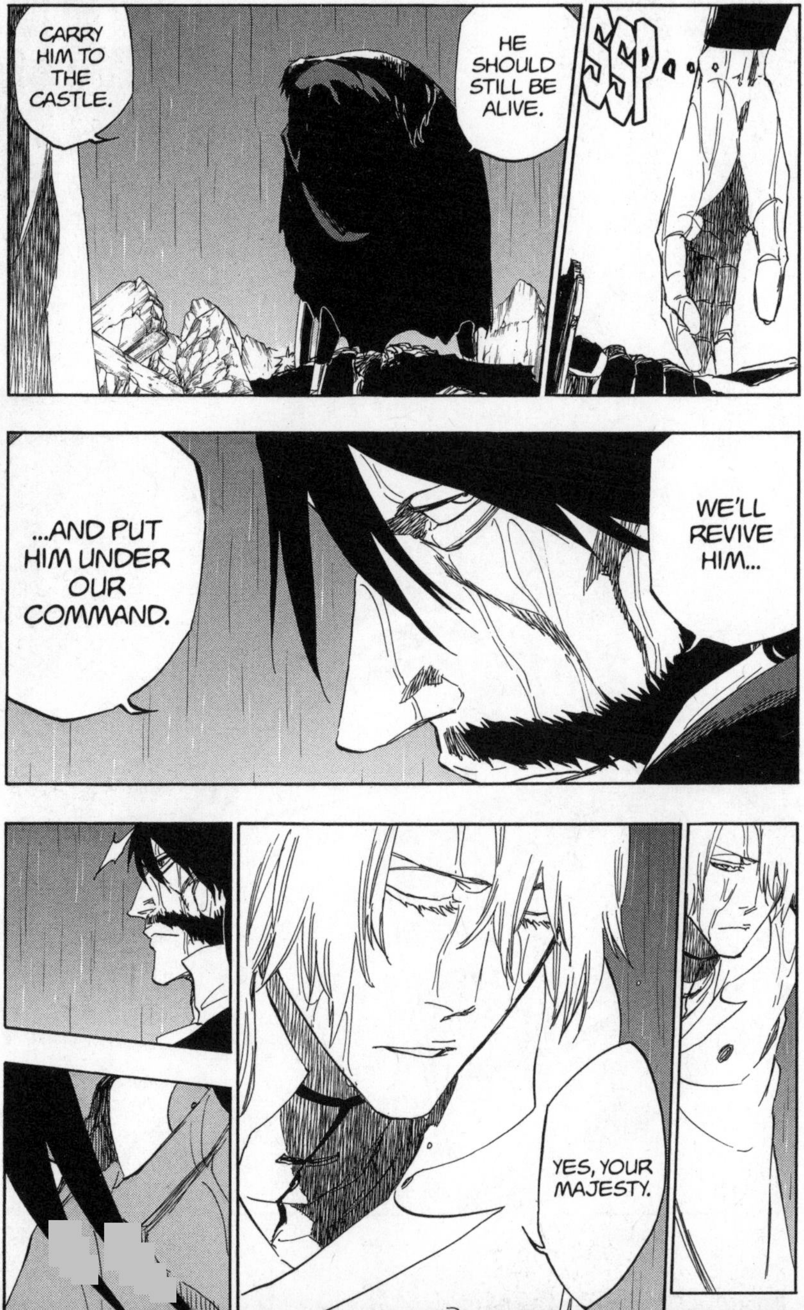
SSP...
HE SHOULD STILL BE ALIVE.
CARRY HIM TO THE CASTLE.
WE'LL REVIVE HIM...
...AND PUT HIM UNDER OUR COMMAND.
YES, YOUR MAJESTY.

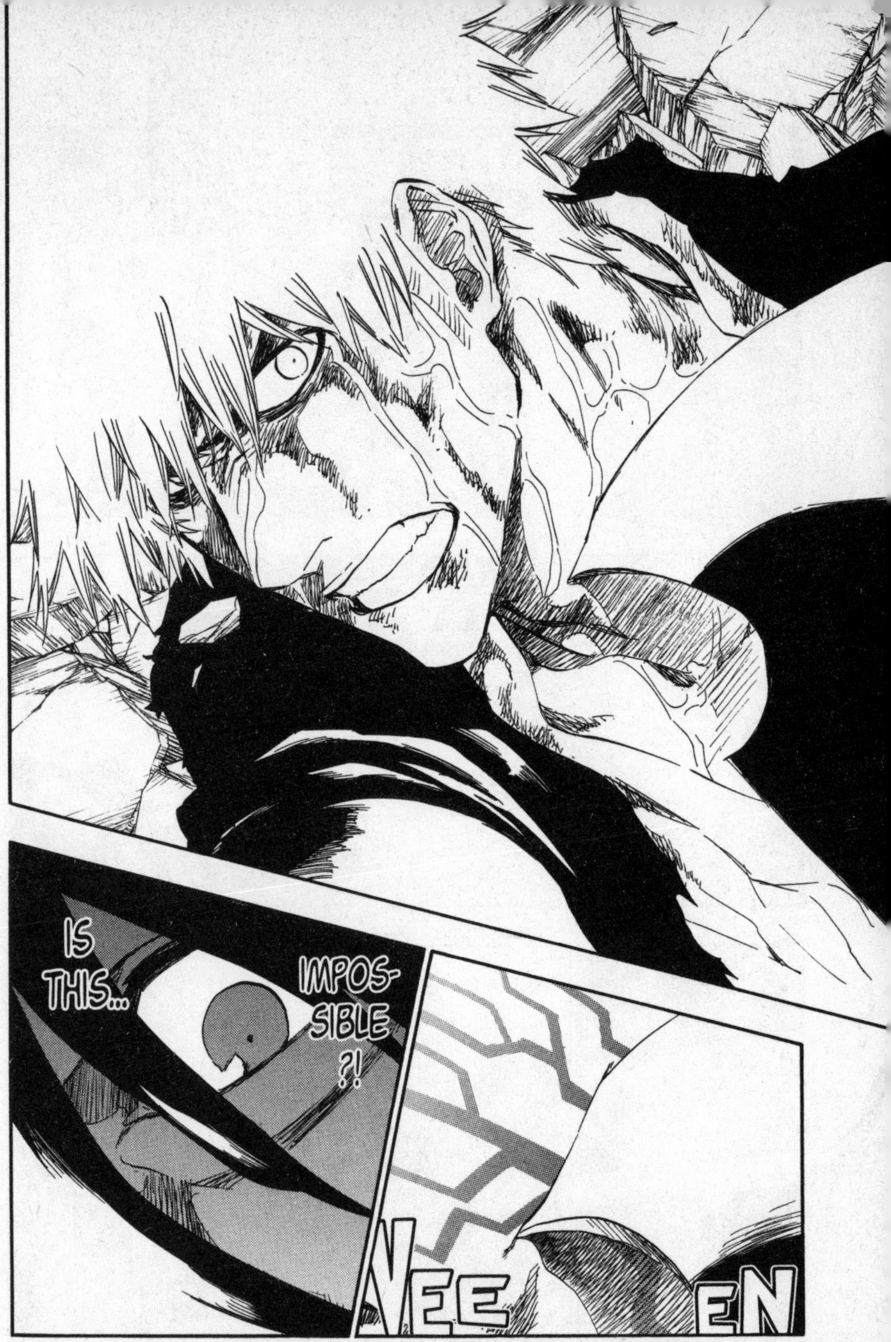
NEE EN
IS THIS...
IMPOS-SIBLE ?!

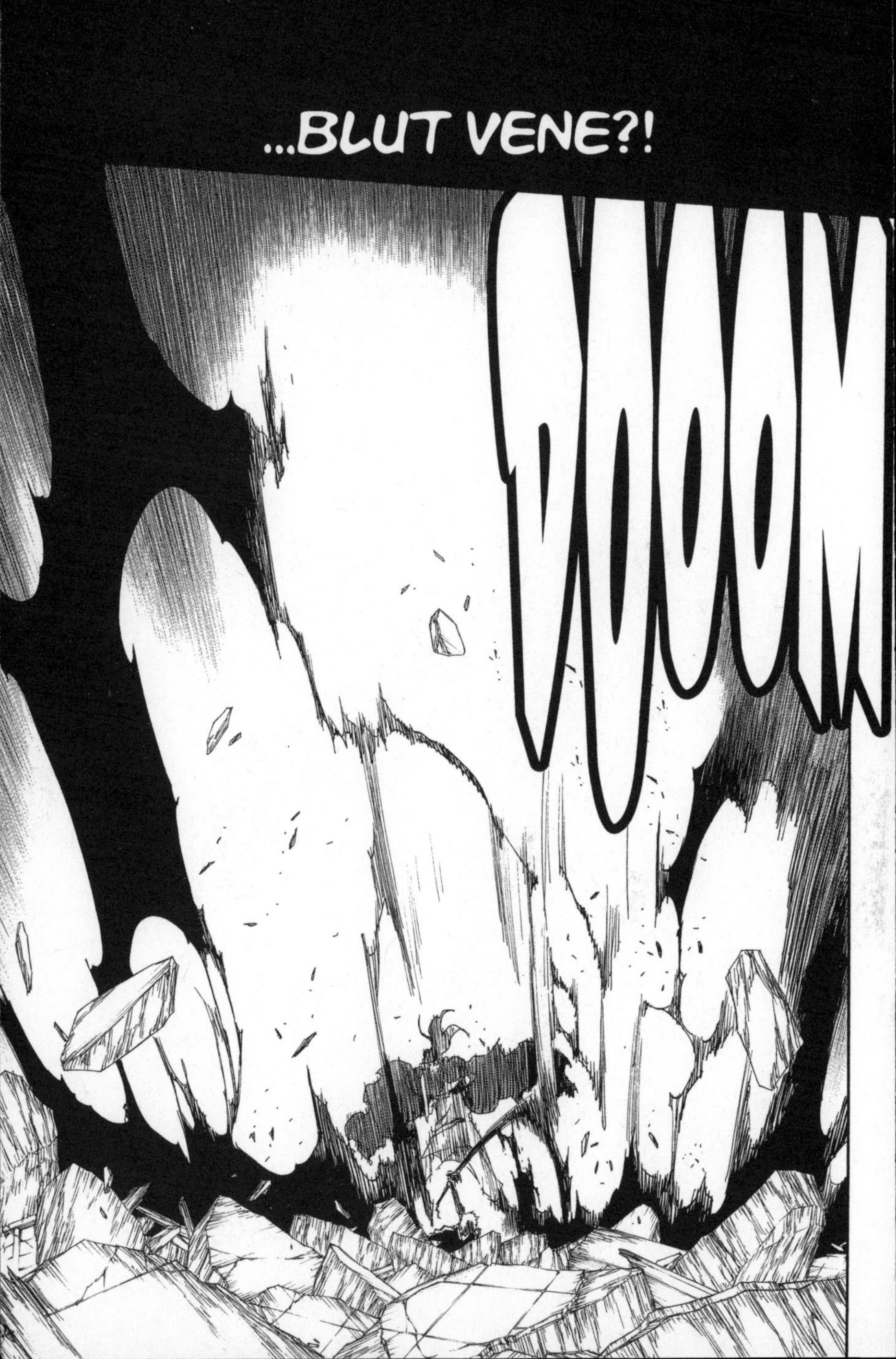
...BLUT VENE?!
DOOOM

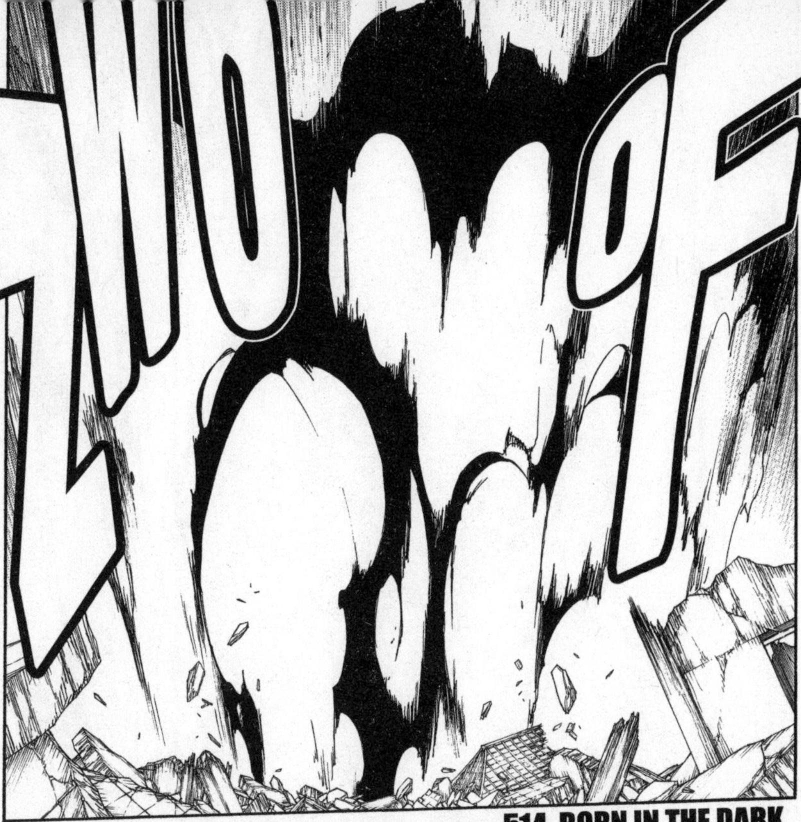
ZWOOOF

514. BORN IN THE DARK

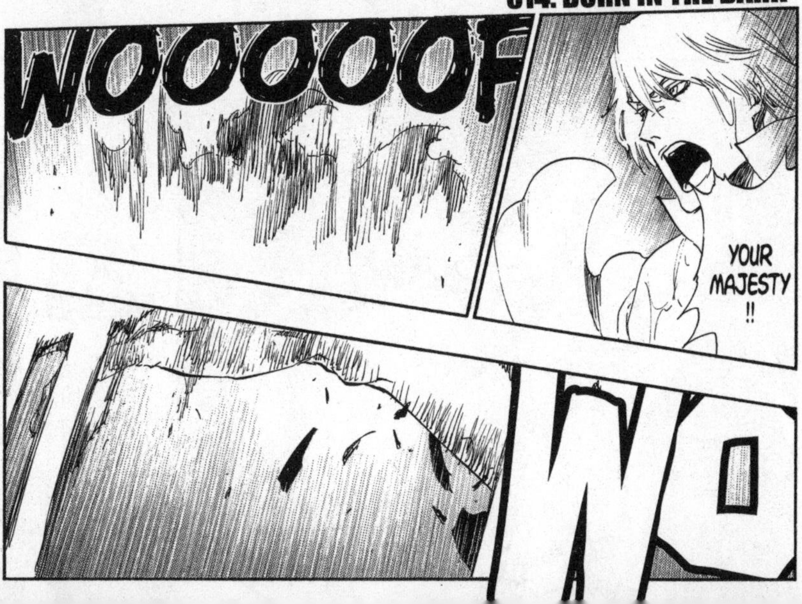
YOUR MAJESTY !!
WOOOOOF
WO

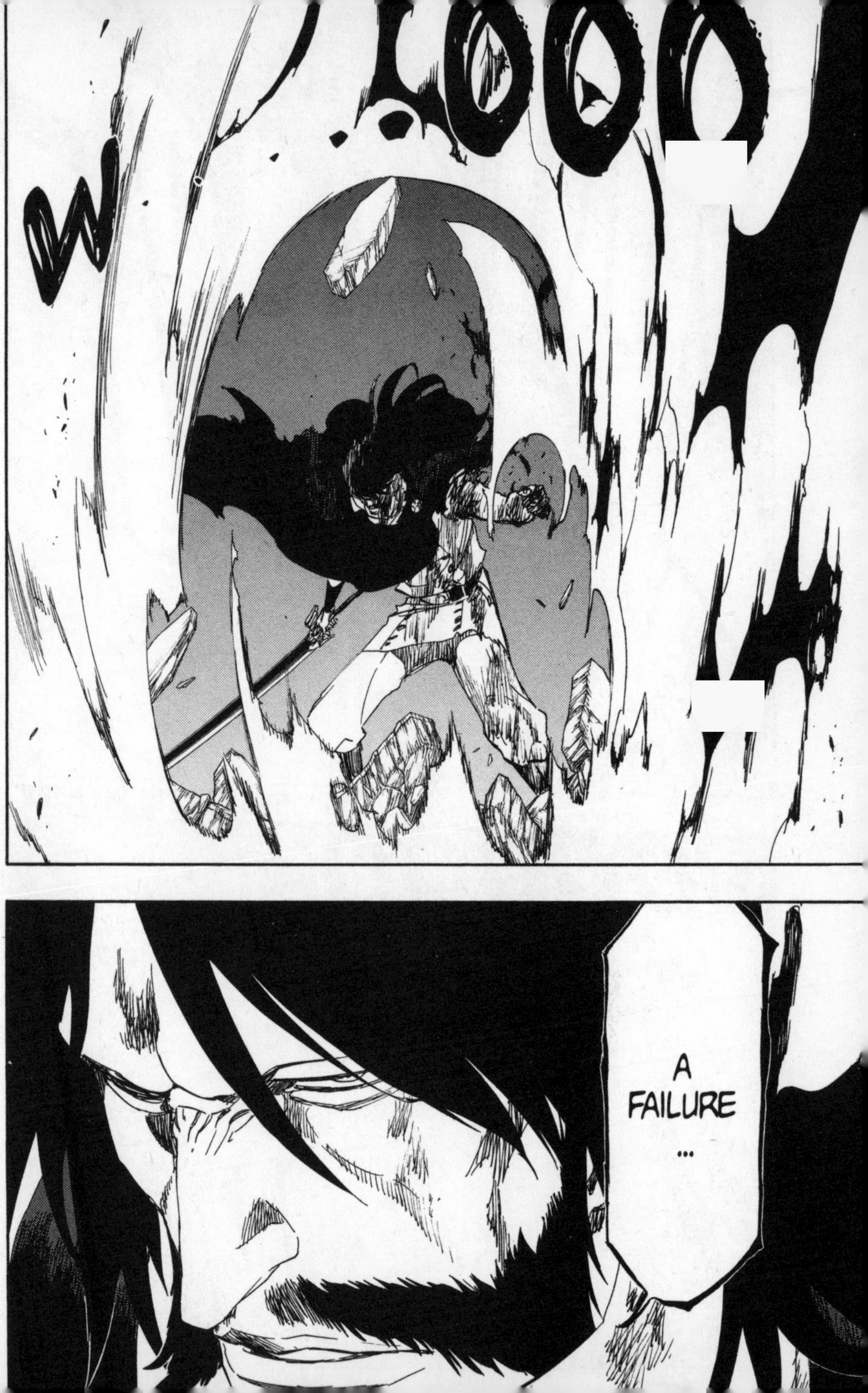
A FAILURE ...

READ THIS WAY

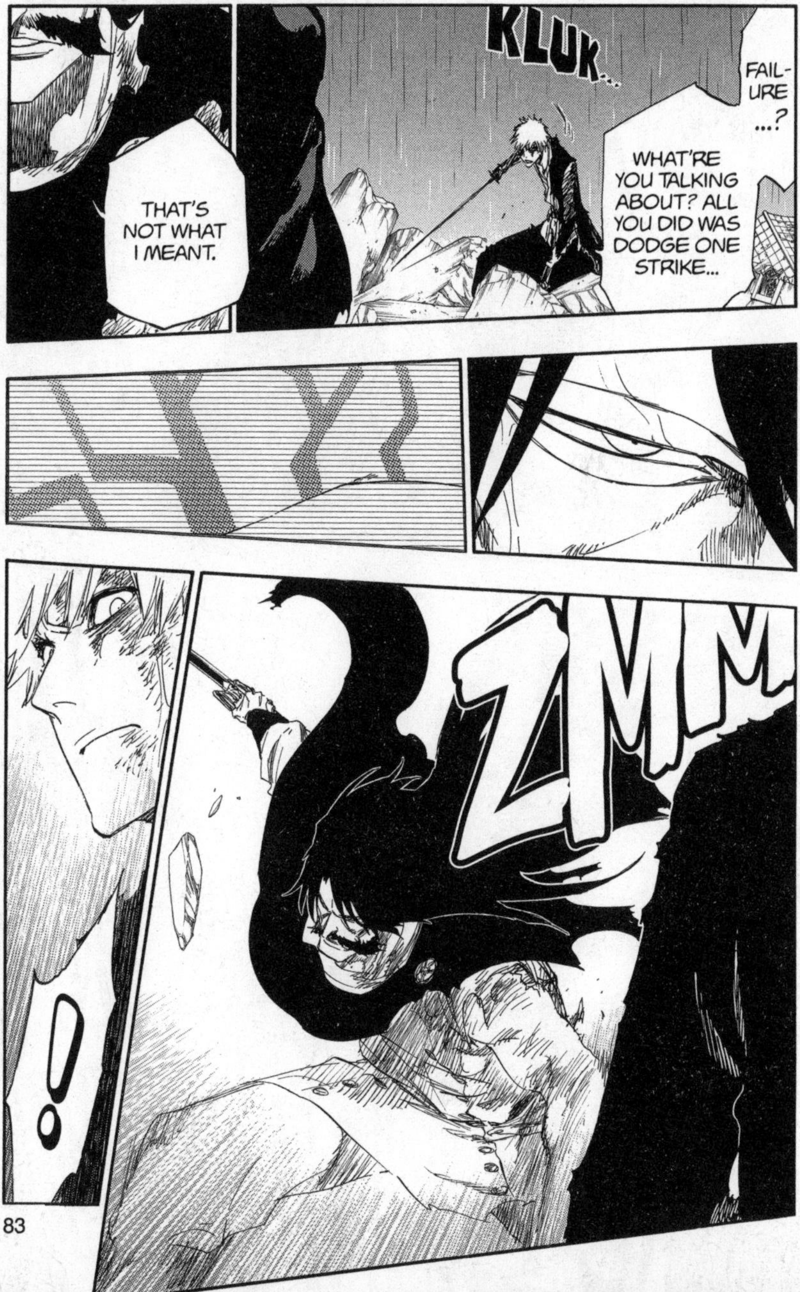

KLUK...
FAIL-URE ...?
WHAT'RE YOU TALKING ABOUT? ALL YOU DID WAS DODGE ONE STRIKE...
THAT'S NOT WHAT I MEANT.
ZMM
!

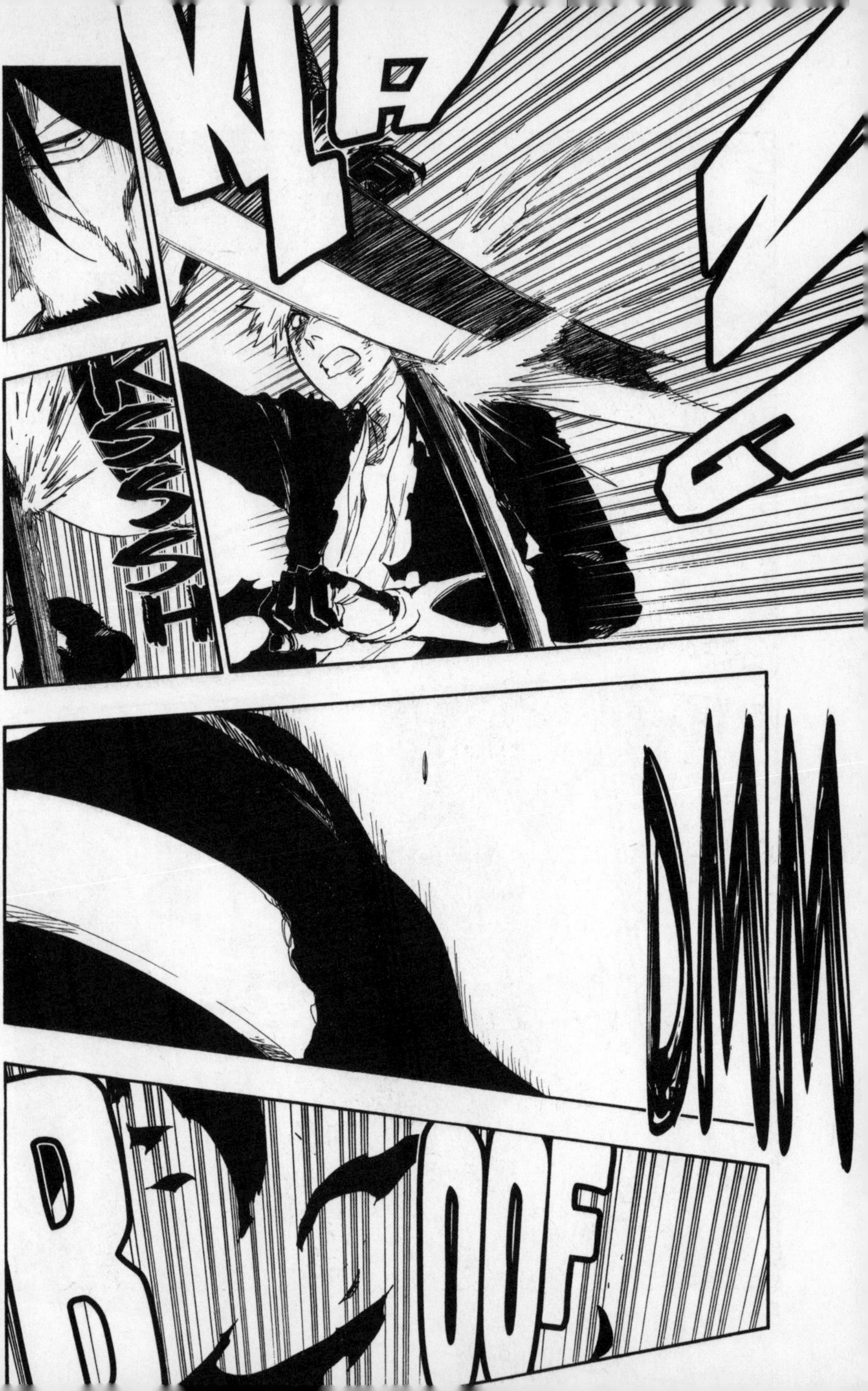
KLANG
KSSSH
DMM
BOOF

READ THIS WAY

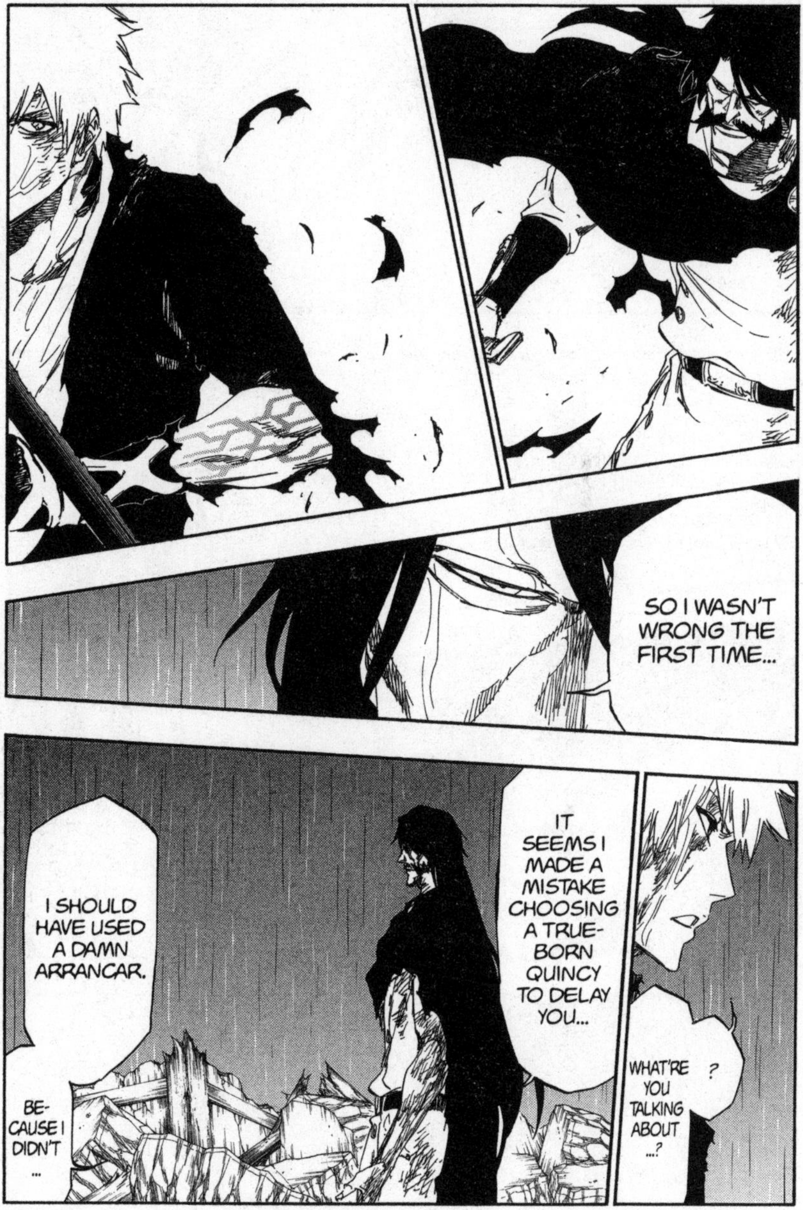
SO I WASN'T WRONG THE FIRST TIME...
?
WHAT'RE YOU TALKING ABOUT ...?
IT SEEMS I MADE A MISTAKE CHOOSING A TRUE-BORN QUINCY TO DELAY YOU...
I SHOULD HAVE USED A DAMN ARRANCAR.
BE-CAUSE I DIDN'T ...

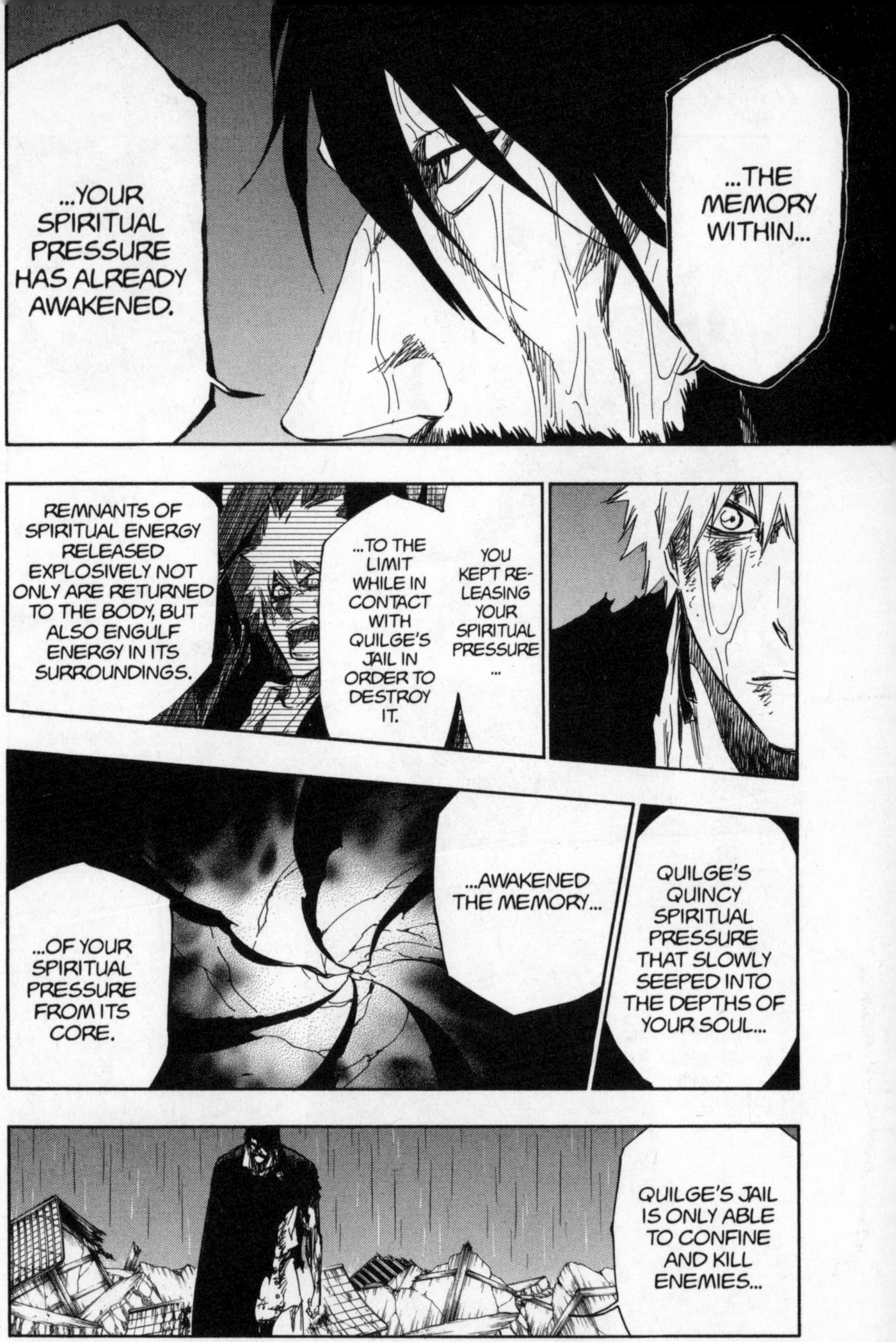
...THE MEMORY WITHIN...
...YOUR SPIRITUAL PRESSURE HAS ALREADY AWAKENED.
YOU KEPT RE-LEASING YOUR SPIRITUAL PRESSURE ...
...TO THE LIMIT WHILE IN CONTACT WITH QUILGE'S JAIL IN ORDER TO DESTROY IT.
REMNANTS OF SPIRITUAL ENERGY RELEASED EXPLOSIVELY NOT ONLY ARE RETURNED TO THE BODY, BUT ALSO ENGULF ENERGY IN ITS SURROUNDINGS.
QUILGE'S QUINCY SPIRITUAL PRESSURE THAT SLOWLY SEEPED INTO THE DEPTHS OF YOUR SOUL...
...AWAKENED THE MEMORY...
...OF YOUR SPIRITUAL PRESSURE FROM ITS CORE.
QUILGE'S JAIL IS ONLY ABLE TO CONFINE AND KILL ENEMIES...

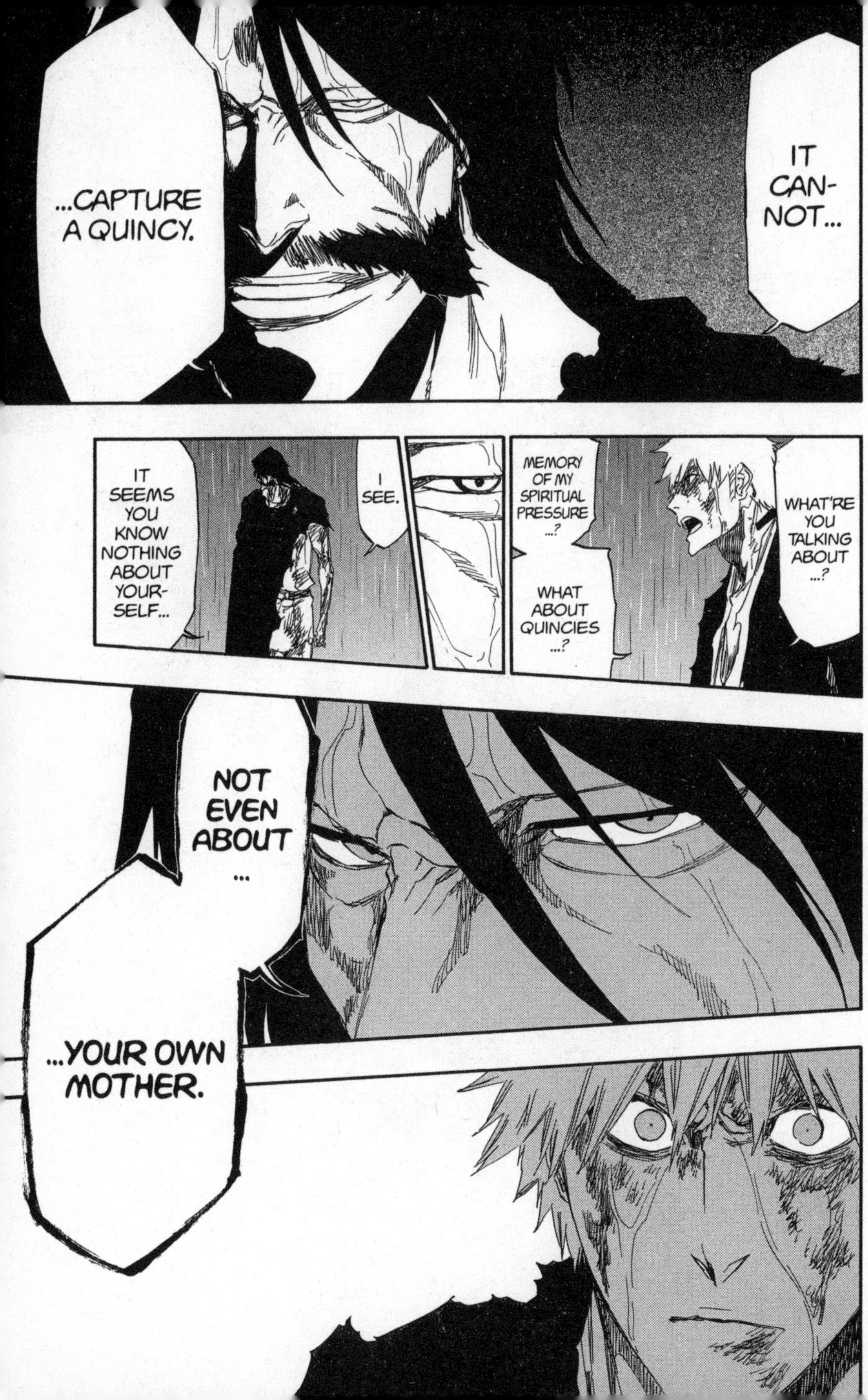
IT CAN-NOT...
...CAPTURE A QUINCY.
MEMORY OF MY SPIRITUAL PRESSURE ...?
WHAT ABOUT QUINCIES ...?
WHAT'RE YOU TALKING ABOUT ...?
I SEE.
IT SEEMS YOU KNOW NOTHING ABOUT YOUR-SELF...
NOT EVEN ABOUT ...
...YOUR OWN MOTHER.

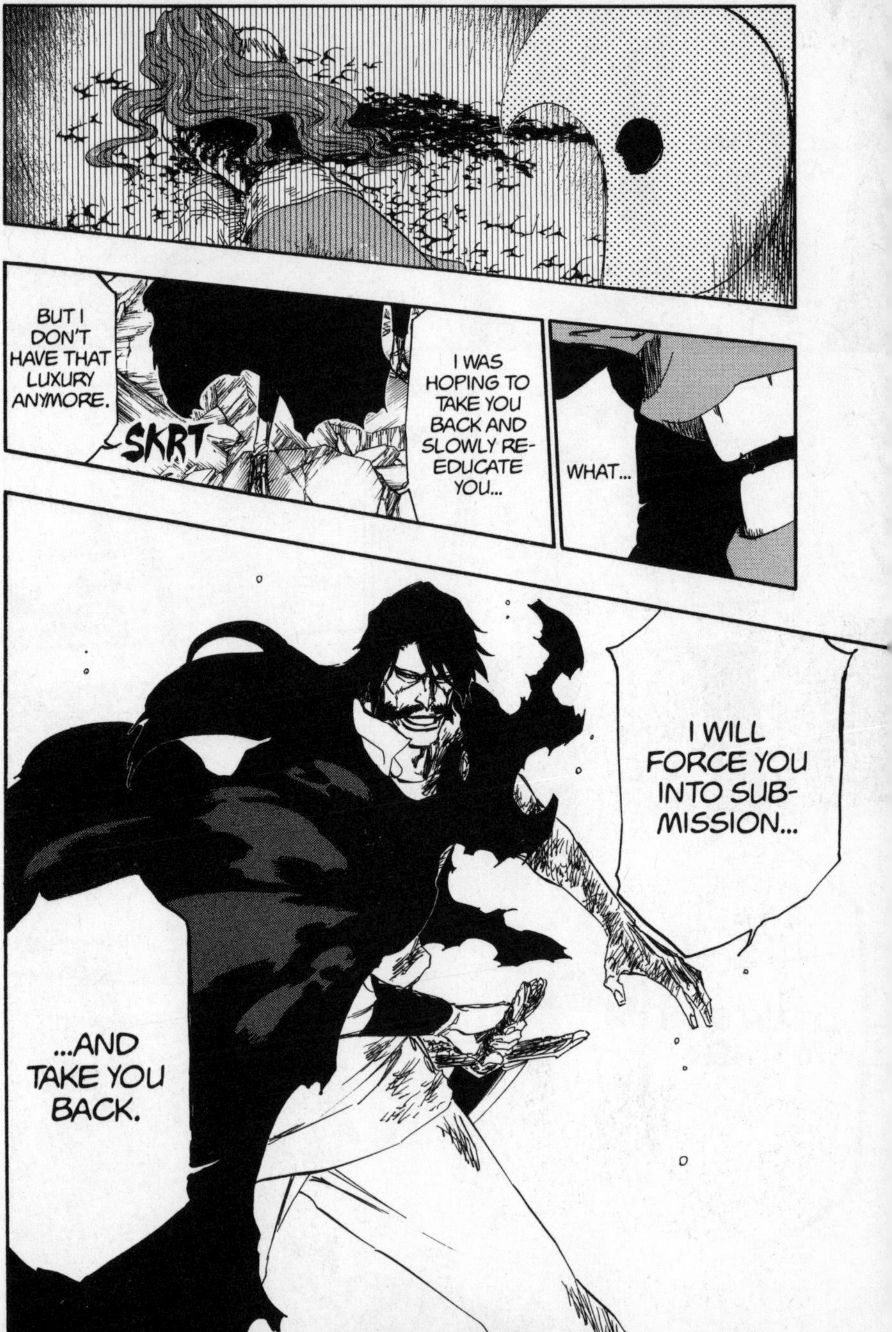
WHAT...
I WAS HOPING TO TAKE YOU BACK AND SLOWLY RE-EDUCATE YOU...
SKRT
BUT I DON'T HAVE THAT LUXURY ANYMORE.
I WILL FORCE YOU INTO SUB-MISSION...
...AND TAKE YOU BACK.

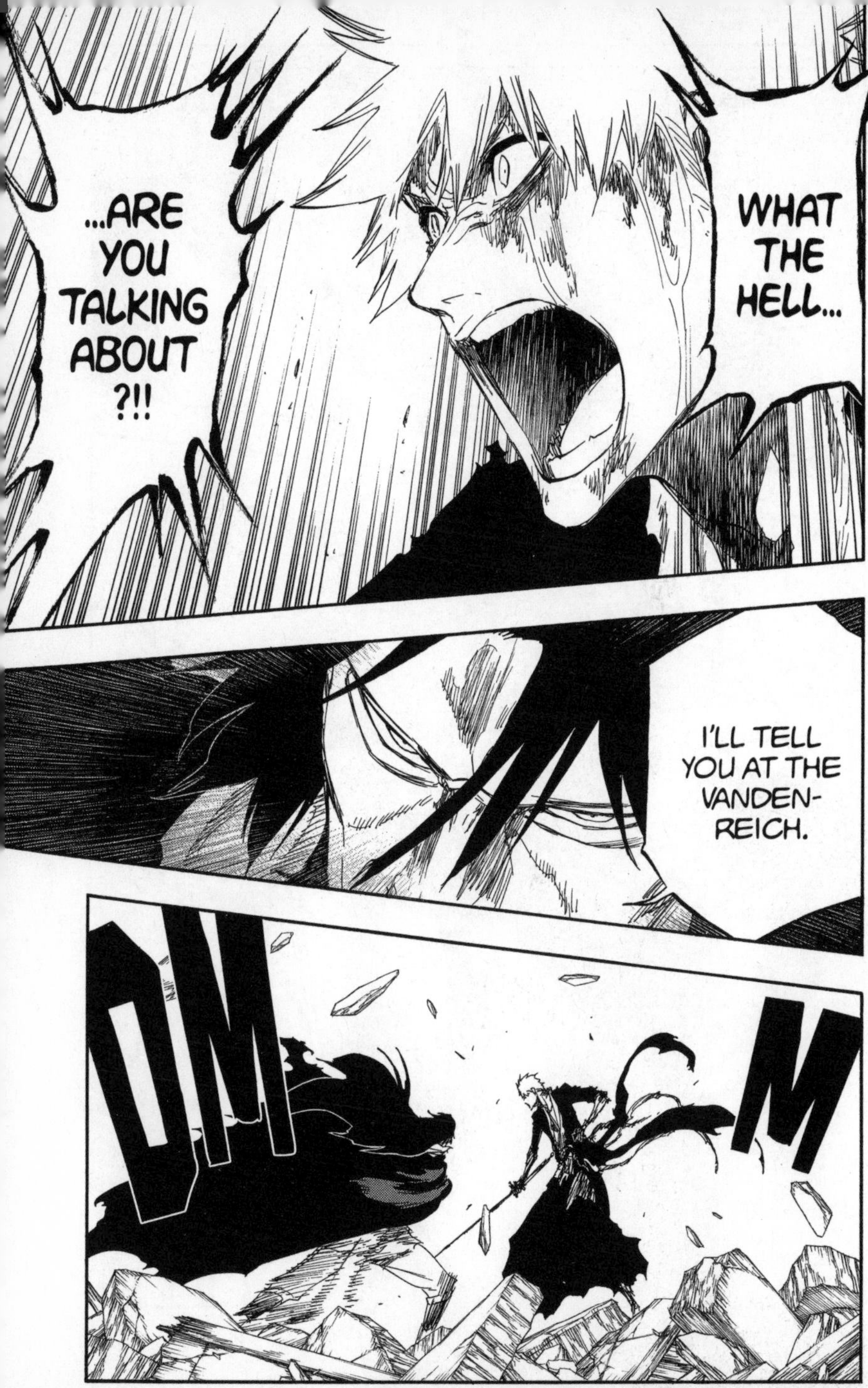
WHAT THE HELL...
...ARE YOU TALKING ABOUT ?!!
I'LL TELL YOU AT THE VANDEN-REICH.
DM
M

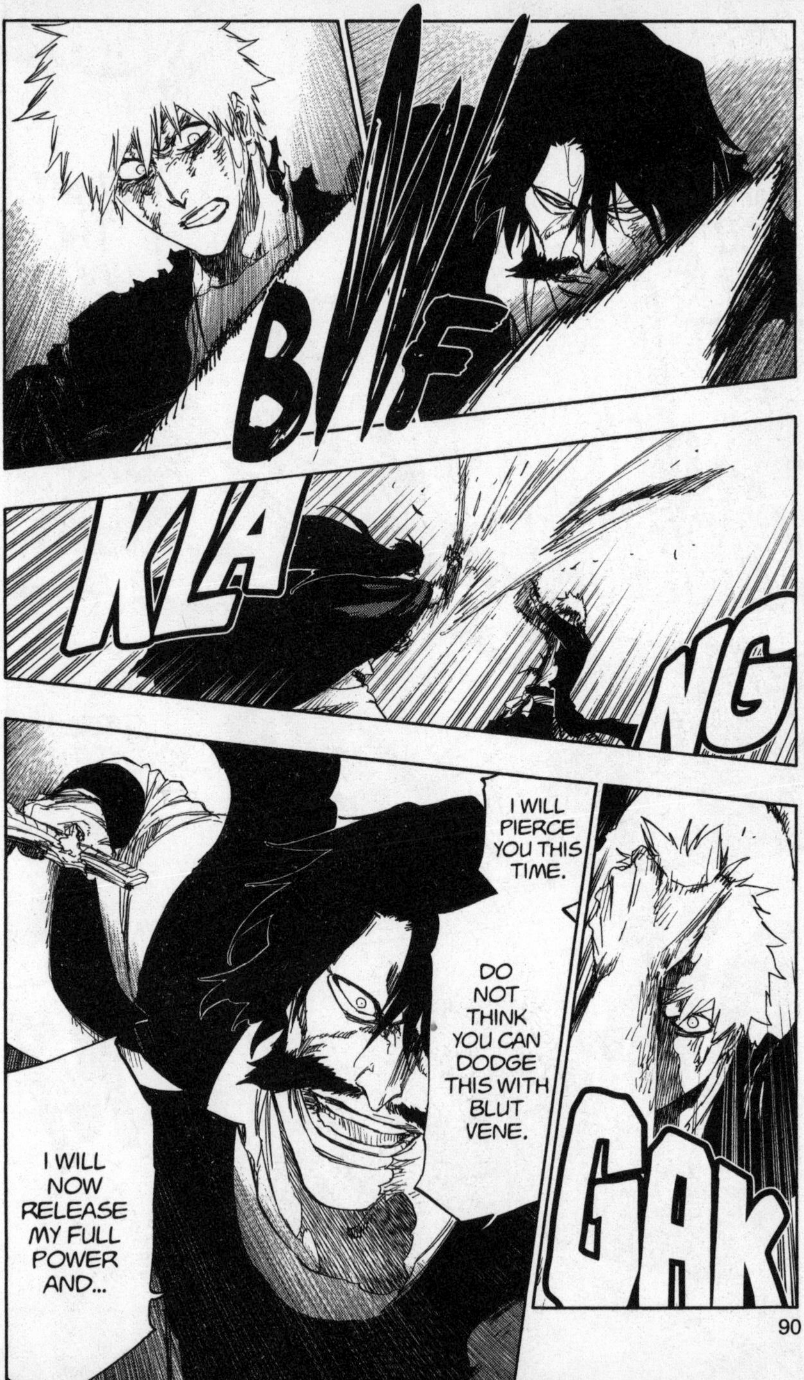
BIFF
KLANG
GAK
I WILL PIERCE YOU THIS TIME.
DO NOT THINK YOU CAN DODGE THIS WITH BLUT VENE.
I WILL NOW RELEASE MY FULL POWER AND...

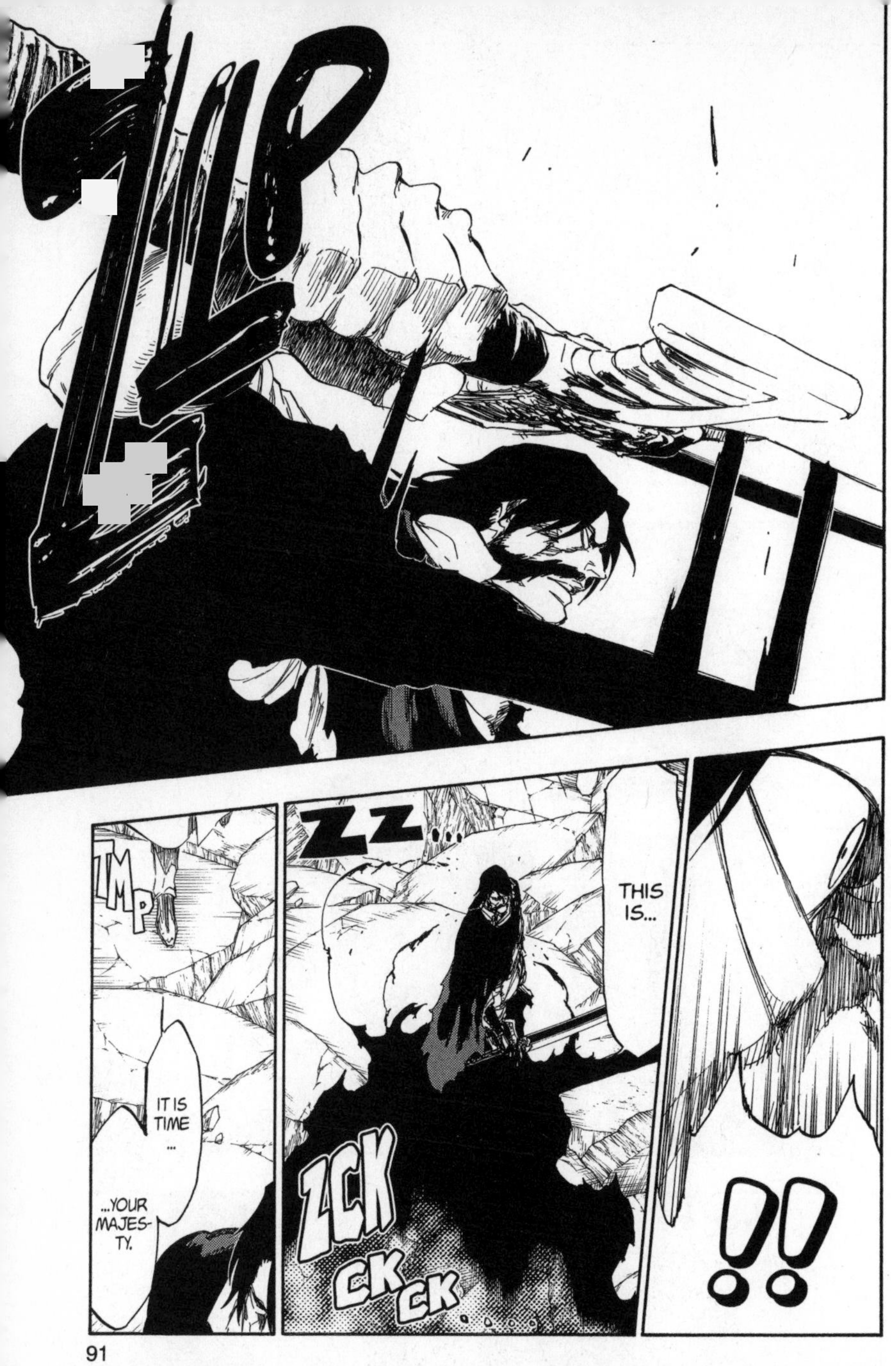
!!
ZZ...
THIS IS...
ZCK CK CK
TMP
IT IS TIME ...
...YOUR MAJES-TY.

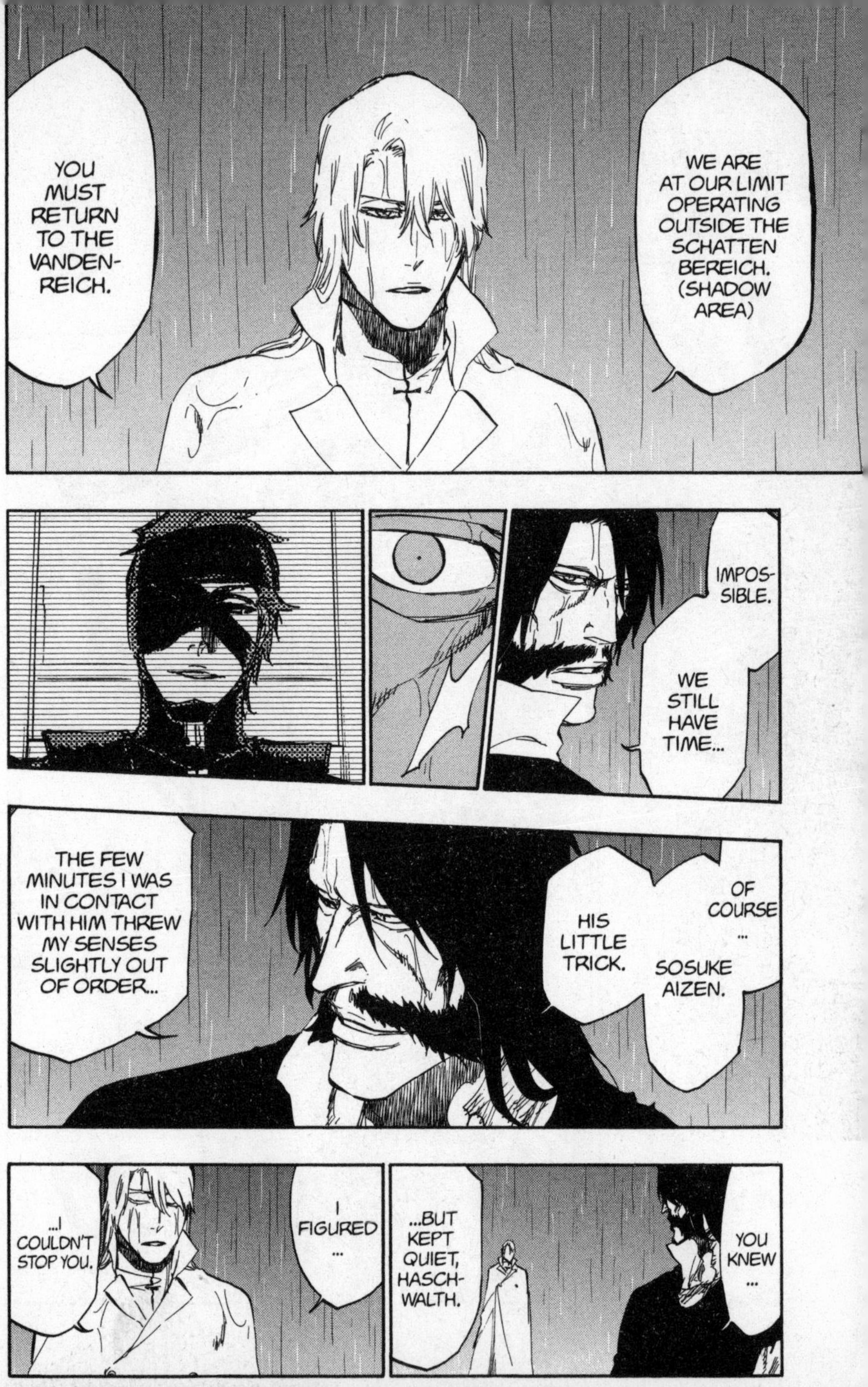
WE ARE AT OUR LIMIT OPERATING OUTSIDE THE SCHATTEN BEREICH. (SHADOW AREA)
YOU MUST RETURN TO THE VANDEN-REICH.
IMPOSSIBLE.
WE STILL HAVE TIME...
OF COURSE... SOSUKE AIZEN.
HIS LITTLE TRICK.
THE FEW MINUTES I WAS IN CONTACT WITH HIM THREW MY SENSES SLIGHTLY OUT OF ORDER...
YOU KNEW...
...BUT KEPT QUIET, HASCH-WALTH.
I FIGURED...
...I COULDN'T STOP YOU.

READ THIS WAY

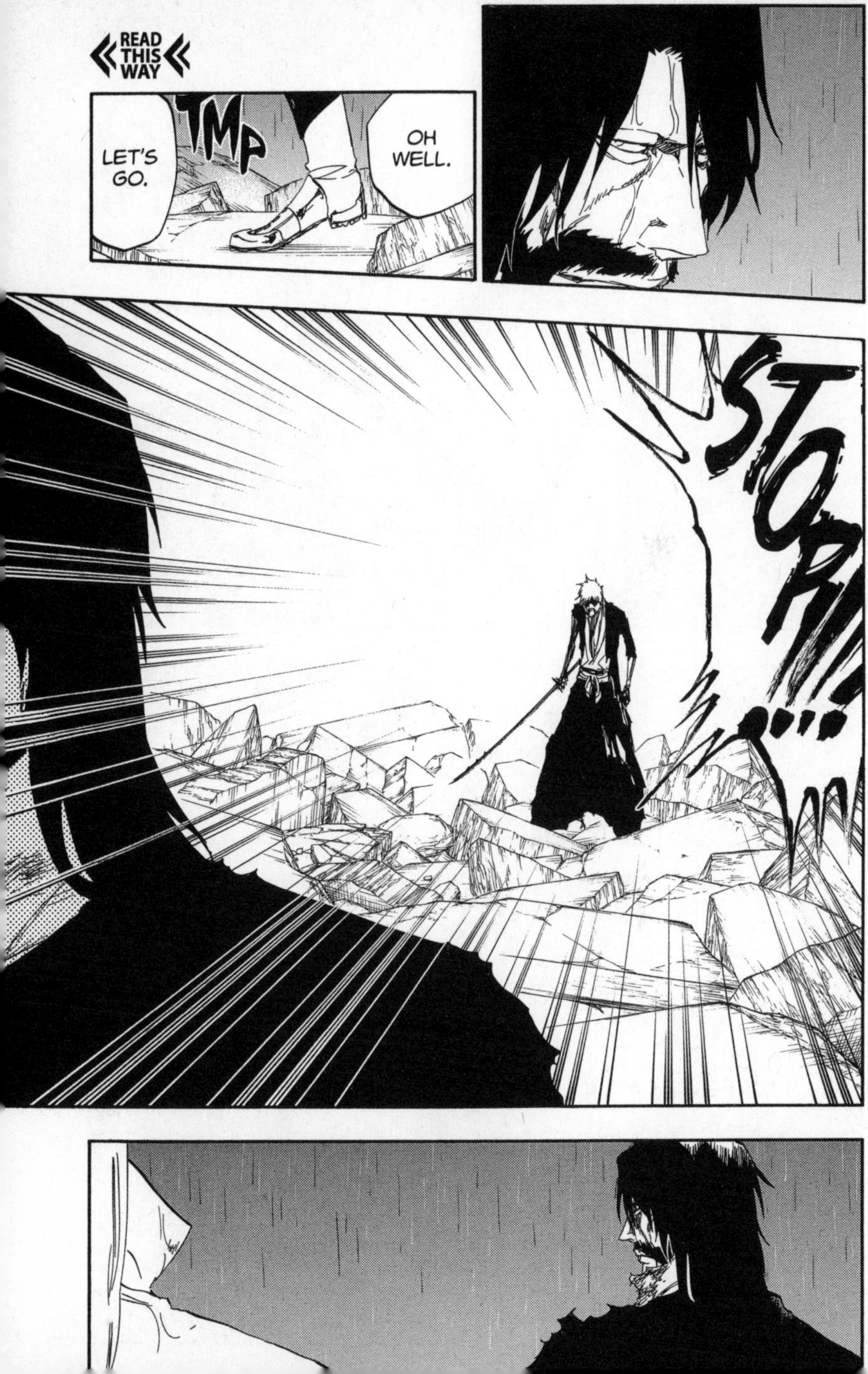
OH WELL.
TMP
LET'S GO.
STOP!!...

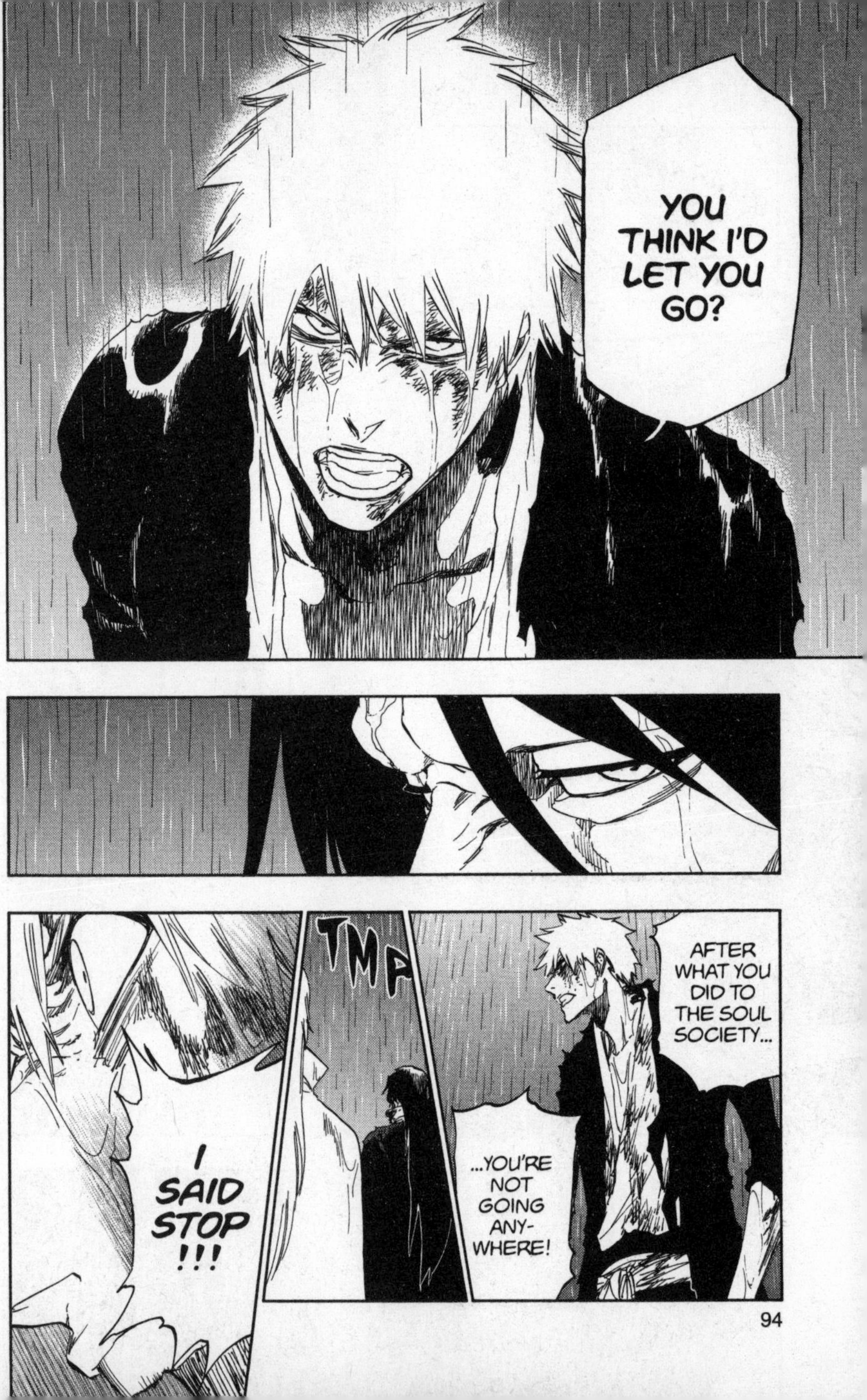
YOU THINK I'D LET YOU GO?
AFTER WHAT YOU DID TO THE SOUL SOCIETY...
...YOU'RE NOT GOING ANY-WHERE!
TMP
I SAID STOP!!!

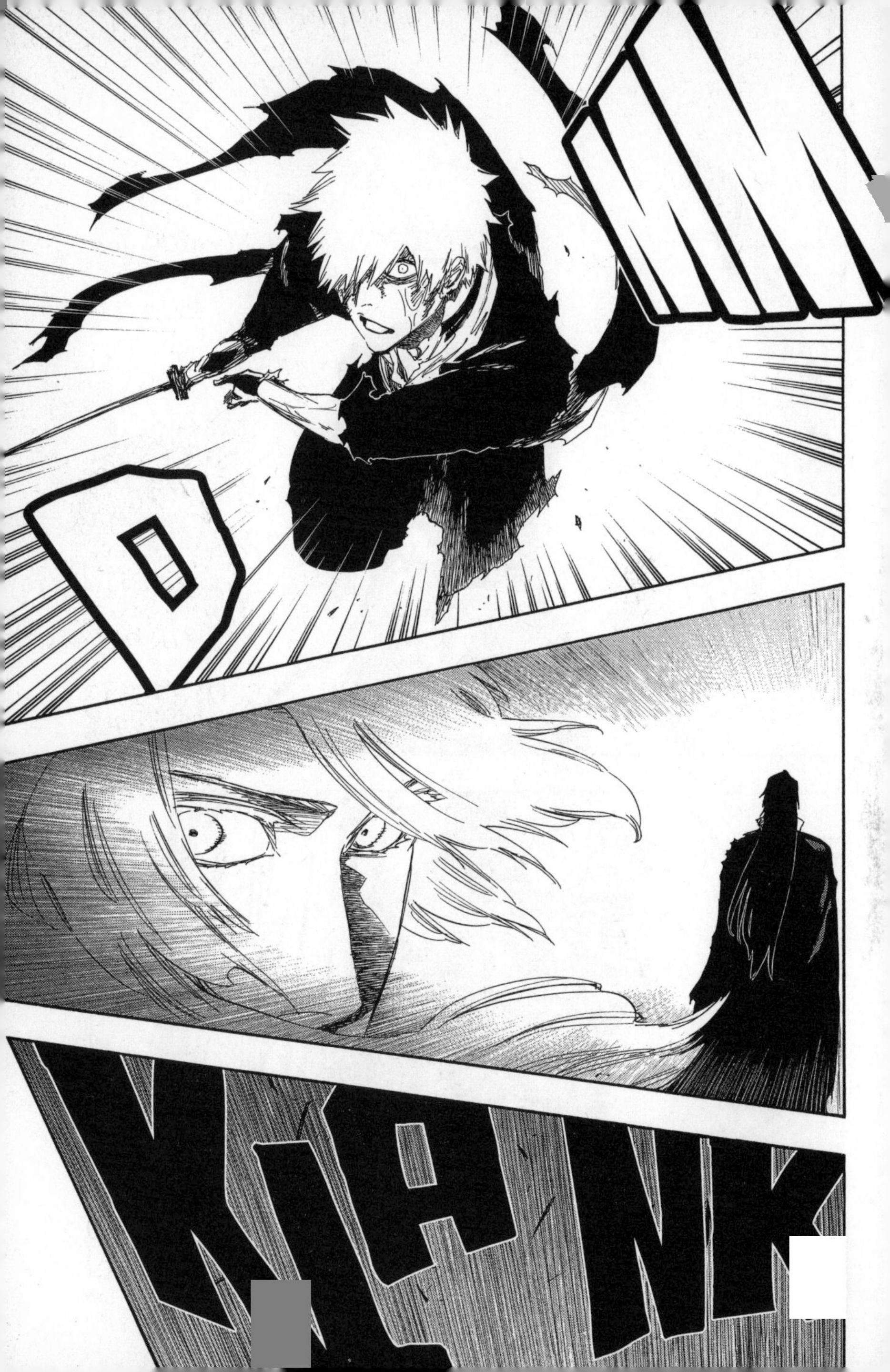

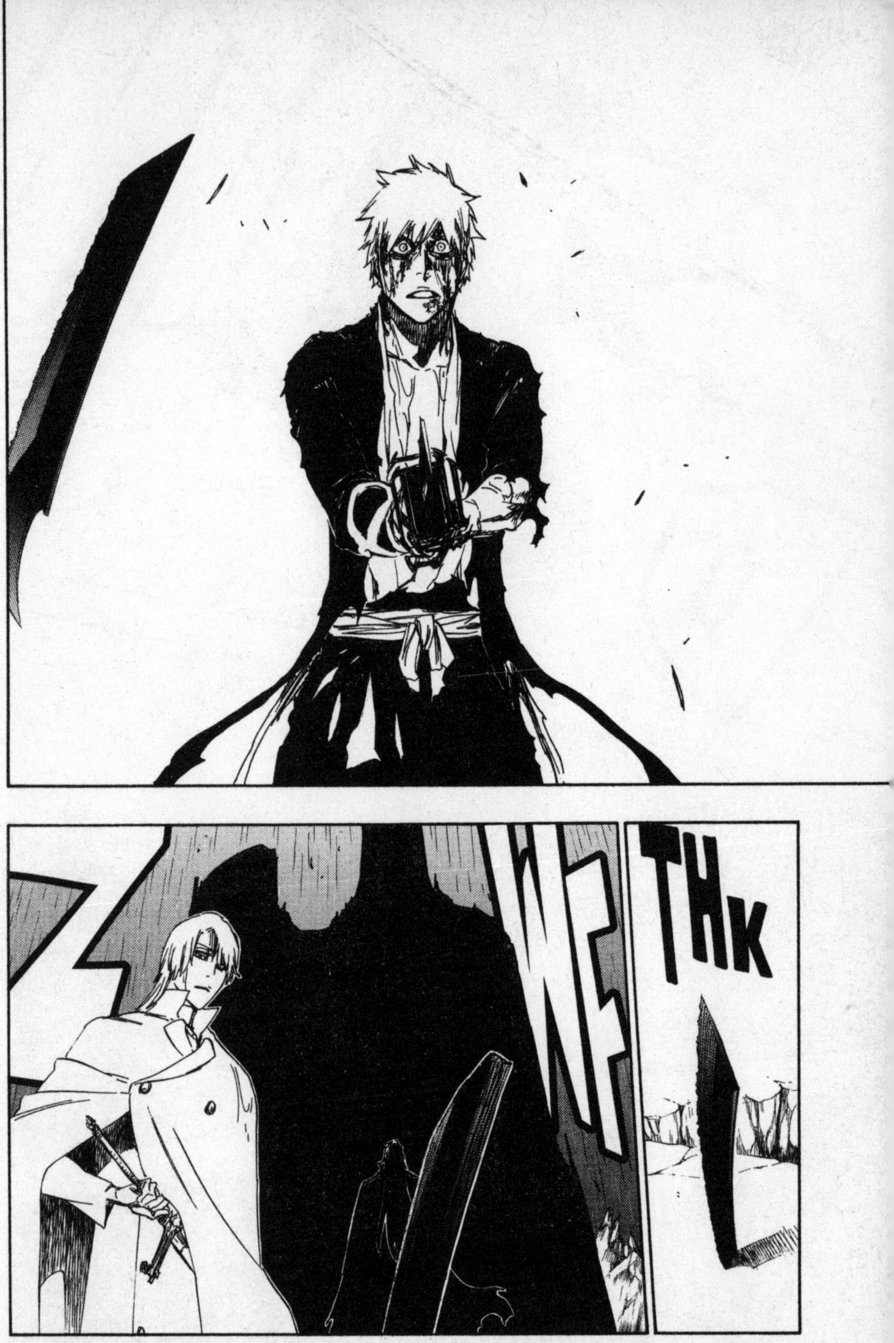
THK

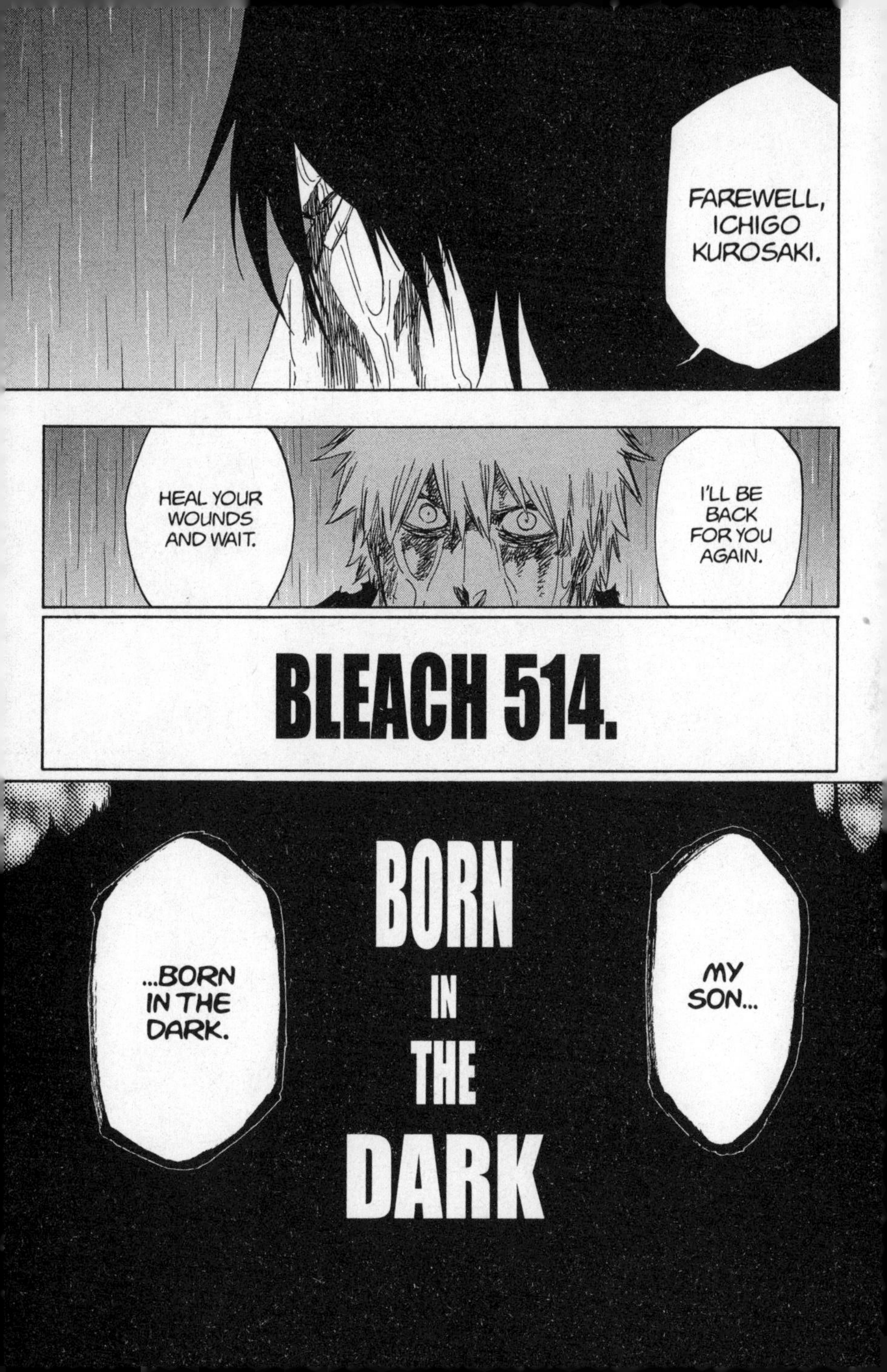
FAREWELL, ICHIGO KUROSAKI.
I'LL BE BACK FOR YOU AGAIN.
HEAL YOUR WOUNDS AND WAIT.
BLEACH 514.
MY SON...
BORN IN THE DARK
...BORN IN THE DARK.

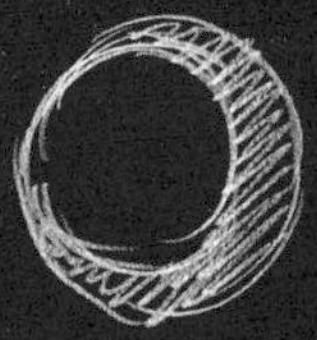

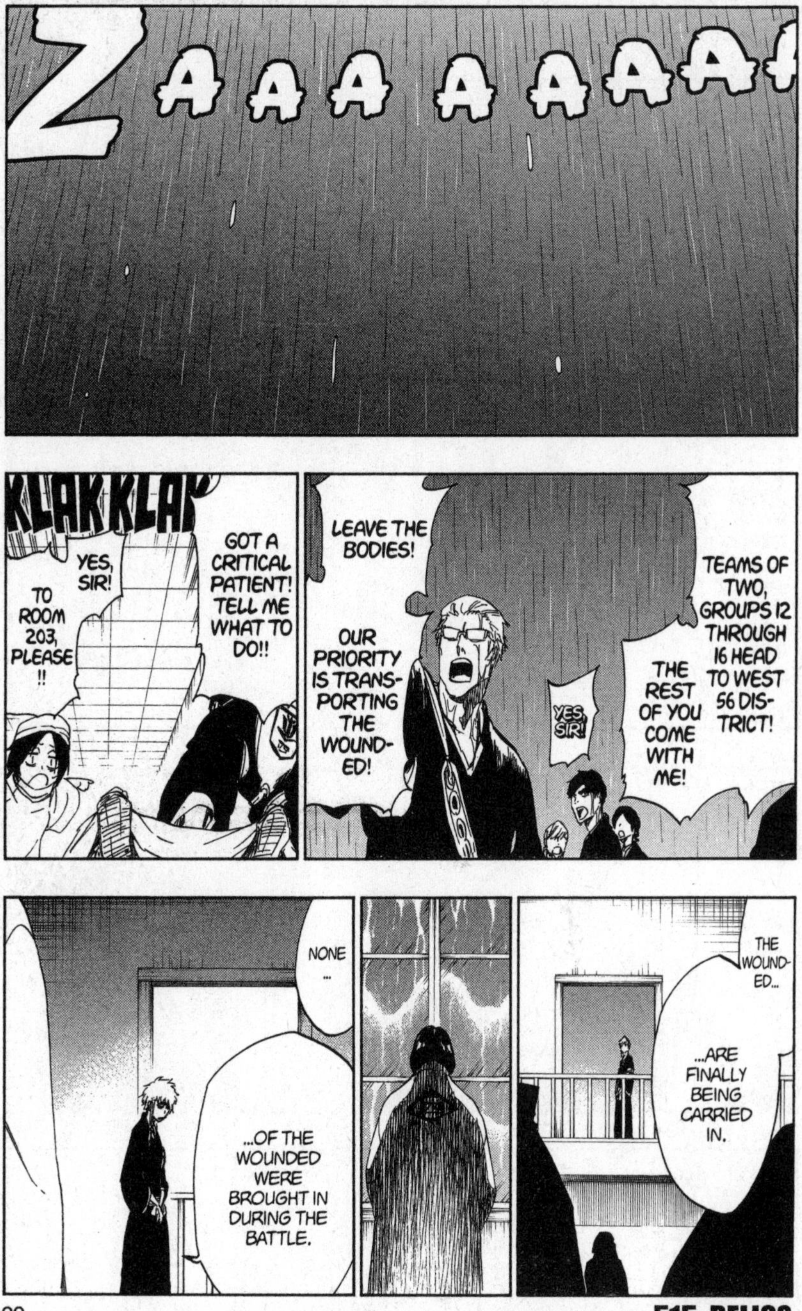
ZAAAAAAA
TEAMS OF TWO, GROUPS 12 THROUGH 16 HEAD TO WEST 56 DISTRICT!
THE REST OF YOU COME WITH ME!
YES, SIR!
LEAVE THE BODIES!
OUR PRIORITY IS TRANSPORTING THE WOUNDED!
KLAK KLAK
GOT A CRITICAL PATIENT! TELL ME WHAT TO DO!!
YES, SIR!
TO ROOM 203, PLEASE!!
THE WOUNDED...
...ARE FINALLY BEING CARRIED IN.
NONE...
...OF THE WOUNDED WERE BROUGHT IN DURING THE BATTLE.

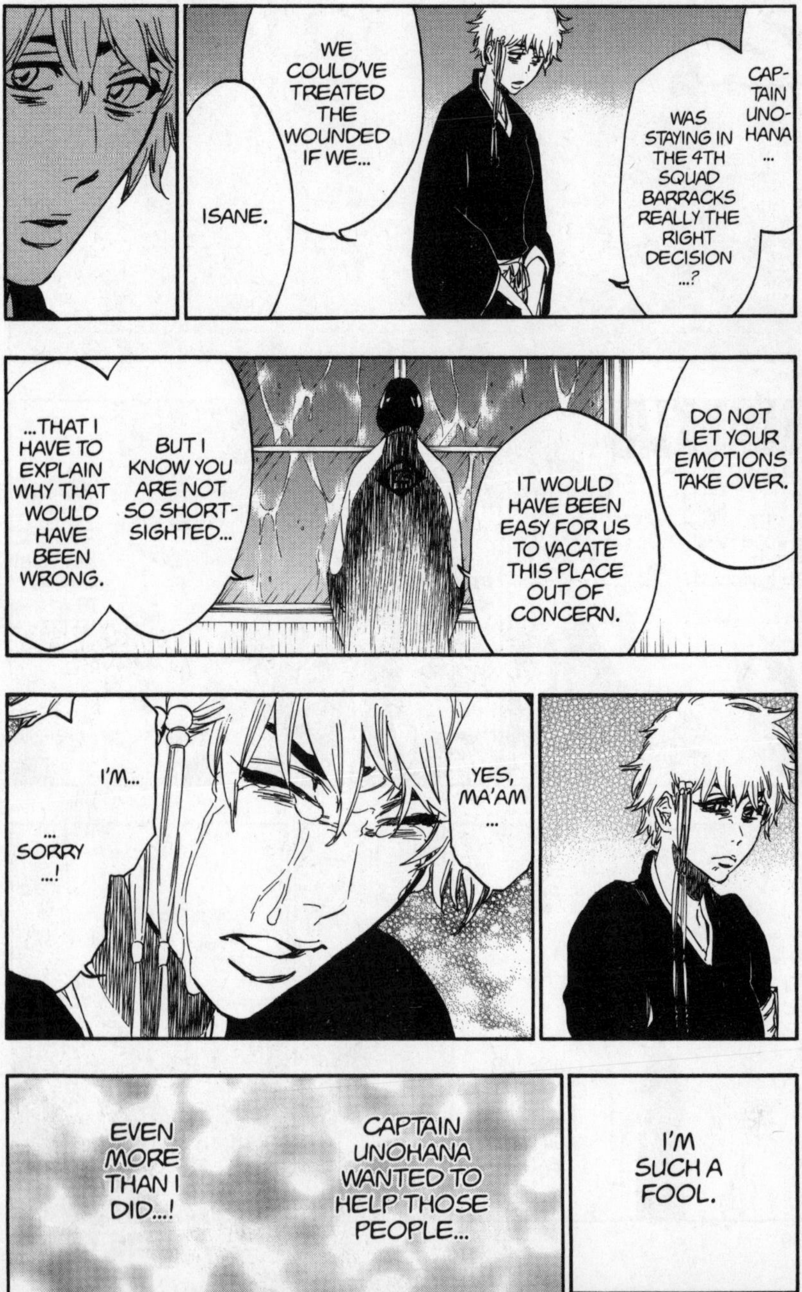
CAPTAIN UNOHANA...
WAS STAYING IN THE 4TH SQUAD BARRACKS REALLY THE RIGHT DECISION...?
WE COULD'VE TREATED THE WOUNDED IF WE...
ISANE.
DO NOT LET YOUR EMOTIONS TAKE OVER.
IT WOULD HAVE BEEN EASY FOR US TO VACATE THIS PLACE OUT OF CONCERN.
BUT I KNOW YOU ARE NOT SO SHORT-SIGHTED...
...THAT I HAVE TO EXPLAIN WHY THAT WOULD HAVE BEEN WRONG.
YES, MA'AM...
I'M...
...SORRY...!
I'M SUCH A FOOL.
CAPTAIN UNOHANA WANTED TO HELP THOSE PEOPLE...
EVEN MORE THAN I DID...!

READ THIS WAY

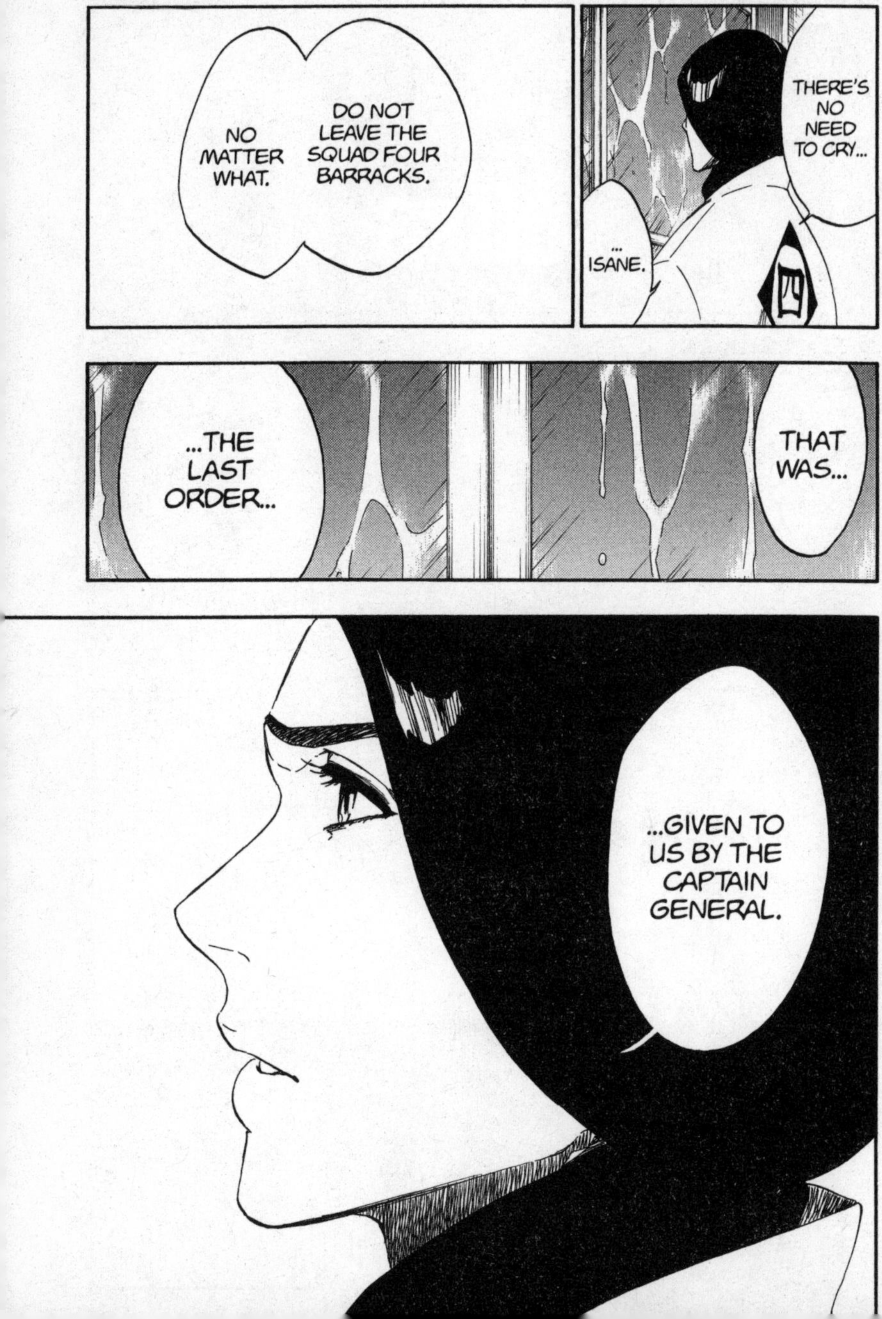
THERE'S NO NEED TO CRY...
... ISANE.
DO NOT LEAVE THE SQUAD FOUR BARRACKS.
NO MATTER WHAT.
THAT WAS...
...THE LAST ORDER...
...GIVEN TO US BY THE CAPTAIN GENERAL.

relics

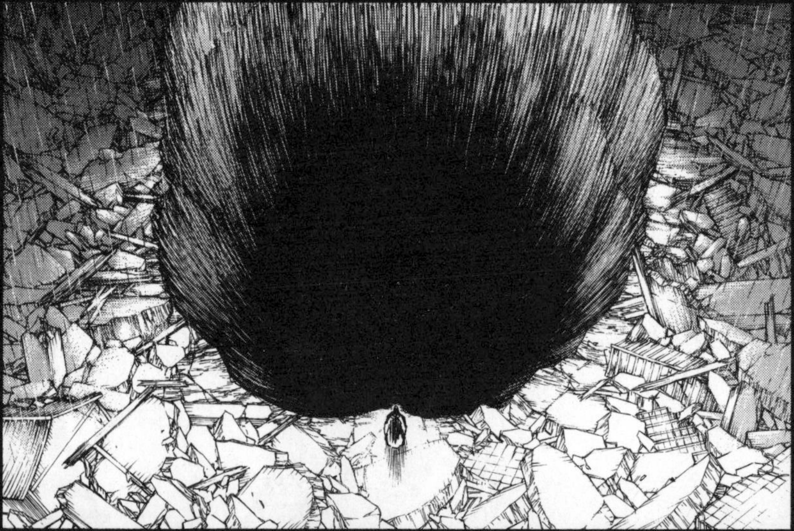

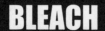

BLEACH 515.

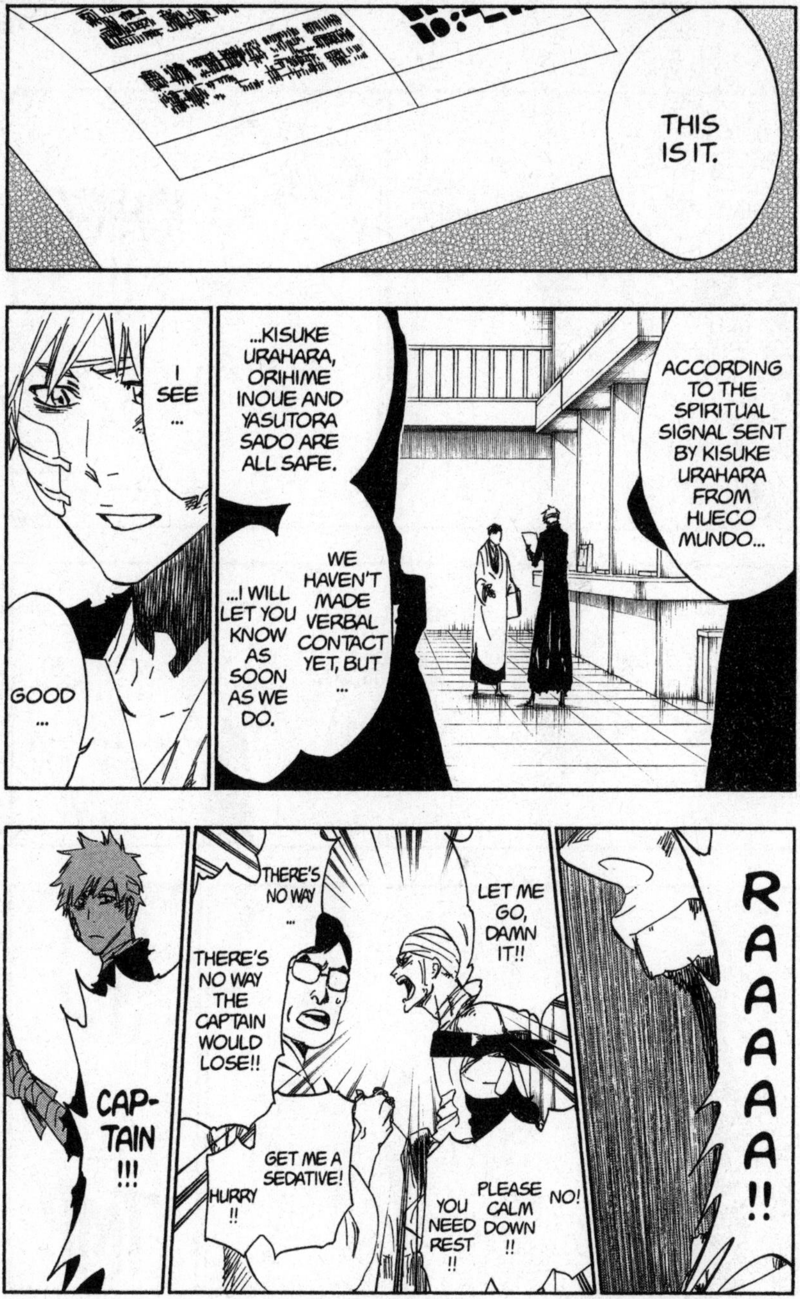
THIS IS IT.
ACCORDING TO THE SPIRITUAL SIGNAL SENT BY KISUKE URAHARA FROM HUECO MUNDO...
...KISUKE URAHARA, ORIHIME INOUE AND YASUTORA SADO ARE ALL SAFE.
WE HAVEN'T MADE VERBAL CONTACT YET, BUT ...
...I WILL LET YOU KNOW AS SOON AS WE DO.
I SEE ...
GOOD ...
RAAAAA!!
LET ME GO, DAMN IT!!
NO!
PLEASE CALM DOWN !!
YOU NEED REST !!
THERE'S NO WAY ...
THERE'S NO WAY THE CAPTAIN WOULD LOSE!!
GET ME A SEDATIVE!
HURRY !!
CAP-TAIN !!!

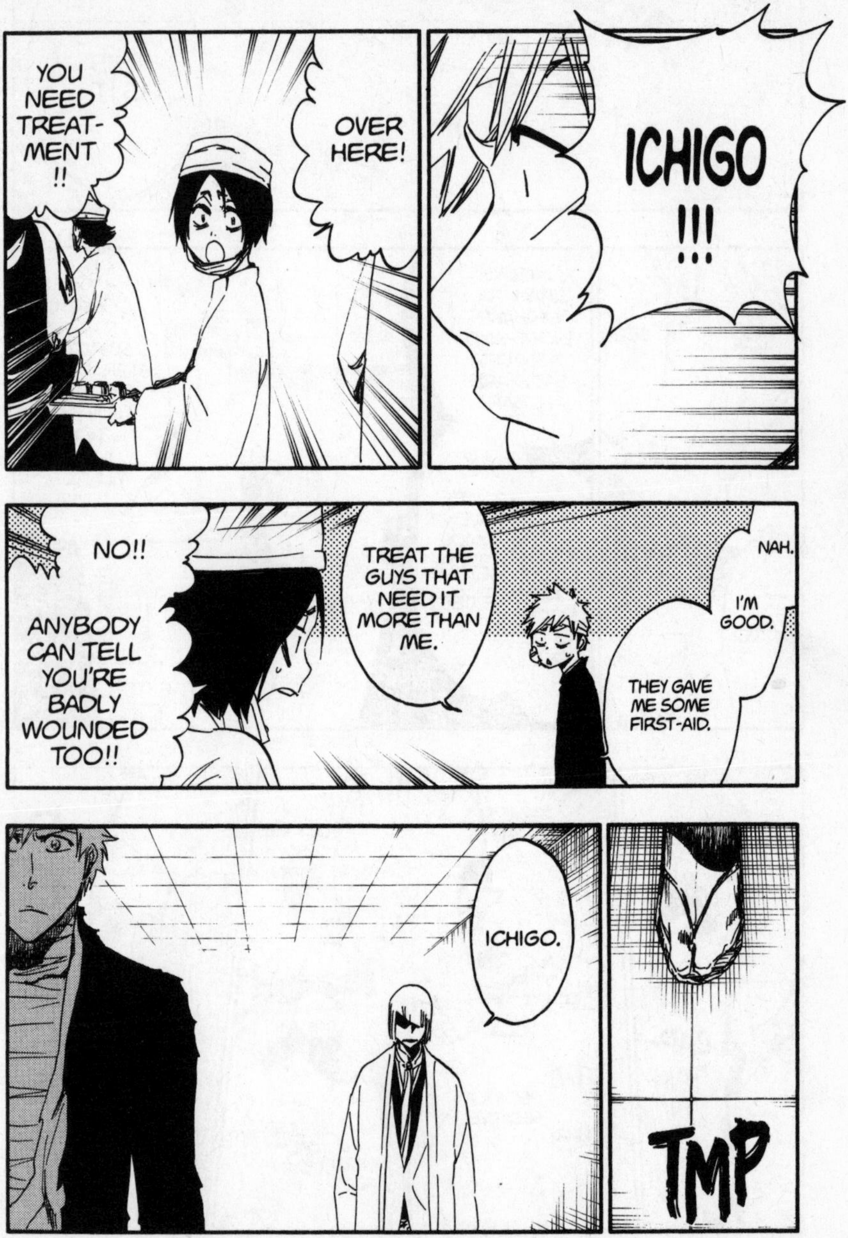
ICHIGO !!!
OVER HERE!
YOU NEED TREAT- MENT !!
NAH.
I'M GOOD.
THEY GAVE ME SOME FIRST-AID.
TREAT THE GUYS THAT NEED IT MORE THAN ME.
NO!!
ANYBODY CAN TELL YOU'RE BADLY WOUNDED TOO!!
TMP
ICHIGO.

READ THIS WAY

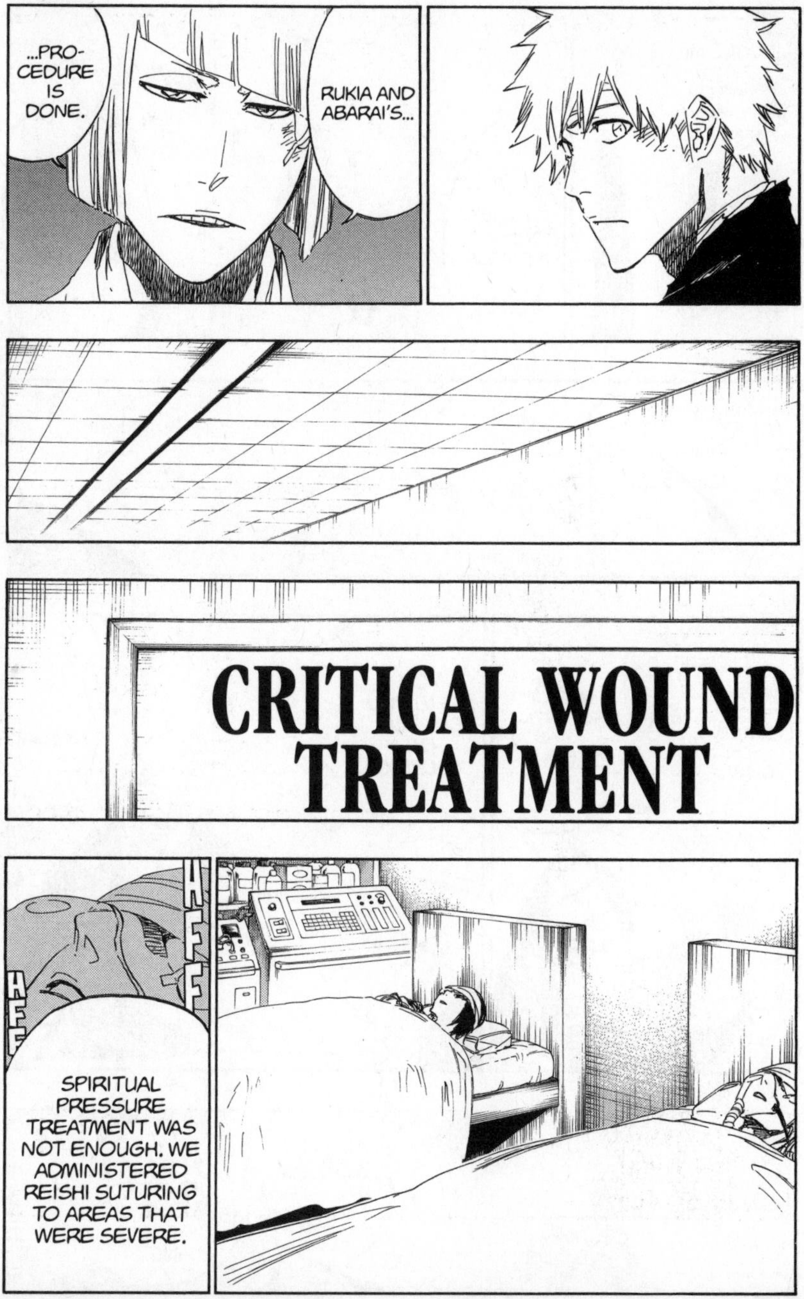
RUKIA AND ABARAI'S...
...PRO-CEDURE IS DONE.
CRITICAL WOUND TREATMENT
HAFF
HAFF
SPIRITUAL PRESSURE TREATMENT WAS NOT ENOUGH. WE ADMINISTERED REISHI SUTURING TO AREAS THAT WERE SEVERE.

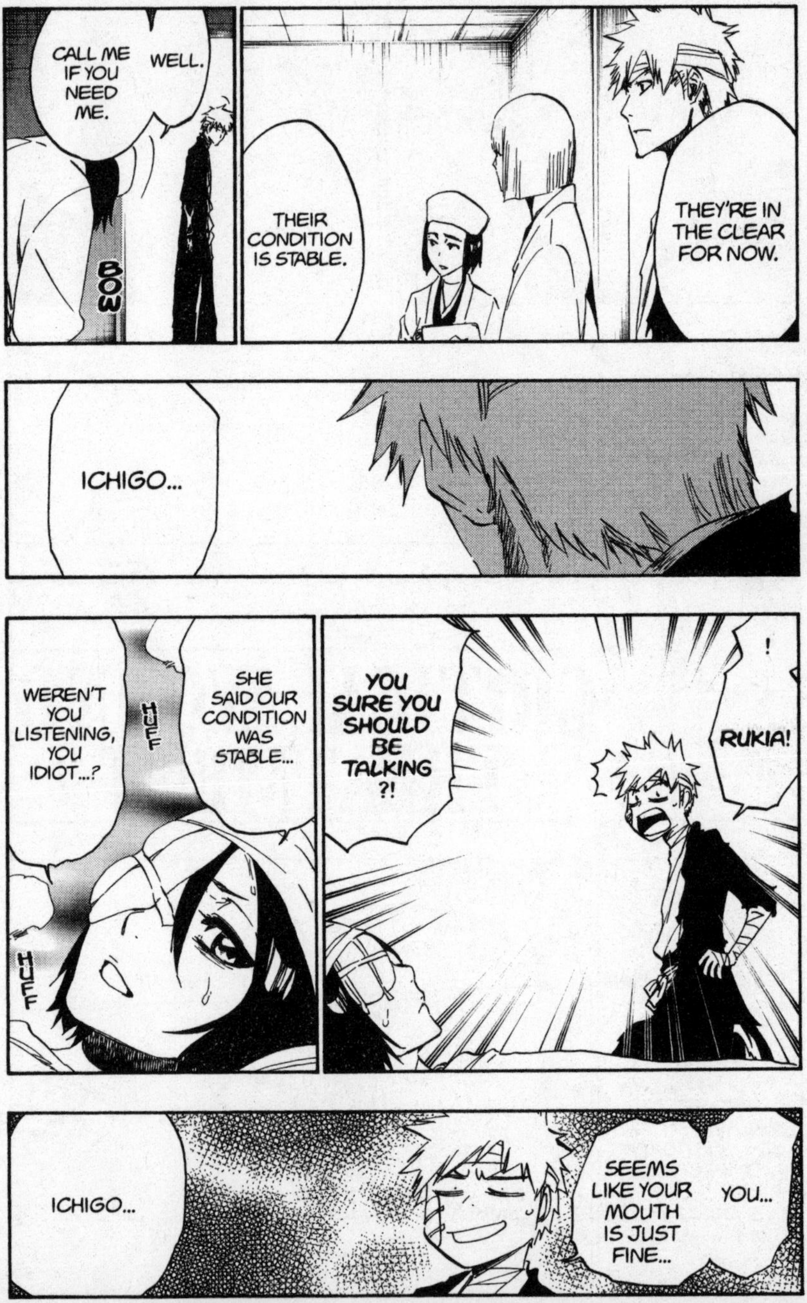
THEY'RE IN THE CLEAR FOR NOW.
THEIR CONDITION IS STABLE.
WELL.
CALL ME IF YOU NEED ME.
BOW
ICHIGO...
!
RUKIA!
YOU SURE YOU SHOULD BE TALKING?!
SHE SAID OUR CONDITION WAS STABLE...
HUFF
WEREN'T YOU LISTENING, YOU IDIOT...?
HUFF
YOU...
SEEMS LIKE YOUR MOUTH IS JUST FINE...
ICHIGO...

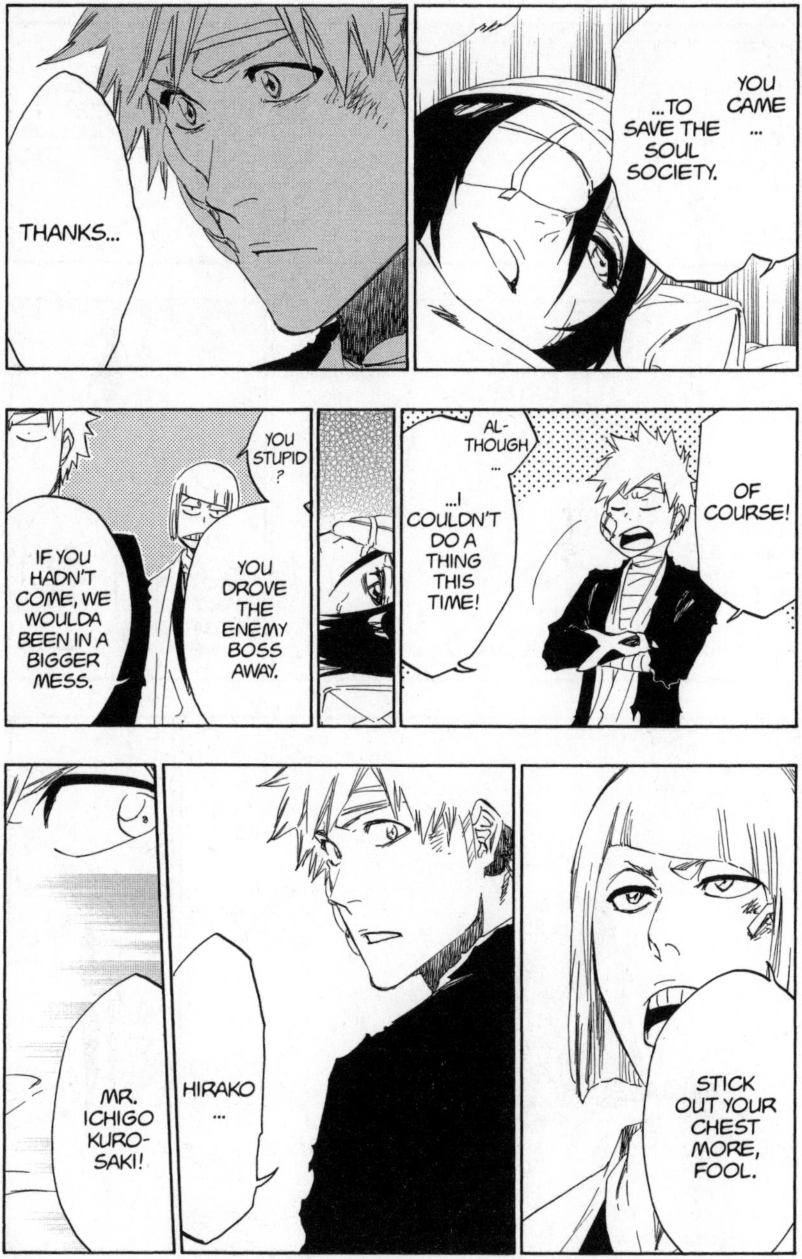
YOU CAME ...
...TO SAVE THE SOUL SOCIETY.
THANKS...
OF COURSE!
AL-THOUGH ...
...I COULDN'T DO A THING THIS TIME!
YOU STUPID?
YOU DROVE THE ENEMY BOSS AWAY.
IF YOU HADN'T COME, WE WOULDA BEEN IN A BIGGER MESS.
STICK OUT YOUR CHEST MORE, FOOL.
HIRAKO ...
MR. ICHIGO KURO-SAKI!

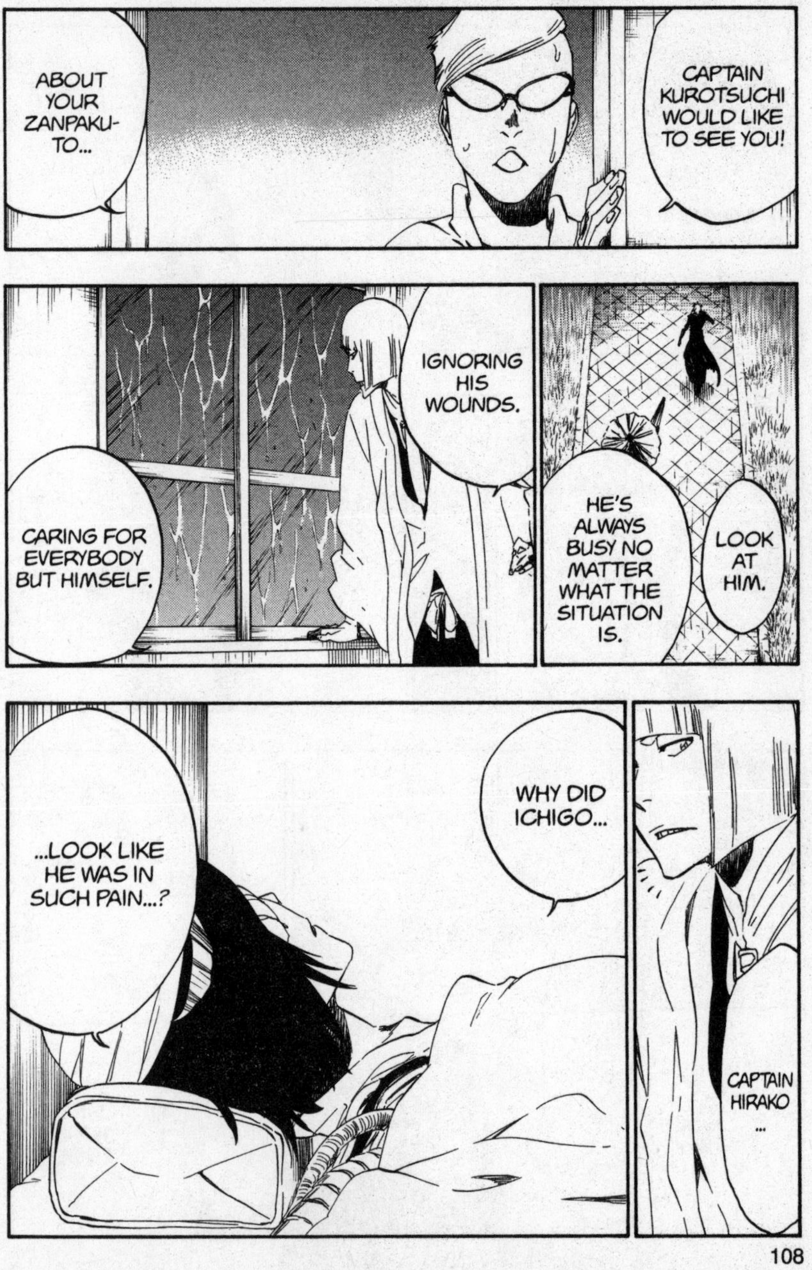
CAPTAIN KUROTSUCHI WOULD LIKE TO SEE YOU!
ABOUT YOUR ZANPAKU-TO...
LOOK AT HIM.
HE'S ALWAYS BUSY NO MATTER WHAT THE SITUATION IS.
IGNORING HIS WOUNDS.
CARING FOR EVERYBODY BUT HIMSELF.
CAPTAIN HIRAKO ...
WHY DID ICHIGO...
...LOOK LIKE HE WAS IN SUCH PAIN...?

READ THIS WAY

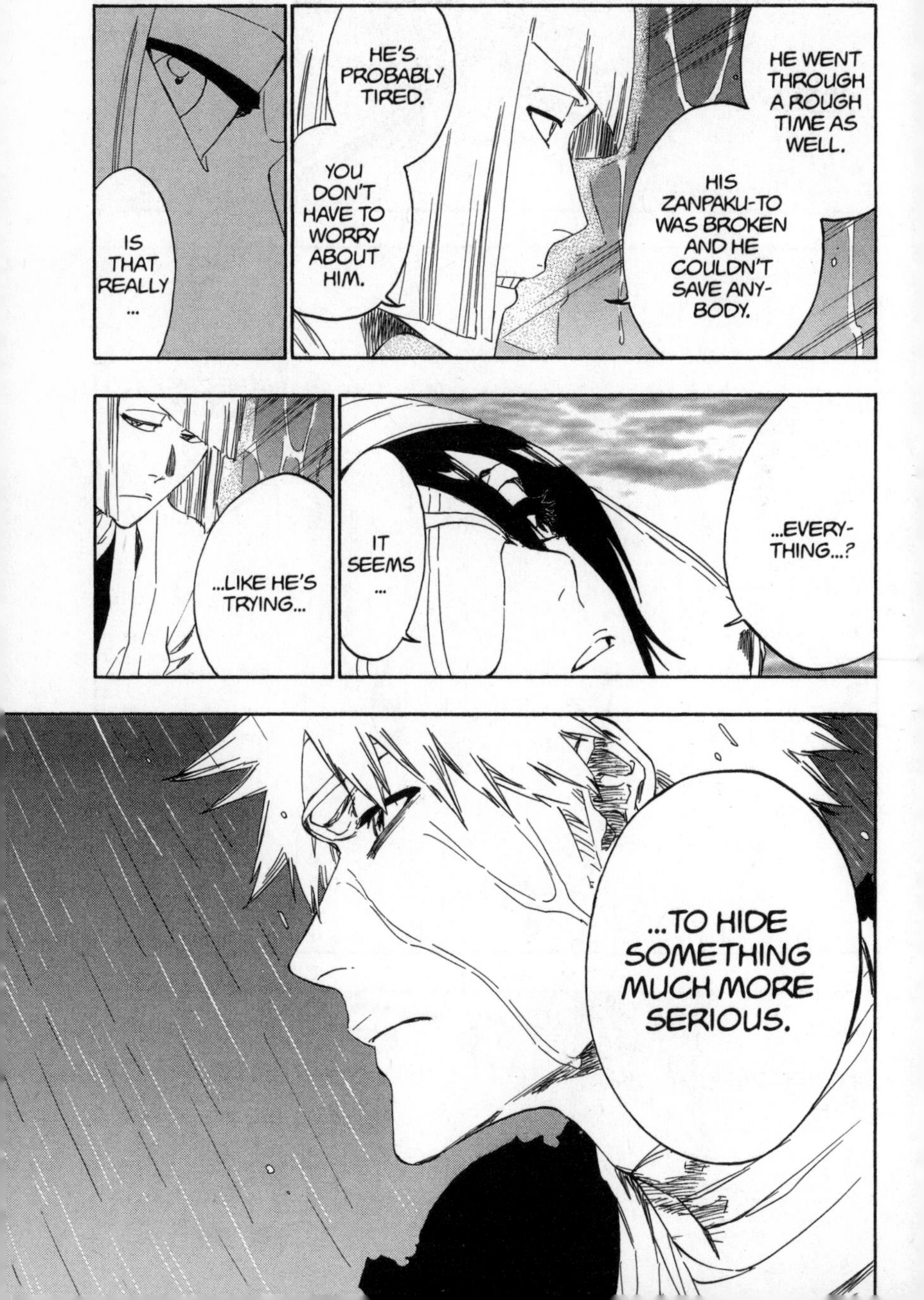
HE WENT THROUGH A ROUGH TIME AS WELL.
HIS ZANPAKU-TO WAS BROKEN AND HE COULDN'T SAVE ANYBODY.
HE'S PROBABLY TIRED.
YOU DON'T HAVE TO WORRY ABOUT HIM.
IS THAT REALLY ...
...EVERYTHING...?
IT SEEMS ...
...LIKE HE'S TRYING...
...TO HIDE SOMETHING MUCH MORE SERIOUS.

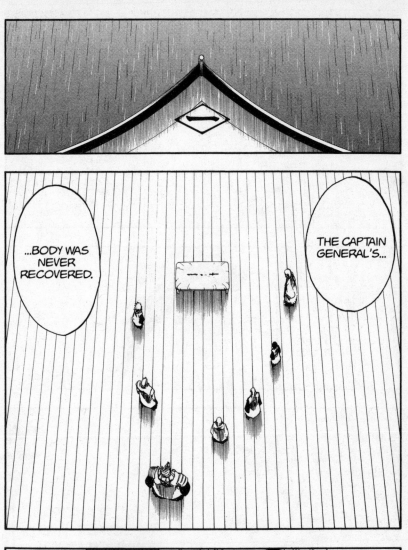

...THE CAPTAIN GENERAL'S...

...BODY WAS NEVER RECOVERED.

...DESTROYED EVERYTHING.

THE ENEMY...

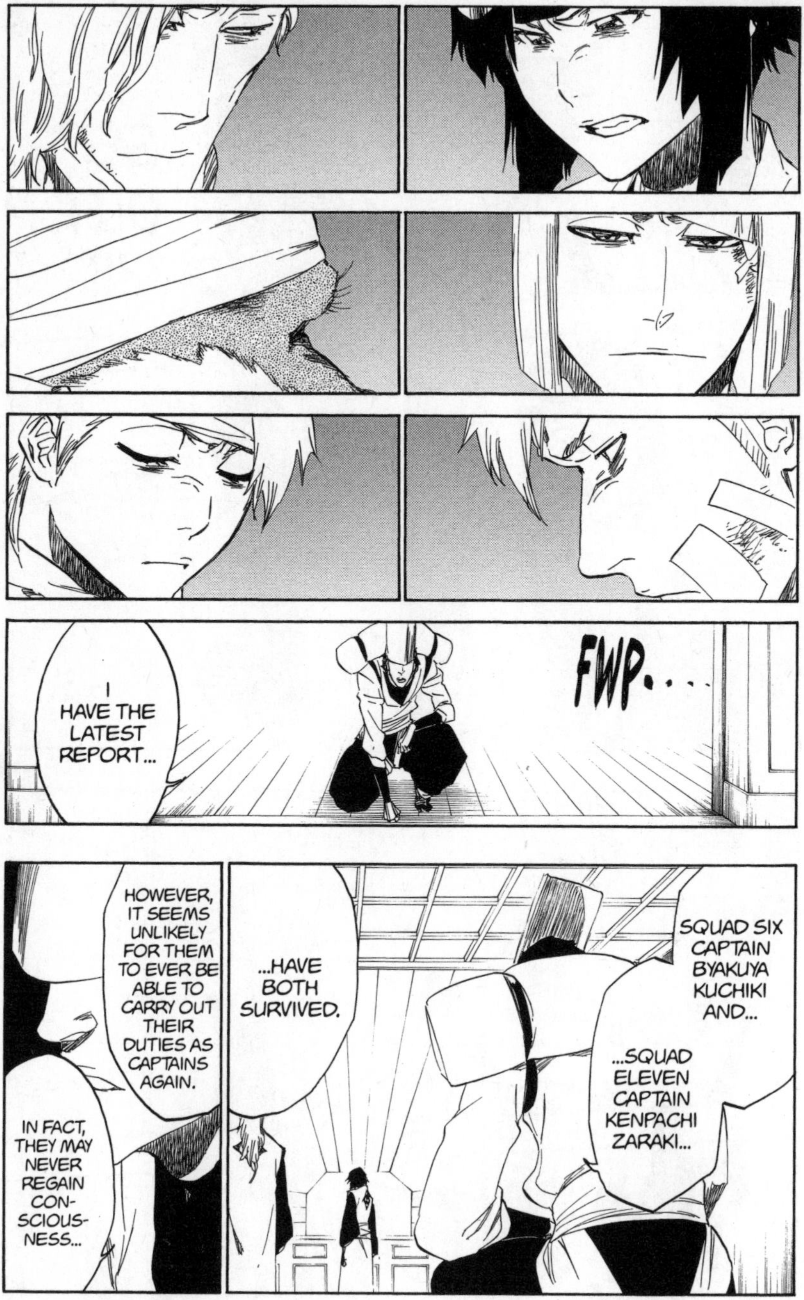
FWP....
I HAVE THE LATEST REPORT...
SQUAD SIX CAPTAIN BYAKUYA KUCHIKI AND...
...SQUAD ELEVEN CAPTAIN KENPACHI ZARAKI...
...HAVE BOTH SURVIVED.
HOWEVER, IT SEEMS UNLIKELY FOR THEM TO EVER BE ABLE TO CARRY OUT THEIR DUTIES AS CAPTAINS AGAIN.
IN FACT, THEY MAY NEVER REGAIN CON-SCIOUS-NESS...

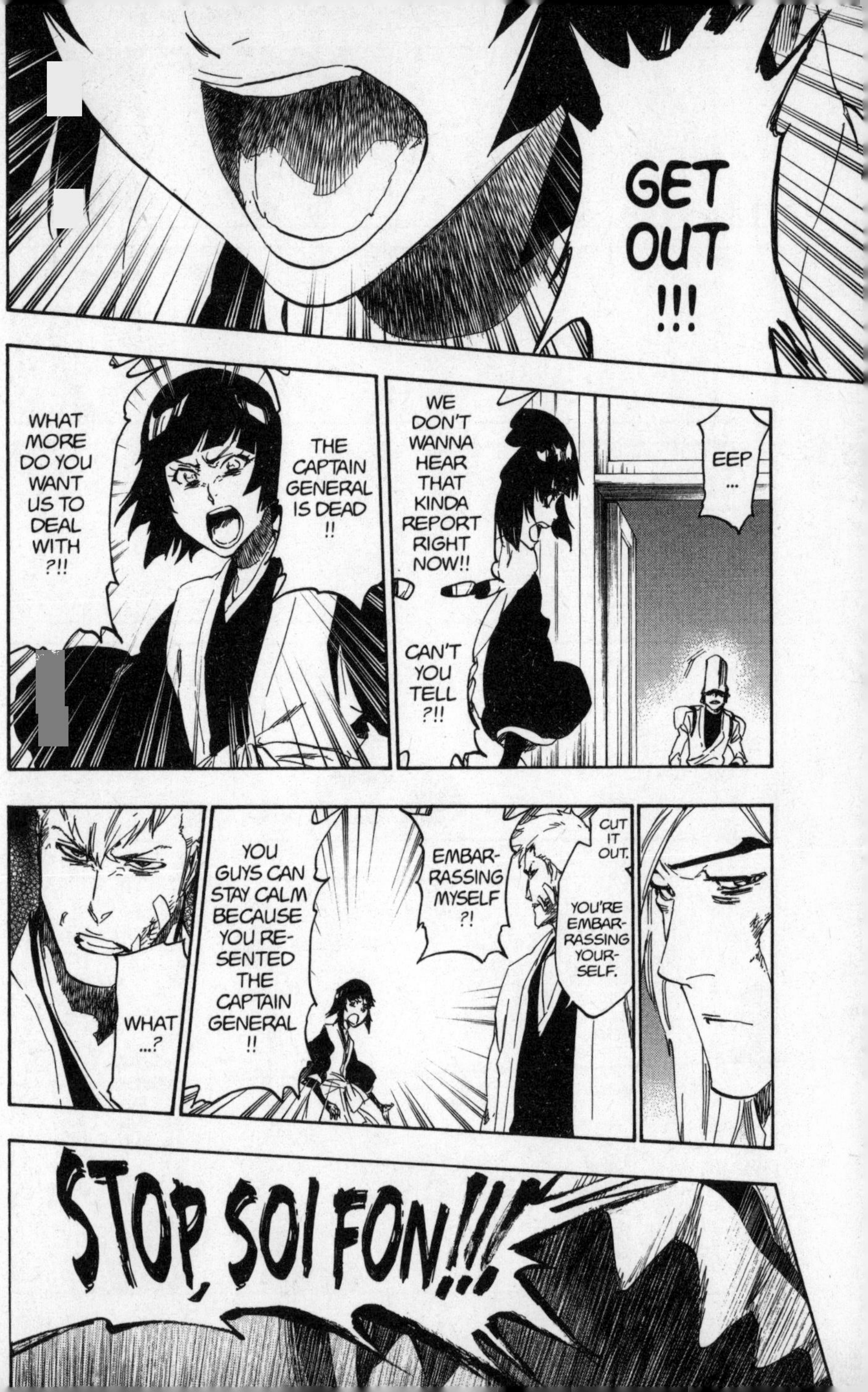
GET OUT !!!
EEP ...
WE DON'T WANNA HEAR THAT KINDA REPORT RIGHT NOW!!
CAN'T YOU TELL ?!!
THE CAPTAIN GENERAL IS DEAD !!
WHAT MORE DO YOU WANT US TO DEAL WITH ?!!
CUT IT OUT.
YOU'RE EMBAR-RASSING YOUR-SELF.
EMBAR-RASSING MYSELF ?!
YOU GUYS CAN STAY CALM BECAUSE YOU RE-SENTED THE CAPTAIN GENERAL !!
WHAT ...?
STOP, SOI FON!!!

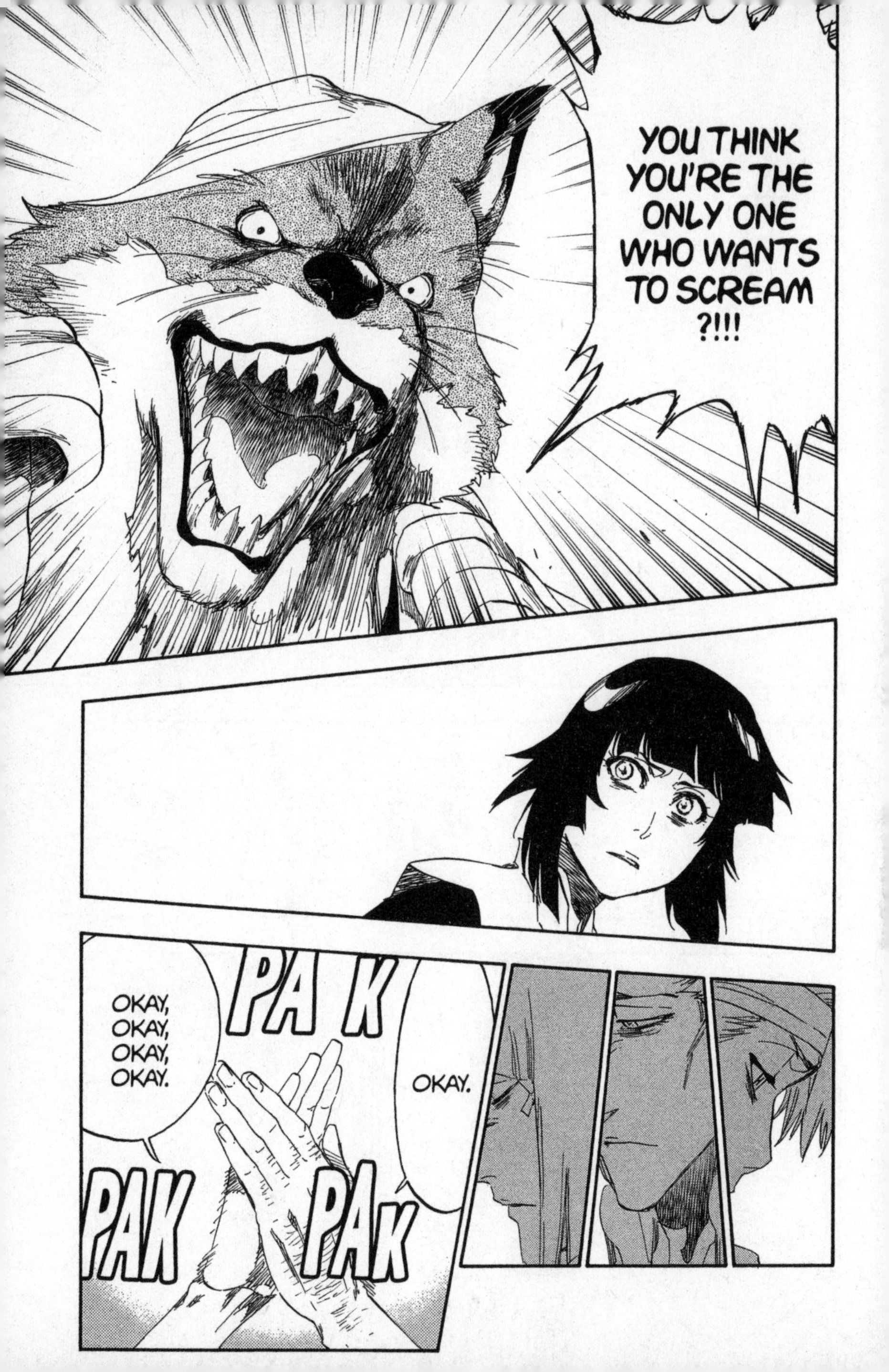
YOU THINK YOU'RE THE ONLY ONE WHO WANTS TO SCREAM ?!!!
PA K
OKAY.
OKAY, OKAY, OKAY, OKAY.
PAk
PAK

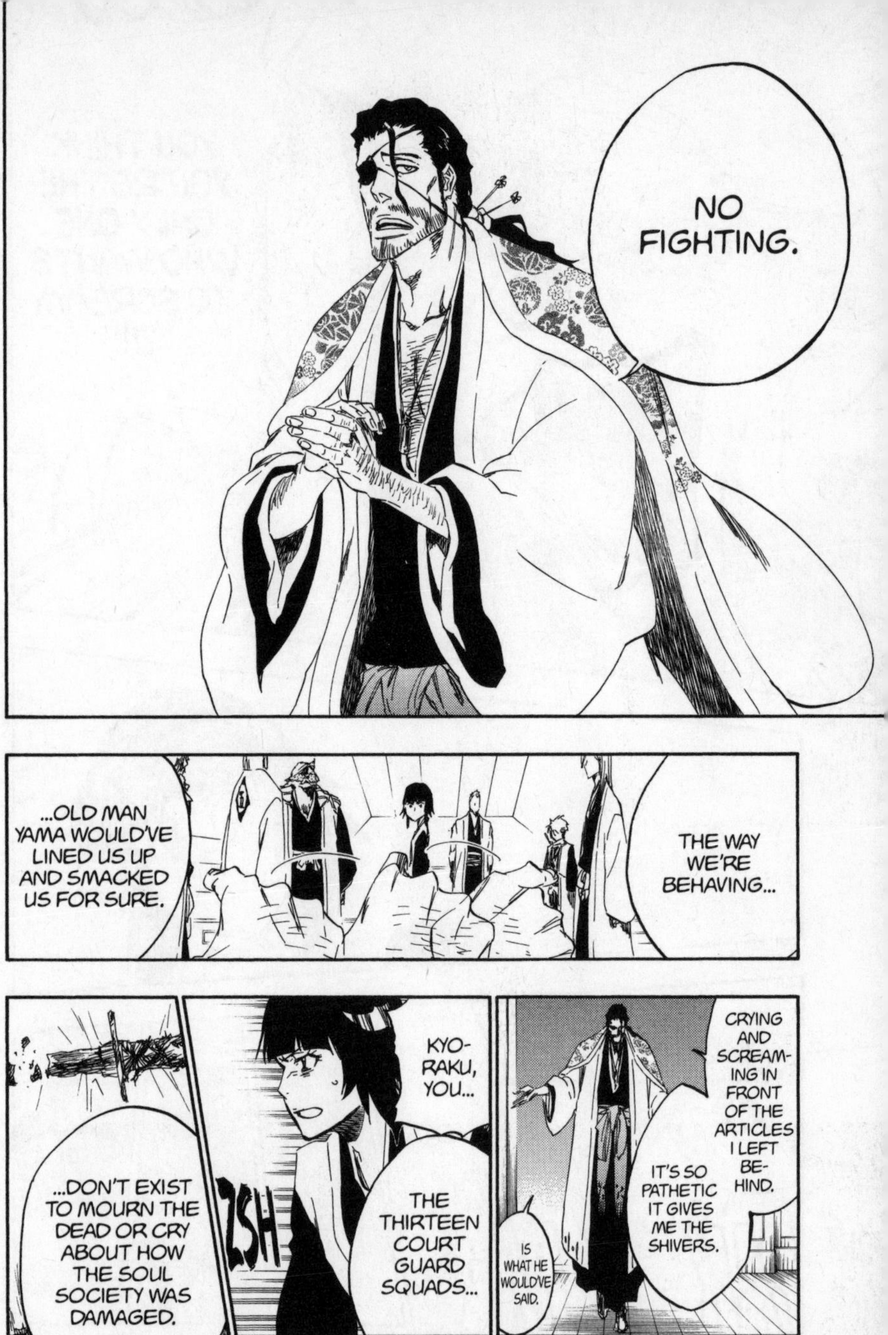
NO FIGHTING.
THE WAY WE'RE BEHAVING...
...OLD MAN YAMA WOULD'VE LINED US UP AND SMACKED US FOR SURE.
CRYING AND SCREAMING IN FRONT OF THE ARTICLES I LEFT BEHIND.
IT'S SO PATHETIC IT GIVES ME THE SHIVERS.
IS WHAT HE WOULD'VE SAID.
KYORAKU, YOU...
THE THIRTEEN COURT GUARD SQUADS...
ZSH
...DON'T EXIST TO MOURN THE DEAD OR CRY ABOUT HOW THE SOUL SOCIETY WAS DAMAGED.

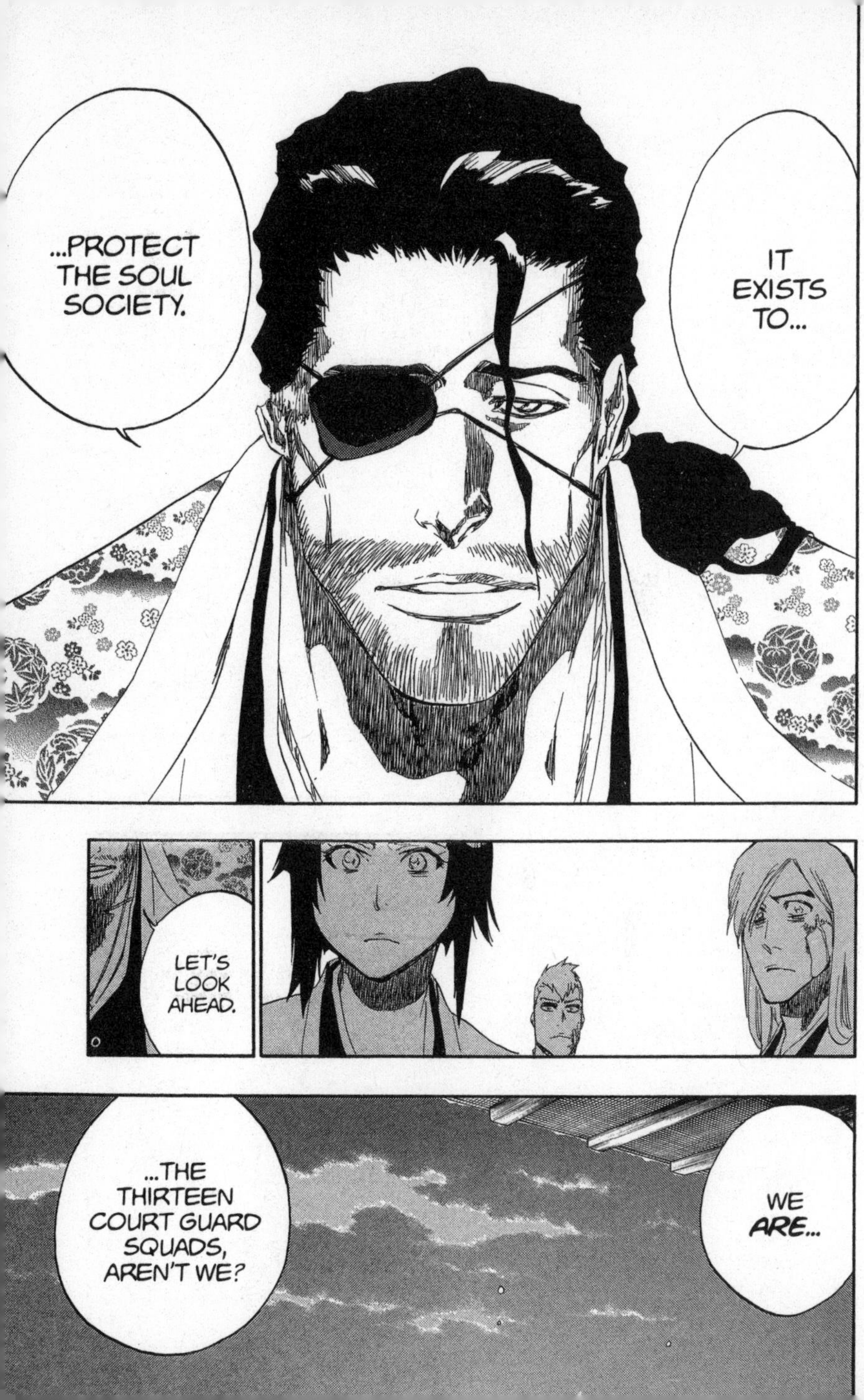
IT EXISTS TO...
...PROTECT THE SOUL SOCIETY.
LET'S LOOK AHEAD.
WE ARE...
...THE THIRTEEN COURT GUARD SQUADS, AREN'T WE?

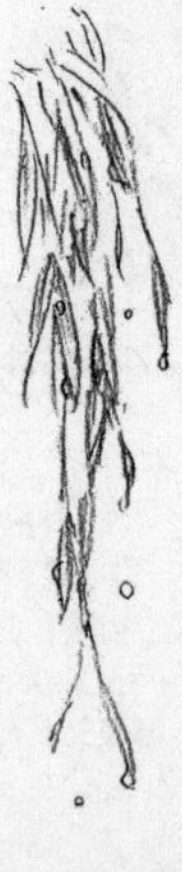

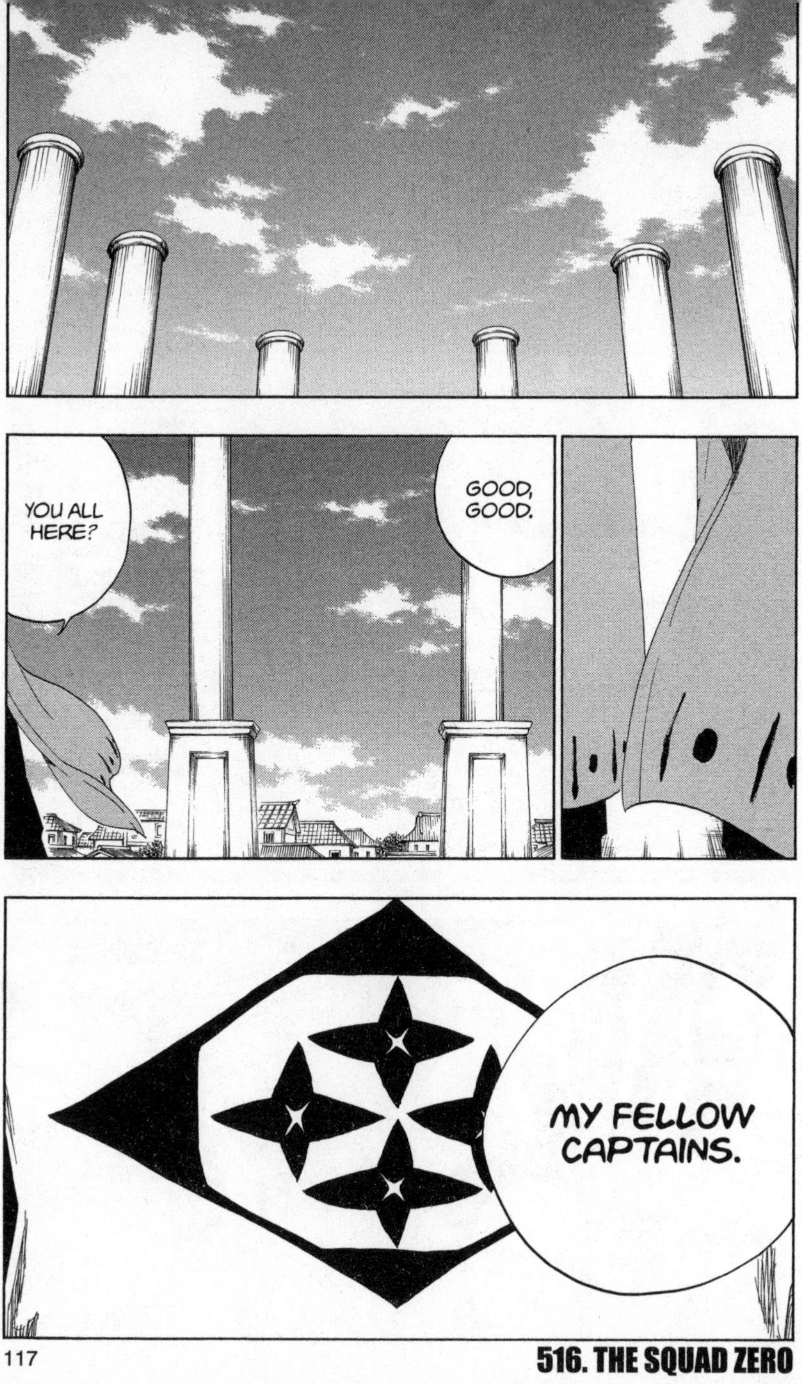
GOOD, GOOD.
YOU ALL HERE?
MY FELLOW CAPTAINS.

516. THE SQUAD ZERO

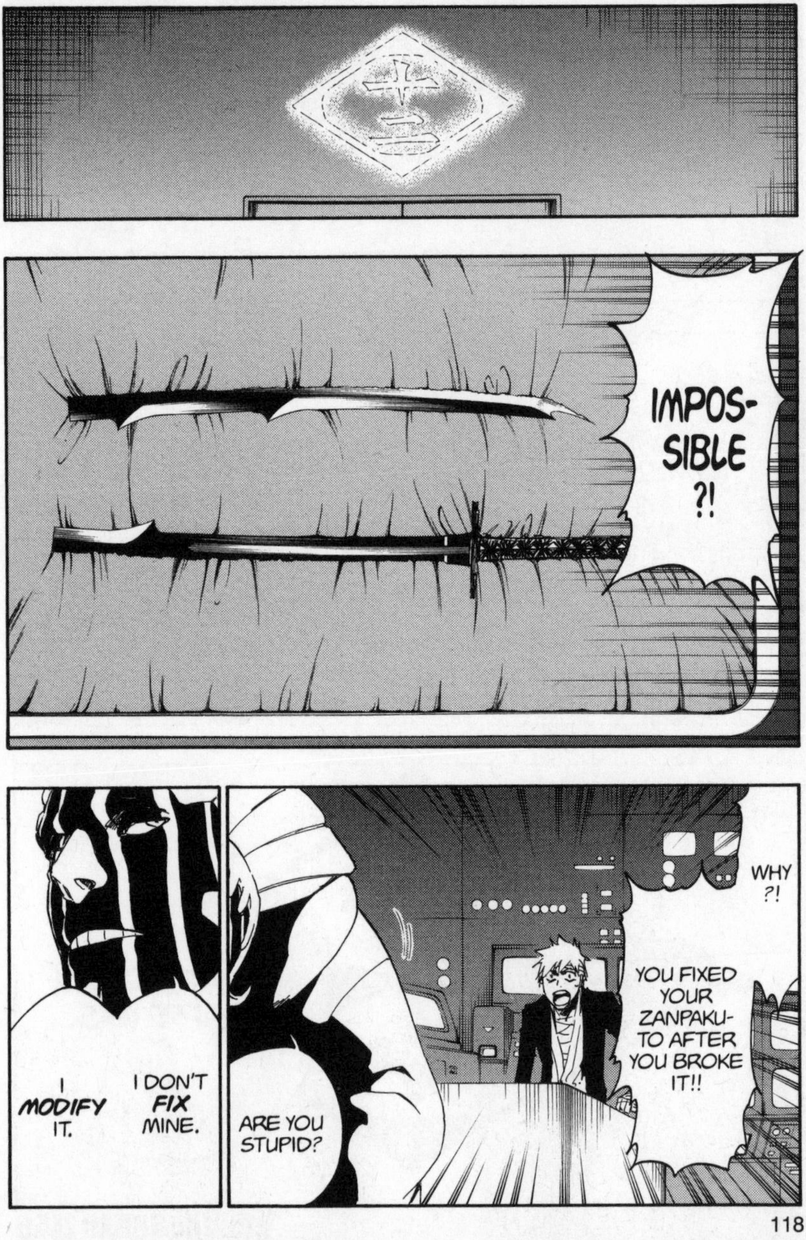
IMPOSSIBLE?!
WHY?!
YOU FIXED YOUR ZANPAKU-TO AFTER YOU BROKE IT!!
ARE YOU STUPID?
I DON'T *FIX* MINE.
I *MODIFY* IT.

READ THIS WAY

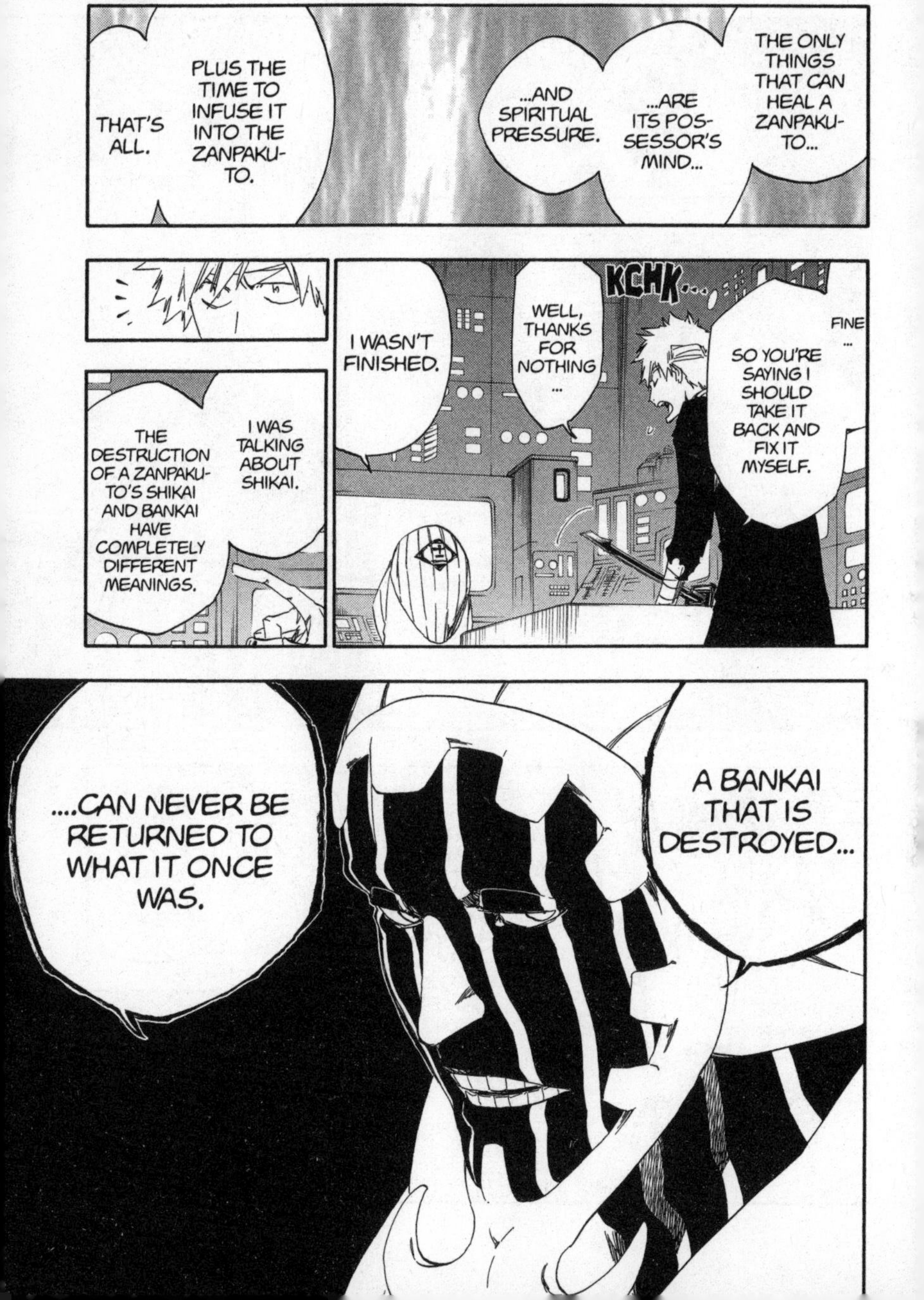
THE ONLY THINGS THAT CAN HEAL A ZANPAKU-TO...
...ARE ITS POS-SESSOR'S MIND...
...AND SPIRITUAL PRESSURE.
PLUS THE TIME TO INFUSE IT INTO THE ZANPAKU-TO.
THAT'S ALL.
KCHK...
FINE...
SO YOU'RE SAYING I SHOULD TAKE IT BACK AND FIX IT MYSELF.
WELL, THANKS FOR NOTHING...
I WASN'T FINISHED.
I WAS TALKING ABOUT SHIKAI.
THE DESTRUCTION OF A ZANPAKU-TO'S SHIKAI AND BANKAI HAVE COMPLETELY DIFFERENT MEANINGS.
A BANKAI THAT IS DESTROYED...
...CAN NEVER BE RETURNED TO WHAT IT ONCE WAS.

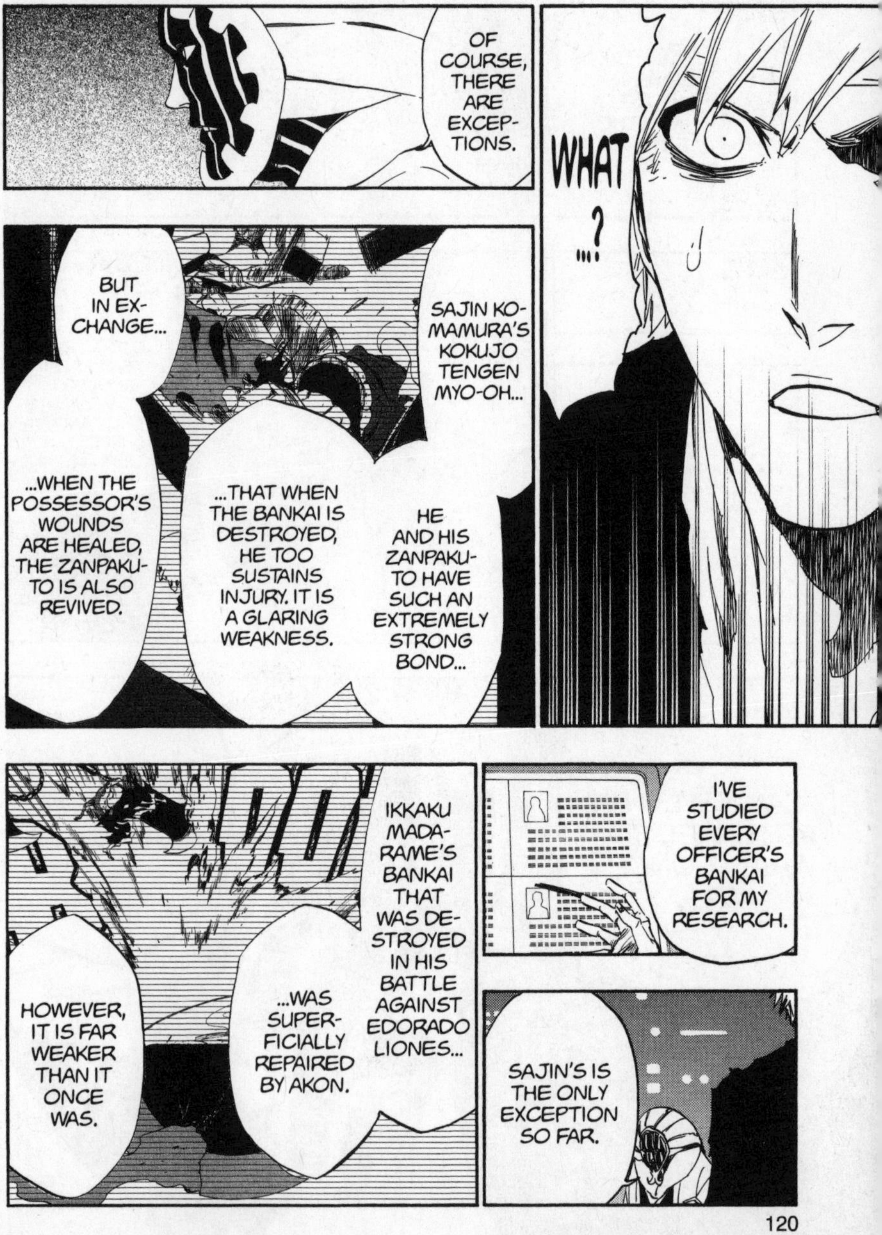
WHAT ...?
OF COURSE, THERE ARE EXCEPTIONS.
SAJIN KOMAMURA'S KOKUJO TENGEN MYO-OH...
HE AND HIS ZANPAKUTO HAVE SUCH AN EXTREMELY STRONG BOND...
BUT IN EXCHANGE...
...THAT WHEN THE BANKAI IS DESTROYED, HE TOO SUSTAINS INJURY. IT IS A GLARING WEAKNESS.
...WHEN THE POSSESSOR'S WOUNDS ARE HEALED, THE ZANPAKUTO IS ALSO REVIVED.
I'VE STUDIED EVERY OFFICER'S BANKAI FOR MY RESEARCH.
SAJIN'S IS THE ONLY EXCEPTION SO FAR.
IKKAKU MADARAME'S BANKAI THAT WAS DESTROYED IN HIS BATTLE AGAINST EDORADO LIONES...
...WAS SUPERFICIALLY REPAIRED BY AKON.
HOWEVER, IT IS FAR WEAKER THAN IT ONCE WAS.

READ THIS WAY

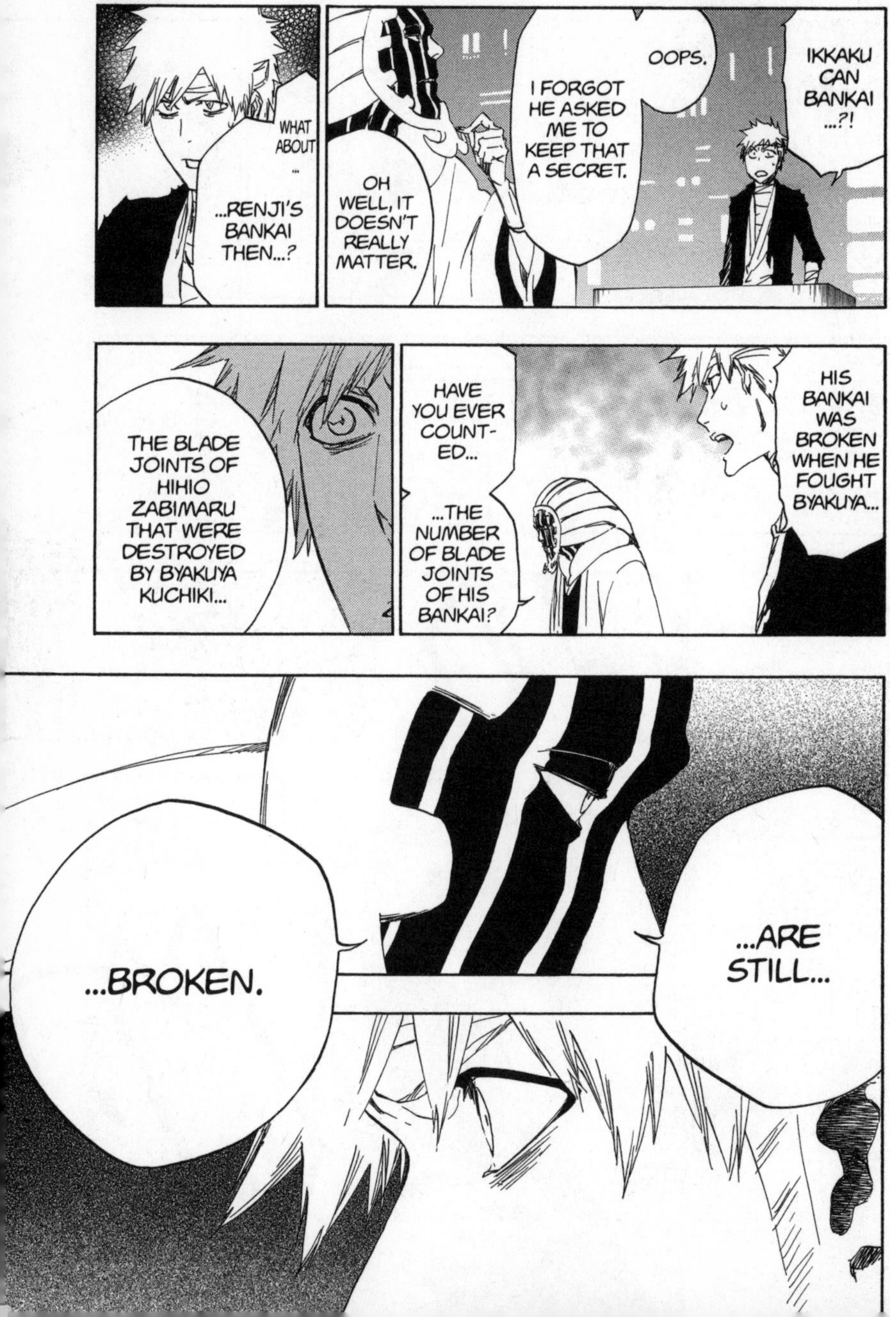
IKKAKU CAN BANKAI ...?!
OOPS.
I FORGOT HE ASKED ME TO KEEP THAT A SECRET.
OH WELL, IT DOESN'T REALLY MATTER.
WHAT ABOUT ...
...RENJI'S BANKAI THEN...?
HIS BANKAI WAS BROKEN WHEN HE FOUGHT BYAKUYA...
HAVE YOU EVER COUNT-ED...
...THE NUMBER OF BLADE JOINTS OF HIS BANKAI?
THE BLADE JOINTS OF HIHIO ZABIMARU THAT WERE DESTROYED BY BYAKUYA KUCHIKI...
...ARE STILL...
...BROKEN.

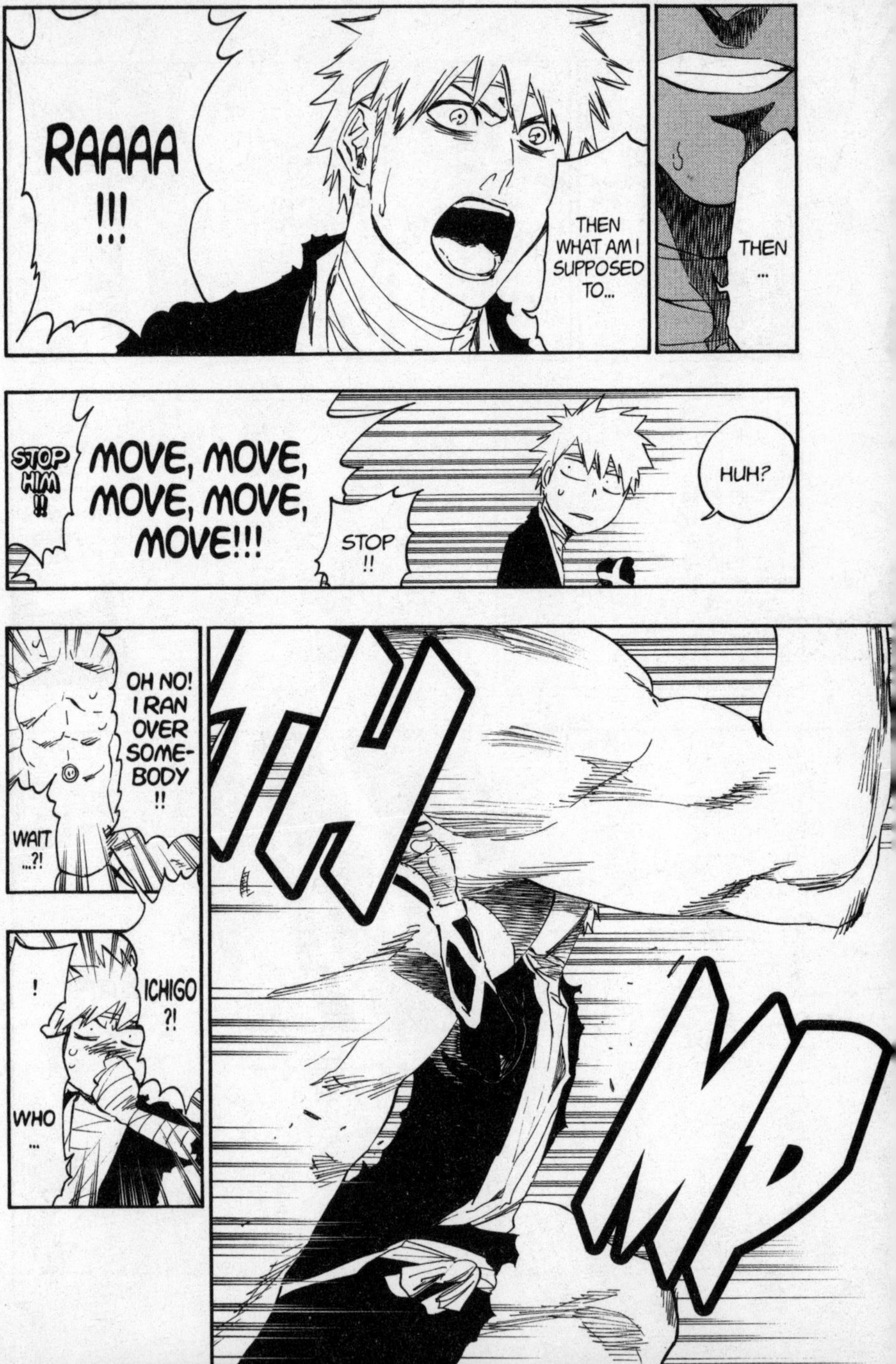
THEN ...
THEN WHAT AM I SUPPOSED TO...
RAAAA !!!
HUH?
STOP !!
MOVE, MOVE, MOVE, MOVE, MOVE!!!
STOP HIM !!
OH NO! I RAN OVER SOME-BODY !!
WAIT ...?!
ICHIGO ?!
!
WHO ...

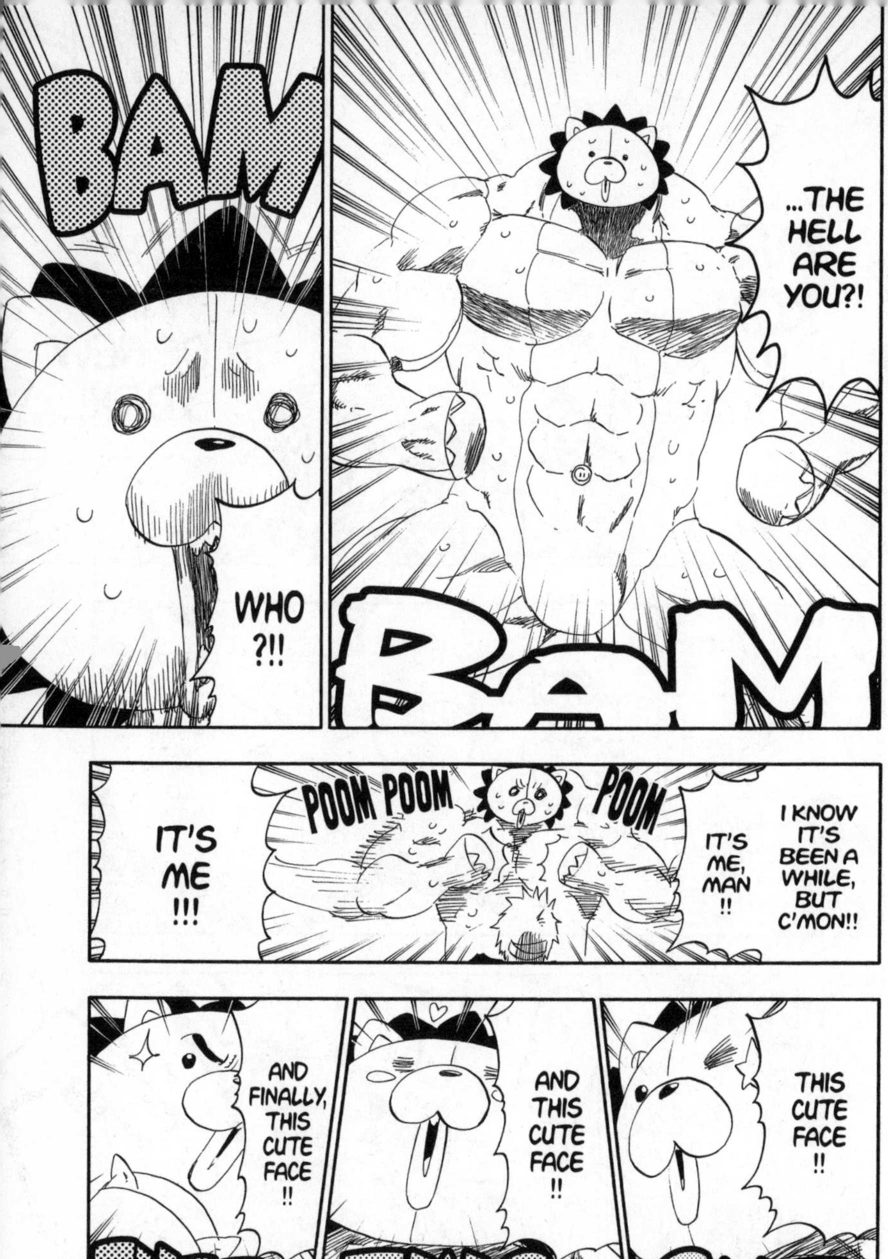
...THE HELL ARE YOU?!
BAM
BAM
WHO ?!!
I KNOW IT'S BEEN A WHILE, BUT C'MON!!
IT'S ME, MAN !!
POOM POOM POOM
IT'S ME !!!
THIS CUTE FACE !!
ONE
AND THIS CUTE FACE !!
TWO
AND FINALLY, THIS CUTE FACE !!
THREE

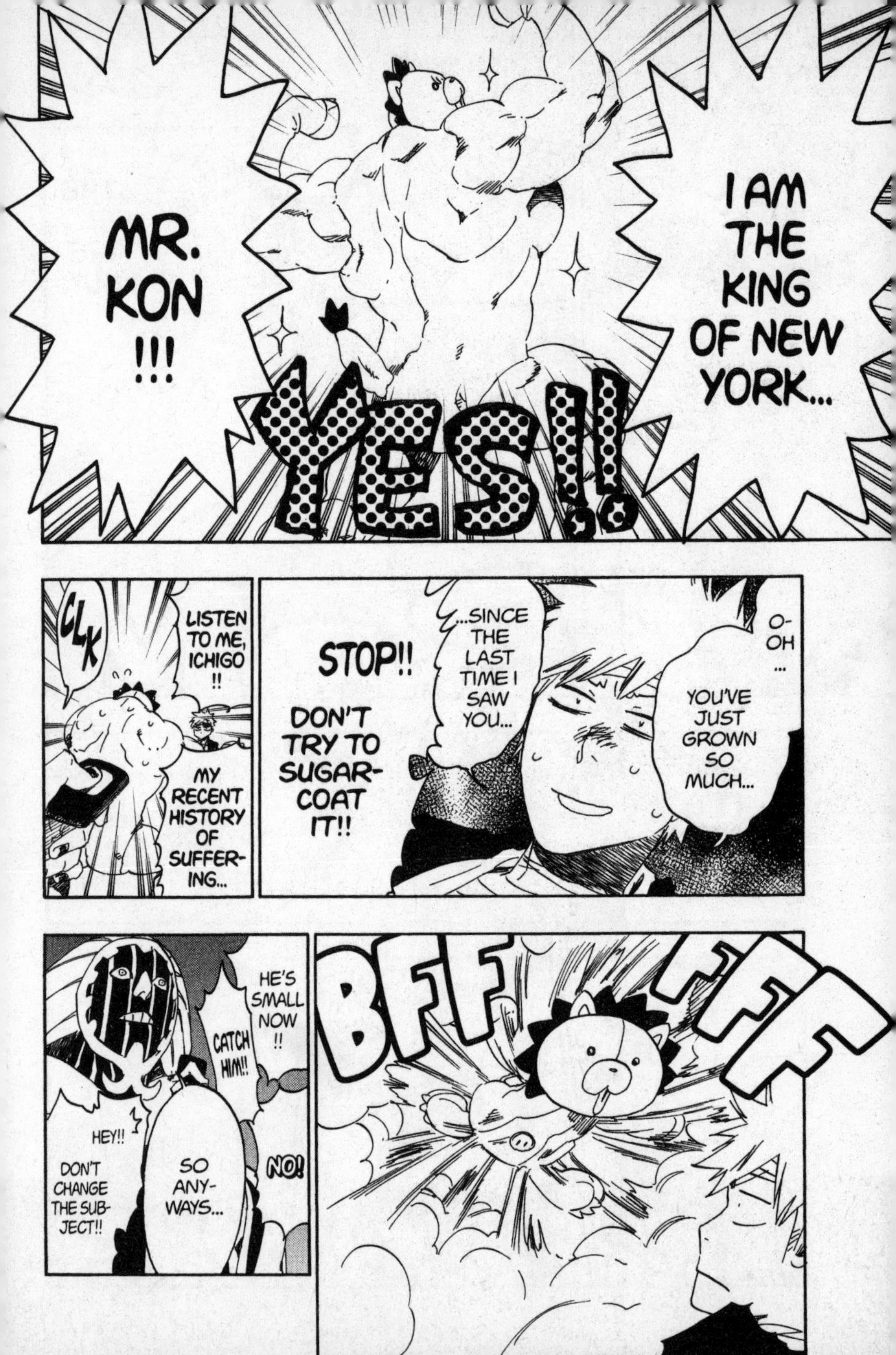

I AM THE KING OF NEW YORK...
MR. KON!!!
YES!!
O-OH... YOU'VE JUST GROWN SO MUCH...
...SINCE THE LAST TIME I SAW YOU...
STOP!!
DON'T TRY TO SUGAR-COAT IT!!
LISTEN TO ME, ICHIGO!!
CLK
MY RECENT HISTORY OF SUFFERING...
BFFFFF
HE'S SMALL NOW!!
CATCH HIM!!
NO!
SO ANYWAYS...
HEY!!
DON'T CHANGE THE SUBJECT!!

READ THIS WAY

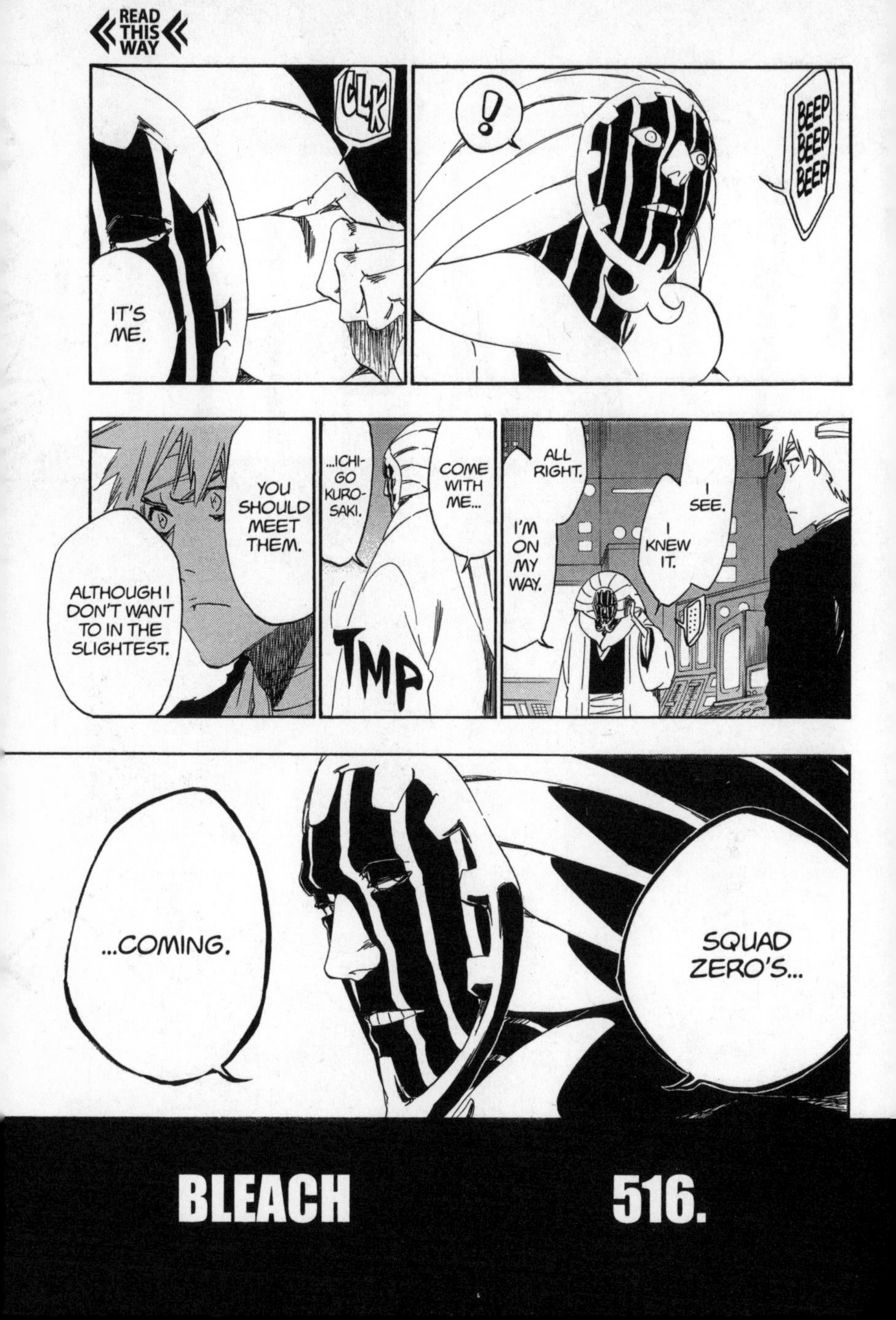
!
BEEP BEEP BEEP
CLK
IT'S ME.
I SEE.
I KNEW IT.
ALL RIGHT.
I'M ON MY WAY.
COME WITH ME...
...ICHIGO KUROSAKI.
TMP
YOU SHOULD MEET THEM.
ALTHOUGH I DON'T WANT TO IN THE SLIGHTEST.
SQUAD ZERO'S...
...COMING.

BLEACH 516.

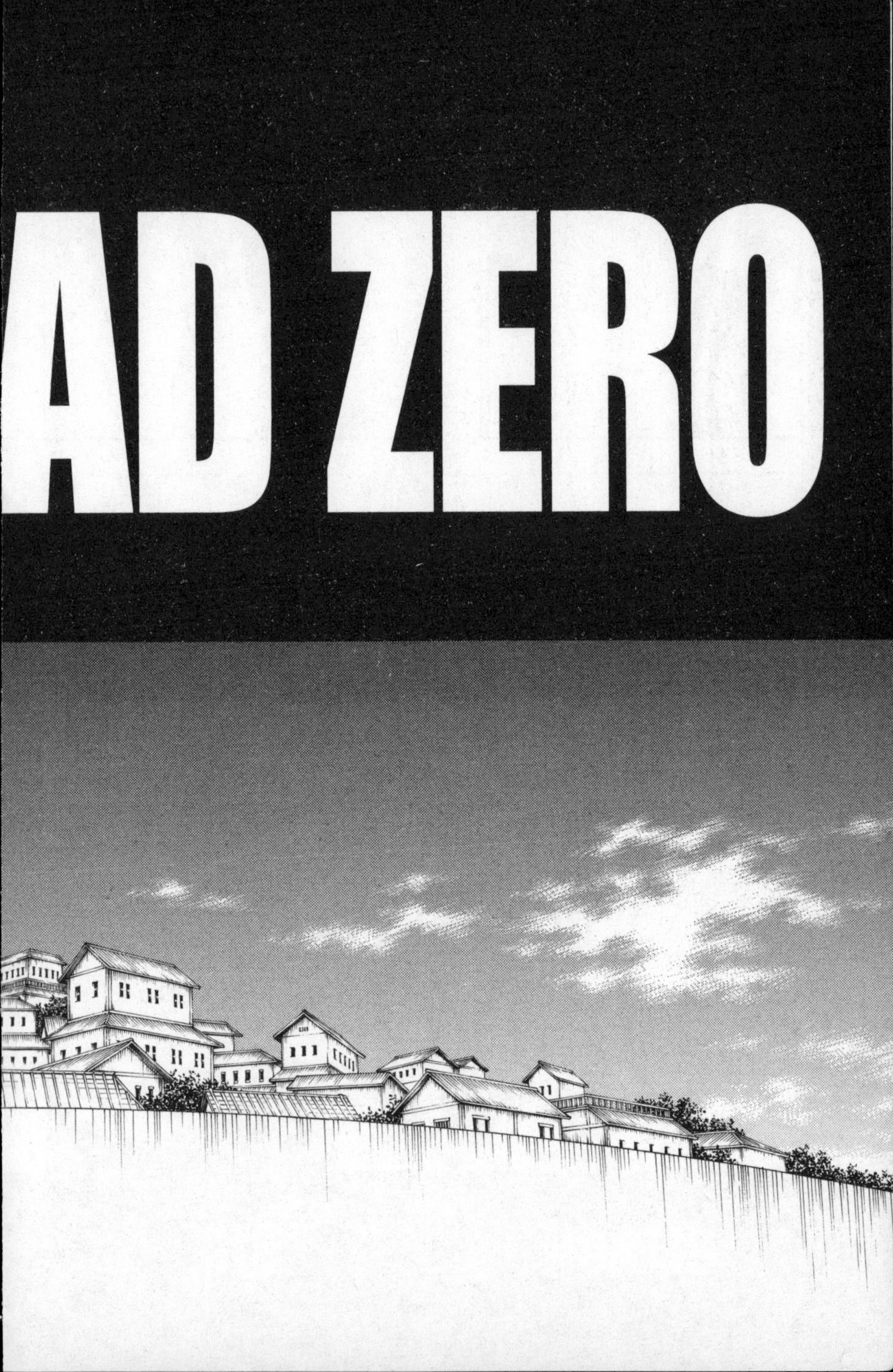
AD ZERO

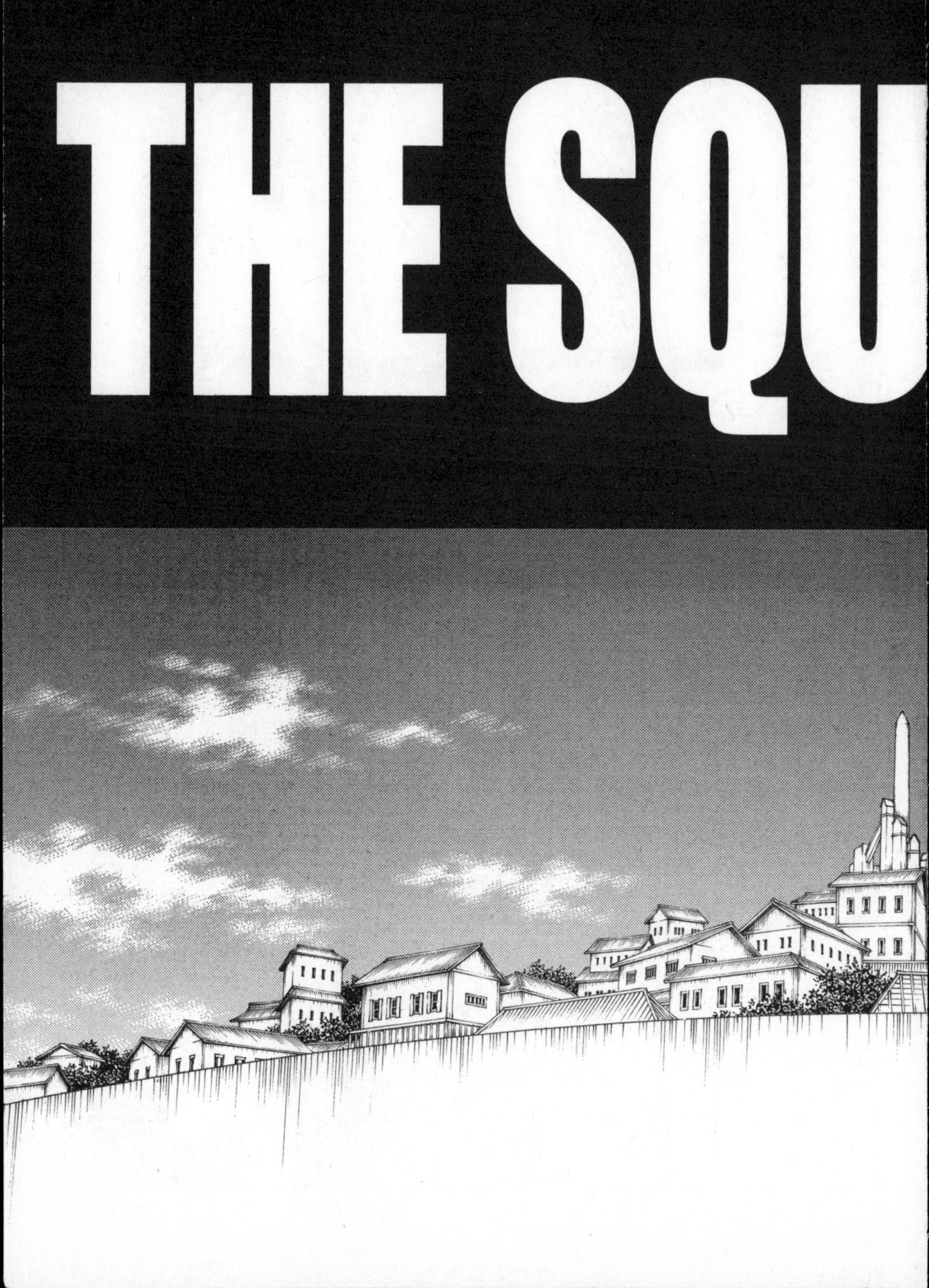
THE SQU

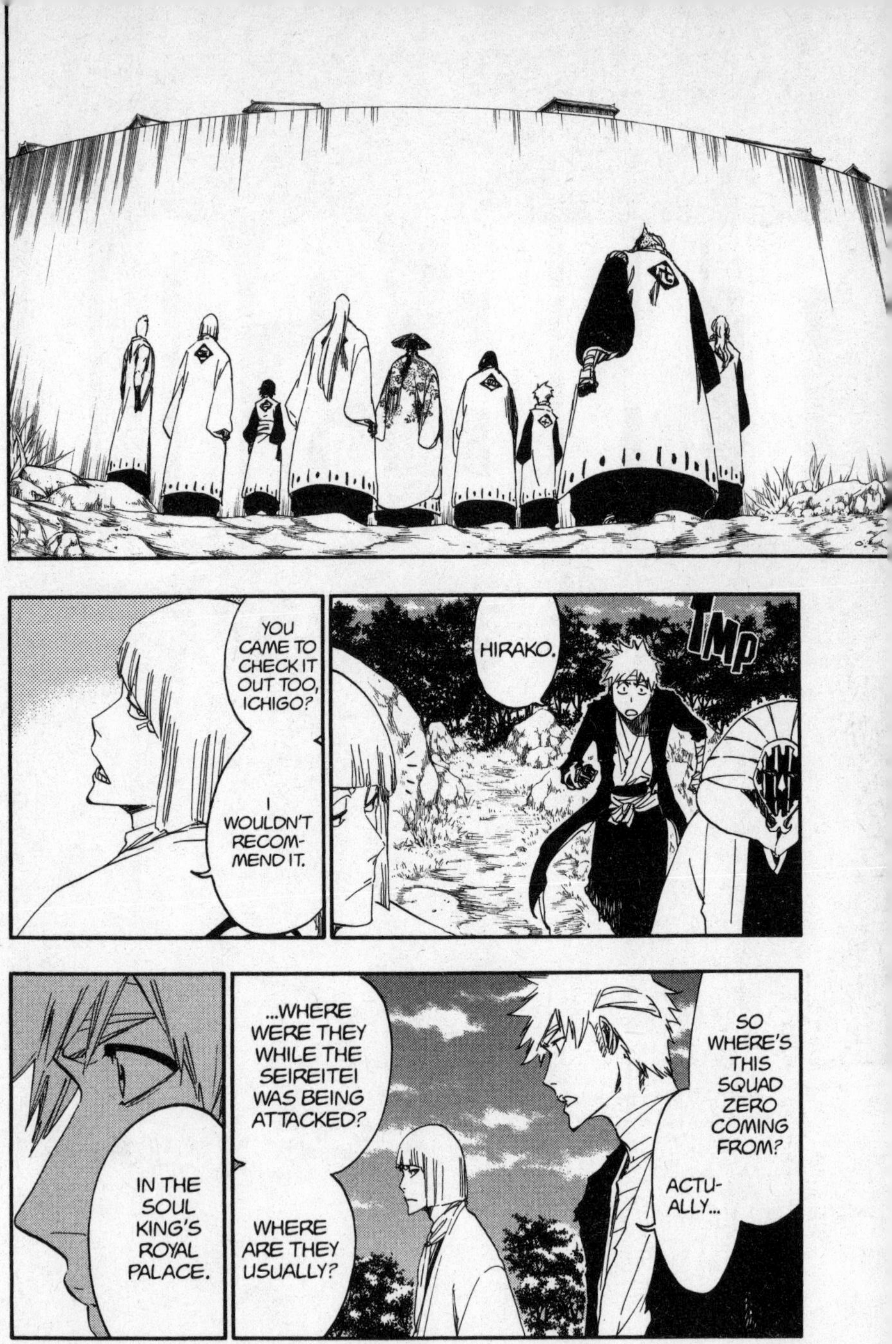
TMP
HIRAKO.
YOU CAME TO CHECK IT OUT TOO, ICHIGO?
I WOULDN'T RECOMMEND IT.
SO WHERE'S THIS SQUAD ZERO COMING FROM?
...WHERE WERE THEY WHILE THE SEIREITEI WAS BEING ATTACKED?
ACTUALLY...
WHERE ARE THEY USUALLY?
IN THE SOUL KING'S ROYAL PALACE.

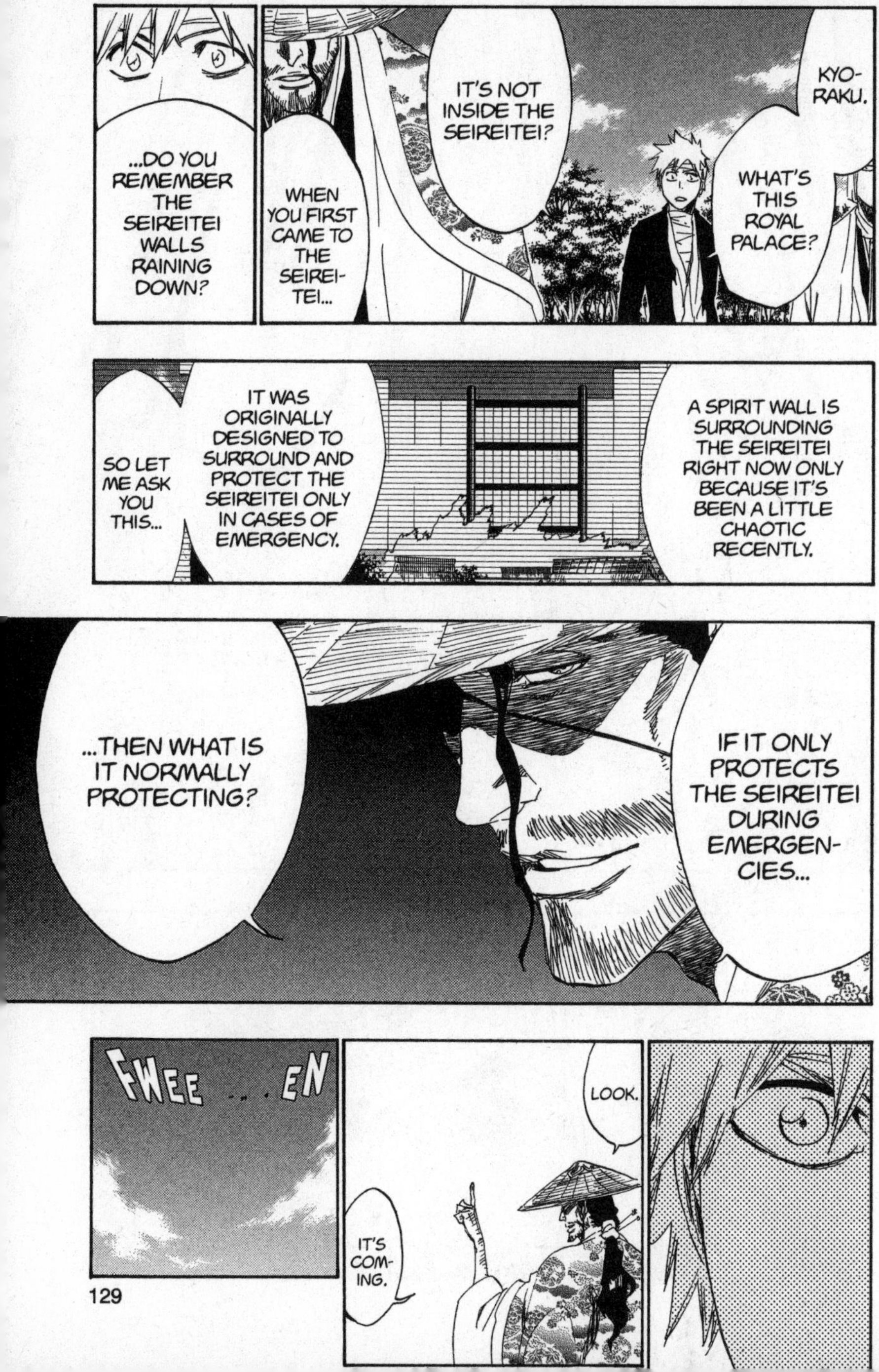
KYO-RAKU.
WHAT'S THIS ROYAL PALACE?
IT'S NOT INSIDE THE SEIREITEI?
WHEN YOU FIRST CAME TO THE SEIREI-TEI...
...DO YOU REMEMBER THE SEIREITEI WALLS RAINING DOWN?
A SPIRIT WALL IS SURROUNDING THE SEIREITEI RIGHT NOW ONLY BECAUSE IT'S BEEN A LITTLE CHAOTIC RECENTLY.
IT WAS ORIGINALLY DESIGNED TO SURROUND AND PROTECT THE SEIREITEI ONLY IN CASES OF EMERGENCY.
SO LET ME ASK YOU THIS...
IF IT ONLY PROTECTS THE SEIREITEI DURING EMERGEN-CIES...
...THEN WHAT IS IT NORMALLY PROTECTING?
LOOK.
IT'S COM-ING.
FWEE ... EN

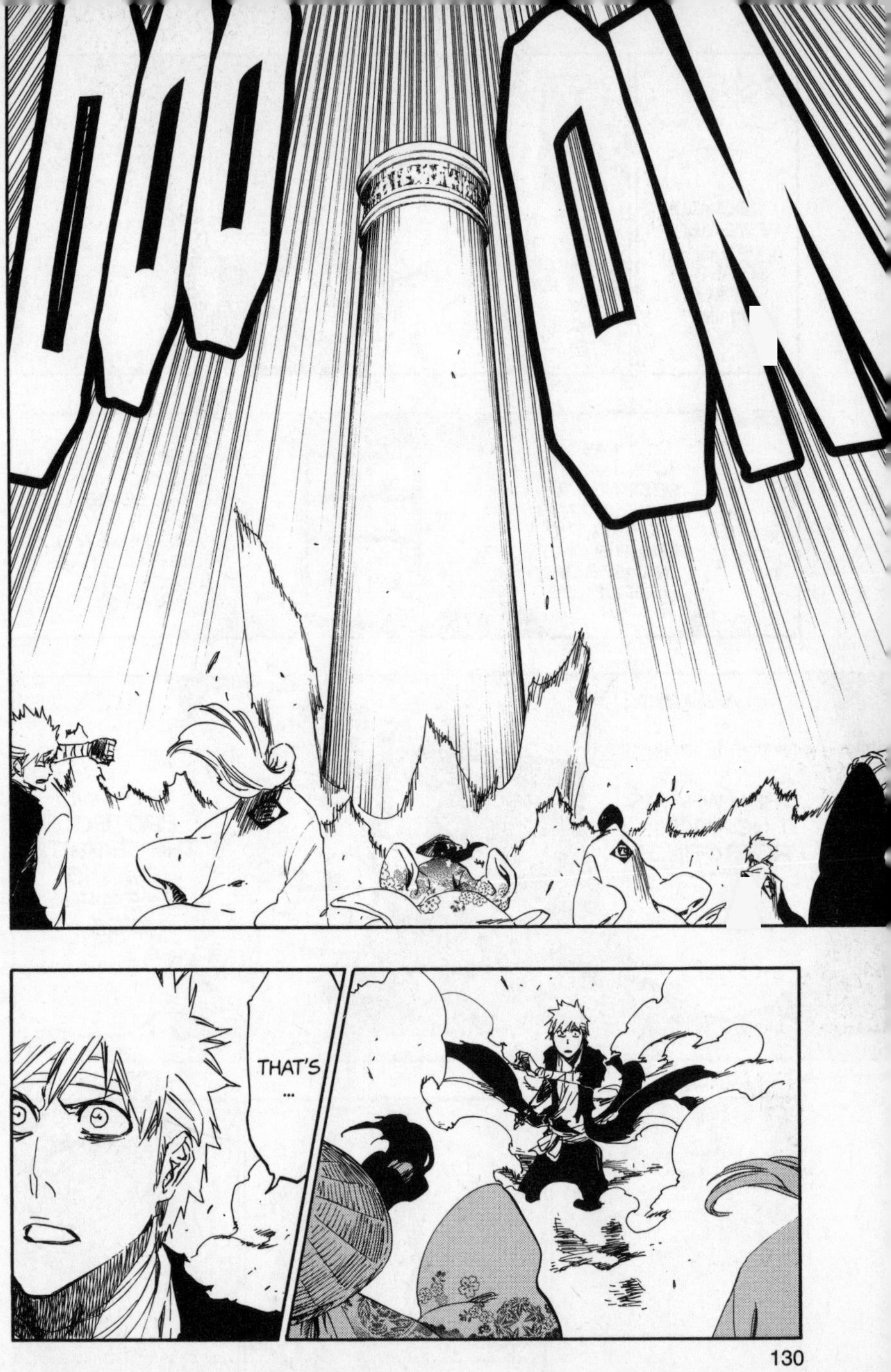
THAT'S ...

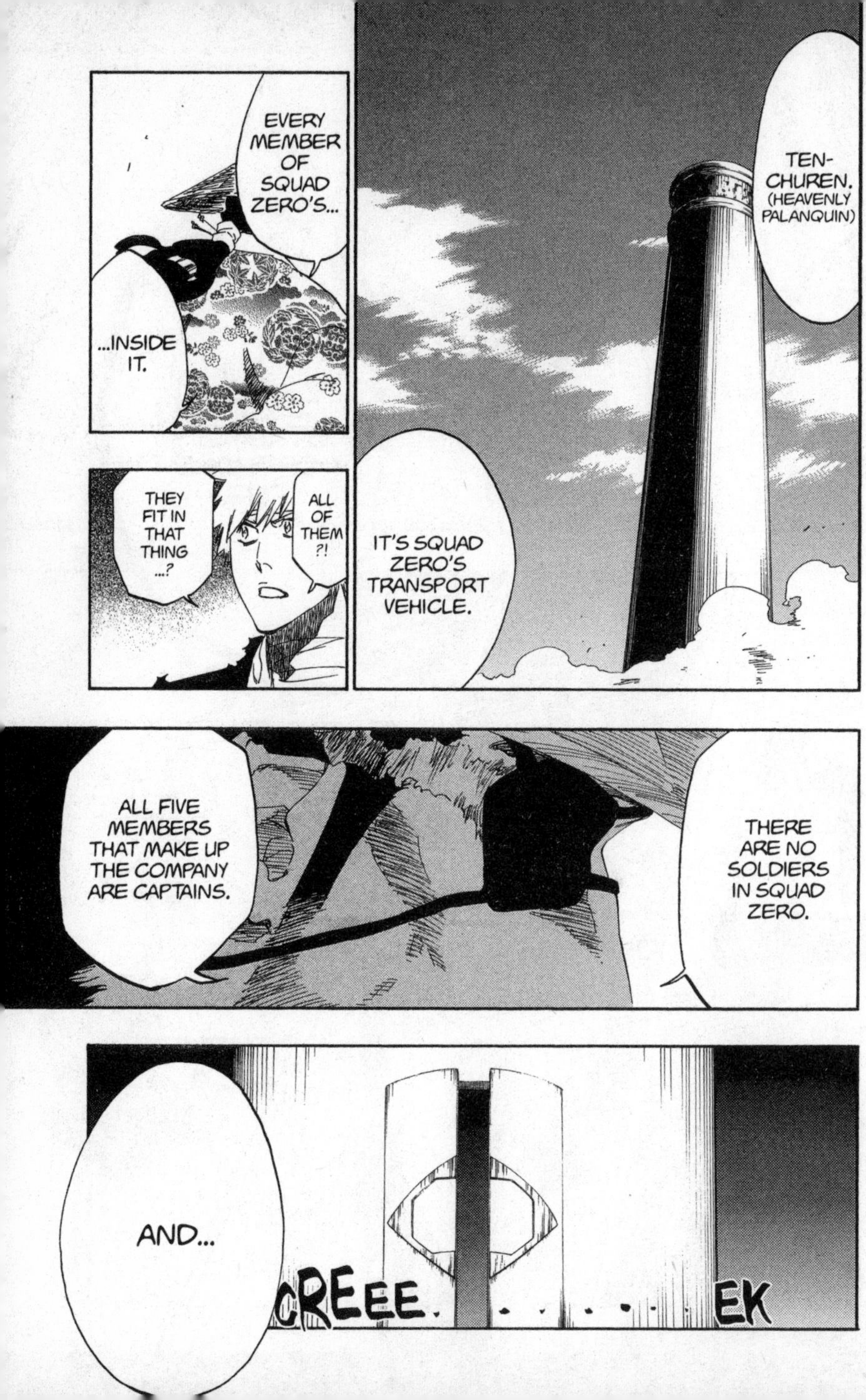
TEN-CHUREN. (HEAVENLY PALANQUIN)
IT'S SQUAD ZERO'S TRANSPORT VEHICLE.
EVERY MEMBER OF SQUAD ZERO'S...
...INSIDE IT.
ALL OF THEM ?!
THEY FIT IN THAT THING ...?
THERE ARE NO SOLDIERS IN SQUAD ZERO.
ALL FIVE MEMBERS THAT MAKE UP THE COMPANY ARE CAPTAINS.
AND...
CREEE.......EK

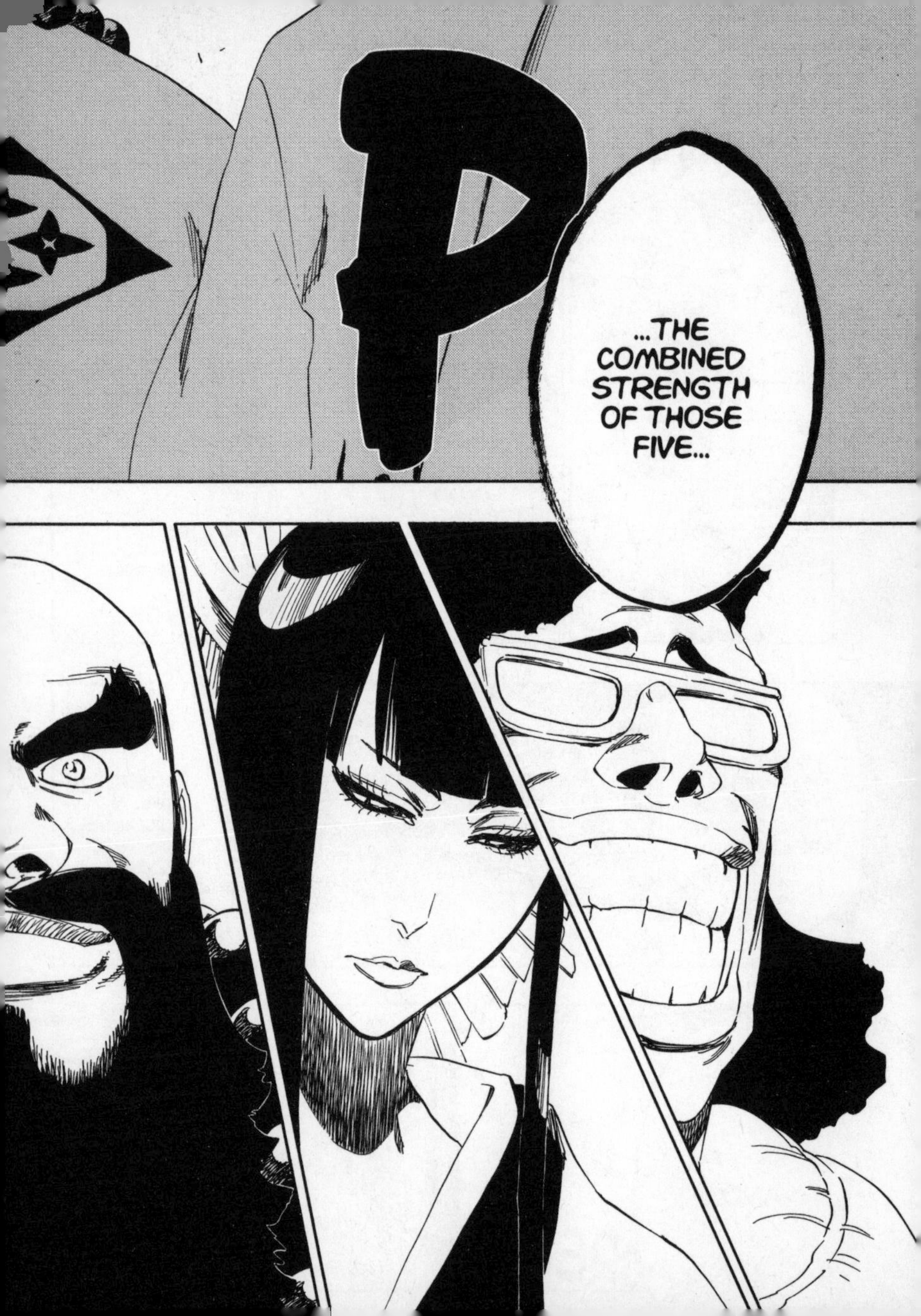
...THE COMBINED STRENGTH OF THOSE FIVE...

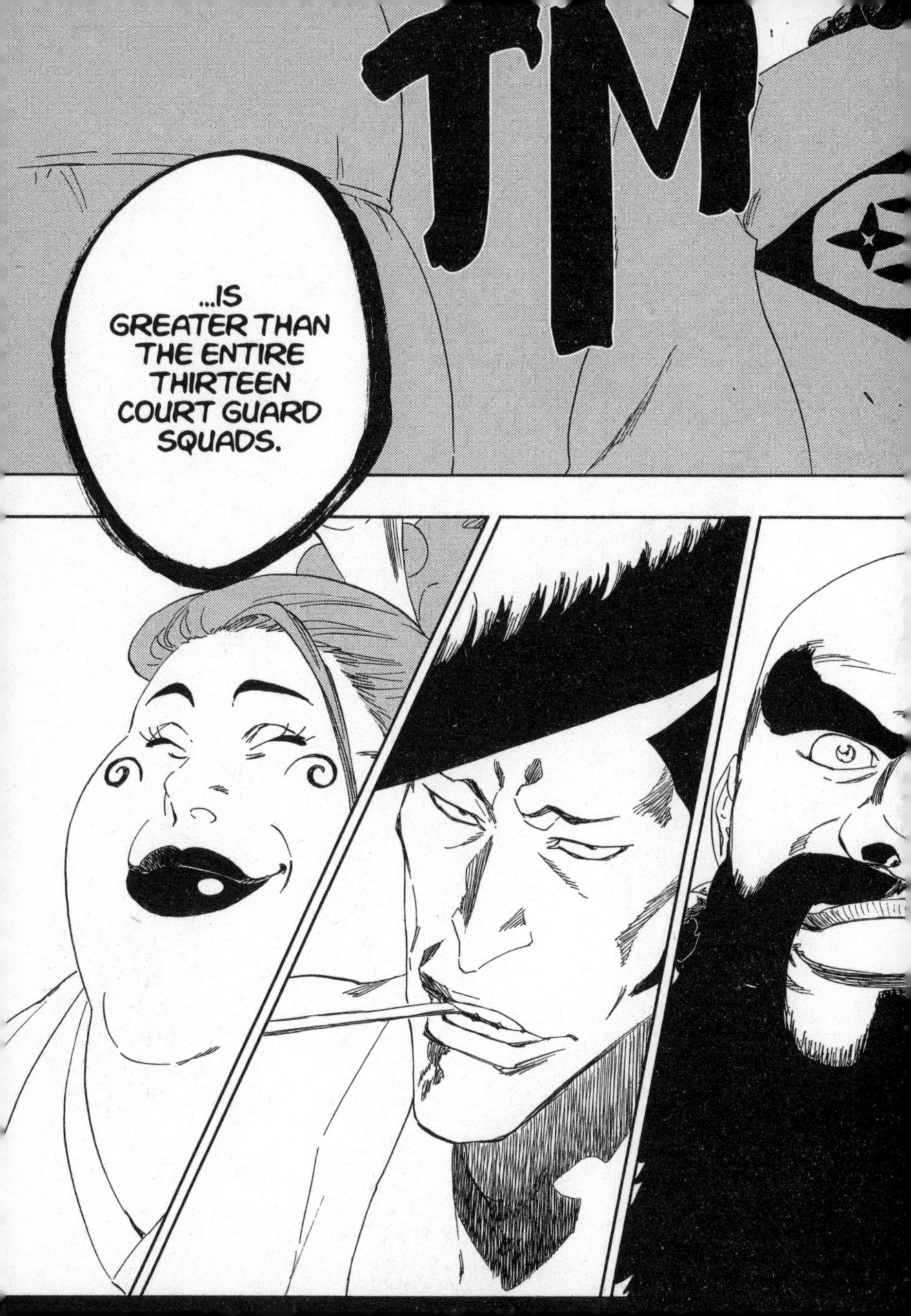
...IS GREATER THAN THE ENTIRE THIRTEEN COURT GUARD SQUADS.

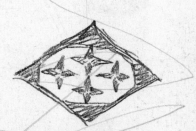

SQUAD ZERO'S FLOWER
THE WINTER DAPHNE

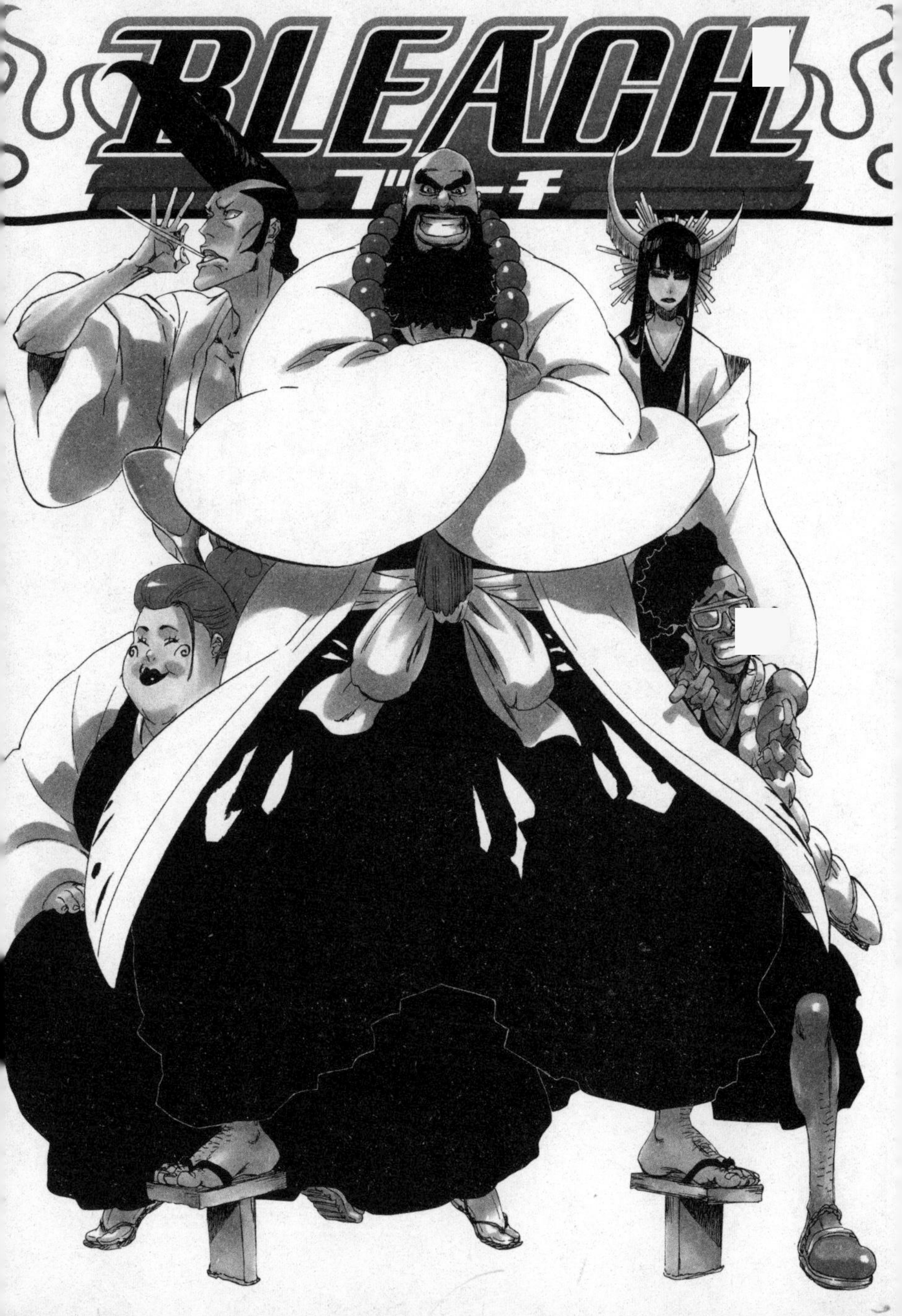
BLEACH

BLEACH
ブリーチ

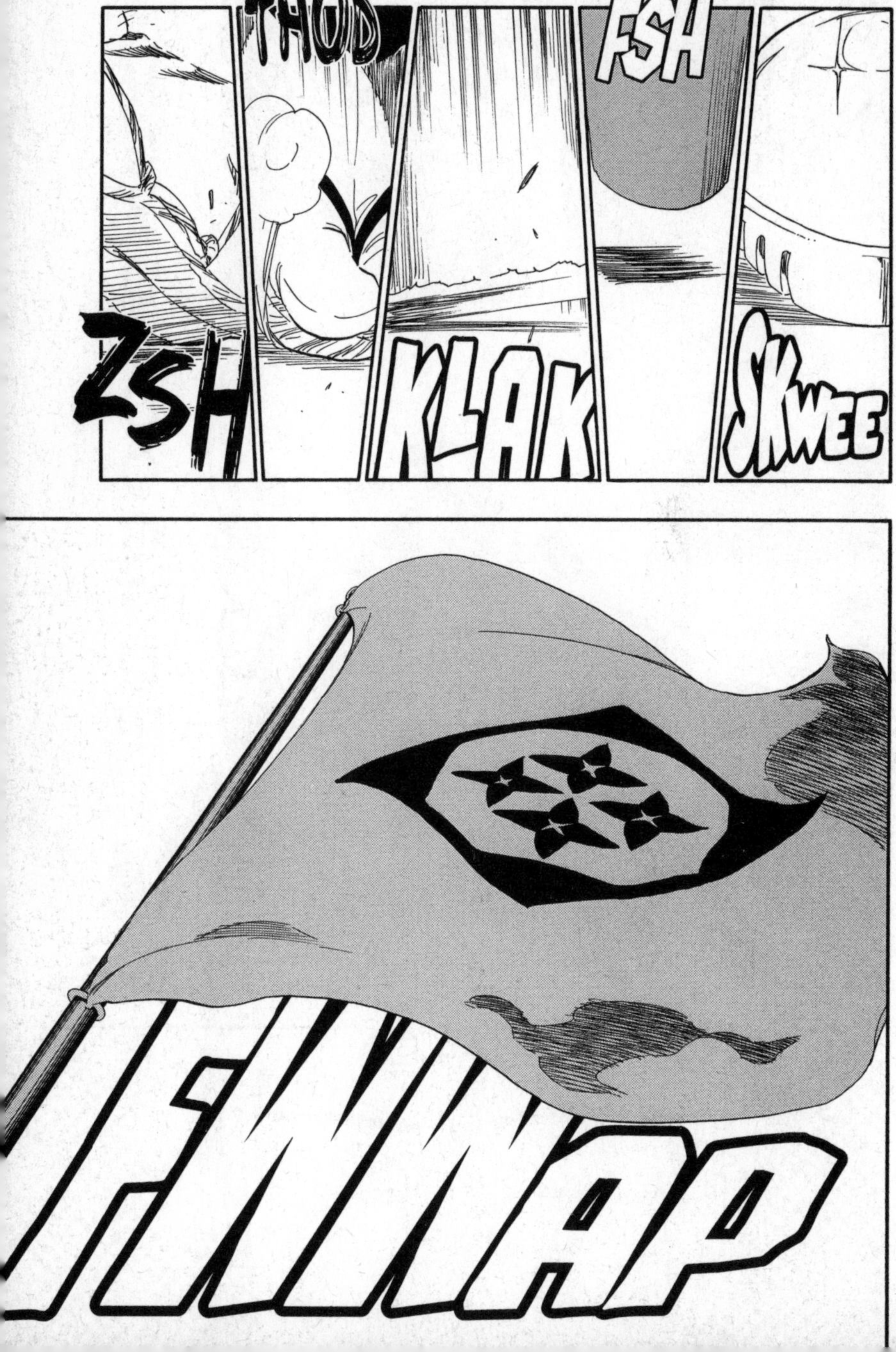
SKWEE
FSH
KLAK
THUD
ZSH
FWAP

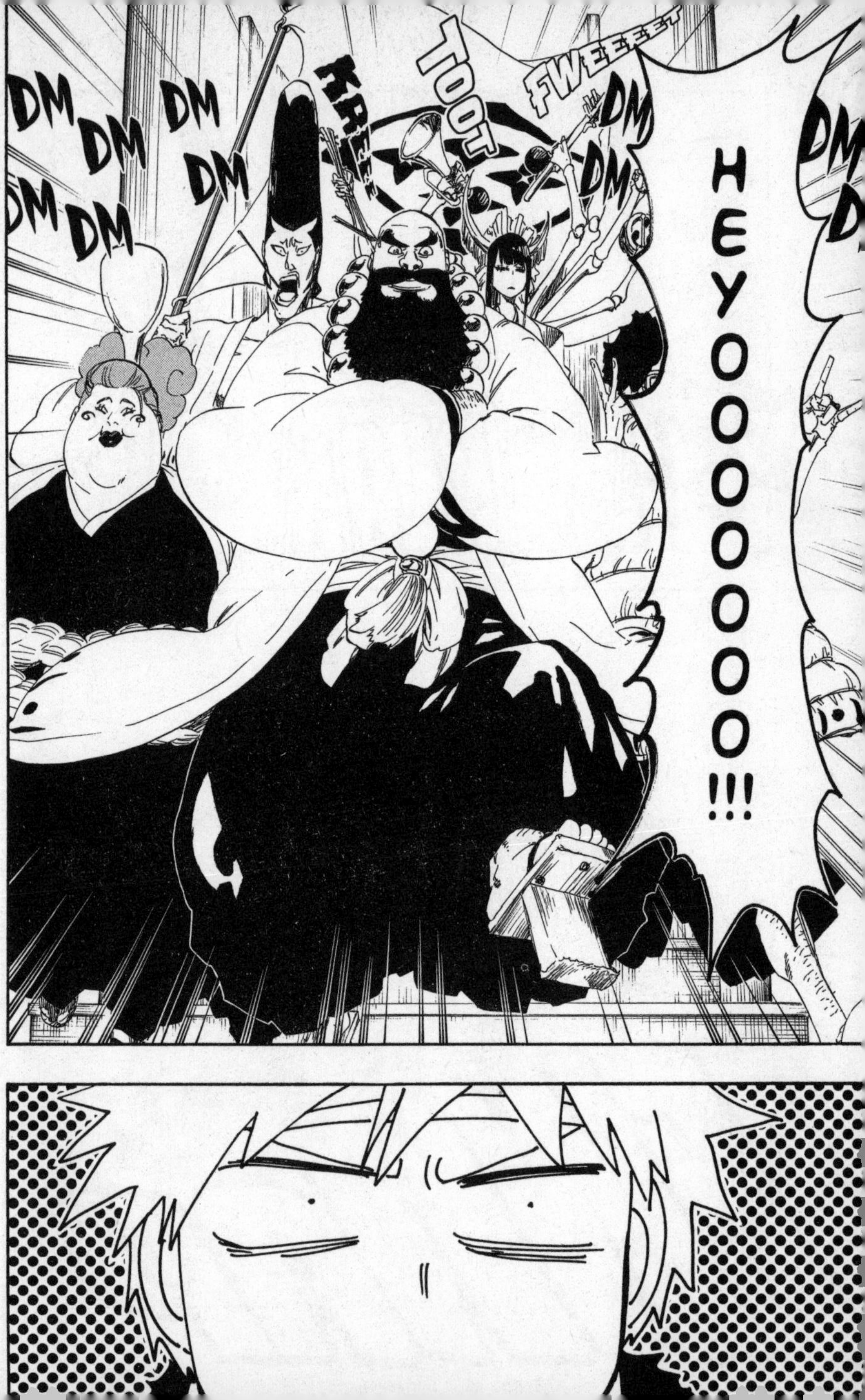

DM
HEYOOOOOOO!!!
FWEEEEET
DM
DM
TOOT
KREE
DM
DM
DM
DM
DM
DM
DM

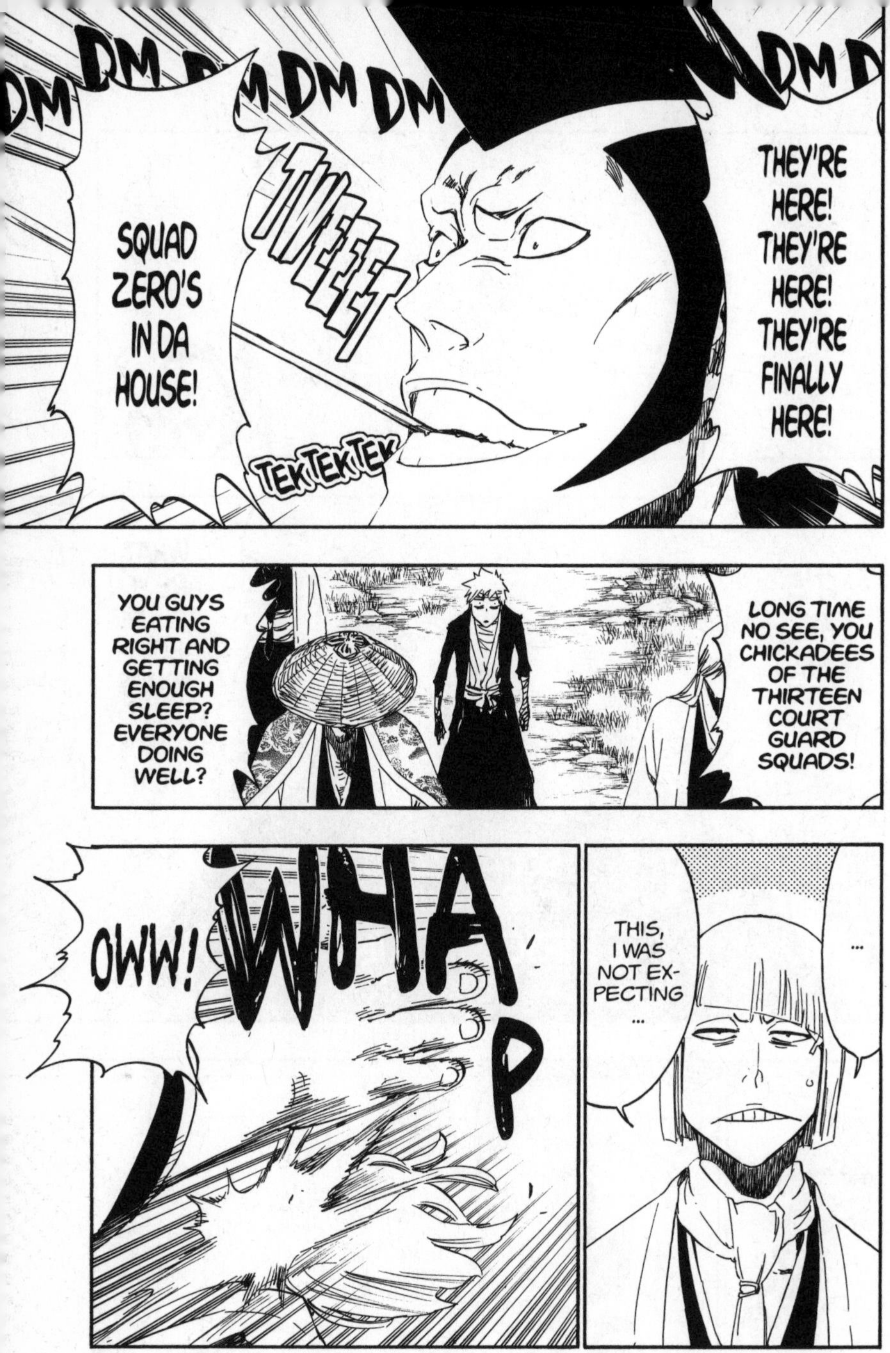
THEY'RE HERE! THEY'RE HERE! THEY'RE FINALLY HERE!
DM DM
DM DM DM DM
TWEEET
SQUAD ZERO'S IN DA HOUSE!
TEK TEK TEK
LONG TIME NO SEE, YOU CHICKADEES OF THE THIRTEEN COURT GUARD SQUADS!
YOU GUYS EATING RIGHT AND GETTING ENOUGH SLEEP? EVERYONE DOING WELL?
...
THIS, I WAS NOT EX-PECTING ...
WHAP
OWW!

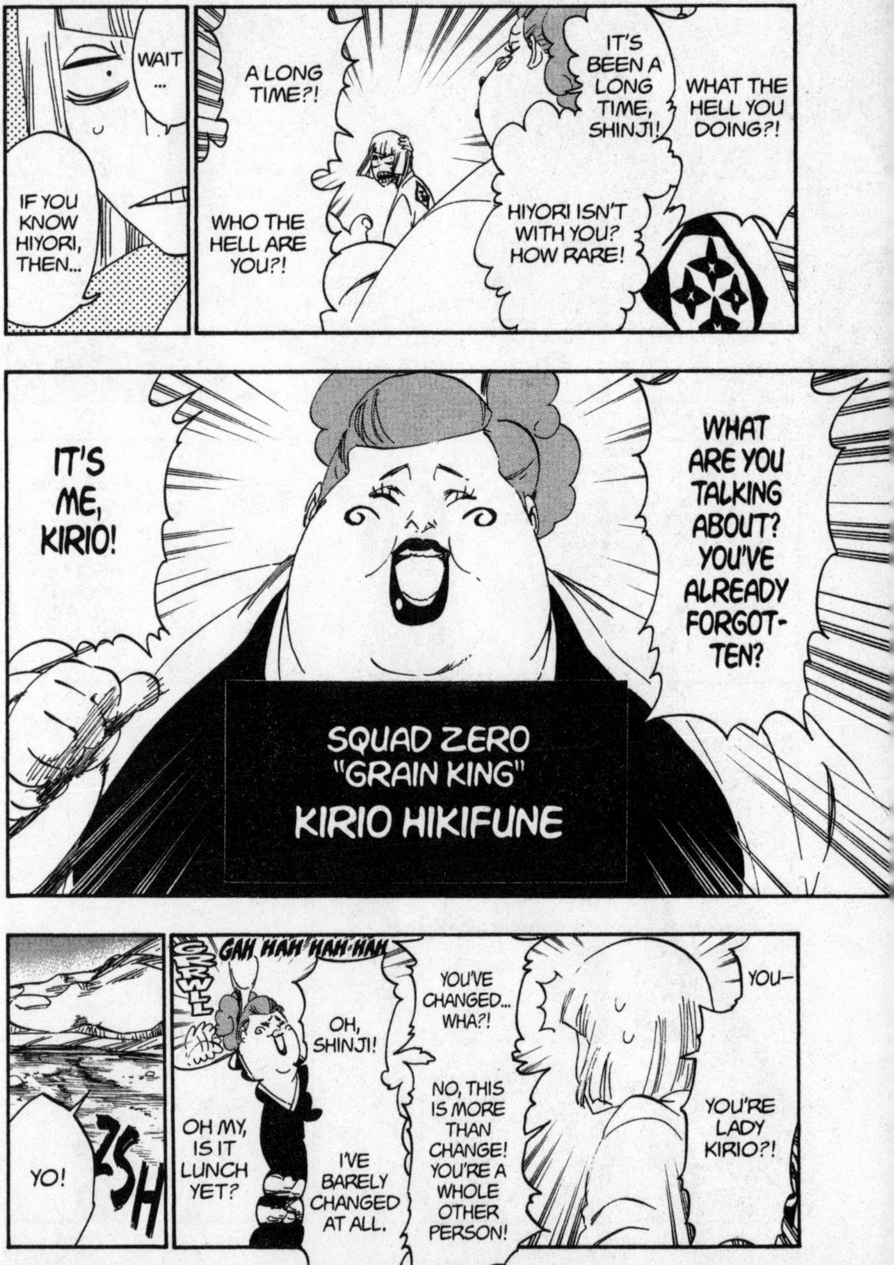
WHAT THE HELL YOU DOING?!
IT'S BEEN A LONG TIME, SHINJI!
HIYORI ISN'T WITH YOU? HOW RARE!
A LONG TIME?!
WHO THE HELL ARE YOU?!
WAIT ...
IF YOU KNOW HIYORI, THEN...
WHAT ARE YOU TALKING ABOUT? YOU'VE ALREADY FORGOT-TEN?
IT'S ME, KIRIO!
SQUAD ZERO "GRAIN KING"
KIRIO HIKIFUNE
YOU—
YOU'RE LADY KIRIO?!
YOU'VE CHANGED... WHA?!
NO, THIS IS MORE THAN CHANGE! YOU'RE A WHOLE OTHER PERSON!
GAH HAH HAH HAH
GRWLL
OH, SHINJI!
I'VE BARELY CHANGED AT ALL.
OH MY, IS IT LUNCH YET?
YO!
ZSH

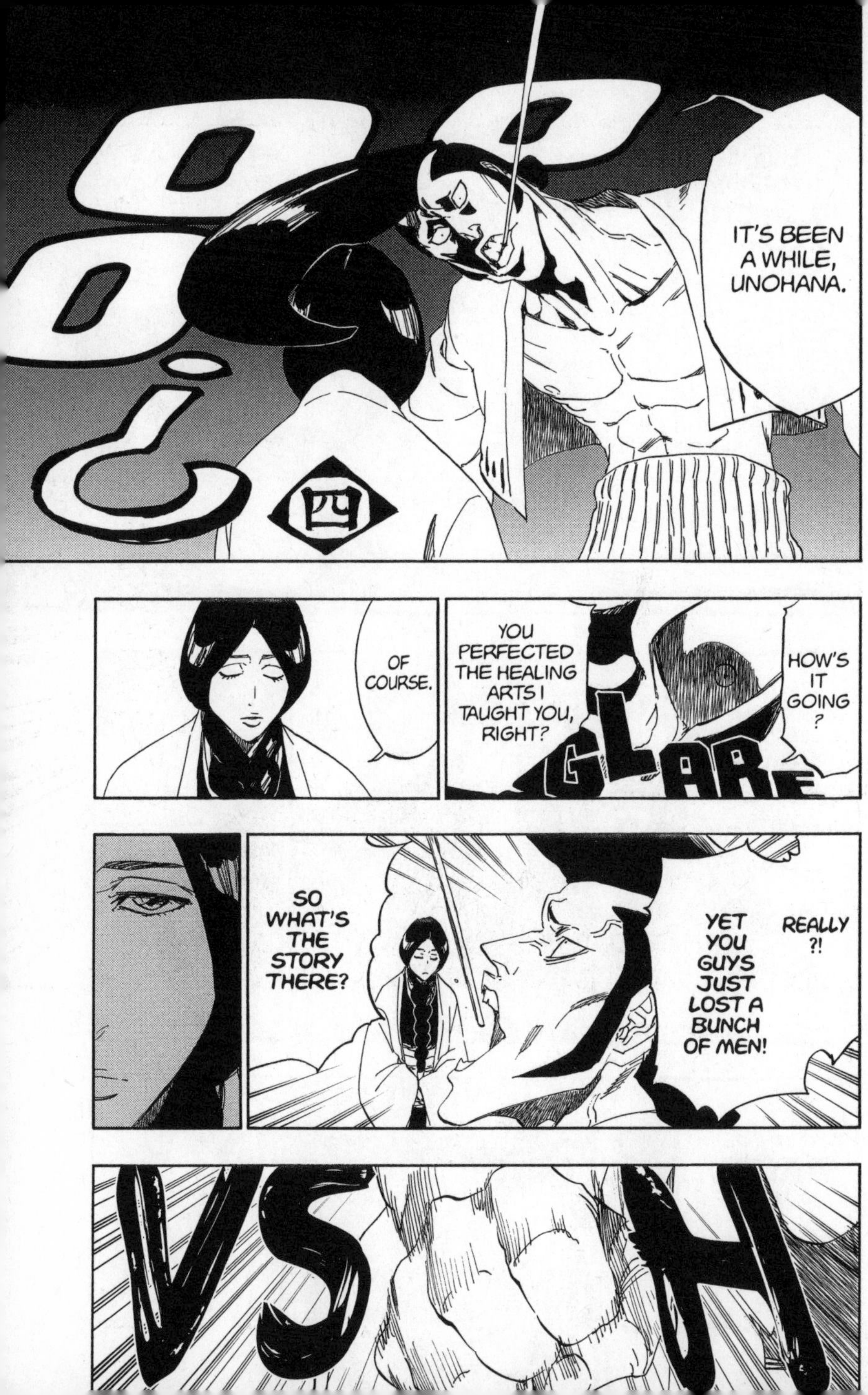
IT'S BEEN A WHILE, UNOHANA.
HOW'S IT GOING?
YOU PERFECTED THE HEALING ARTS I TAUGHT YOU, RIGHT?
GLARE
OF COURSE.
REALLY?!
YET YOU GUYS JUST LOST A BUNCH OF MEN!
SO WHAT'S THE STORY THERE?

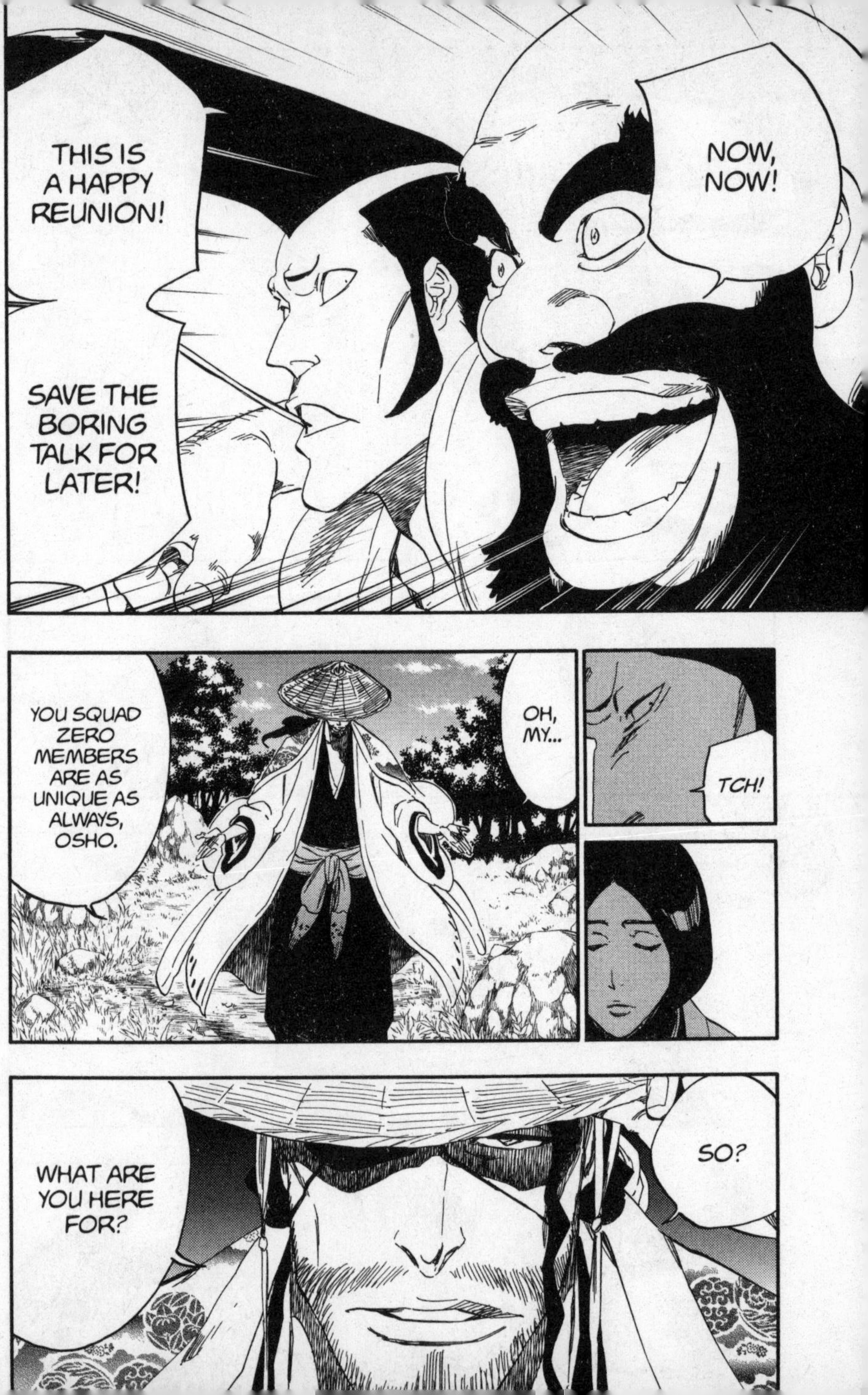
NOW, NOW!
THIS IS A HAPPY REUNION!
SAVE THE BORING TALK FOR LATER!
TCH!
OH, MY...
YOU SQUAD ZERO MEMBERS ARE AS UNIQUE AS ALWAYS, OSHO.
SO?
WHAT ARE YOU HERE FOR?

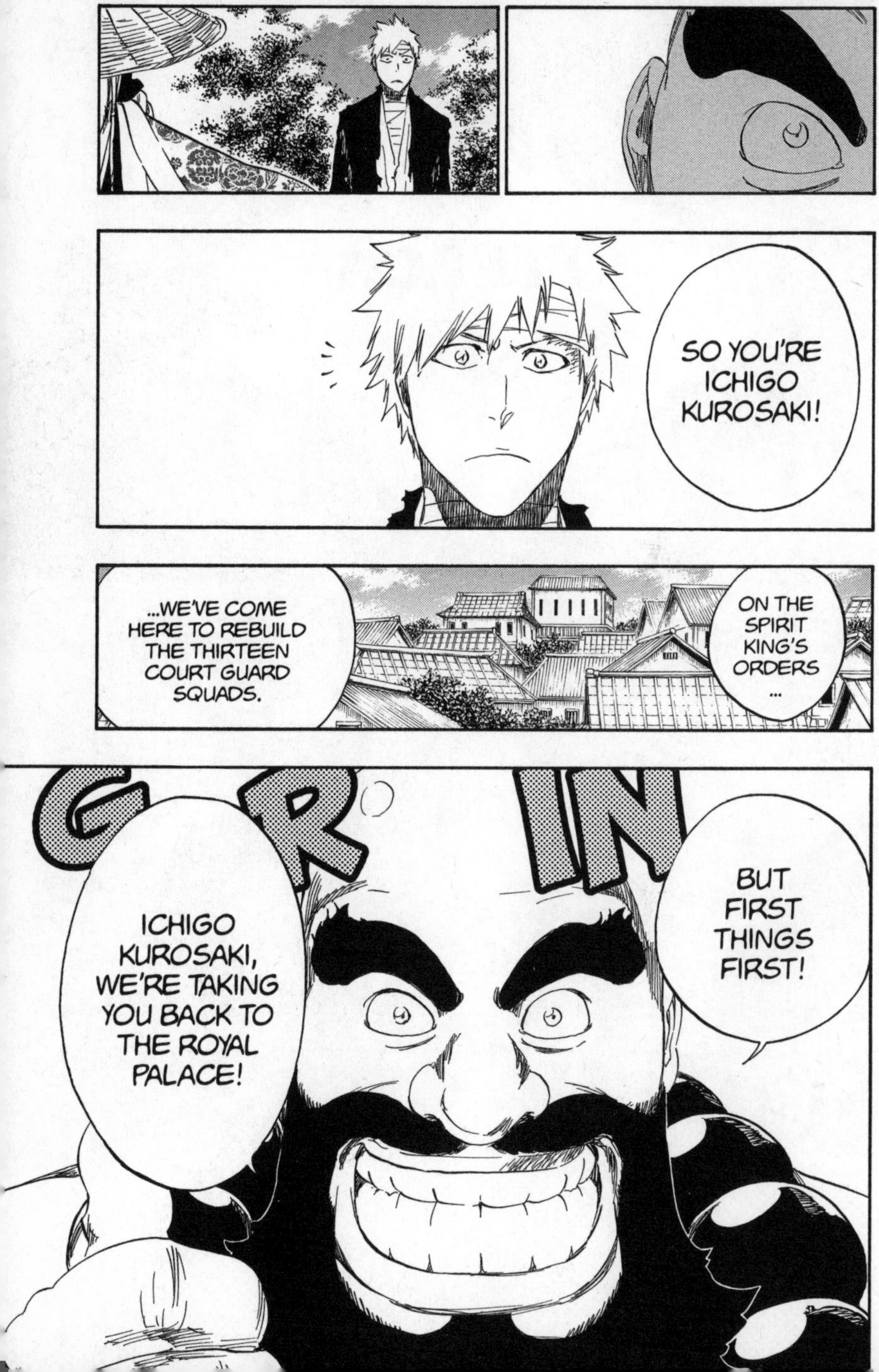
SO YOU'RE ICHIGO KUROSAKI!
ON THE SPIRIT KING'S ORDERS ...
...WE'VE COME HERE TO REBUILD THE THIRTEEN COURT GUARD SQUADS.
GRIN
BUT FIRST THINGS FIRST!
ICHIGO KUROSAKI, WE'RE TAKING YOU BACK TO THE ROYAL PALACE!

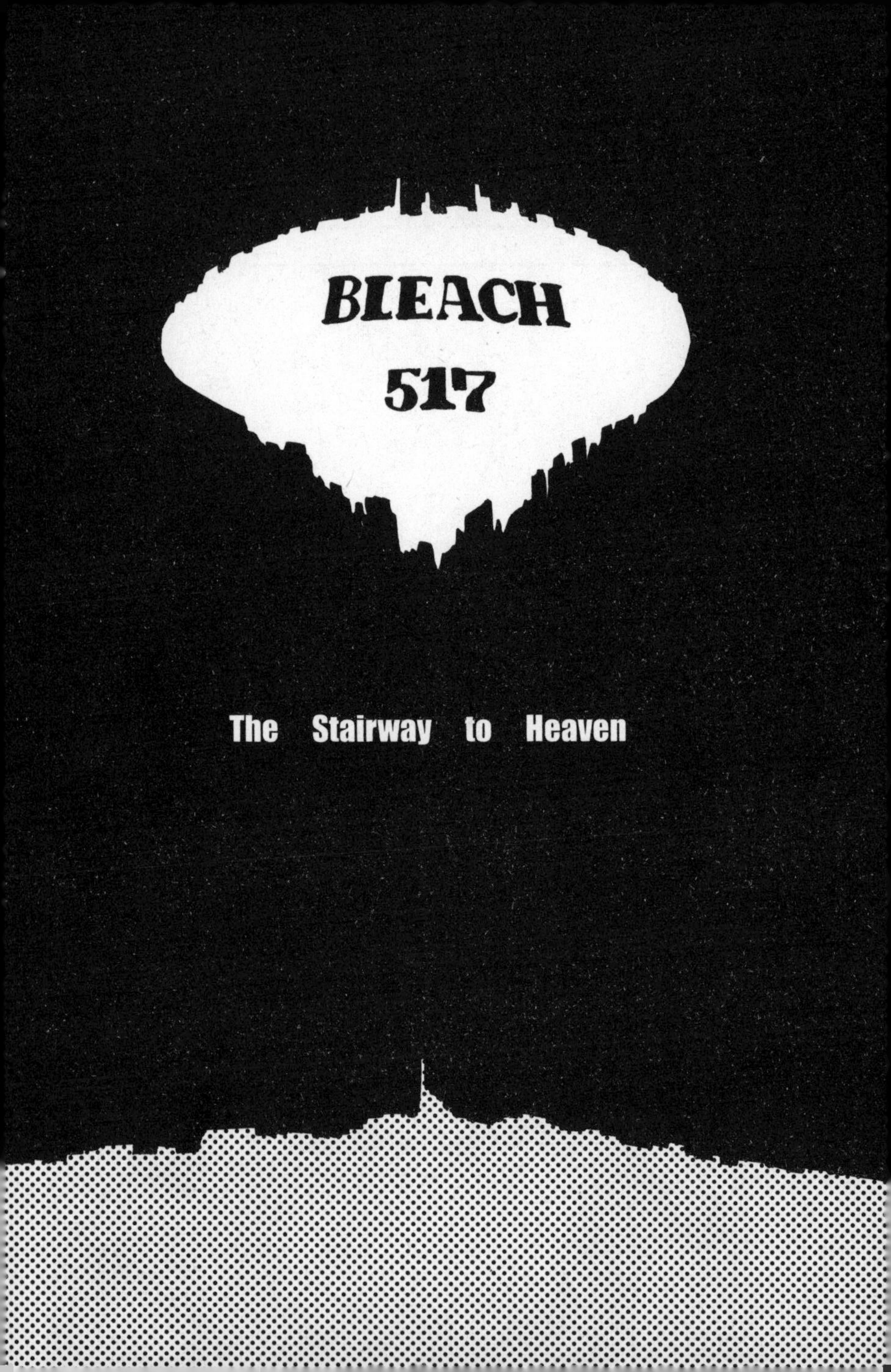
BLEACH
517
The Stairway to Heaven

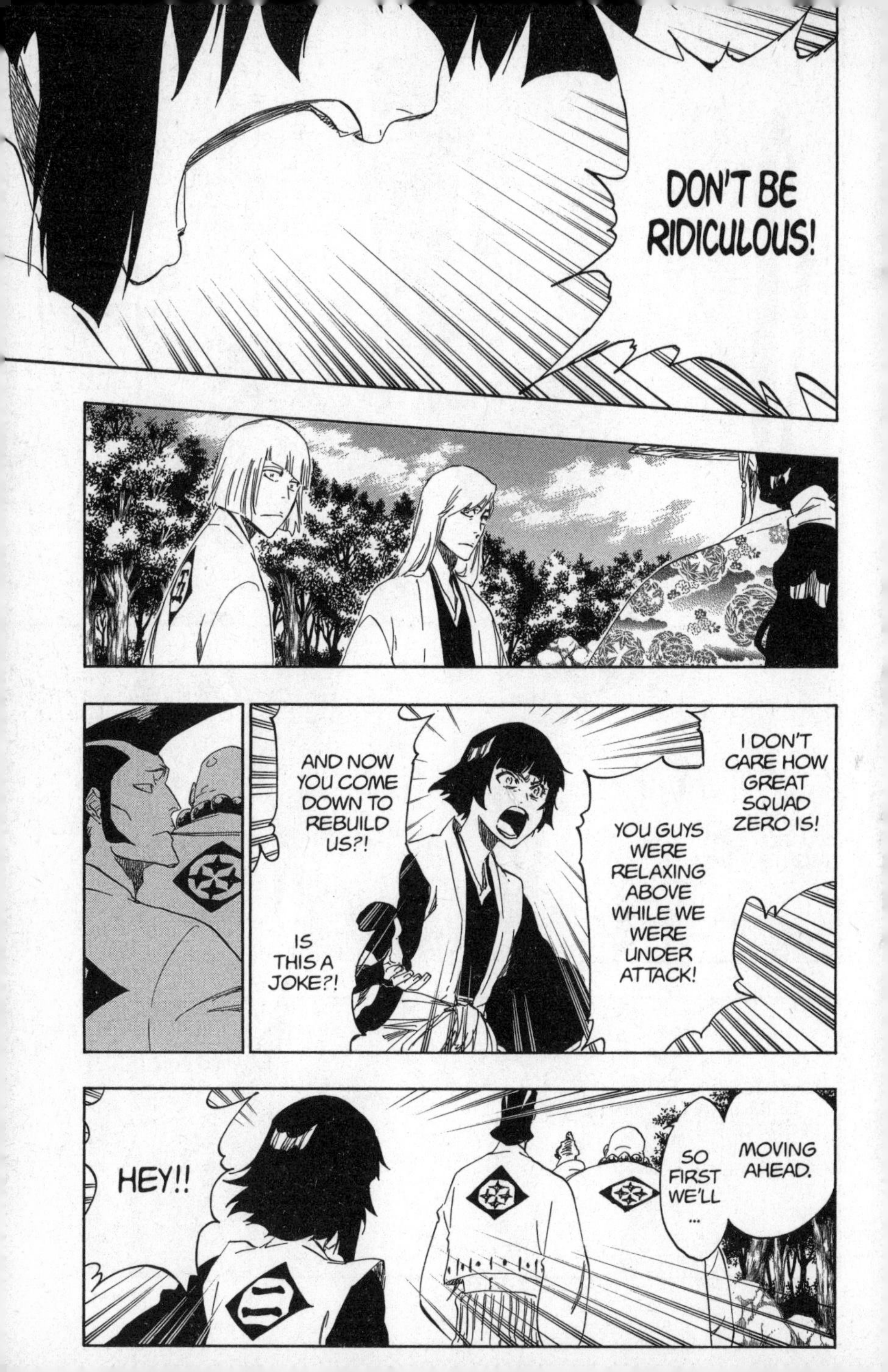
DON'T BE RIDICULOUS!
I DON'T CARE HOW GREAT SQUAD ZERO IS!
YOU GUYS WERE RELAXING ABOVE WHILE WE WERE UNDER ATTACK!
AND NOW YOU COME DOWN TO REBUILD US?!
IS THIS A JOKE?!
MOVING AHEAD.
SO FIRST WE'LL ...
HEY!!

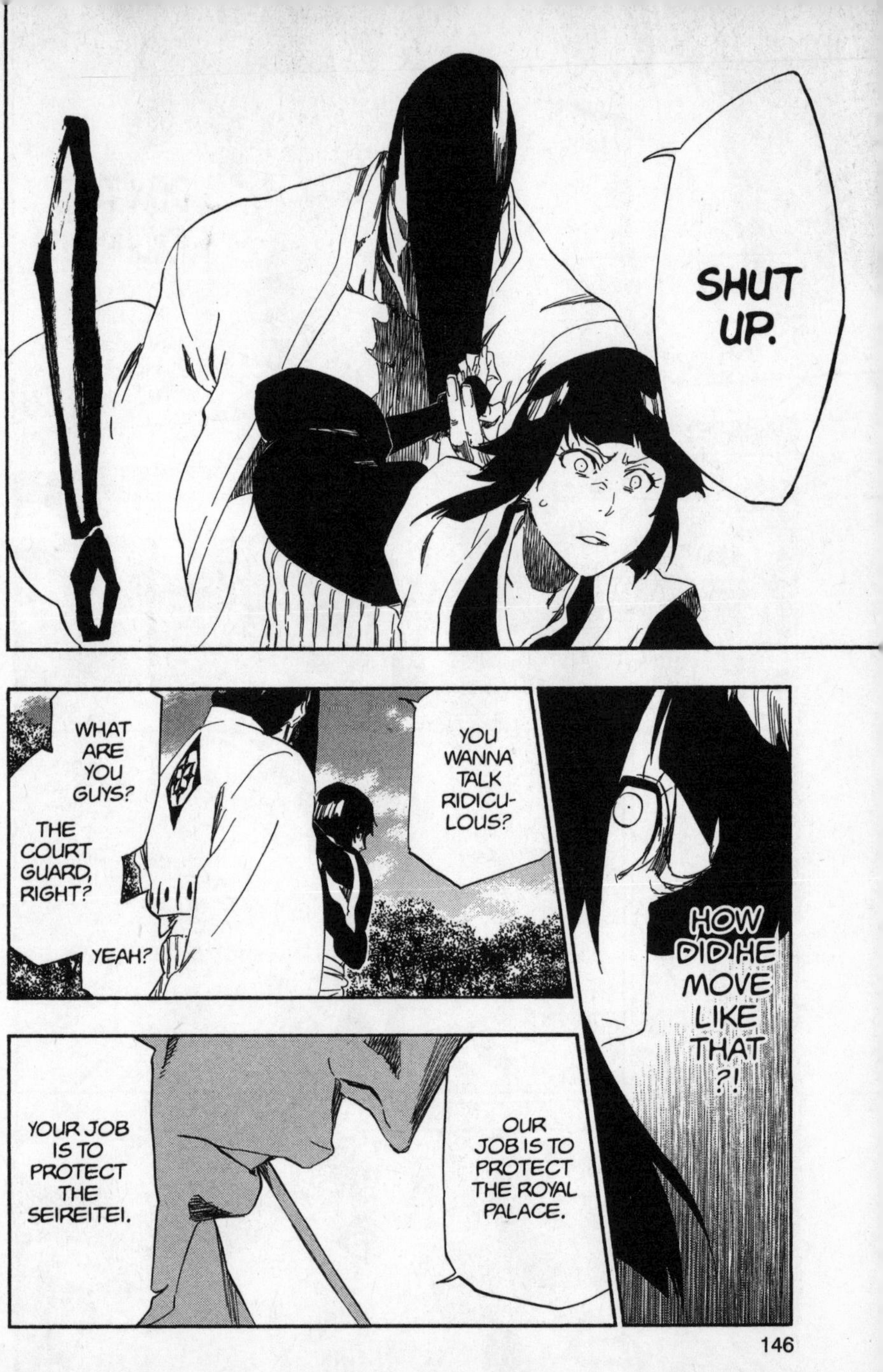
SHUT UP.
HOW DID HE MOVE LIKE THAT?!
YOU WANNA TALK RIDICULOUS?
WHAT ARE YOU GUYS?
THE COURT GUARD, RIGHT?
YEAH?
OUR JOB IS TO PROTECT THE ROYAL PALACE.
YOUR JOB IS TO PROTECT THE SEIREITEI.

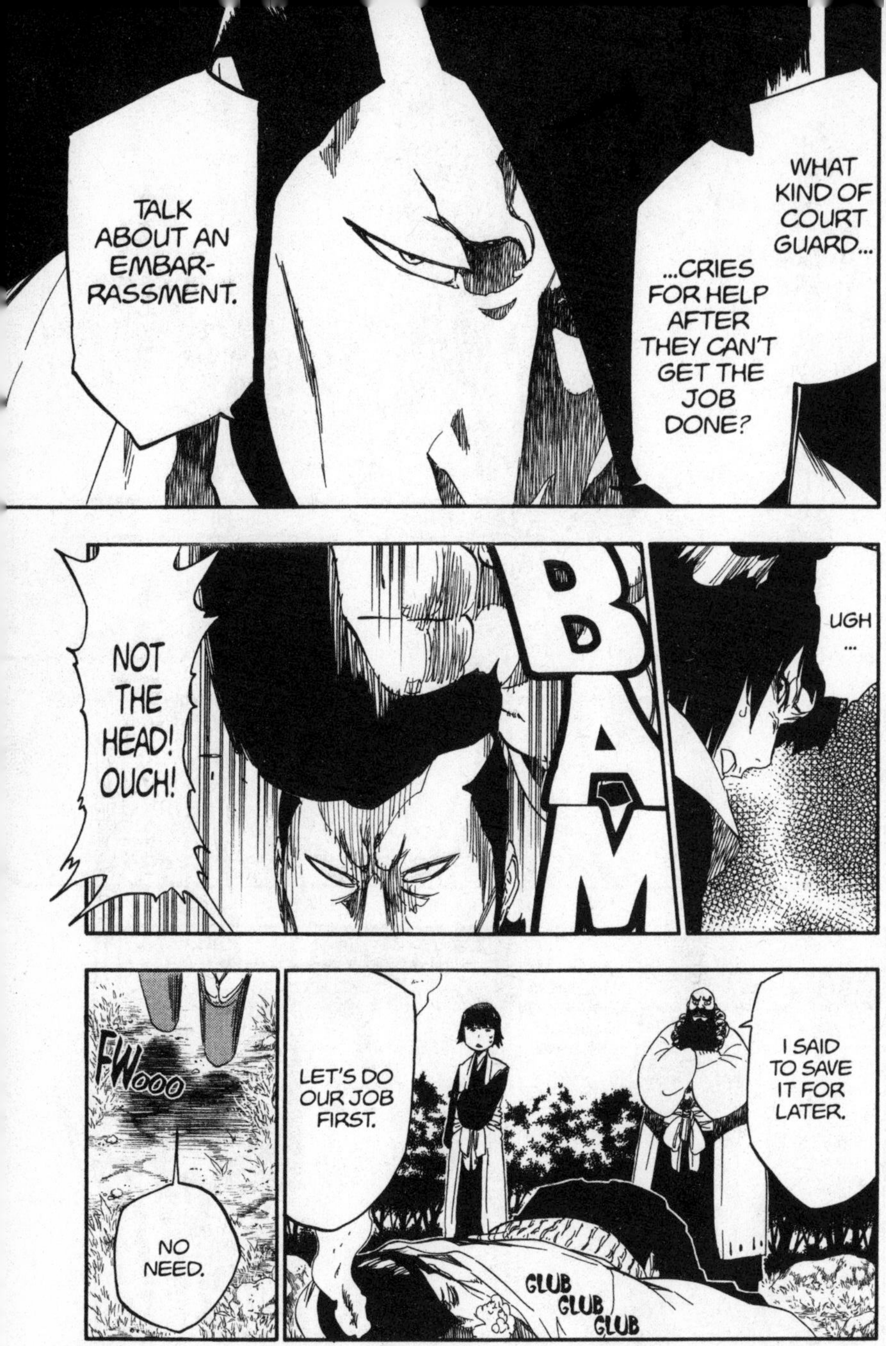
WHAT KIND OF COURT GUARD...
...CRIES FOR HELP AFTER THEY CAN'T GET THE JOB DONE?
TALK ABOUT AN EMBAR-RASSMENT.
UGH ...
BAM
NOT THE HEAD! OUCH!
I SAID TO SAVE IT FOR LATER.
LET'S DO OUR JOB FIRST.
GLUB GLUB GLUB
FWooo
NO NEED.

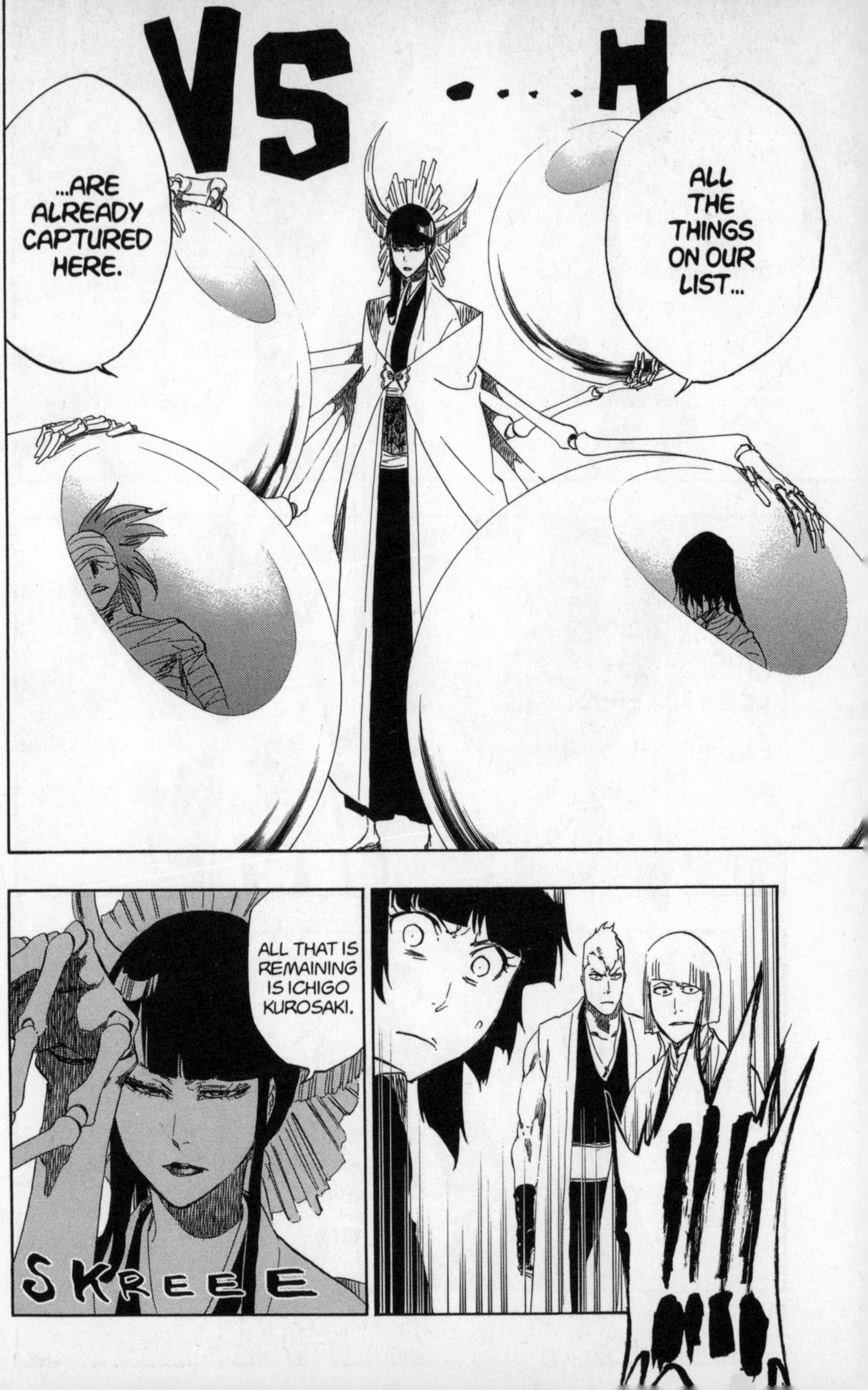
VS...H
ALL THE THINGS ON OUR LIST...
...ARE ALREADY CAPTURED HERE.
ALL THAT IS REMAINING IS ICHIGO KUROSAKI.
SKREEE

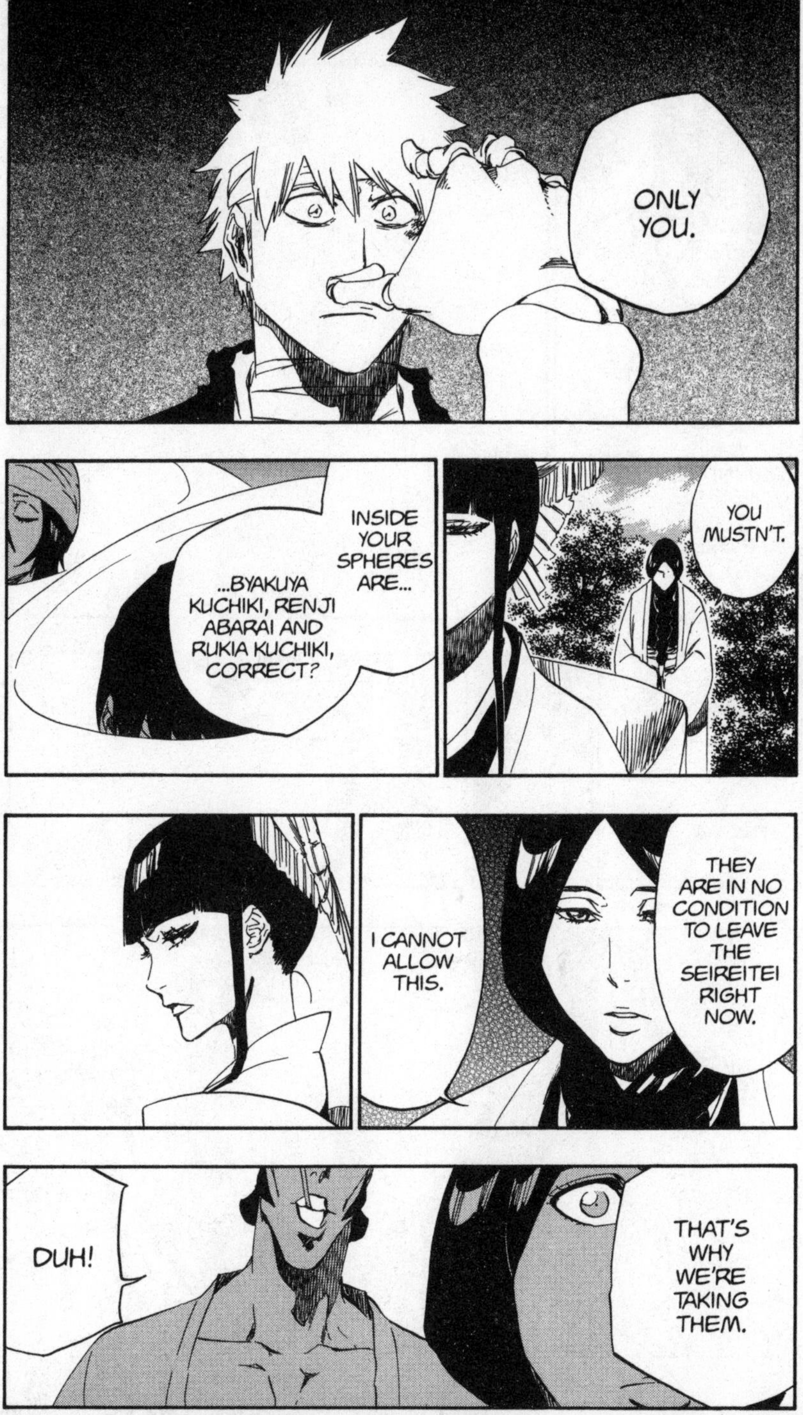
ONLY YOU.
YOU MUSTN'T.
INSIDE YOUR SPHERES ARE...
...BYAKUYA KUCHIKI, RENJI ABARAI AND RUKIA KUCHIKI, CORRECT?
THEY ARE IN NO CONDITION TO LEAVE THE SEIREITEI RIGHT NOW.
I CANNOT ALLOW THIS.
THAT'S WHY WE'RE TAKING THEM.
DUH!

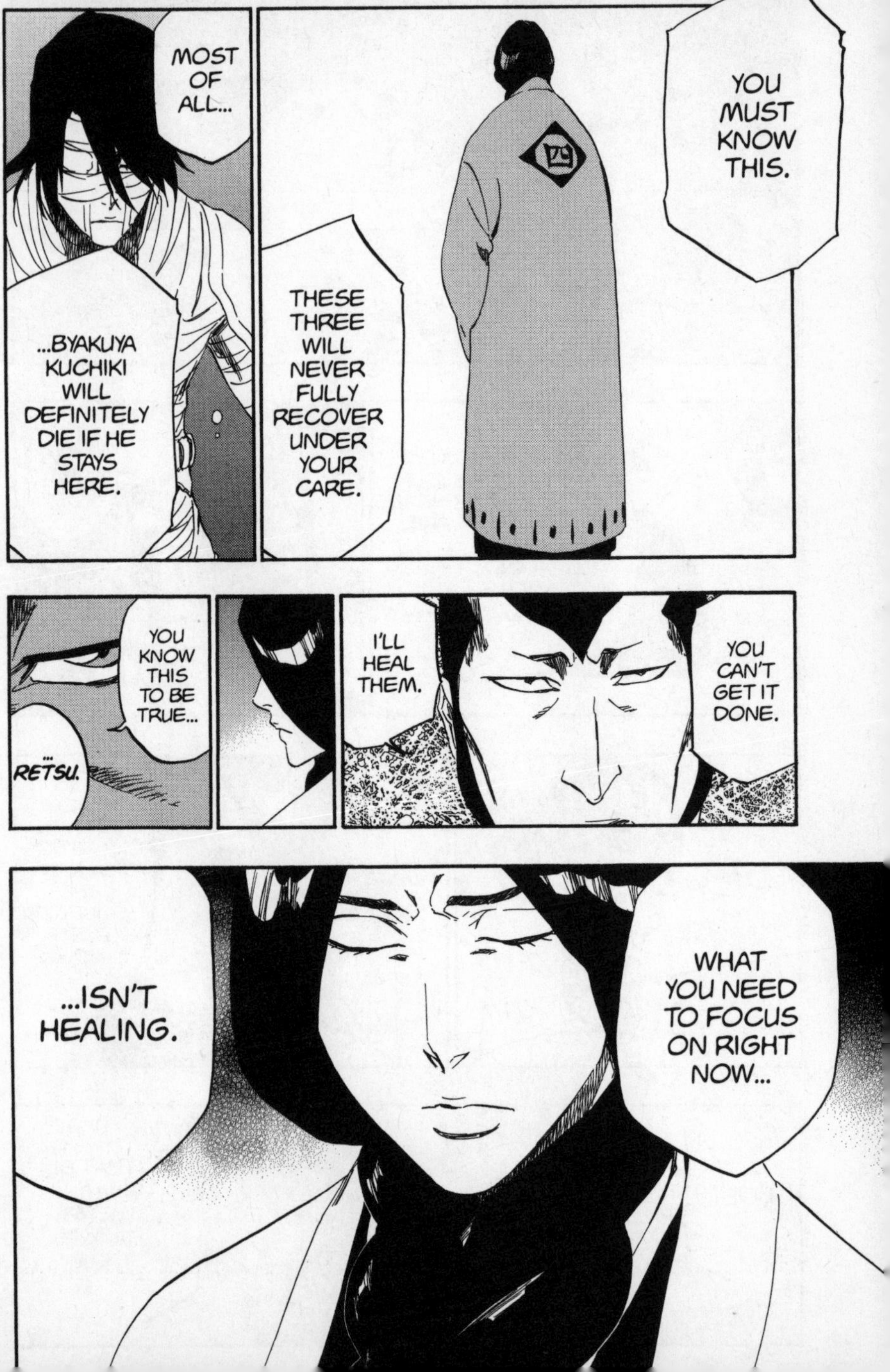
YOU MUST KNOW THIS.
THESE THREE WILL NEVER FULLY RECOVER UNDER YOUR CARE.
MOST OF ALL...
...BYAKUYA KUCHIKI WILL DEFINITELY DIE IF HE STAYS HERE.
YOU CAN'T GET IT DONE.
I'LL HEAL THEM.
YOU KNOW THIS TO BE TRUE...
...RETSU.
WHAT YOU NEED TO FOCUS ON RIGHT NOW...
...ISN'T HEALING.

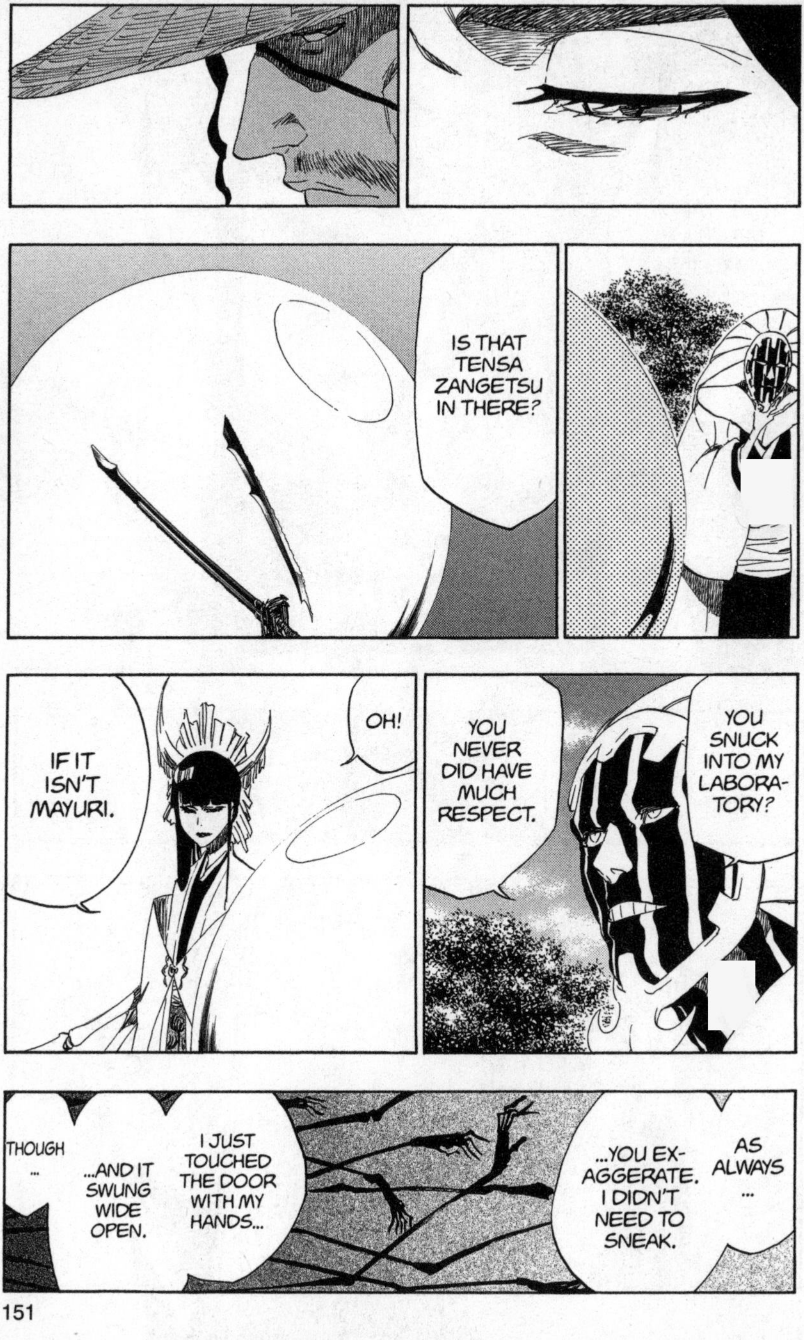
IS THAT TENSA ZANGETSU IN THERE?
YOU SNUCK INTO MY LABORATORY?
YOU NEVER DID HAVE MUCH RESPECT.
OH!
IF IT ISN'T MAYURI.
AS ALWAYS ...
...YOU EXAGGERATE. I DIDN'T NEED TO SNEAK.
I JUST TOUCHED THE DOOR WITH MY HANDS...
...AND IT SWUNG WIDE OPEN.
THOUGH ...

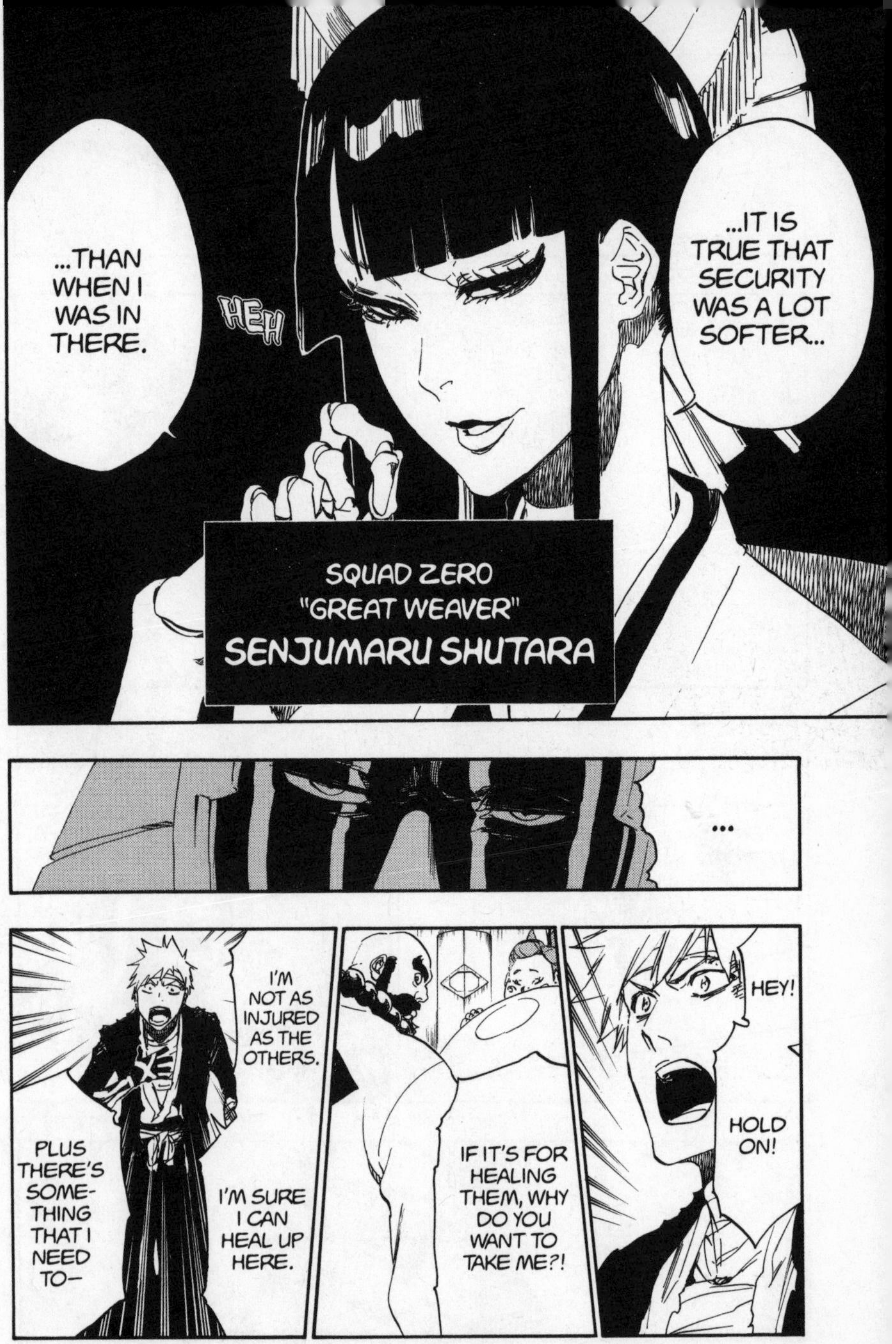
...IT IS TRUE THAT SECURITY WAS A LOT SOFTER...
HEH
...THAN WHEN I WAS IN THERE.
SQUAD ZERO "GREAT WEAVER" SENJUMARU SHUTARA
...
HEY!
HOLD ON!
IF IT'S FOR HEALING THEM, WHY DO YOU WANT TO TAKE ME?!
I'M NOT AS INJURED AS THE OTHERS.
I'M SURE I CAN HEAL UP HERE.
PLUS THERE'S SOME-THING THAT I NEED TO—

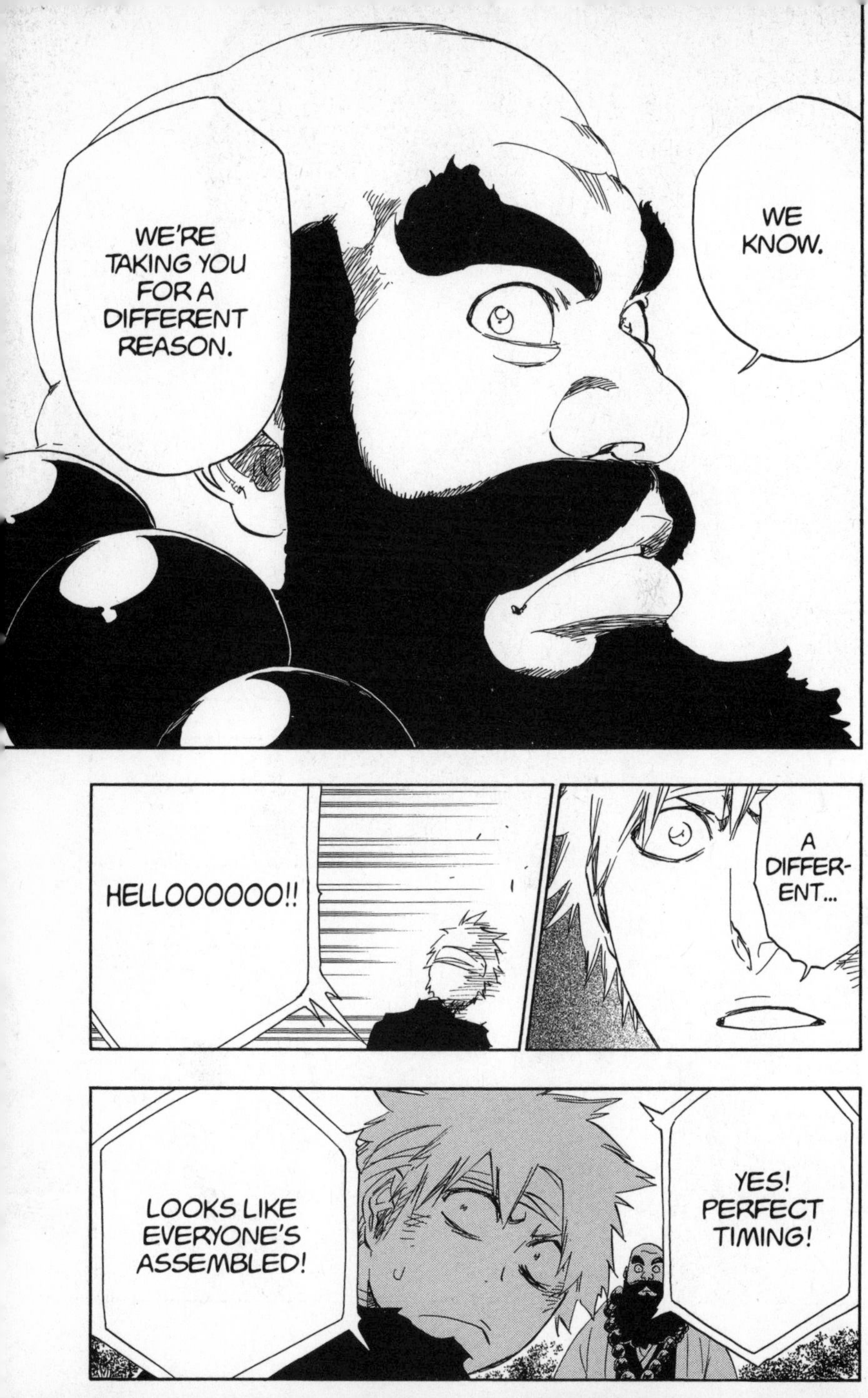
WE KNOW.
WE'RE TAKING YOU FOR A DIFFERENT REASON.
A DIFFER-ENT...
HELLOOOOOO!!
YES! PERFECT TIMING!
LOOKS LIKE EVERYONE'S ASSEMBLED!

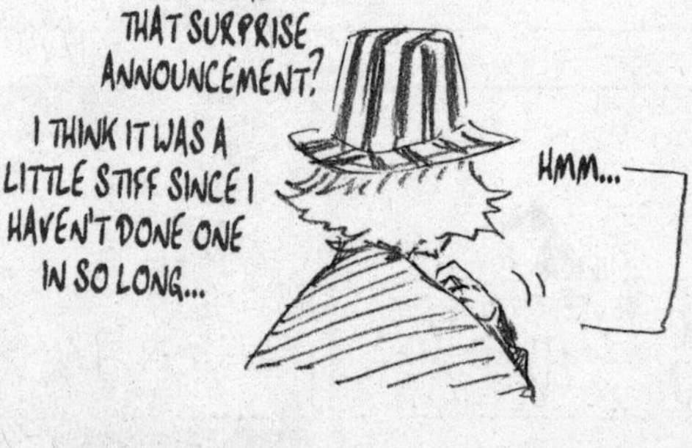
HOW WAS THAT SURPRISE ANNOUNCEMENT?
I THINK IT WAS A LITTLE STIFF SINCE I HAVEN'T DONE ONE IN SO LONG...
HMM...

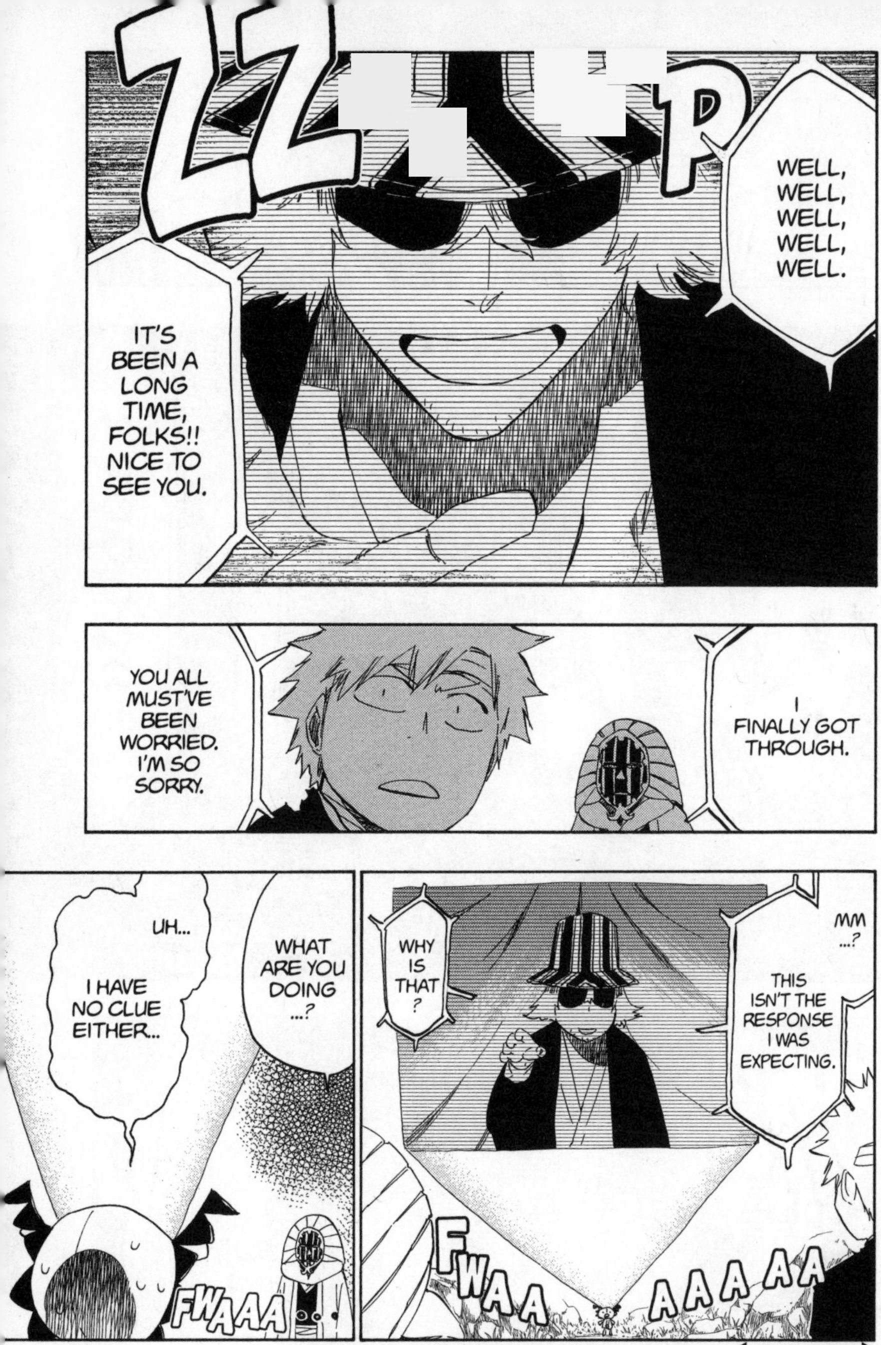
ZZ P
WELL, WELL, WELL, WELL, WELL.
IT'S BEEN A LONG TIME, FOLKS!! NICE TO SEE YOU.
I FINALLY GOT THROUGH.
YOU ALL MUST'VE BEEN WORRIED. I'M SO SORRY.
MM ...?
THIS ISN'T THE RESPONSE I WAS EXPECTING.
WHY IS THAT ?
FWAA AAAAAA
WHAT ARE YOU DOING ...?
UH...
I HAVE NO CLUE EITHER...
FWAAAA

518. THE SHOOTING STAR PROJECT 〔ZERO MIX〕

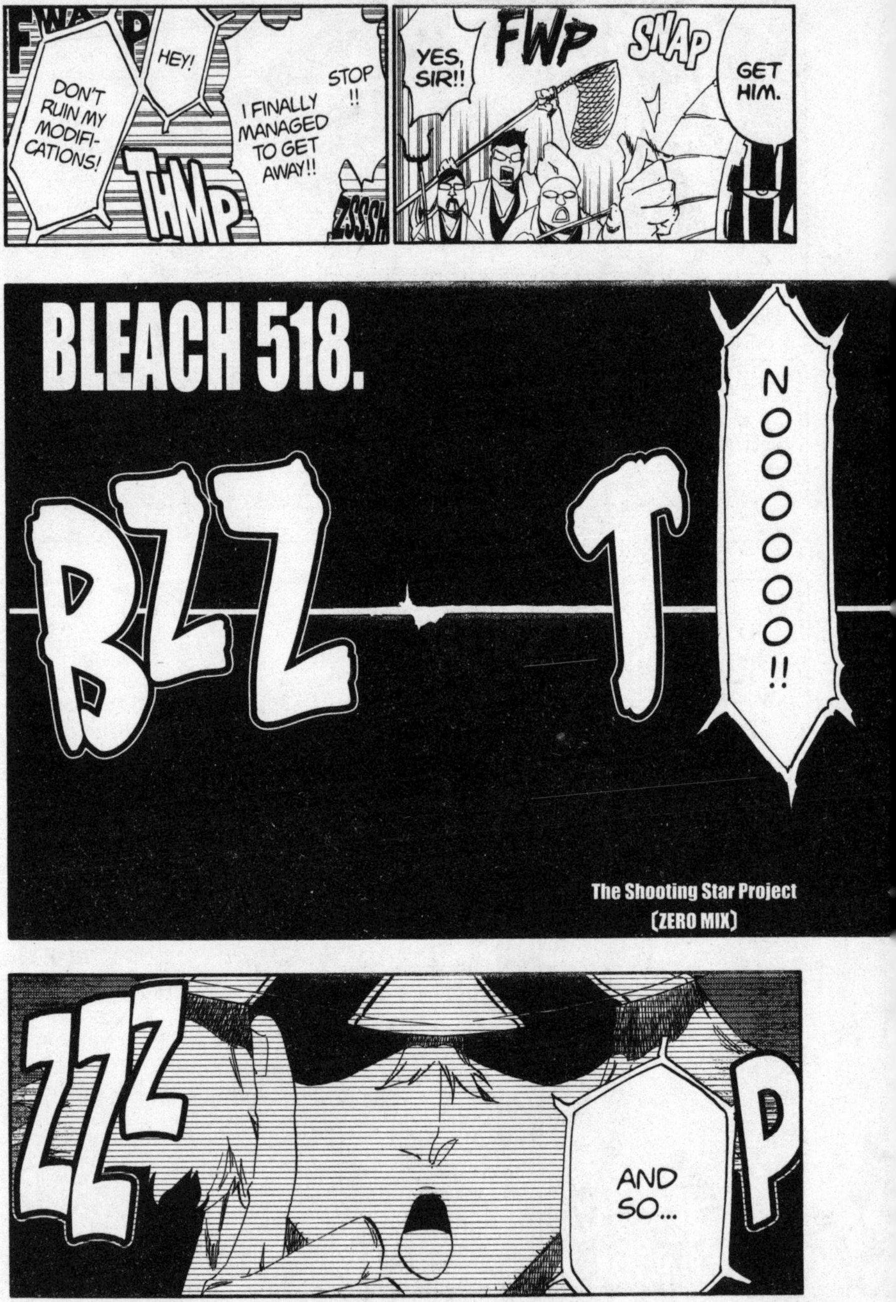

GET HIM.
SNAP
FWP
YES, SIR!!
STOP !!
I FINALLY MANAGED TO GET AWAY!!
HEY!
FWAP
DON'T RUIN MY MODIFI-CATIONS!
THMP
ZSSSH
BLEACH 518.
NOOOOOOO!!
BZZT
The Shooting Star Project
〔ZERO MIX〕
ZZZP
AND SO...

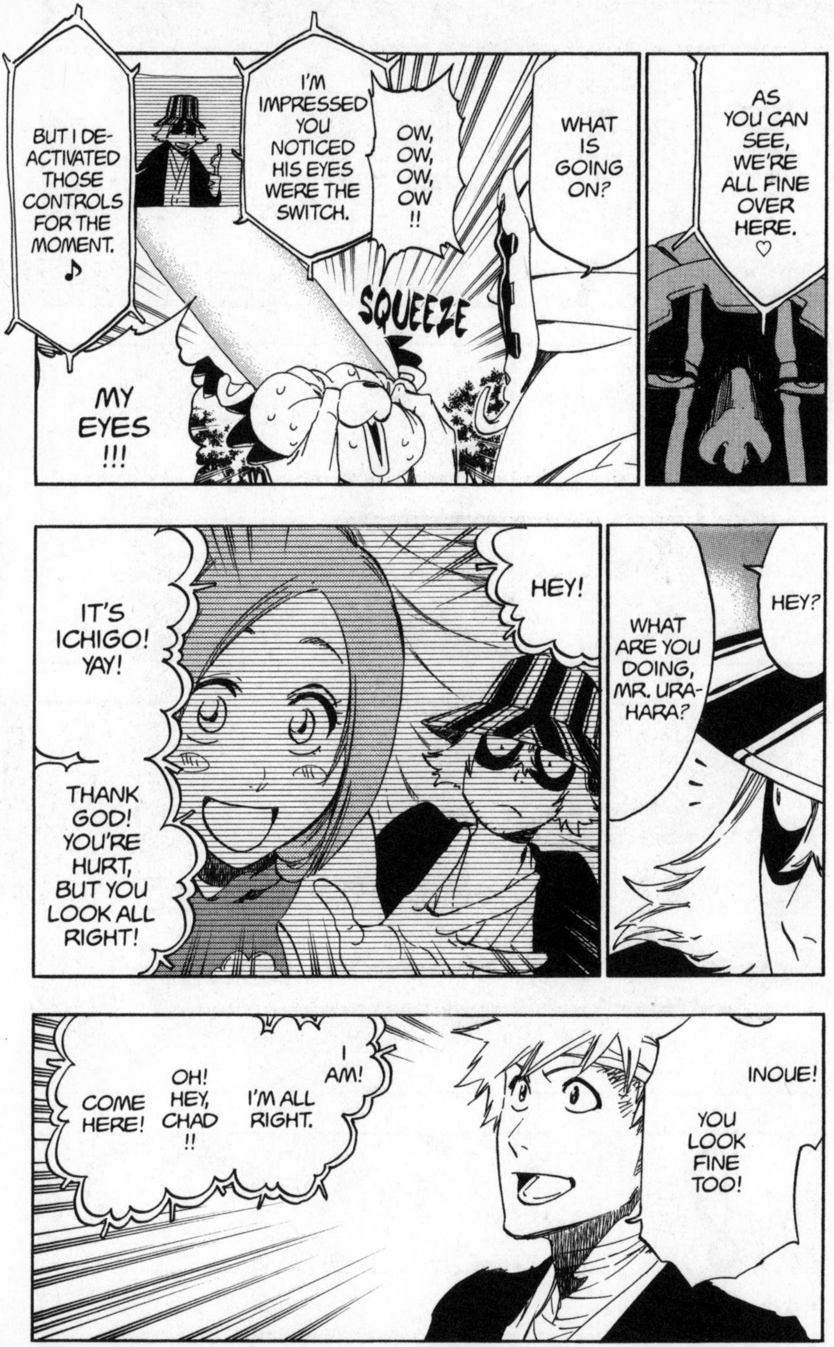
AS YOU CAN SEE, WE'RE ALL FINE OVER HERE. ♡
WHAT IS GOING ON?
OW, OW, OW, OW !!
I'M IMPRESSED YOU NOTICED HIS EYES WERE THE SWITCH.
BUT I DE-ACTIVATED THOSE CONTROLS FOR THE MOMENT. ♪
SQUEEZE
MY EYES !!!
HEY?
WHAT ARE YOU DOING, MR. URA-HARA?
HEY!
IT'S ICHIGO! YAY!
THANK GOD! YOU'RE HURT, BUT YOU LOOK ALL RIGHT!
INOUE!
YOU LOOK FINE TOO!
I AM!
I'M ALL RIGHT.
OH! HEY, CHAD !!
COME HERE!

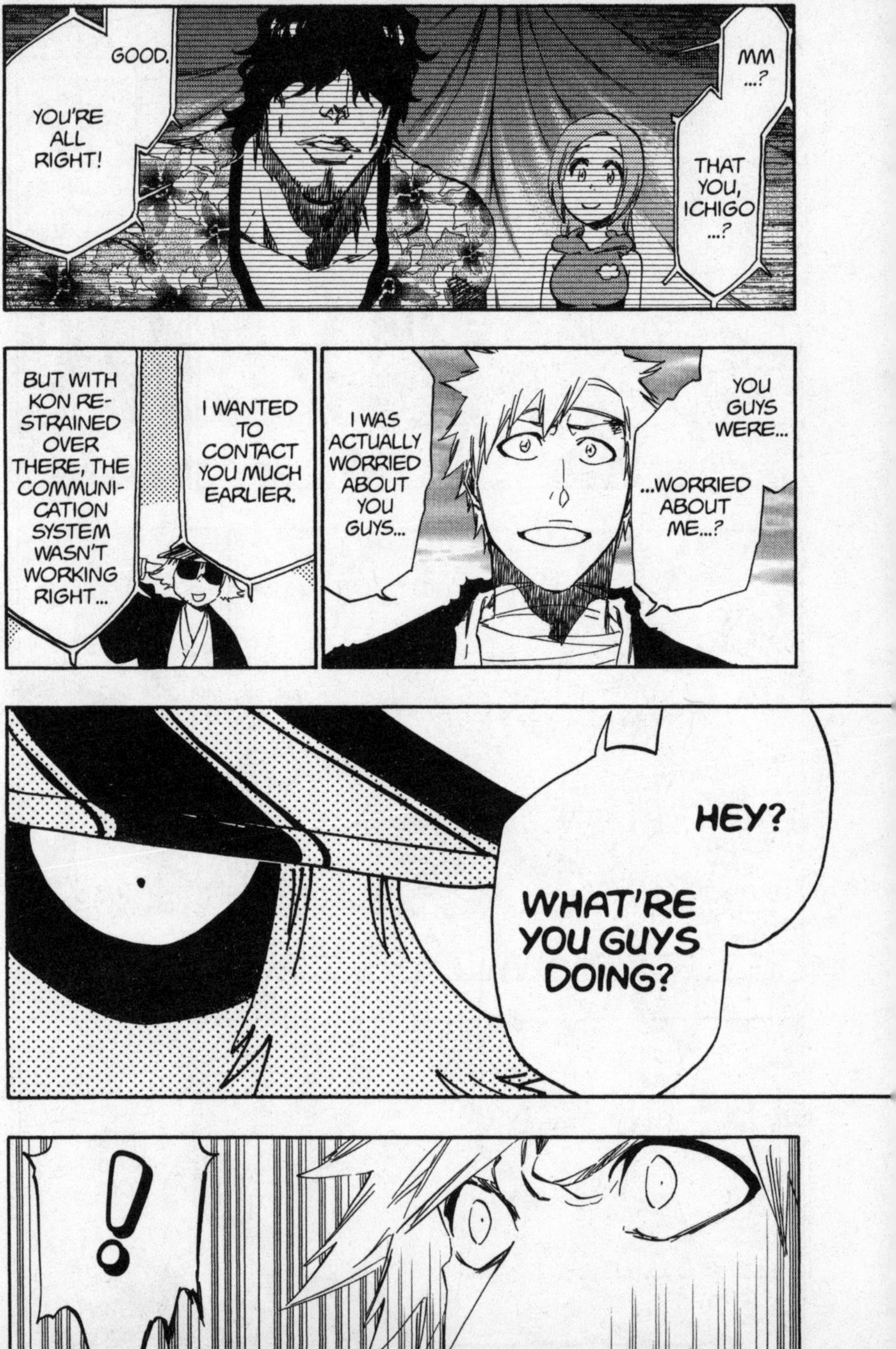
MM ...?
THAT YOU, ICHIGO ...?
GOOD.
YOU'RE ALL RIGHT!
YOU GUYS WERE...
...WORRIED ABOUT ME...?
I WAS ACTUALLY WORRIED ABOUT YOU GUYS...
I WANTED TO CONTACT YOU MUCH EARLIER.
BUT WITH KON RE-STRAINED OVER THERE, THE COMMUNICATION SYSTEM WASN'T WORKING RIGHT...
HEY?
WHAT'RE YOU GUYS DOING?
!

READ THIS WAY

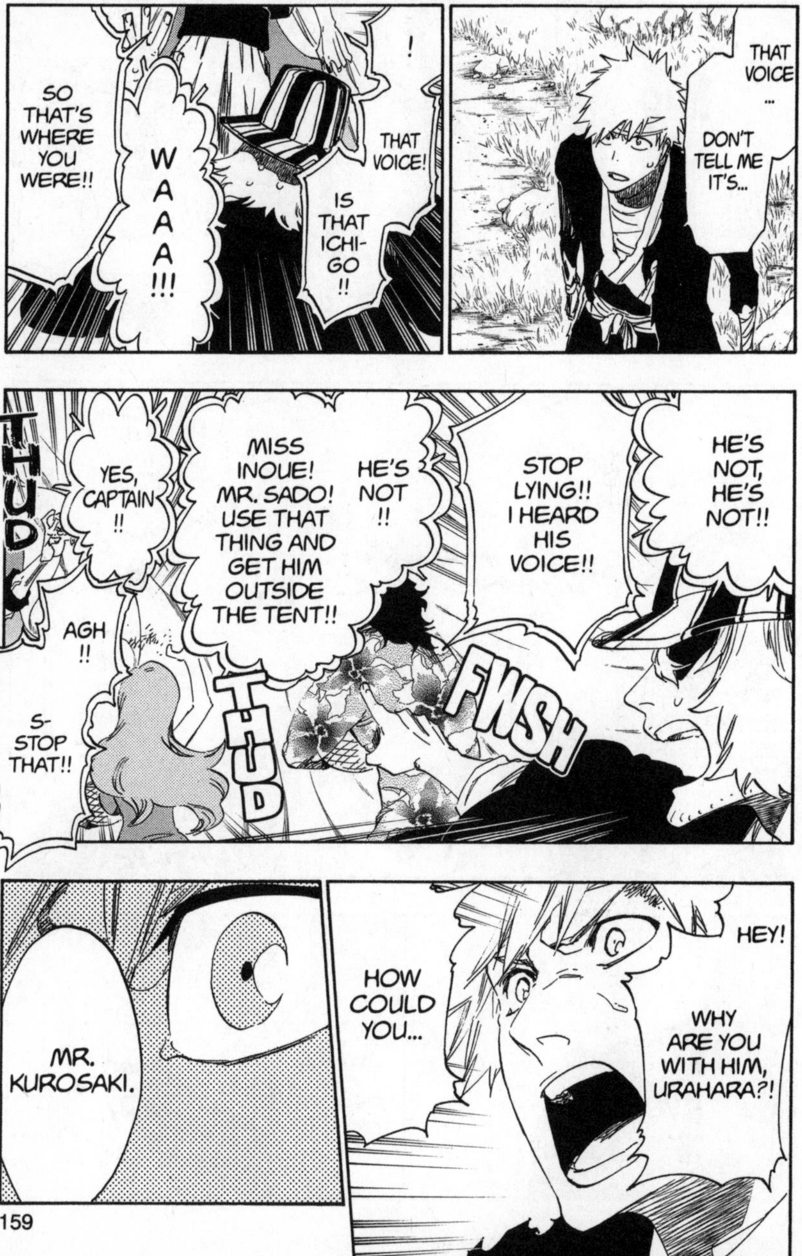
THAT VOICE ...
DON'T TELL ME IT'S...
!
THAT VOICE!
IS THAT ICHI-GO!!
WAAAA!!!
SO THAT'S WHERE YOU WERE!!
HE'S NOT, HE'S NOT!!
STOP LYING!! I HEARD HIS VOICE!!
HE'S NOT!!
MISS INOUE! MR. SADO! USE THAT THING AND GET HIM OUTSIDE THE TENT!!
FWSH
YES, CAPTAIN!!
THUD
AGH!!
THUD
S-STOP THAT!!
HEY!
WHY ARE YOU WITH HIM, URAHARA?!
HOW COULD YOU...
MR. KUROSAKI.

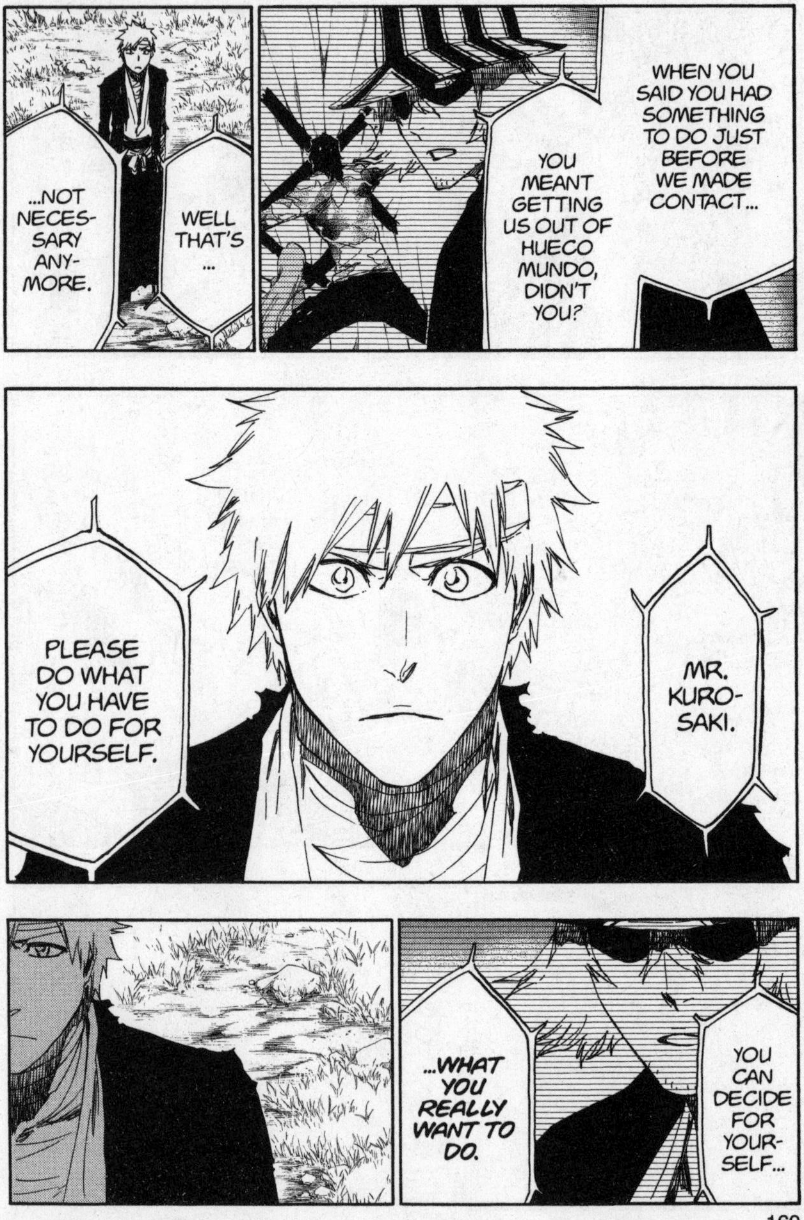
WHEN YOU SAID YOU HAD SOMETHING TO DO JUST BEFORE WE MADE CONTACT...
YOU MEANT GETTING US OUT OF HUECO MUNDO, DIDN'T YOU?
WELL THAT'S ...
...NOT NECES-SARY ANY-MORE.
MR. KURO-SAKI.
PLEASE DO WHAT YOU HAVE TO DO FOR YOURSELF.
YOU CAN DECIDE FOR YOUR-SELF...
...WHAT YOU REALLY WANT TO DO.

READ THIS WAY

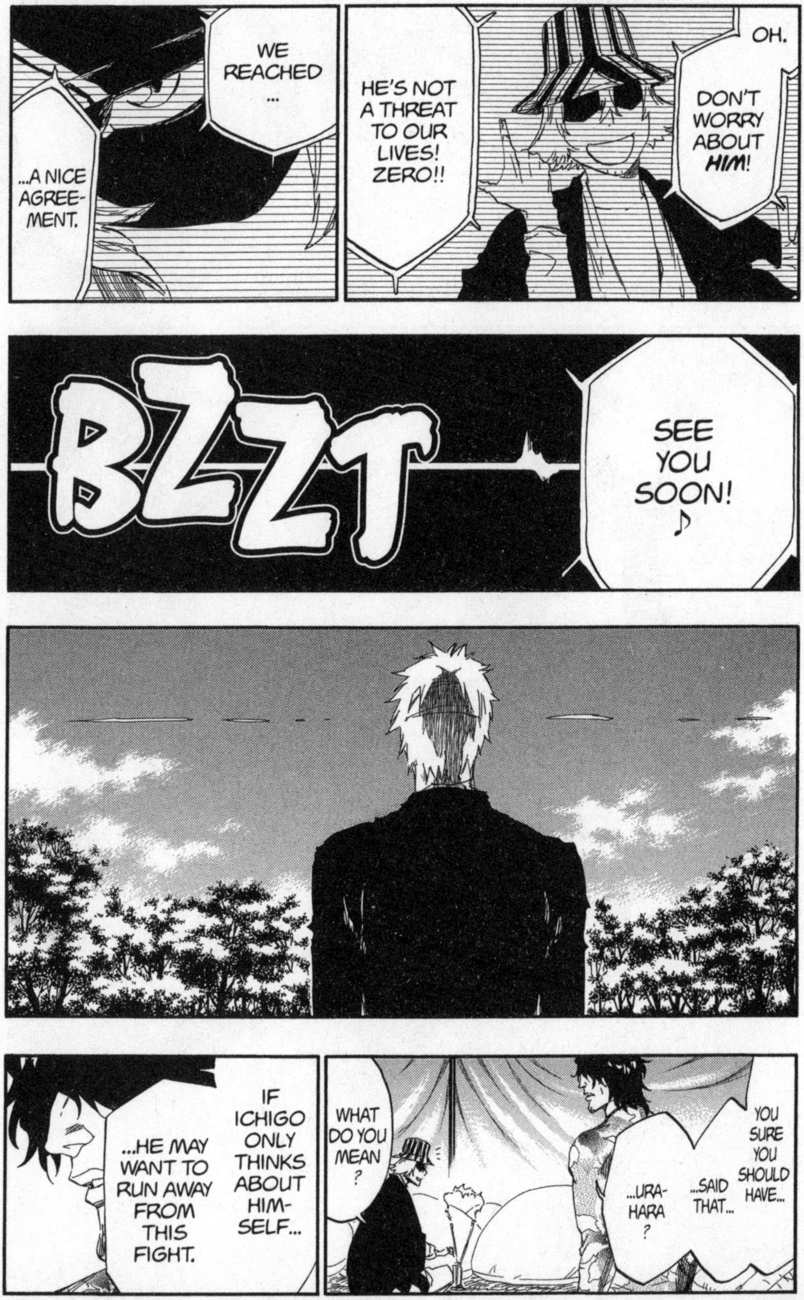
OH.
DON'T WORRY ABOUT HIM!
HE'S NOT A THREAT TO OUR LIVES! ZERO!!
WE REACHED...
...A NICE AGREEMENT.
SEE YOU SOON! ♪
BZZT
YOU SURE YOU SHOULD HAVE...
...SAID THAT...
...URA-HARA?
WHAT DO YOU MEAN?
IF ICHIGO ONLY THINKS ABOUT HIMSELF...
...HE MAY WANT TO RUN AWAY FROM THIS FIGHT.

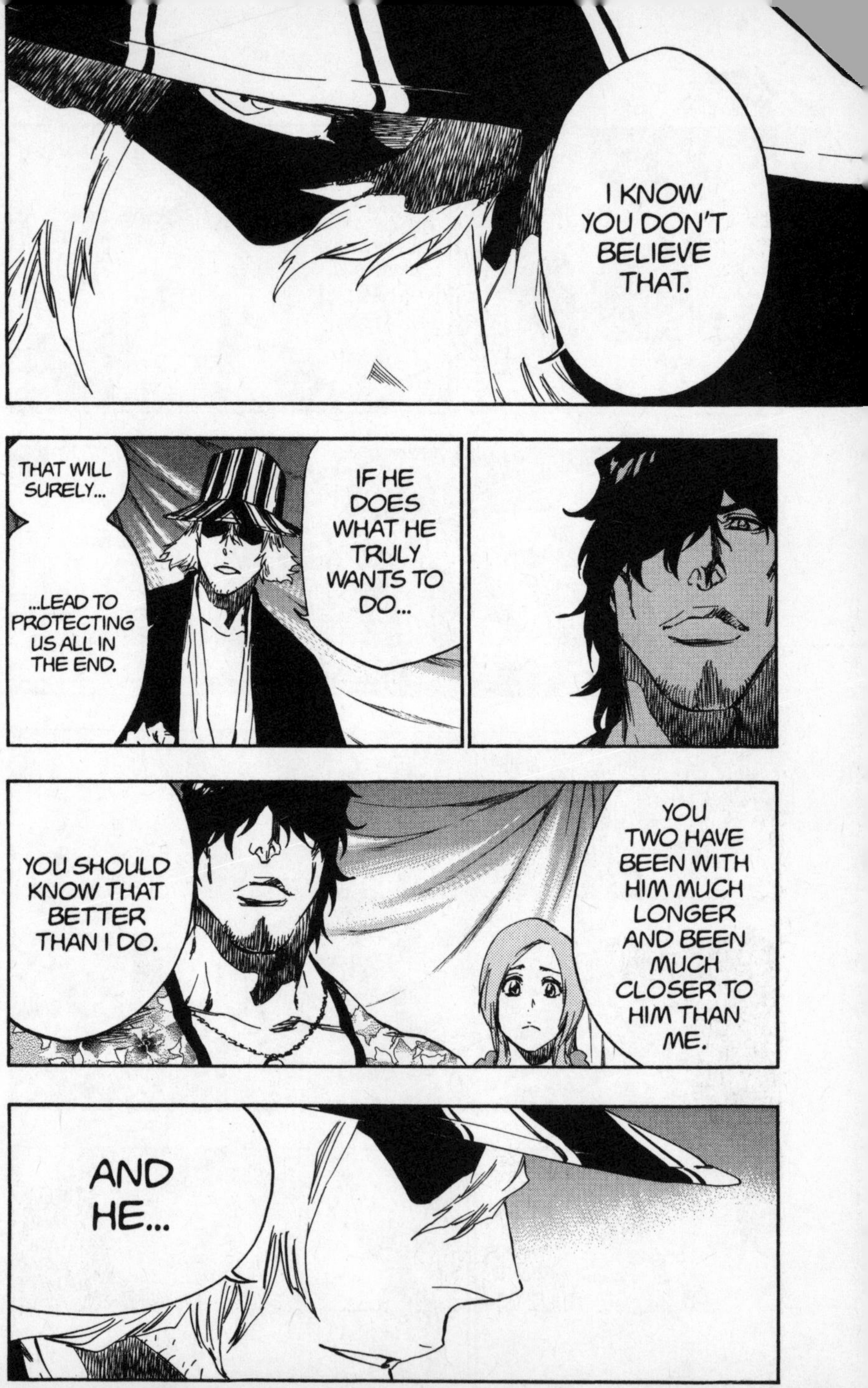
I KNOW YOU DON'T BELIEVE THAT.
IF HE DOES WHAT HE TRULY WANTS TO DO...
THAT WILL SURELY...
...LEAD TO PROTECTING US ALL IN THE END.
YOU TWO HAVE BEEN WITH HIM MUCH LONGER AND BEEN MUCH CLOSER TO HIM THAN ME.
YOU SHOULD KNOW THAT BETTER THAN I DO.
AND HE...

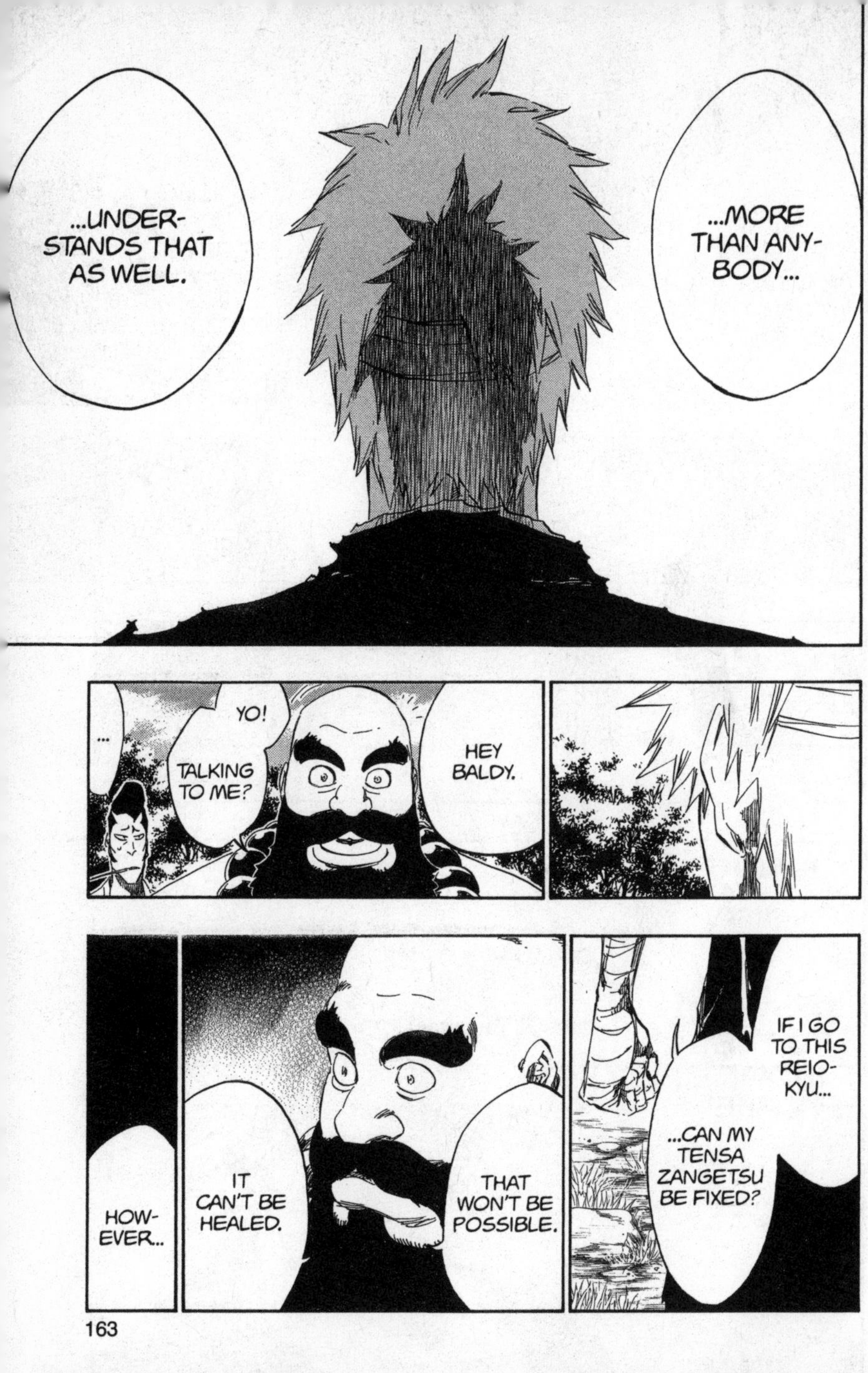
...MORE THAN ANY-BODY...
...UNDER-STANDS THAT AS WELL.
HEY BALDY.
YO! TALKING TO ME?
...
IF I GO TO THIS REIO-KYU...
...CAN MY TENSA ZANGETSU BE FIXED?
THAT WON'T BE POSSIBLE.
IT CAN'T BE HEALED.
HOW-EVER...

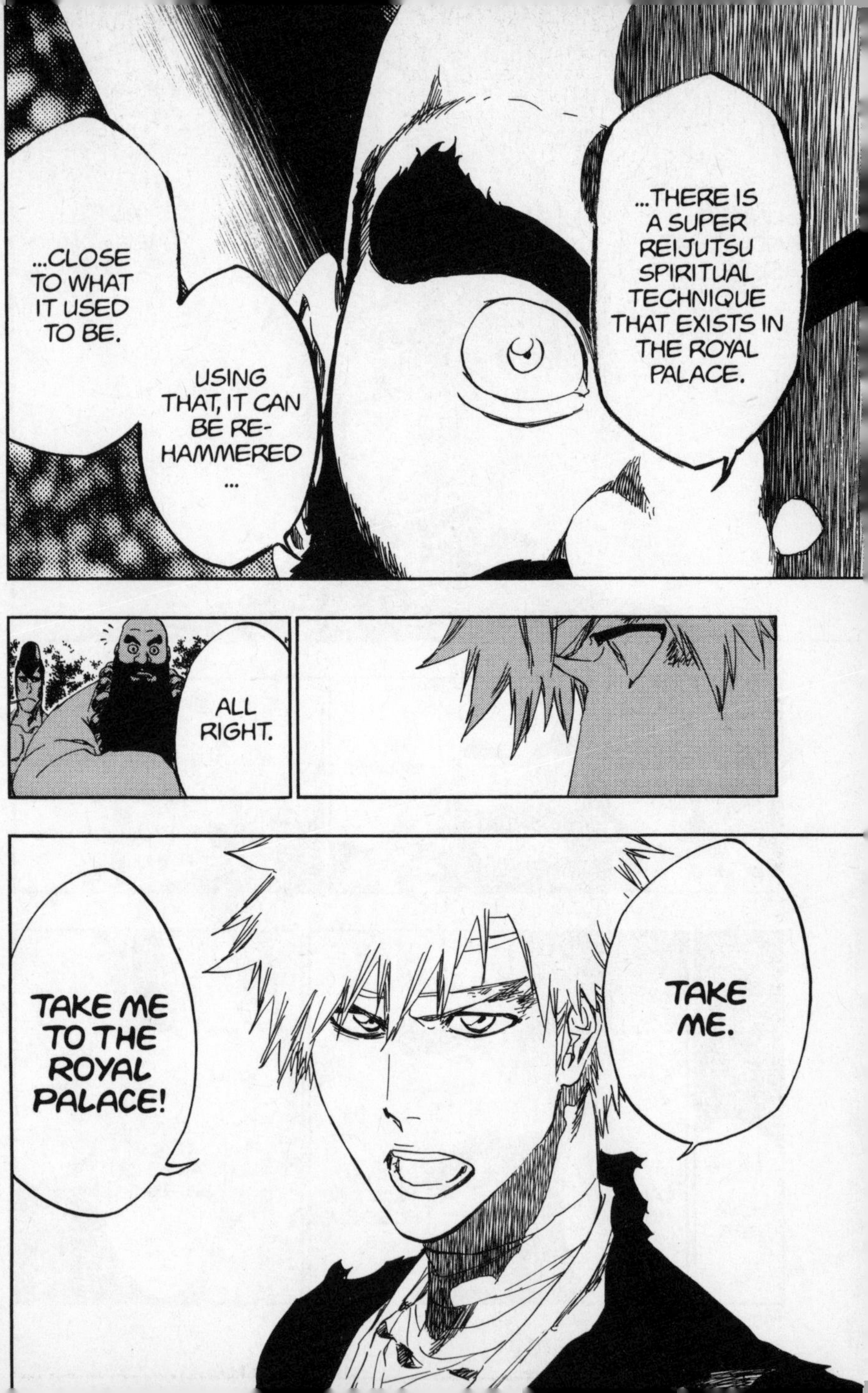
...THERE IS A SUPER REIJUTSU SPIRITUAL TECHNIQUE THAT EXISTS IN THE ROYAL PALACE.
USING THAT, IT CAN BE RE-HAMMERED ...
...CLOSE TO WHAT IT USED TO BE.
ALL RIGHT.
TAKE ME.
TAKE ME TO THE ROYAL PALACE!

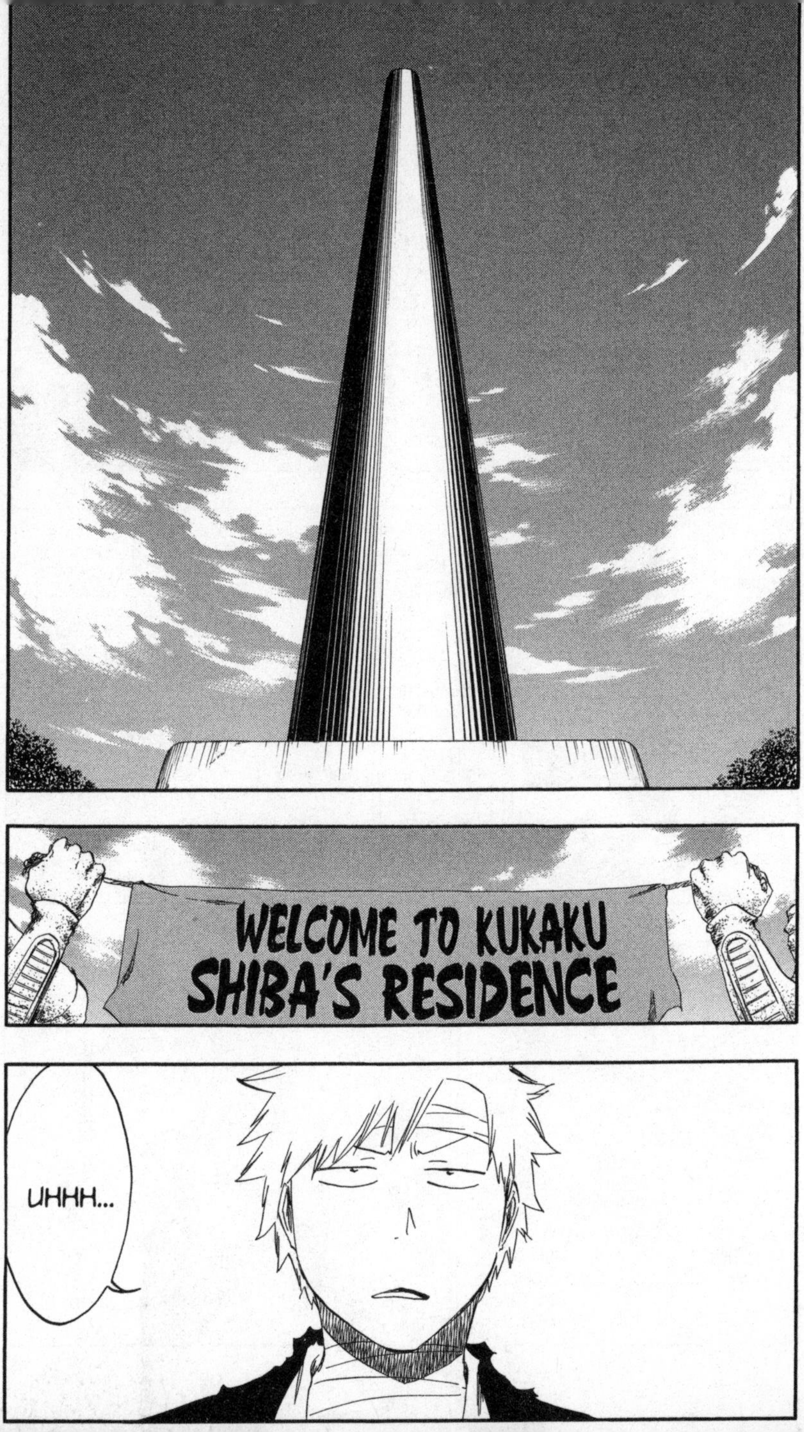
WELCOME TO KUKAKU SHIBA'S RESIDENCE
UHHH...

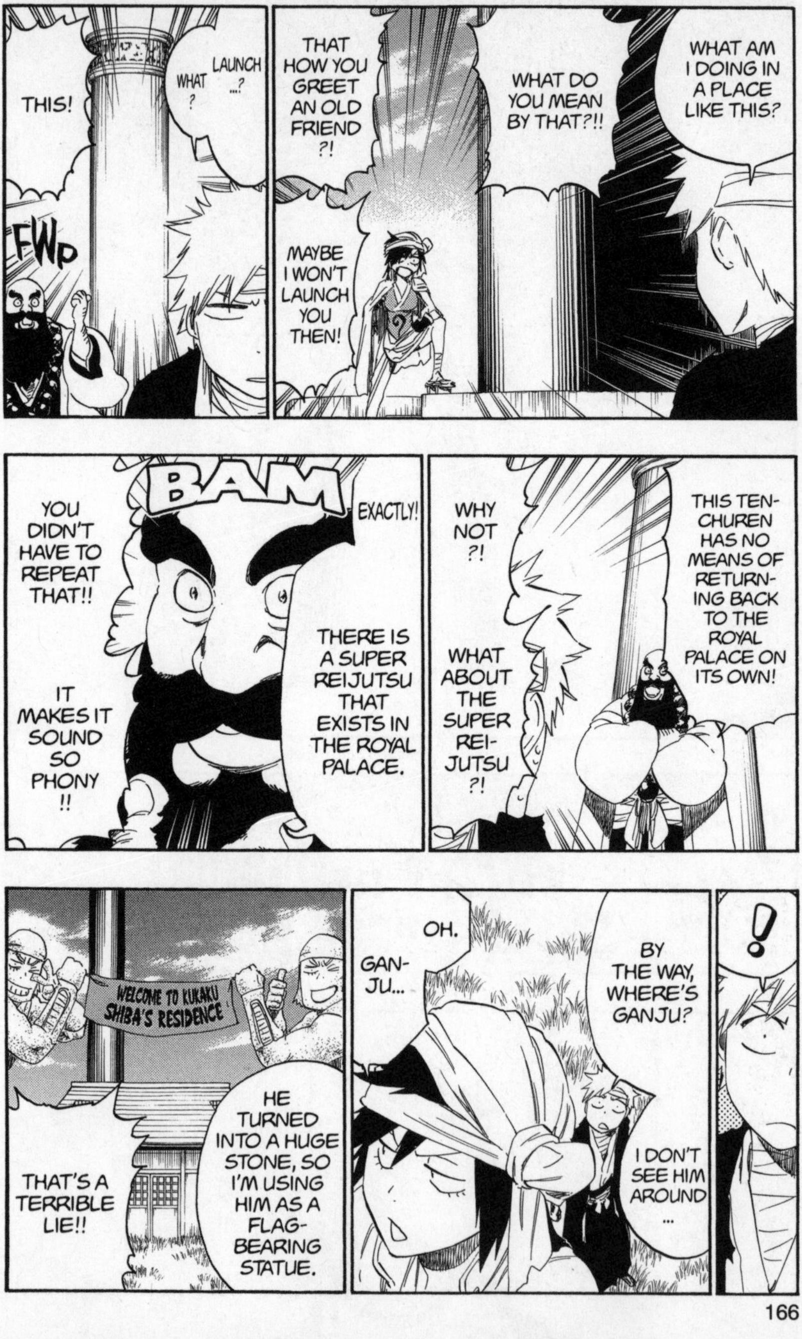

WHAT AM I DOING IN A PLACE LIKE THIS?
WHAT DO YOU MEAN BY THAT?!!
THAT HOW YOU GREET AN OLD FRIEND ?!
MAYBE I WON'T LAUNCH YOU THEN!
LAUNCH ...?
WHAT ?
THIS!
FWP
THIS TEN-CHUREN HAS NO MEANS OF RETURNING BACK TO THE ROYAL PALACE ON ITS OWN!
WHY NOT ?!
WHAT ABOUT THE SUPER REI-JUTSU ?!
EXACTLY!
BAM
THERE IS A SUPER REIJUTSU THAT EXISTS IN THE ROYAL PALACE.
YOU DIDN'T HAVE TO REPEAT THAT!!
IT MAKES IT SOUND SO PHONY !!
!
BY THE WAY, WHERE'S GANJU?
OH.
GANJU...
I DON'T SEE HIM AROUND ...
WELCOME TO KUKAKU SHIBA'S RESIDENCE
HE TURNED INTO A HUGE STONE, SO I'M USING HIM AS A FLAG-BEARING STATUE.
THAT'S A TERRIBLE LIE!!

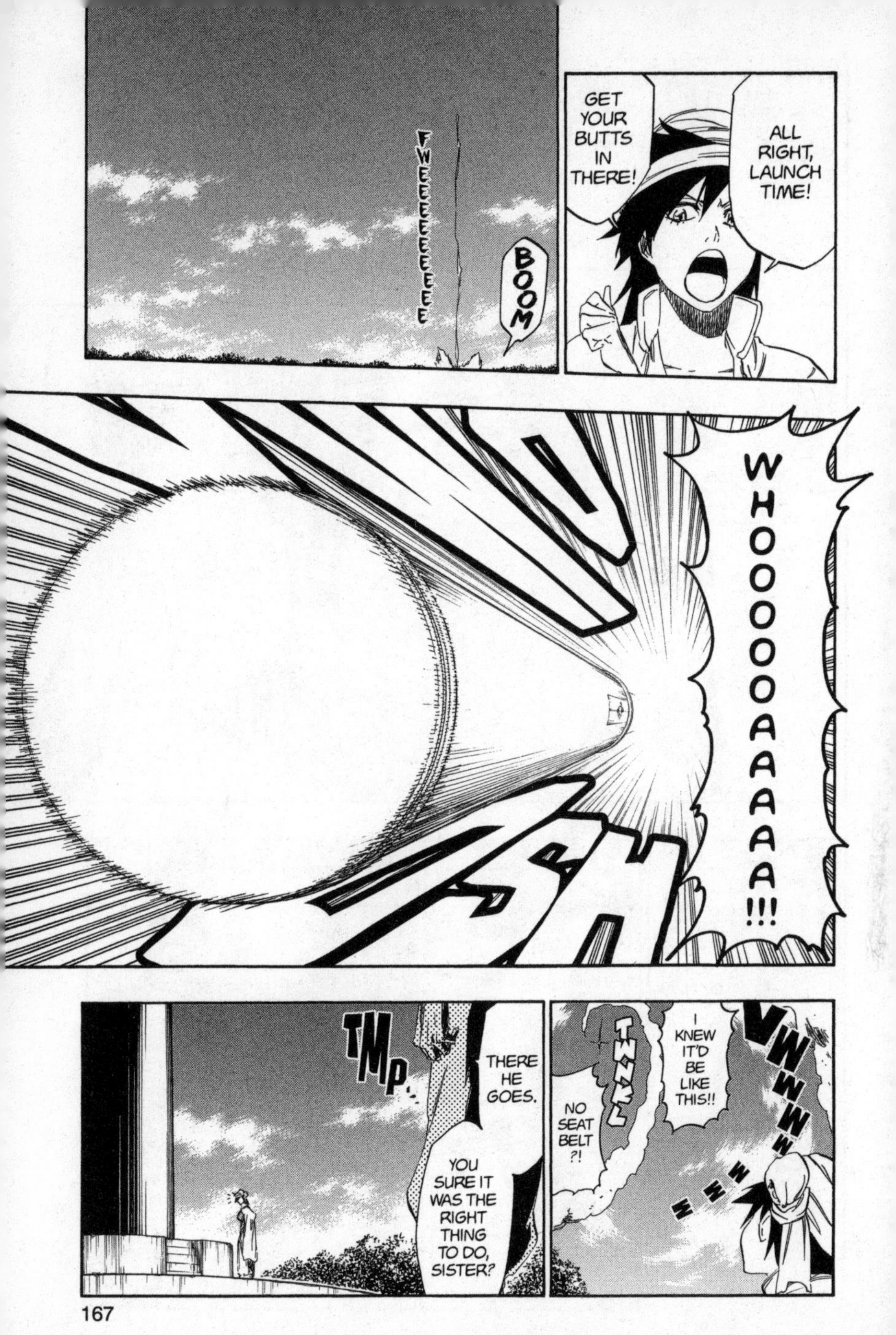
ALL RIGHT, LAUNCH TIME!
GET YOUR BUTTS IN THERE!
FWEEEEEEEEEE
BOOM
WHOOOOOOAAAAAAA!!!
I KNEW IT'D BE LIKE THIS!!
NO SEAT BELT?!
TMP
THERE HE GOES.
YOU SURE IT WAS THE RIGHT THING TO DO, SISTER?

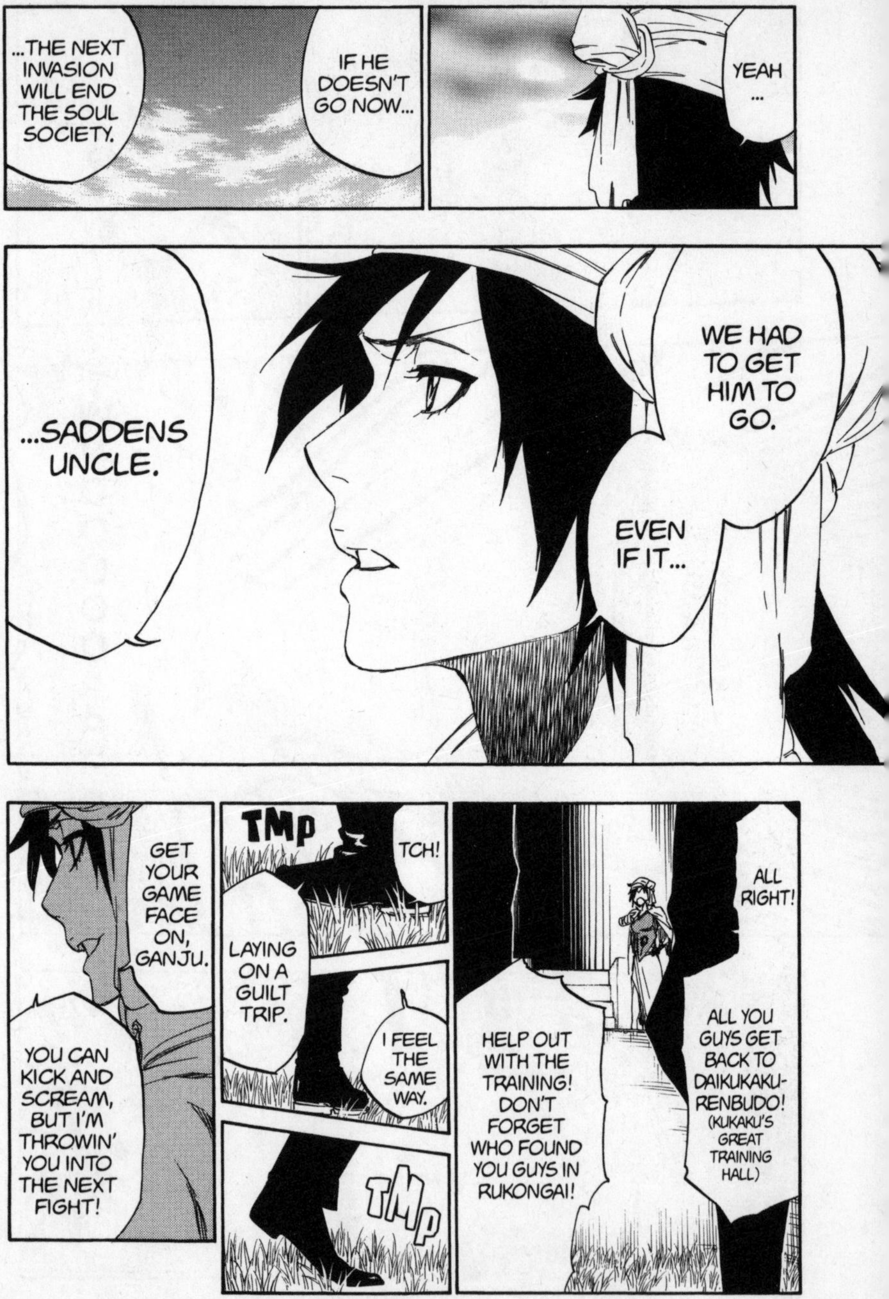
YEAH ...
IF HE DOESN'T GO NOW...
...THE NEXT INVASION WILL END THE SOUL SOCIETY.
WE HAD TO GET HIM TO GO.
EVEN IF IT...
...SADDENS UNCLE.
ALL RIGHT!
ALL YOU GUYS GET BACK TO DAIKUKAKU-RENBUDO!
(KUKAKU'S GREAT TRAINING HALL)
HELP OUT WITH THE TRAINING! DON'T FORGET WHO FOUND YOU GUYS IN RUKONGAI!
TCH!
TMP
LAYING ON A GUILT TRIP.
I FEEL THE SAME WAY.
TMP
GET YOUR GAME FACE ON, GANJU.
YOU CAN KICK AND SCREAM, BUT I'M THROWIN' YOU INTO THE NEXT FIGHT!

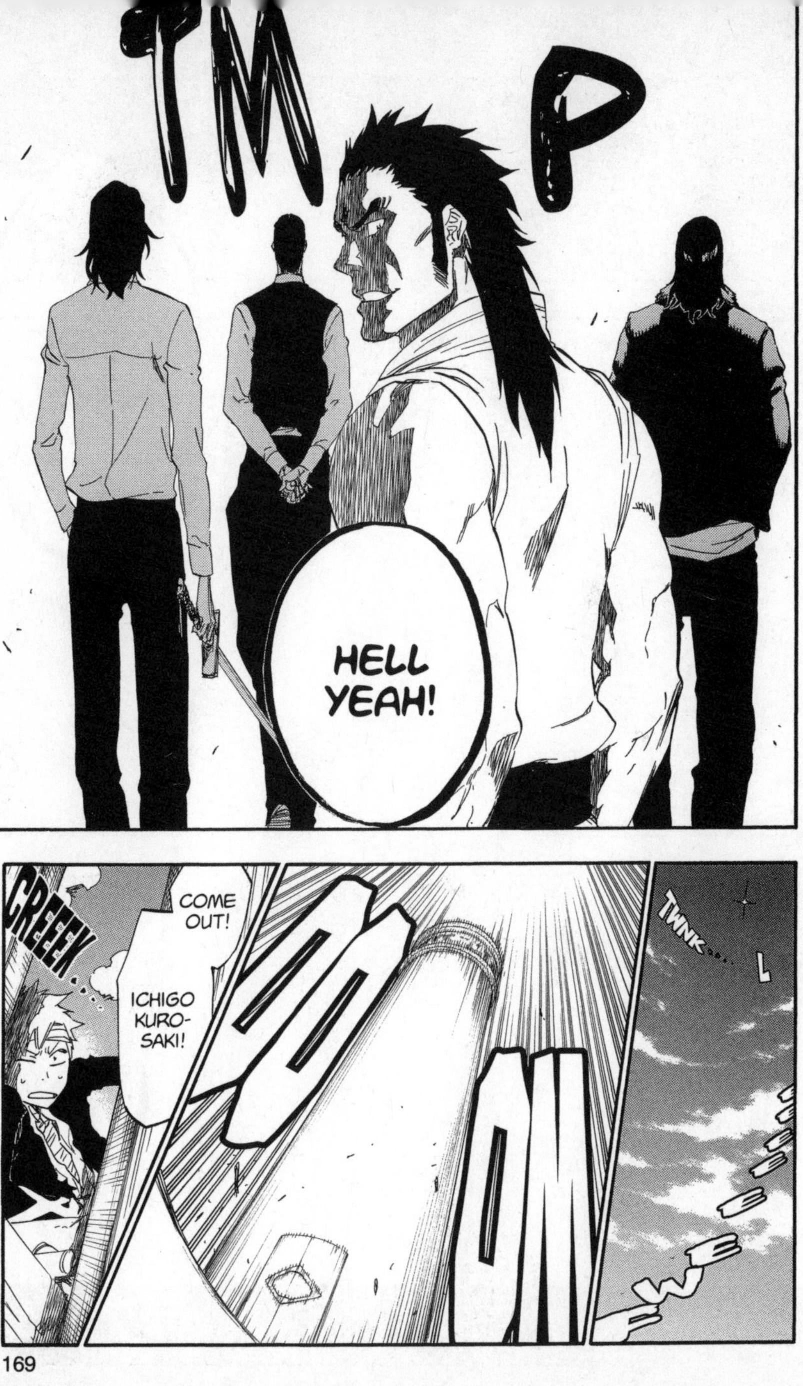
TMP
HELL YEAH!
TWNK... L
COME OUT!
ICHIGO KURO-SAKI!
CREEK

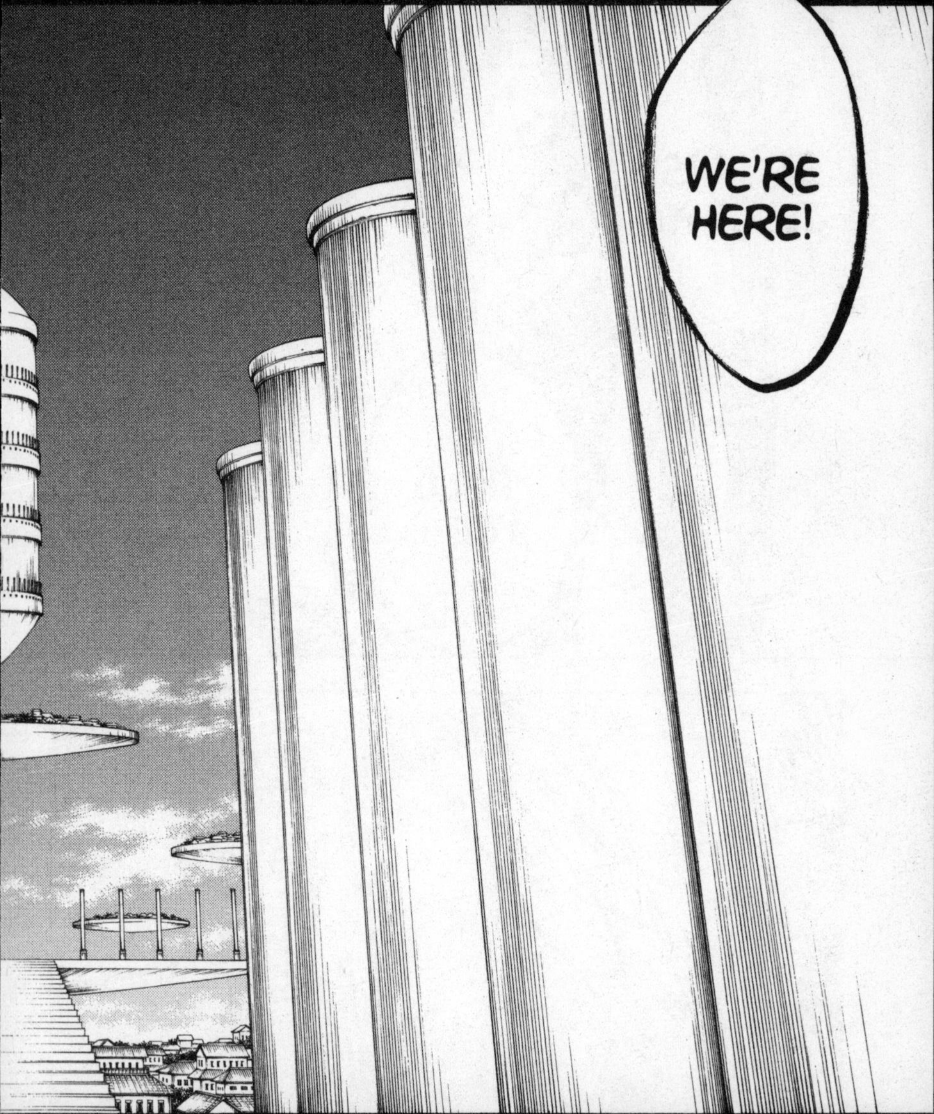
WE'RE HERE!

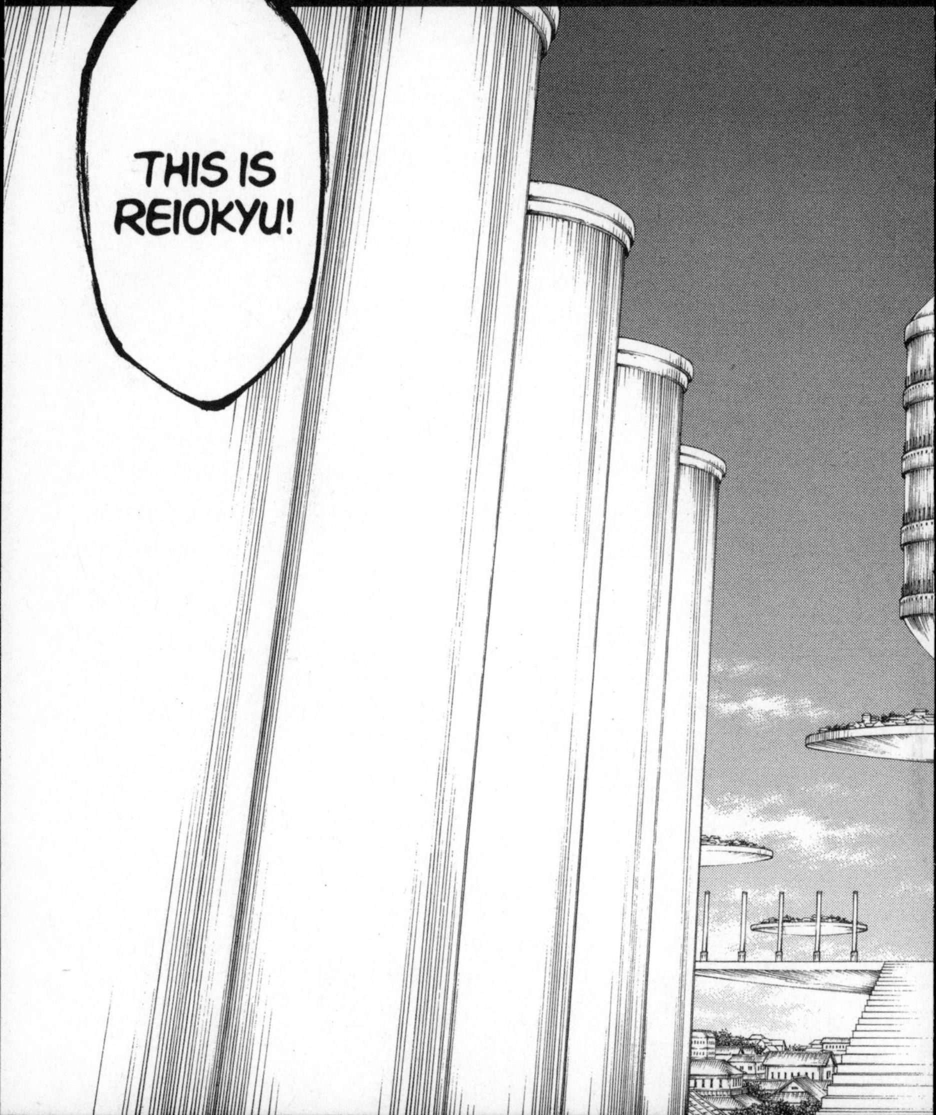
THIS IS REIOKYU!

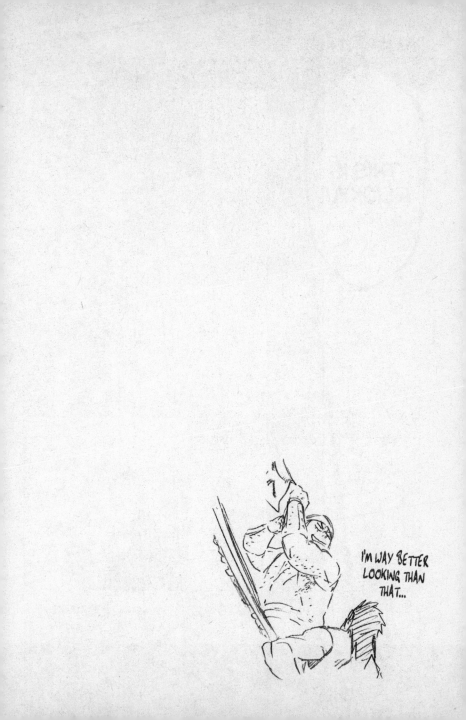

I'M WAY BETTER
LOOKING THAN
THAT...

519. HOT, HOT, HEAT

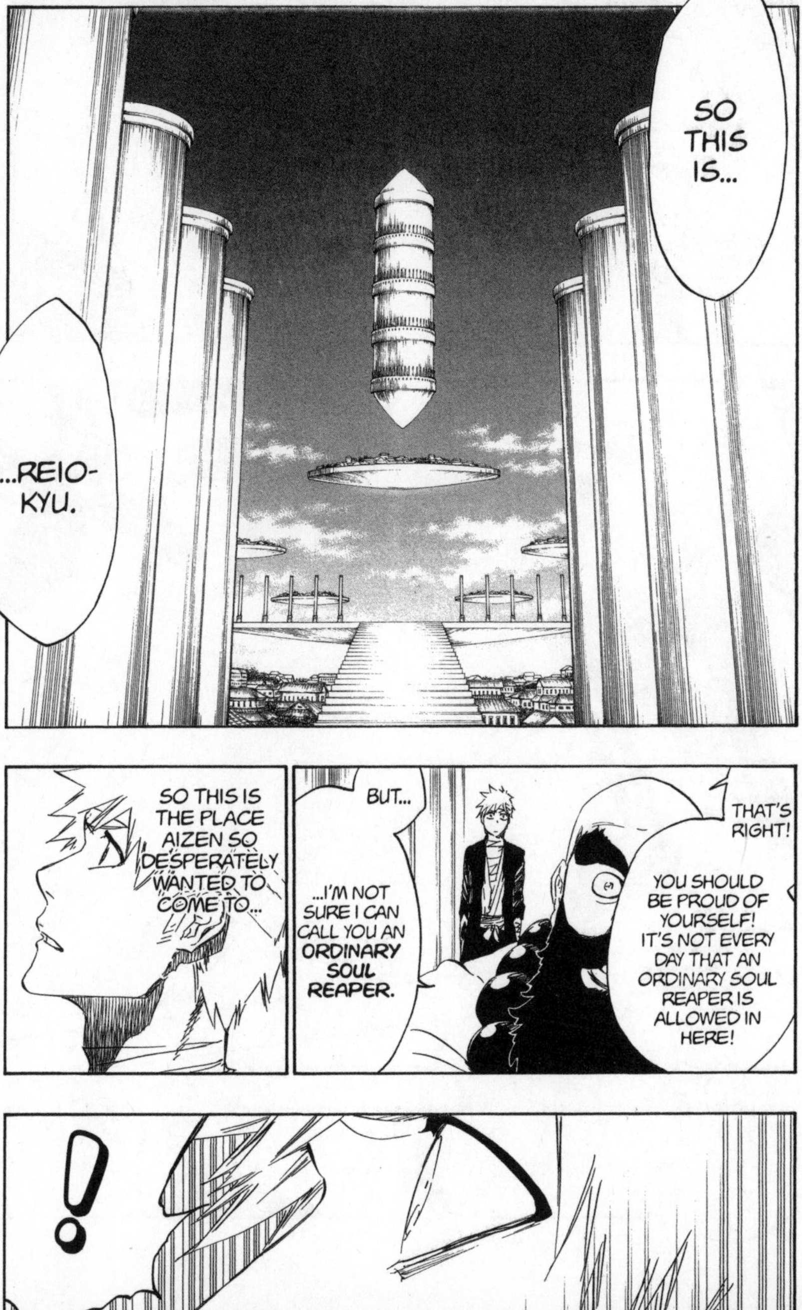
SO THIS IS...
...REIO-KYU.
THAT'S RIGHT!
YOU SHOULD BE PROUD OF YOURSELF! IT'S NOT EVERY DAY THAT AN ORDINARY SOUL REAPER IS ALLOWED IN HERE!
BUT...
...I'M NOT SURE I CAN CALL YOU AN ORDINARY SOUL REAPER.
SO THIS IS THE PLACE AIZEN SO DESPERATELY WANTED TO COME TO...
!

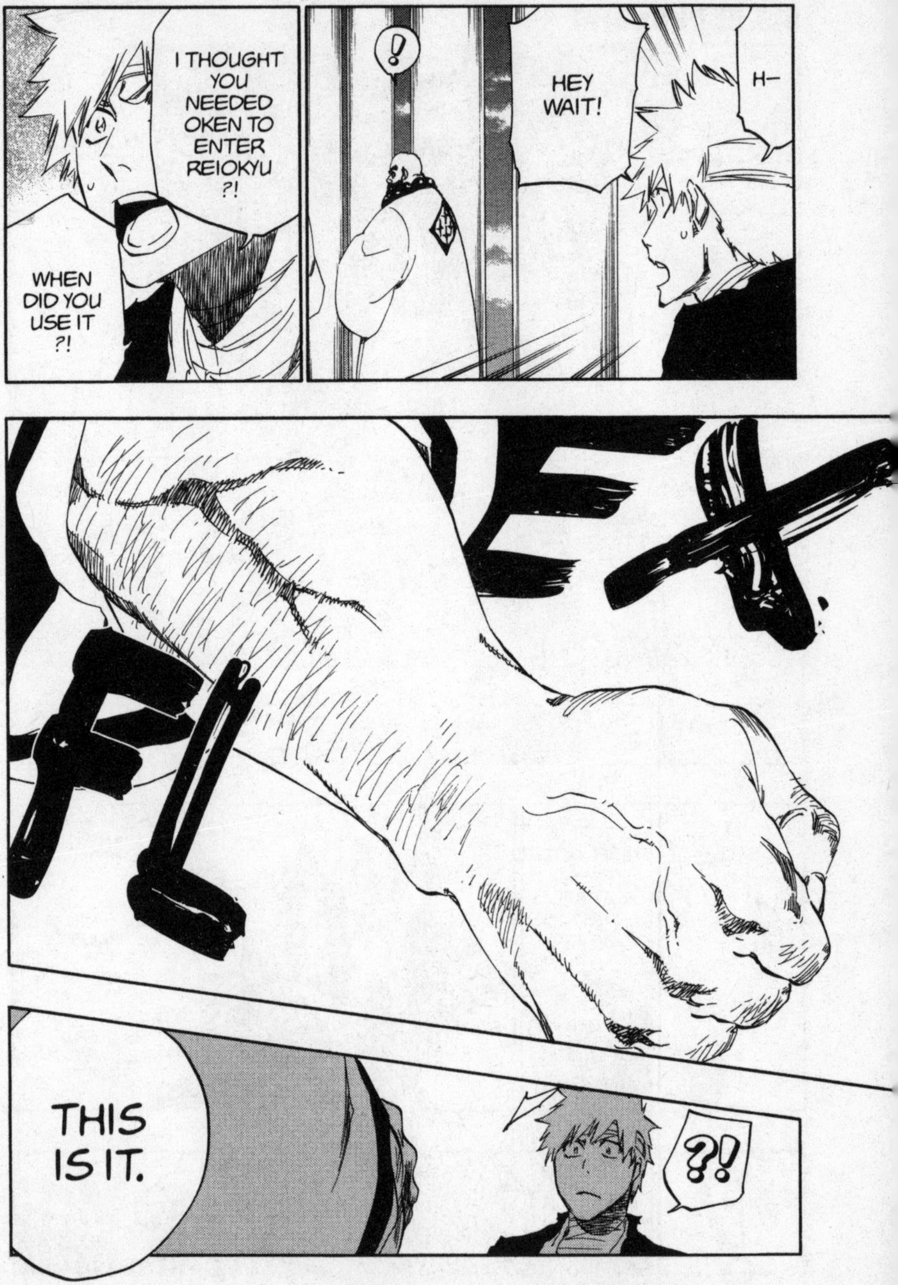
H—
HEY WAIT!
!
I THOUGHT YOU NEEDED OKEN TO ENTER REIOKYU ?!
WHEN DID YOU USE IT ?!
THIS IS IT.
?!

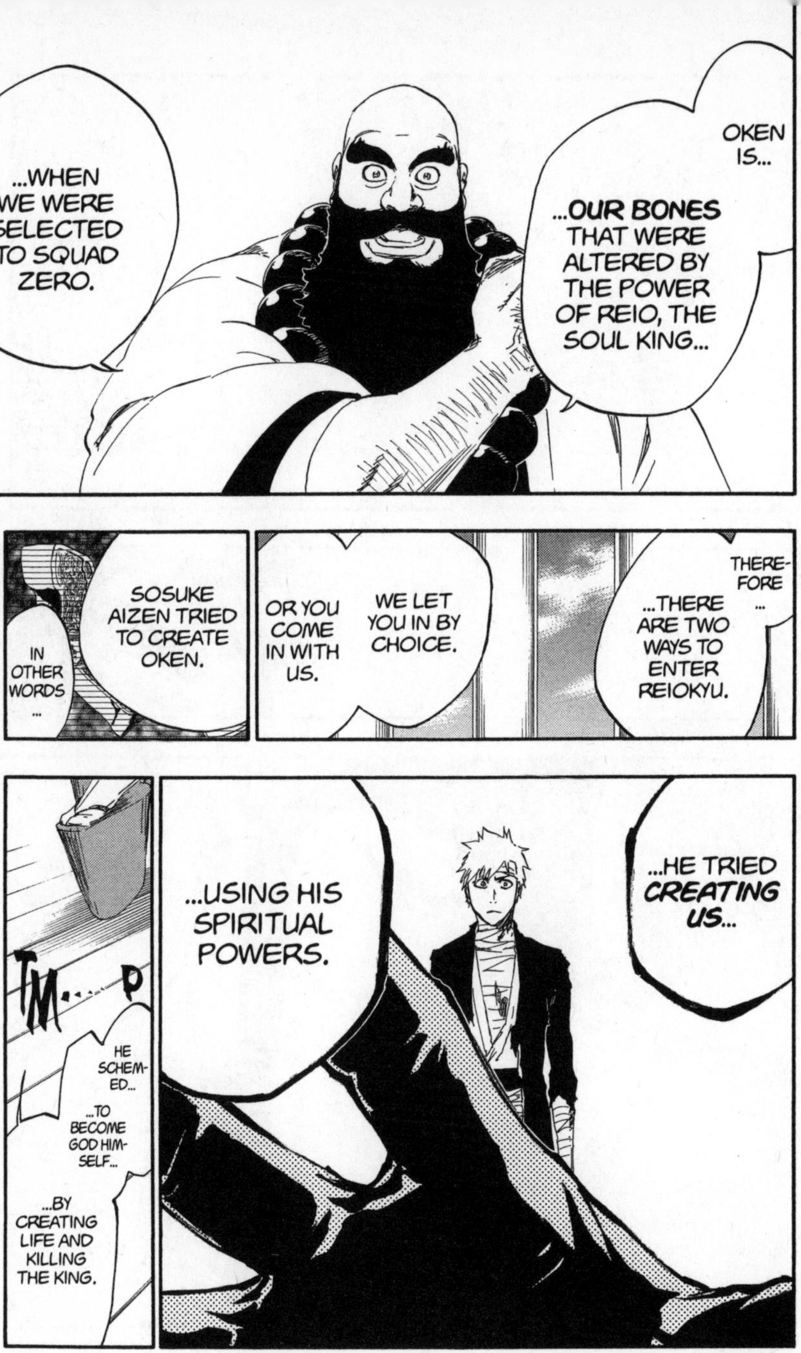
OKEN IS...
...OUR BONES THAT WERE ALTERED BY THE POWER OF REIO, THE SOUL KING...
...WHEN WE WERE SELECTED TO SQUAD ZERO.
THEREFORE...
...THERE ARE TWO WAYS TO ENTER REIOKYU.
WE LET YOU IN BY CHOICE.
OR YOU COME IN WITH US.
SOSUKE AIZEN TRIED TO CREATE OKEN.
IN OTHER WORDS...
...HE TRIED CREATING US...
...USING HIS SPIRITUAL POWERS.
TM... P
HE SCHEMED...
...TO BECOME GOD HIMSELF...
...BY CREATING LIFE AND KILLING THE KING.

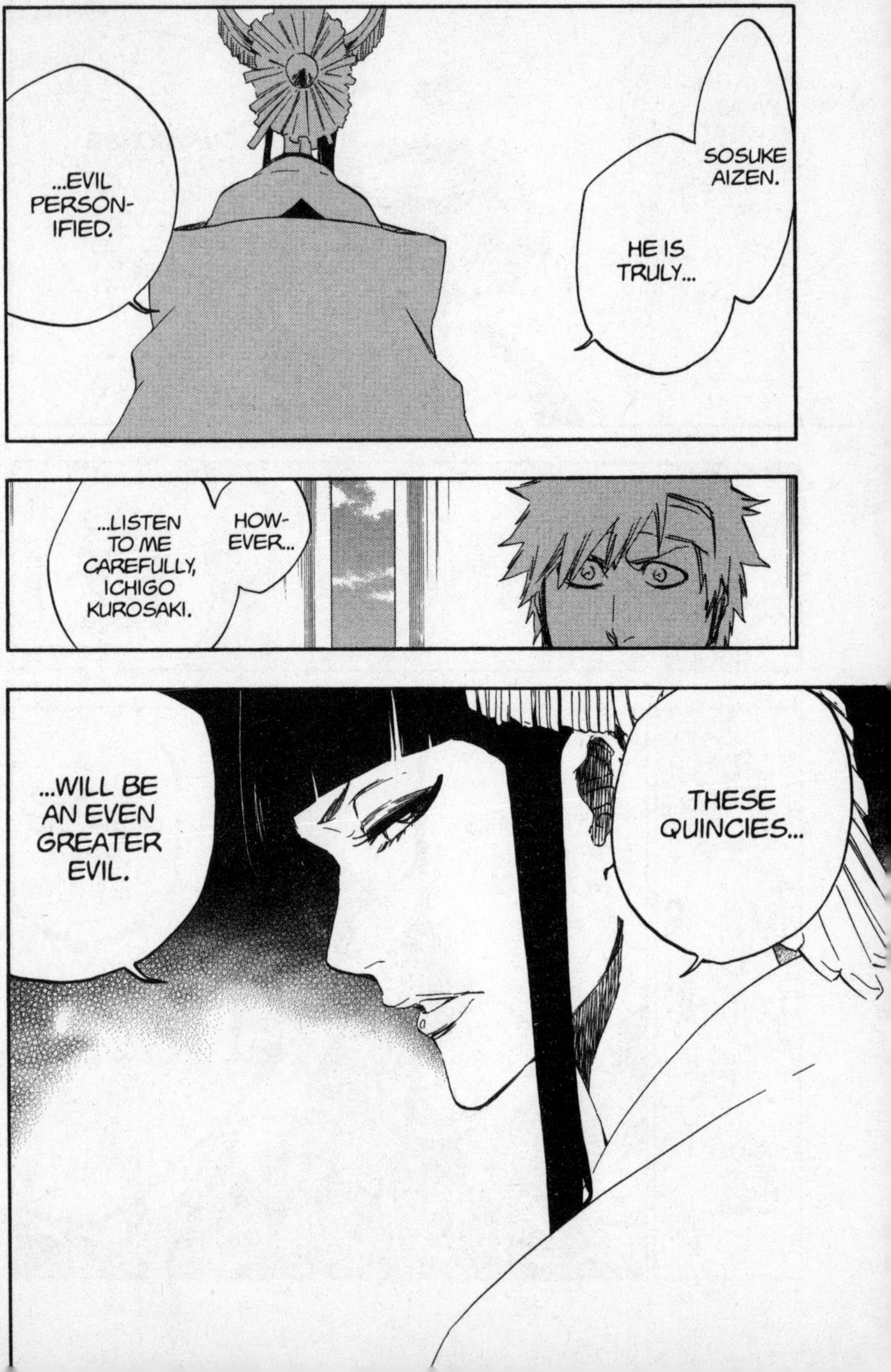
SOSUKE AIZEN.
HE IS TRULY...
...EVIL PERSONIFIED.
HOWEVER...
...LISTEN TO ME CAREFULLY, ICHIGO KUROSAKI.
THESE QUINCIES...
...WILL BE AN EVEN GREATER EVIL.

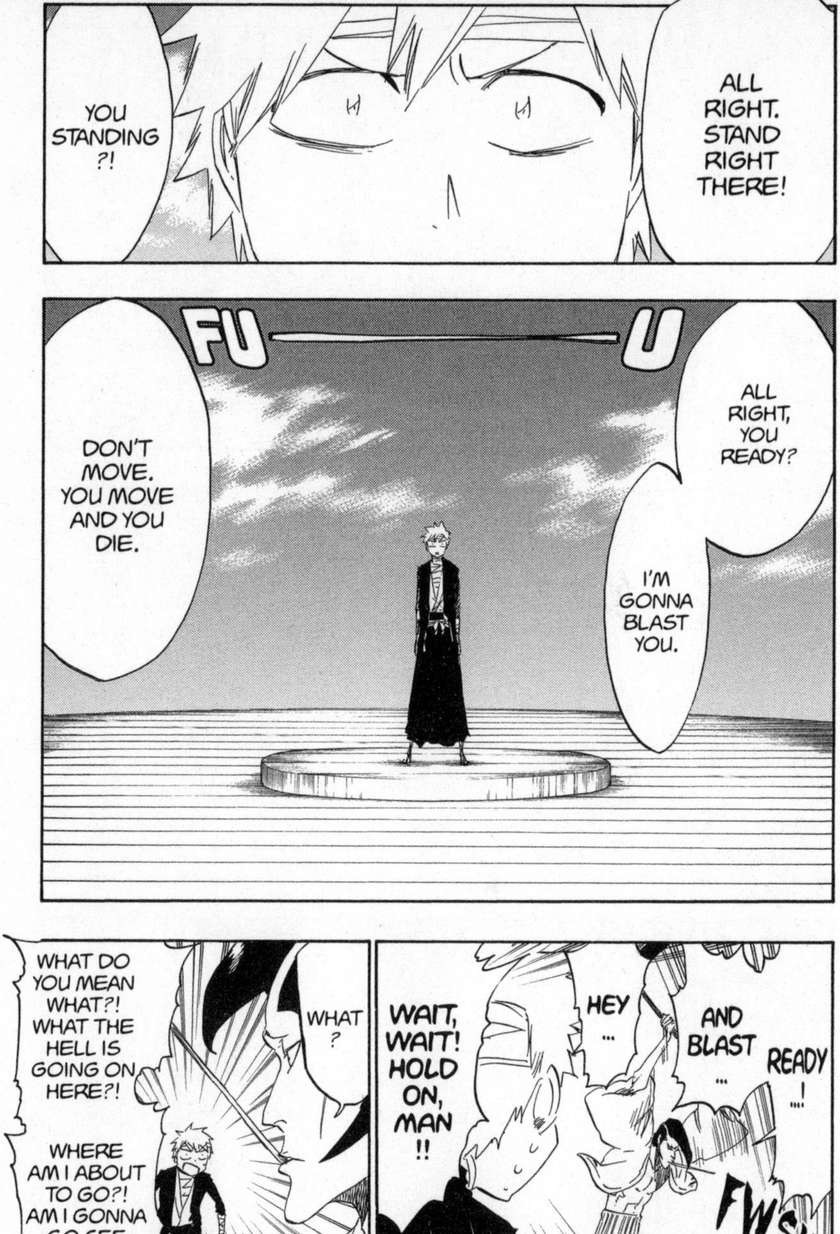
ALL RIGHT. STAND RIGHT THERE!
YOU STANDING ?!
FU——U
ALL RIGHT, YOU READY?
I'M GONNA BLAST YOU.
DON'T MOVE. YOU MOVE AND YOU DIE.
READY ...!
AND BLAST ...
HEY ...
FWSH
WAIT, WAIT! HOLD ON, MAN !!
WHAT ?
WHAT DO YOU MEAN WHAT?! WHAT THE HELL IS GOING ON HERE?!
WHERE AM I ABOUT TO GO?! AM I GONNA GO SEE THE KING?!

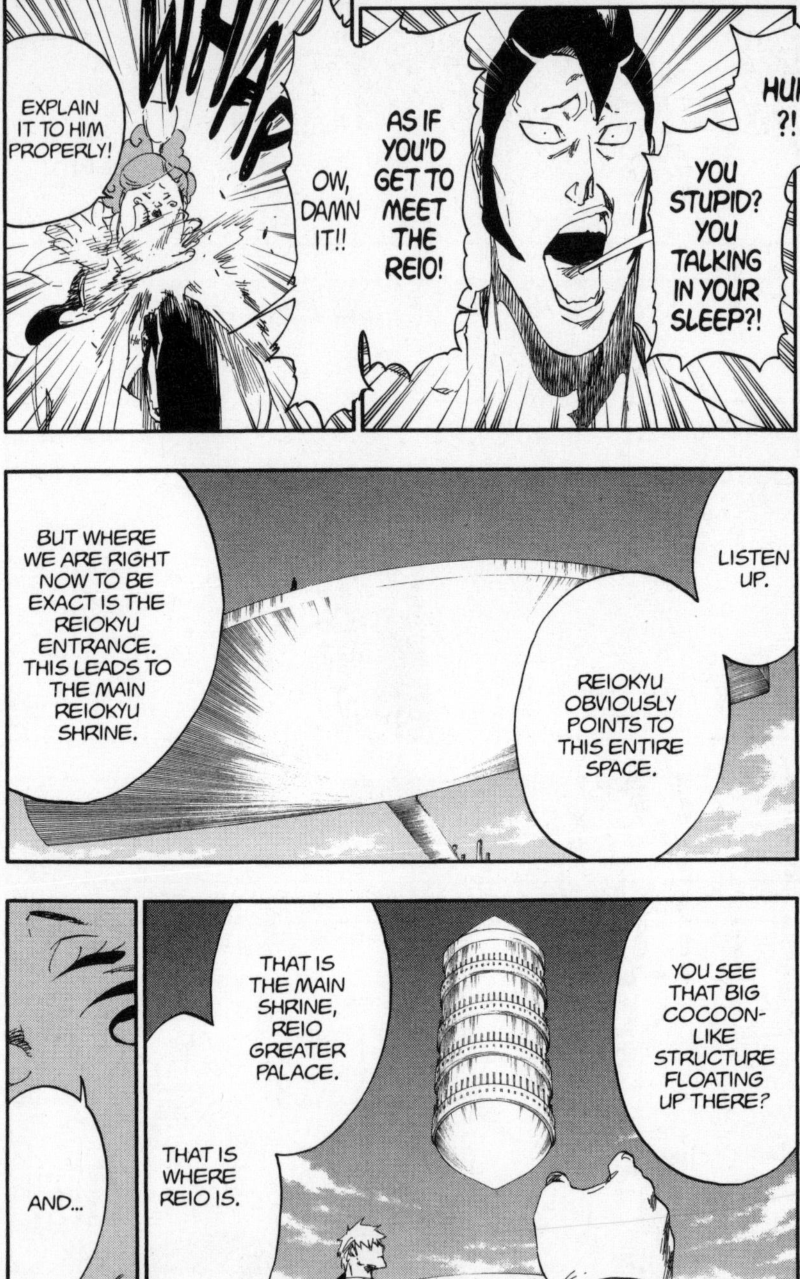
HUH ?!
YOU STUPID? YOU TALKING IN YOUR SLEEP?!
AS IF YOU'D GET TO MEET THE REIO!
WHAP
OW, DAMN IT!!
EXPLAIN IT TO HIM PROPERLY!
LISTEN UP.
REIOKYU OBVIOUSLY POINTS TO THIS ENTIRE SPACE.
BUT WHERE WE ARE RIGHT NOW TO BE EXACT IS THE REIOKYU ENTRANCE. THIS LEADS TO THE MAIN REIOKYU SHRINE.
YOU SEE THAT BIG COCOON-LIKE STRUCTURE FLOATING UP THERE?
THAT IS THE MAIN SHRINE, REIO GREATER PALACE.
THAT IS WHERE REIO IS.
AND...

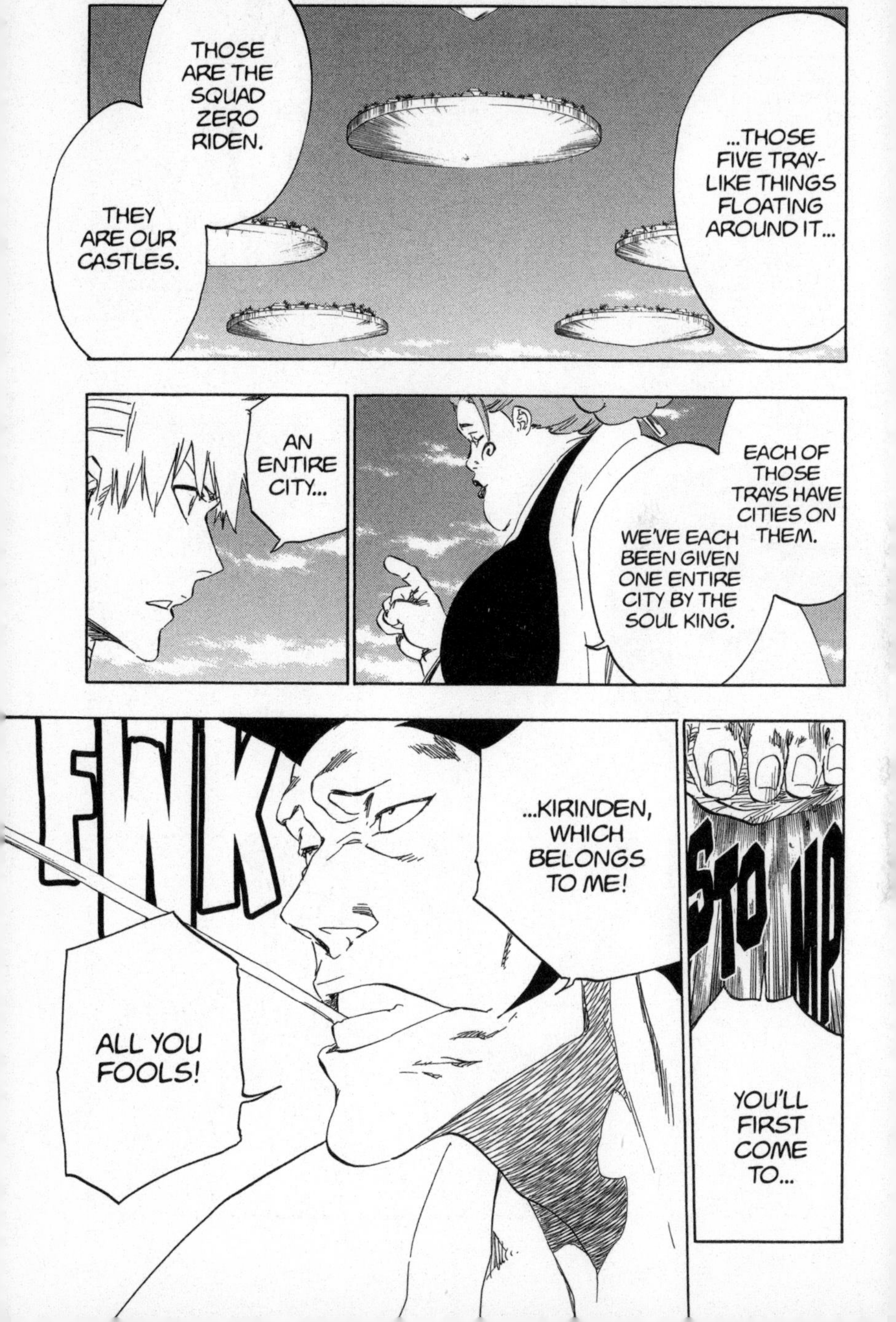
...THOSE FIVE TRAY-LIKE THINGS FLOATING AROUND IT...
THOSE ARE THE SQUAD ZERO RIDEN.
THEY ARE OUR CASTLES.
EACH OF THOSE TRAYS HAVE CITIES ON THEM.
WE'VE EACH BEEN GIVEN ONE ENTIRE CITY BY THE SOUL KING.
AN ENTIRE CITY...
STOMP
YOU'LL FIRST COME TO...
FWK
...KIRINDEN, WHICH BELONGS TO ME!
ALL YOU FOOLS!

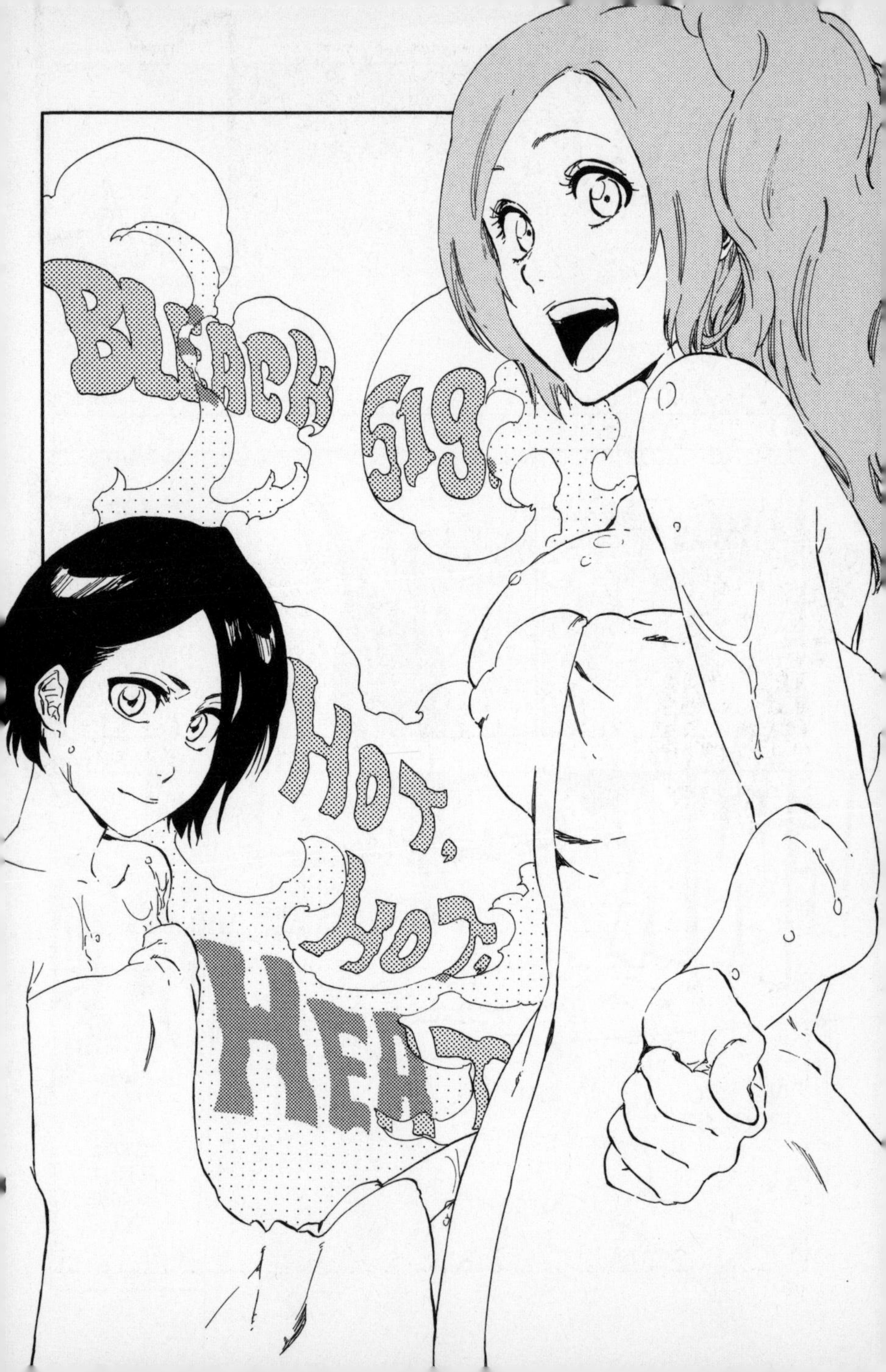
BLEACH 519.
HOT, HOT, HEAT

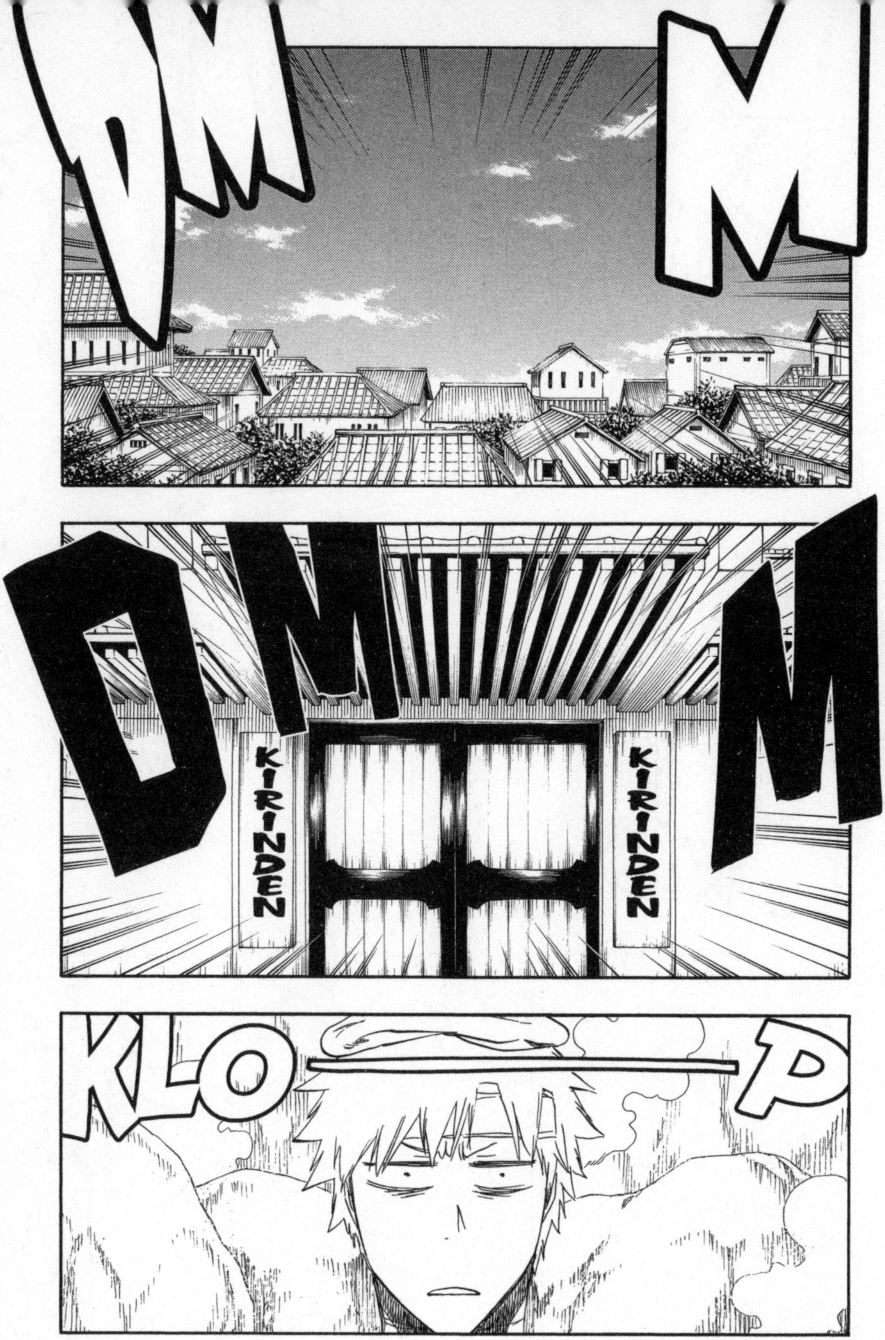
DMM
DMM
KIRINDEN
KIRINDEN
KLO—P

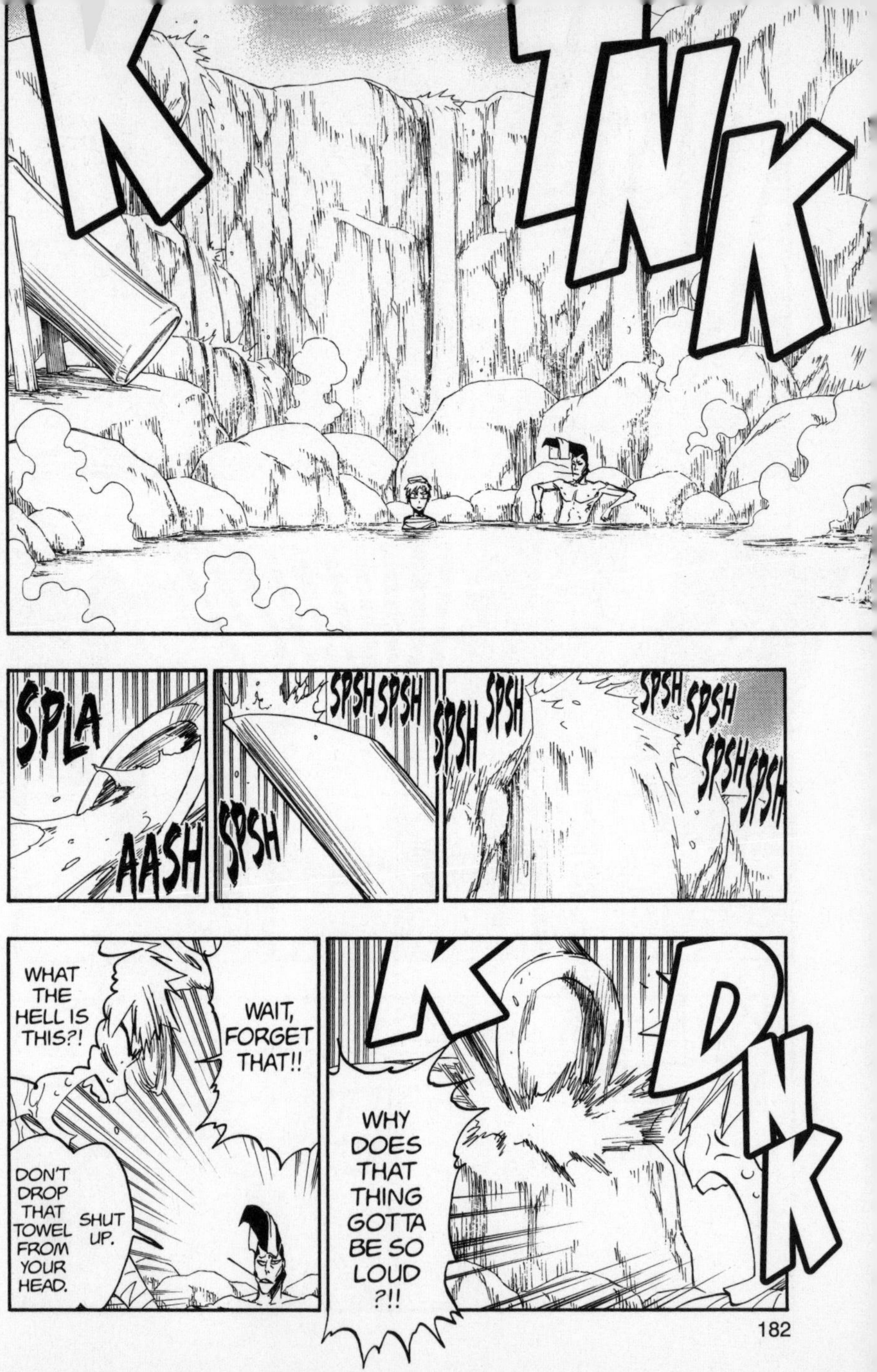
KTNK
SPSH SPSH SPSH SPSH SPSH SPSH
SPSH SPSH SPSH
SPLAASH
KDNK
WHY DOES THAT THING GOTTA BE SO LOUD?!!
WHAT THE HELL IS THIS?!
WAIT, FORGET THAT!!
DON'T DROP THAT TOWEL FROM YOUR HEAD.
SHUT UP.

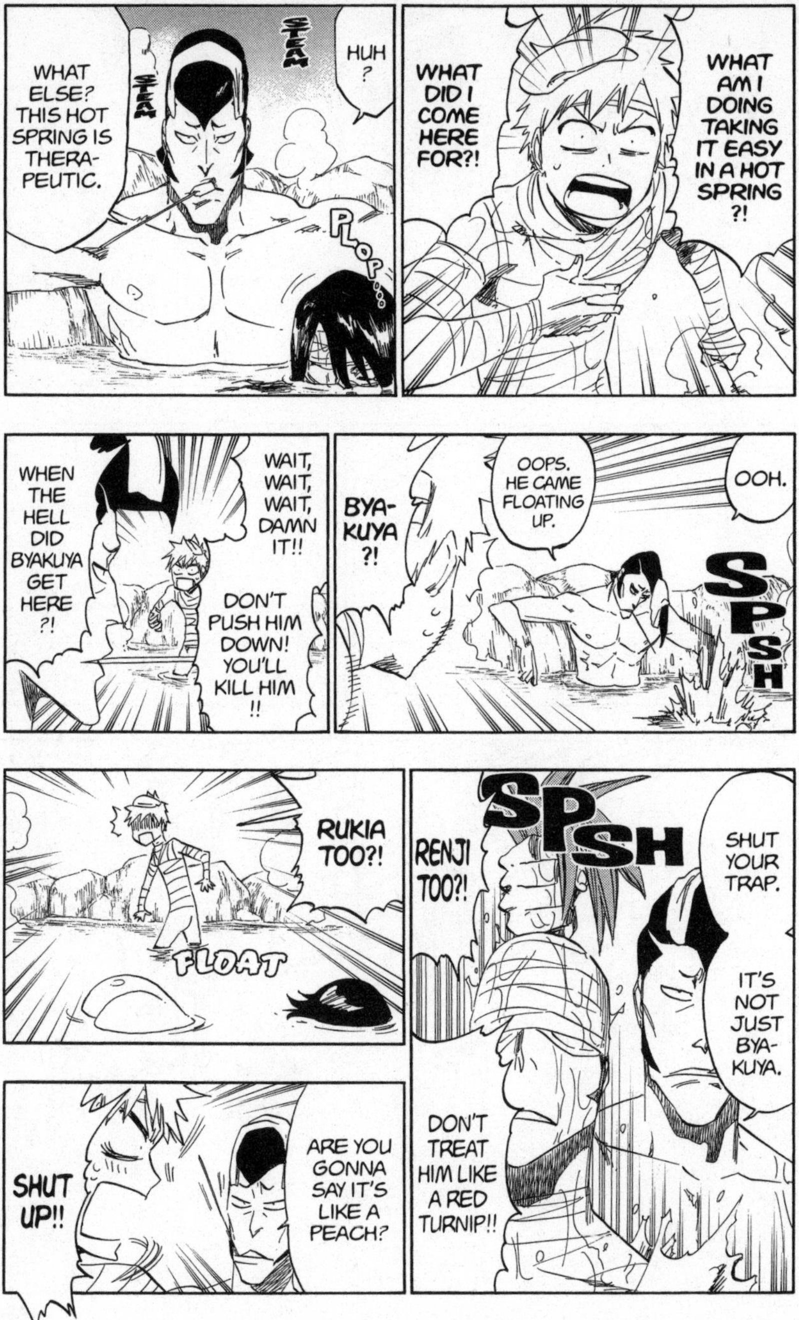
WHAT AM I DOING TAKING IT EASY IN A HOT SPRING?!
WHAT DID I COME HERE FOR?!
HUH?
STEAM
STEAM
WHAT ELSE? THIS HOT SPRING IS THERA-PEUTIC.
PLOP...
OOH.
OOPS. HE CAME FLOATING UP.
BYA-KUYA?!
SPSH
WAIT, WAIT, WAIT, DAMN IT!!
DON'T PUSH HIM DOWN! YOU'LL KILL HIM!!
WHEN THE HELL DID BYAKUYA GET HERE?!
SHUT YOUR TRAP.
SPSH
RENJI TOO?!
IT'S NOT JUST BYA-KUYA.
DON'T TREAT HIM LIKE A RED TURNIP!!
RUKIA TOO?!
FLOAT
ARE YOU GONNA SAY IT'S LIKE A PEACH?
SHUT UP!!

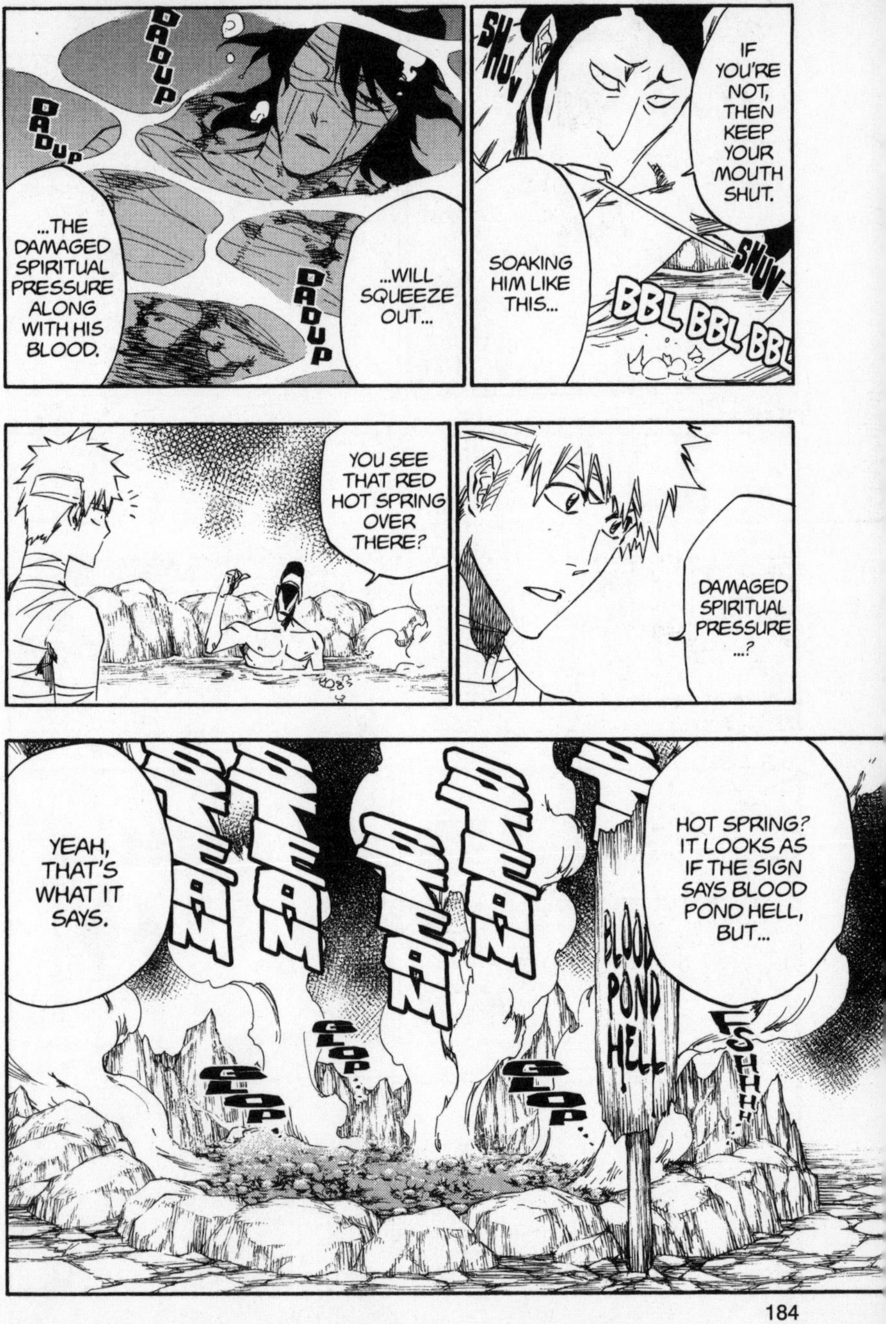
SHUV
IF YOU'RE NOT, THEN KEEP YOUR MOUTH SHUT.
SOAKING HIM LIKE THIS...
SHUV
BBL BBL BBL
DADUP DADUP
...WILL SQUEEZE OUT...
DADUP
...THE DAMAGED SPIRITUAL PRESSURE ALONG WITH HIS BLOOD.
DAMAGED SPIRITUAL PRESSURE ...?
YOU SEE THAT RED HOT SPRING OVER THERE?
HOT SPRING? IT LOOKS AS IF THE SIGN SAYS BLOOD POND HELL, BUT...
BLOOD POND HELL
FSHHHH
STEAM STEAM STEAM STEAM
GLOP... GLOP... GLOP...
YEAH, THAT'S WHAT IT SAYS.

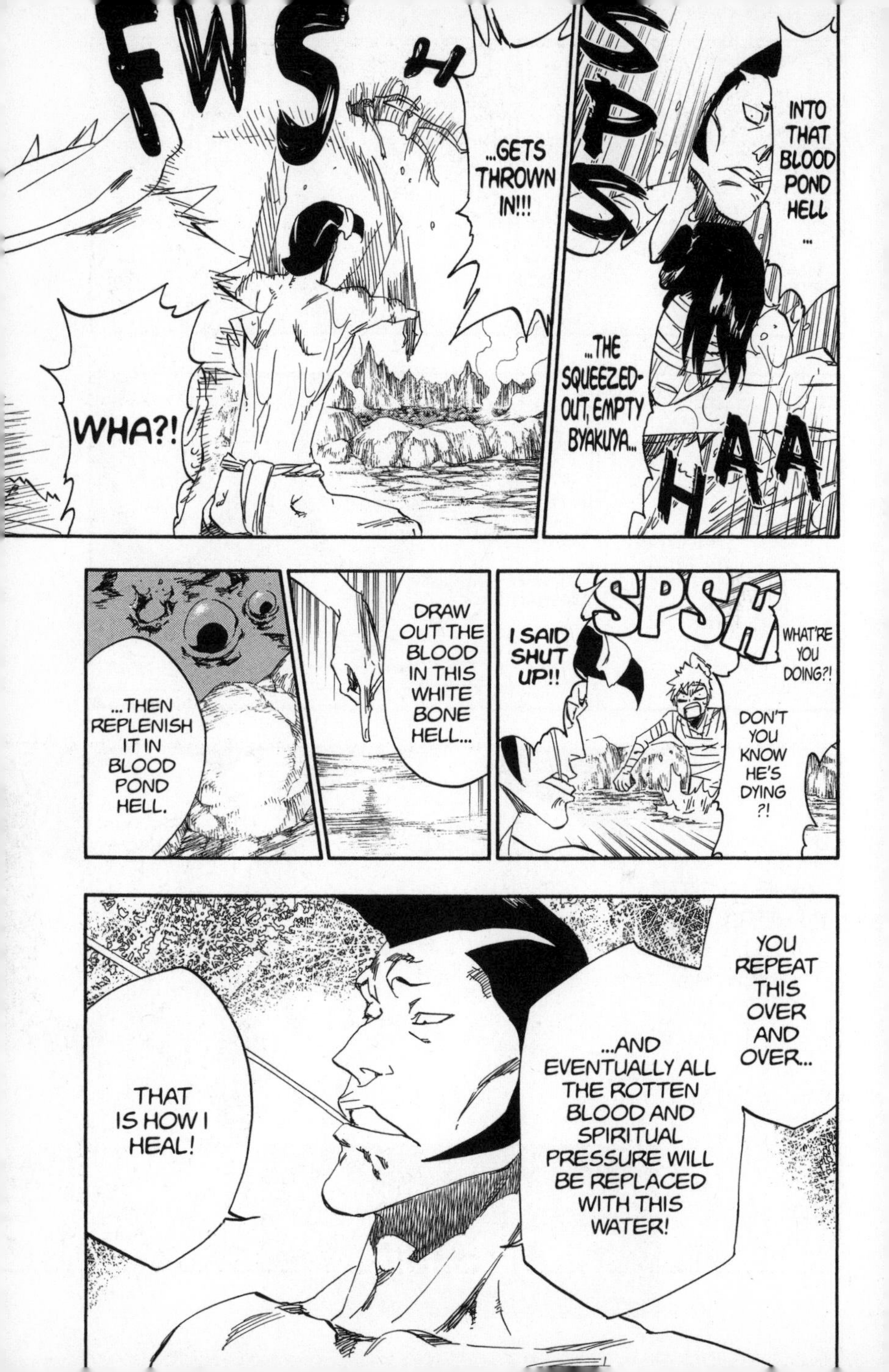
SPS
INTO THAT BLOOD POND HELL ...
...THE SQUEEZED-OUT, EMPTY BYAKUYA...
HAAH
FWSH
...GETS THROWN IN!!!
WHA?!
SPSH
WHAT'RE YOU DOING?!
DON'T YOU KNOW HE'S DYING ?!
I SAID SHUT UP!!
DRAW OUT THE BLOOD IN THIS WHITE BONE HELL...
...THEN REPLENISH IT IN BLOOD POND HELL.
YOU REPEAT THIS OVER AND OVER...
...AND EVENTUALLY ALL THE ROTTEN BLOOD AND SPIRITUAL PRESSURE WILL BE REPLACED WITH THIS WATER!
THAT IS HOW I HEAL!

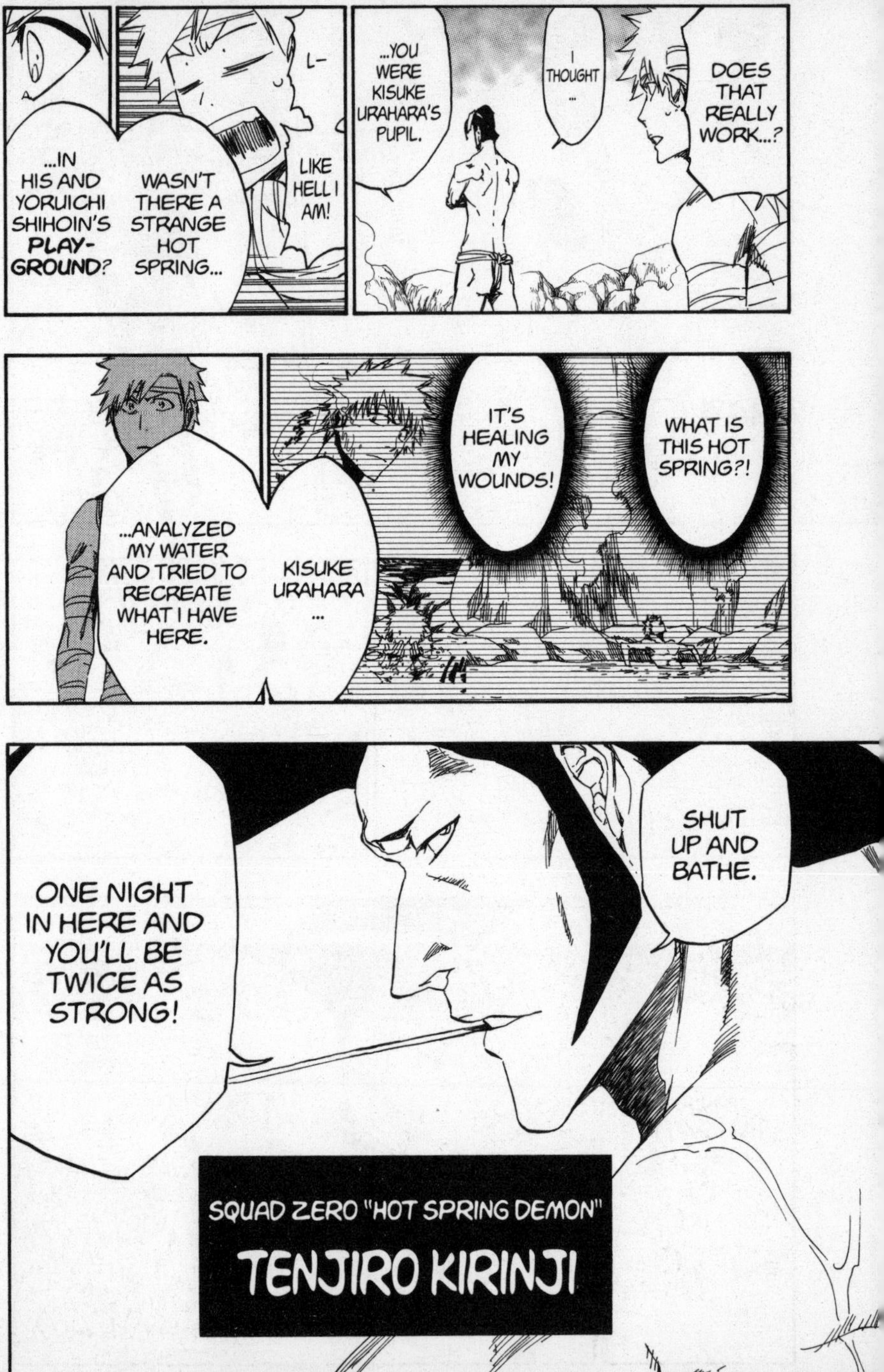
DOES THAT REALLY WORK...?
I THOUGHT...
...YOU WERE KISUKE URAHARA'S PUPIL.
L-
LIKE HELL I AM!
WASN'T THERE A STRANGE HOT SPRING...
...IN HIS AND YORUICHI SHIHOIN'S **PLAY-GROUND**?
WHAT IS THIS HOT SPRING?!
IT'S HEALING MY WOUNDS!
KISUKE URAHARA...
...ANALYZED MY WATER AND TRIED TO RECREATE WHAT I HAVE HERE.
SHUT UP AND BATHE.
ONE NIGHT IN HERE AND YOU'LL BE TWICE AS STRONG!
SQUAD ZERO "HOT SPRING DEMON"
TENJIRO KIRINJI

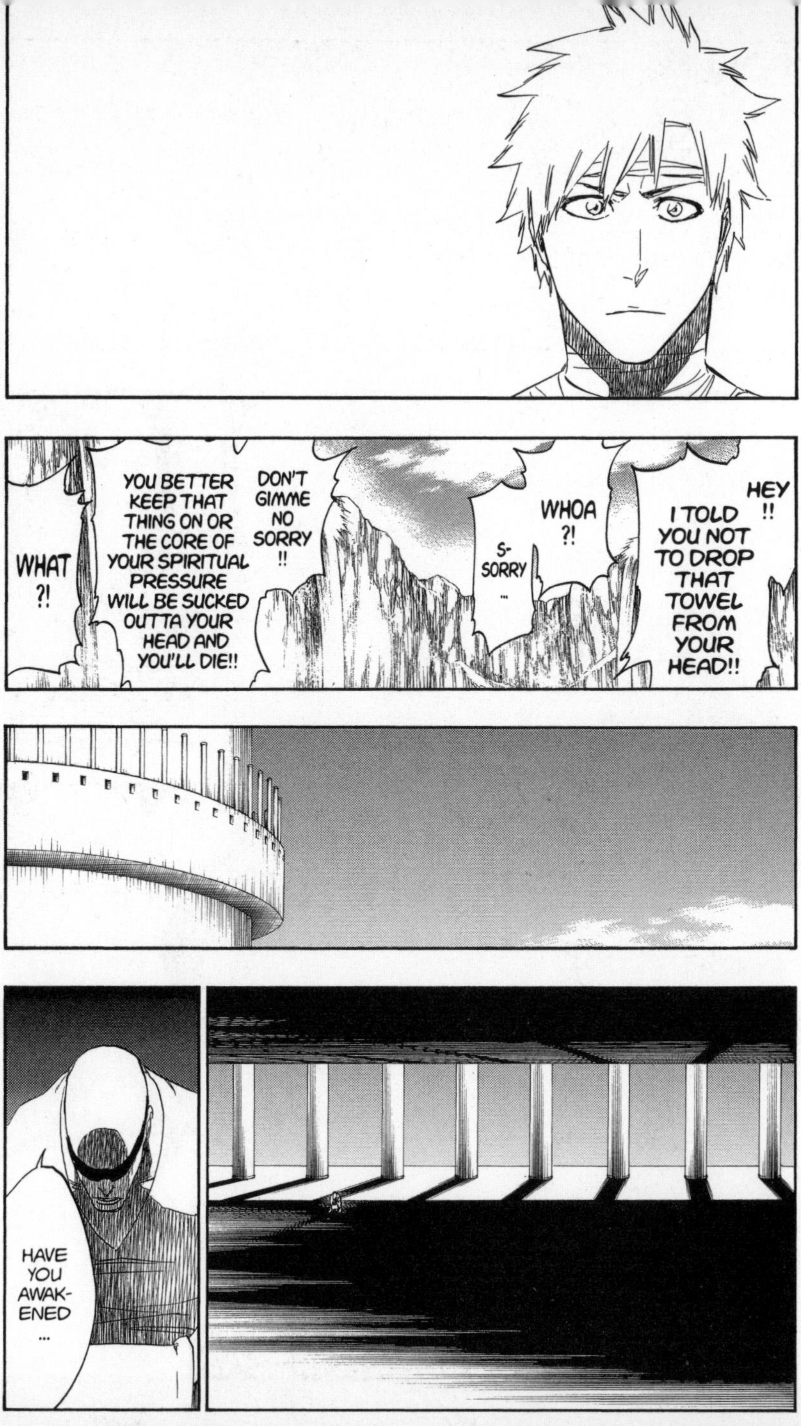
HEY!!
I TOLD YOU NOT TO DROP THAT TOWEL FROM YOUR HEAD!!
WHOA?!
S-SORRY...
DON'T GIMME NO SORRY!!
YOU BETTER KEEP THAT THING ON OR THE CORE OF YOUR SPIRITUAL PRESSURE WILL BE SUCKED OUTTA YOUR HEAD AND YOU'LL DIE!!
WHAT?!
HAVE YOU AWAKENED...

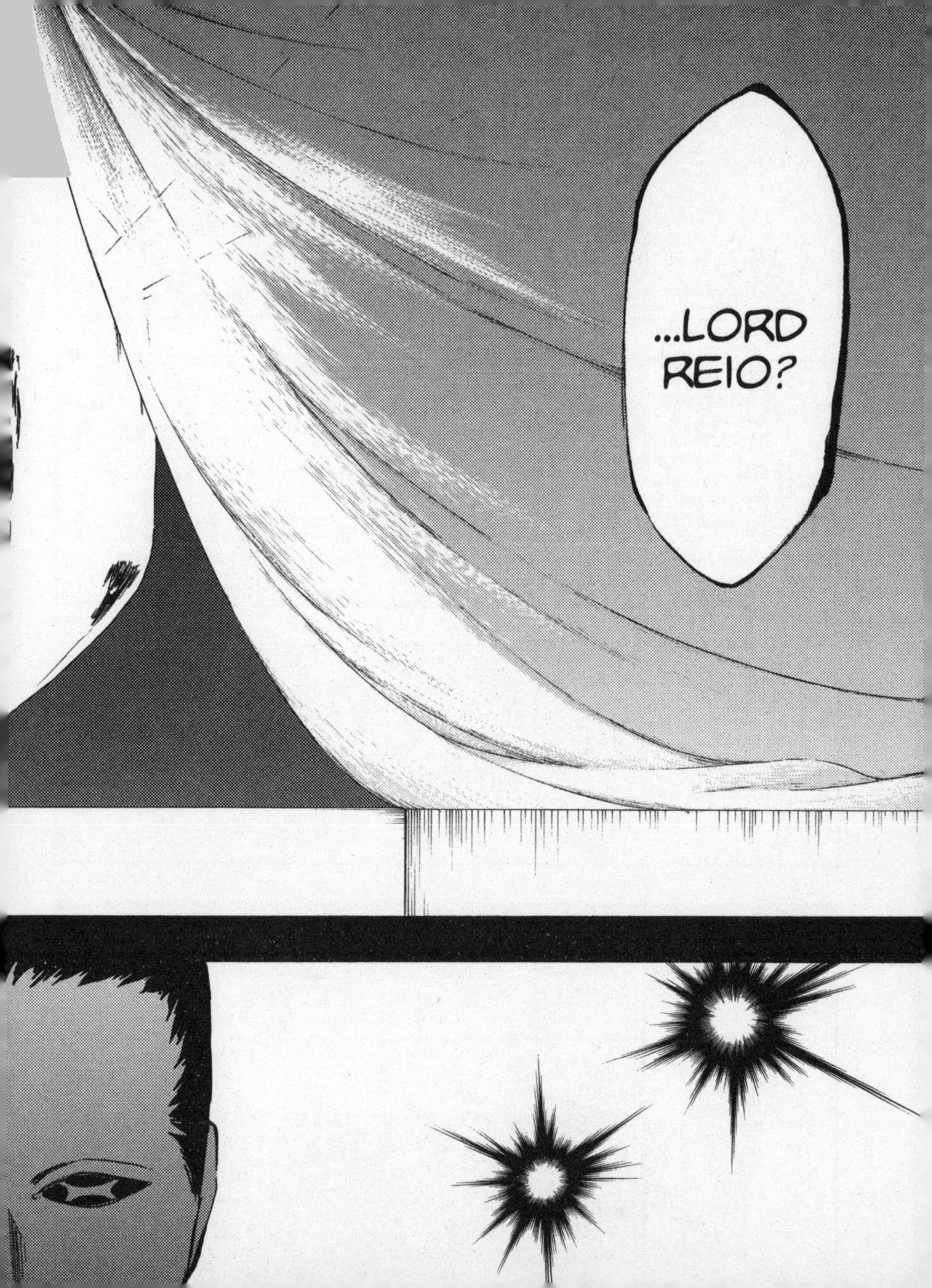
...LORD REIO?

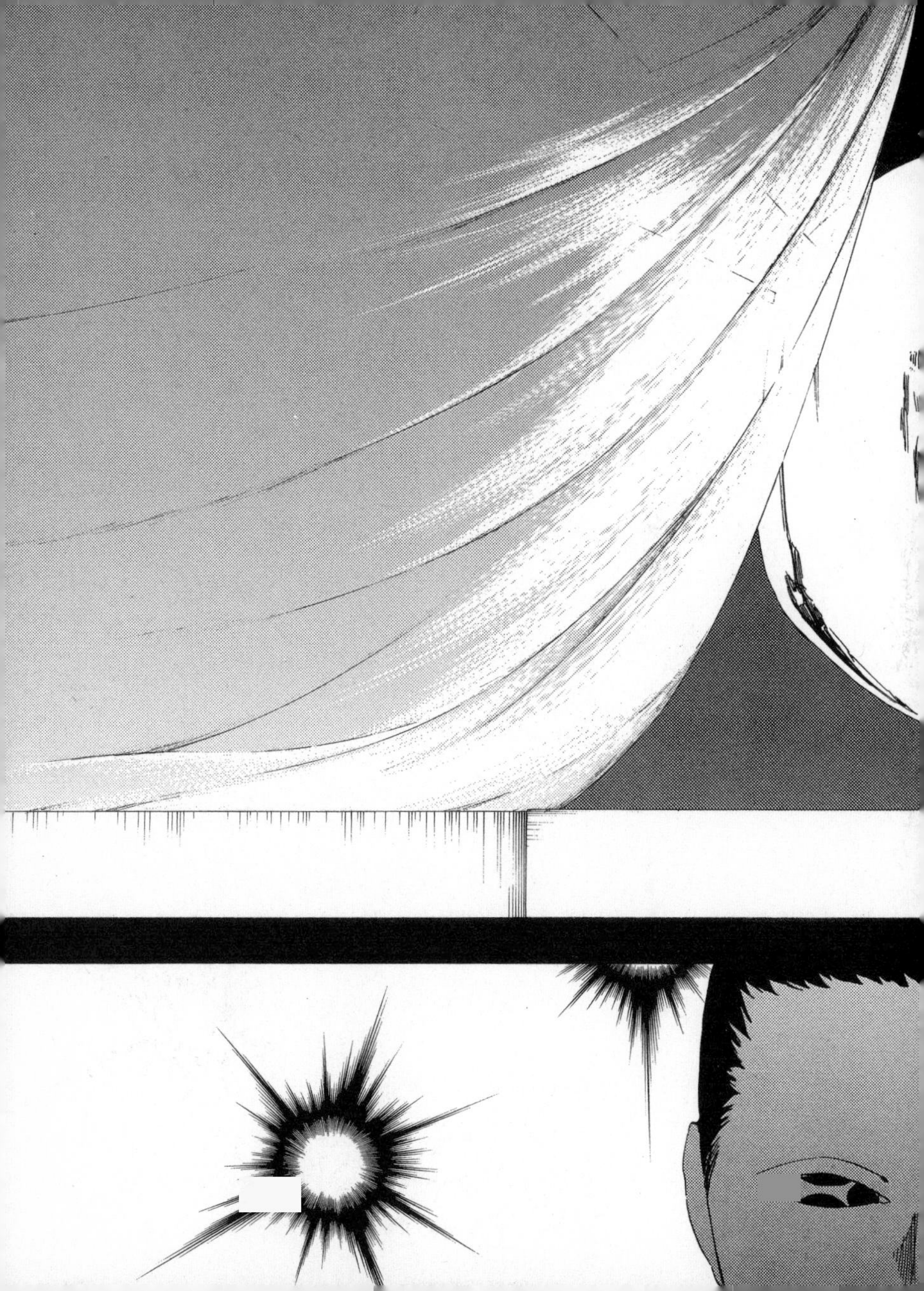

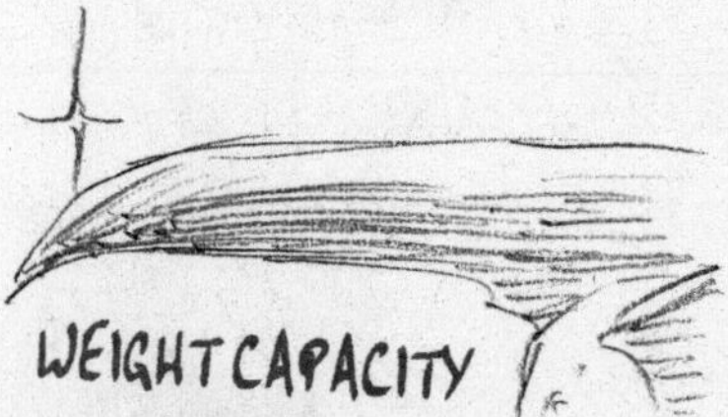
WEIGHT CAPACITY
120 kg

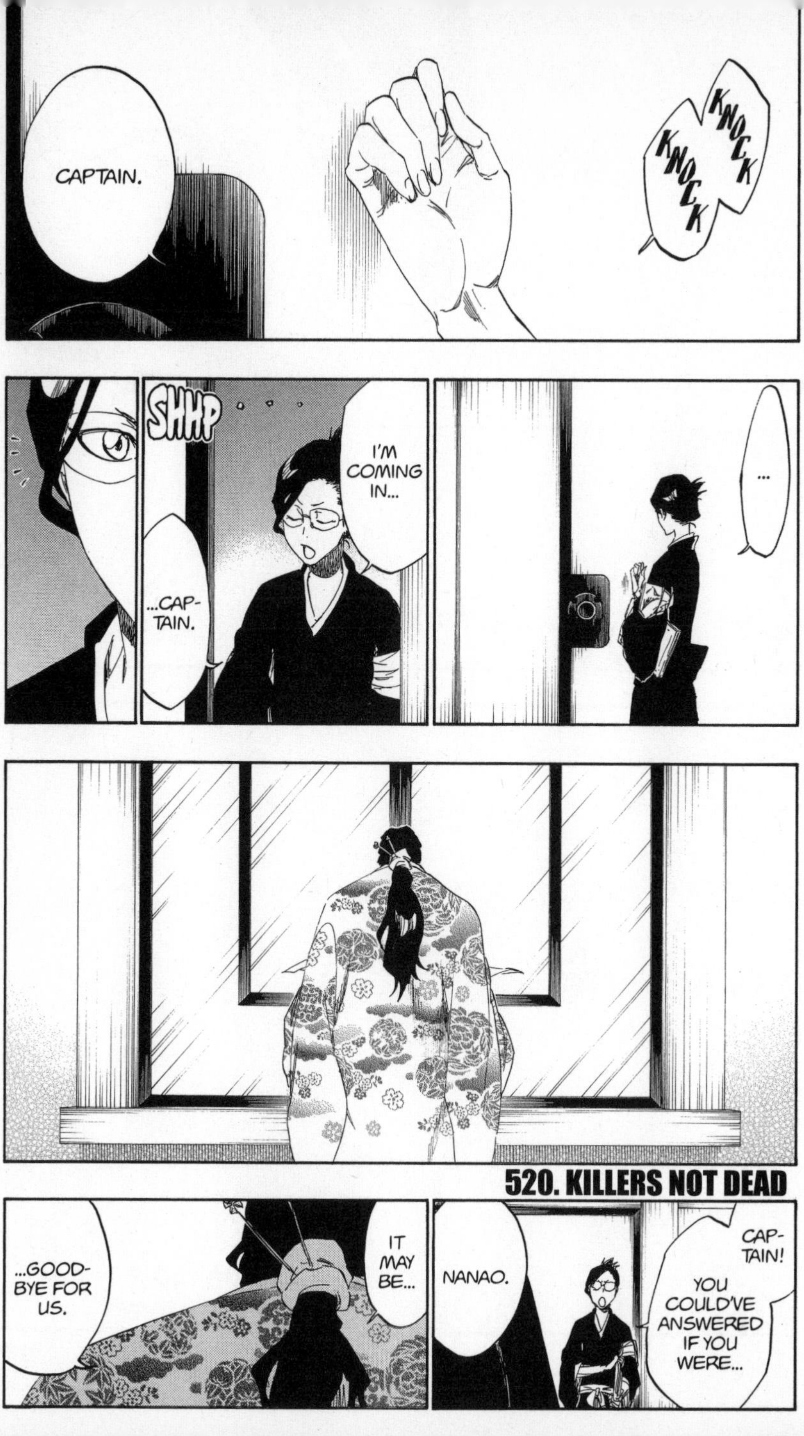
KNOCK
KNOCK
CAPTAIN.
...
I'M COMING IN...
SHHP
...CAPTAIN.
520. KILLERS NOT DEAD
CAPTAIN!
YOU COULD'VE ANSWERED IF YOU WERE...
NANAO.
IT MAY BE...
...GOODBYE FOR US.

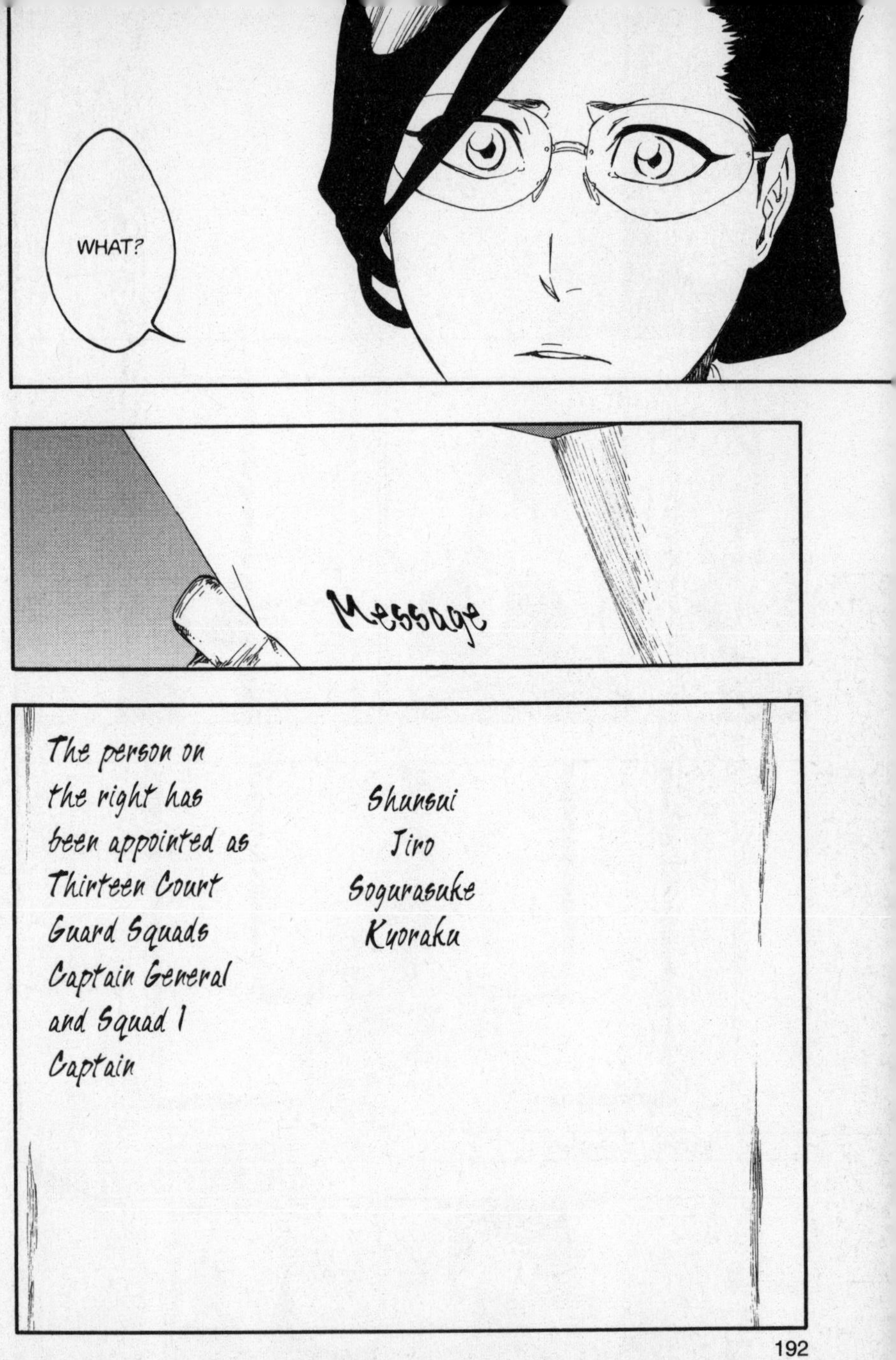
WHAT?
Message
The person on the right has been appointed as Thirteen Court Guard Squads Captain General and Squad 1 Captain
Shunsui Jiro Sogurasuke Kyoraku

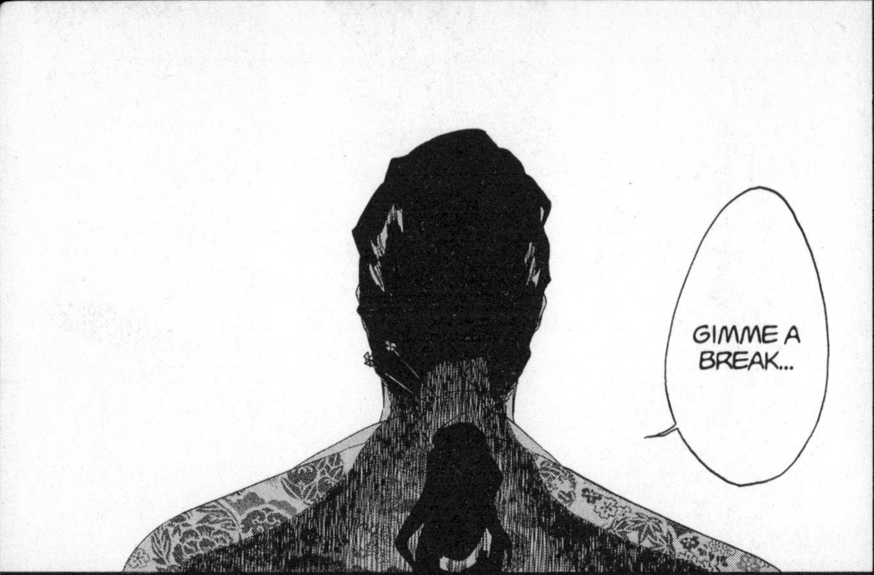
GIMME A BREAK...

BLEACH 520.

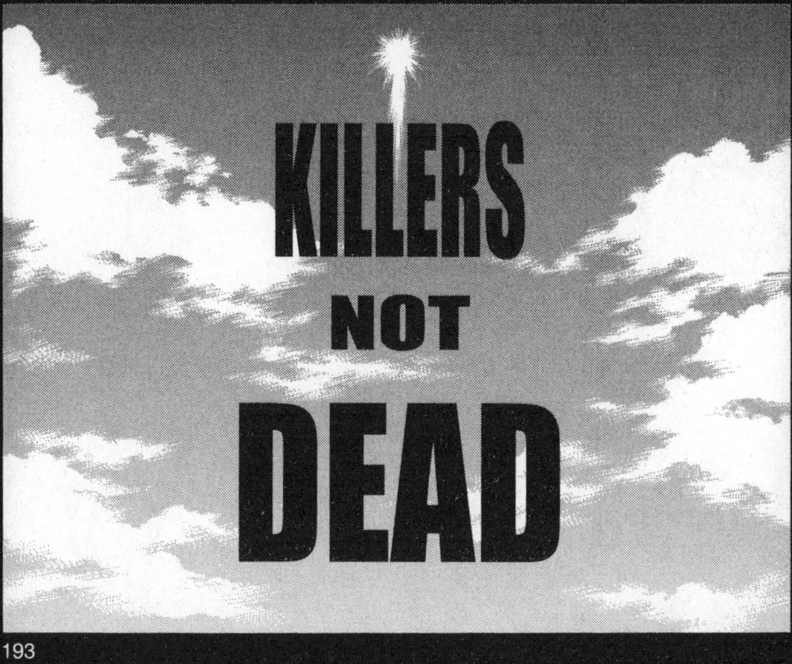
KILLERS NOT DEAD

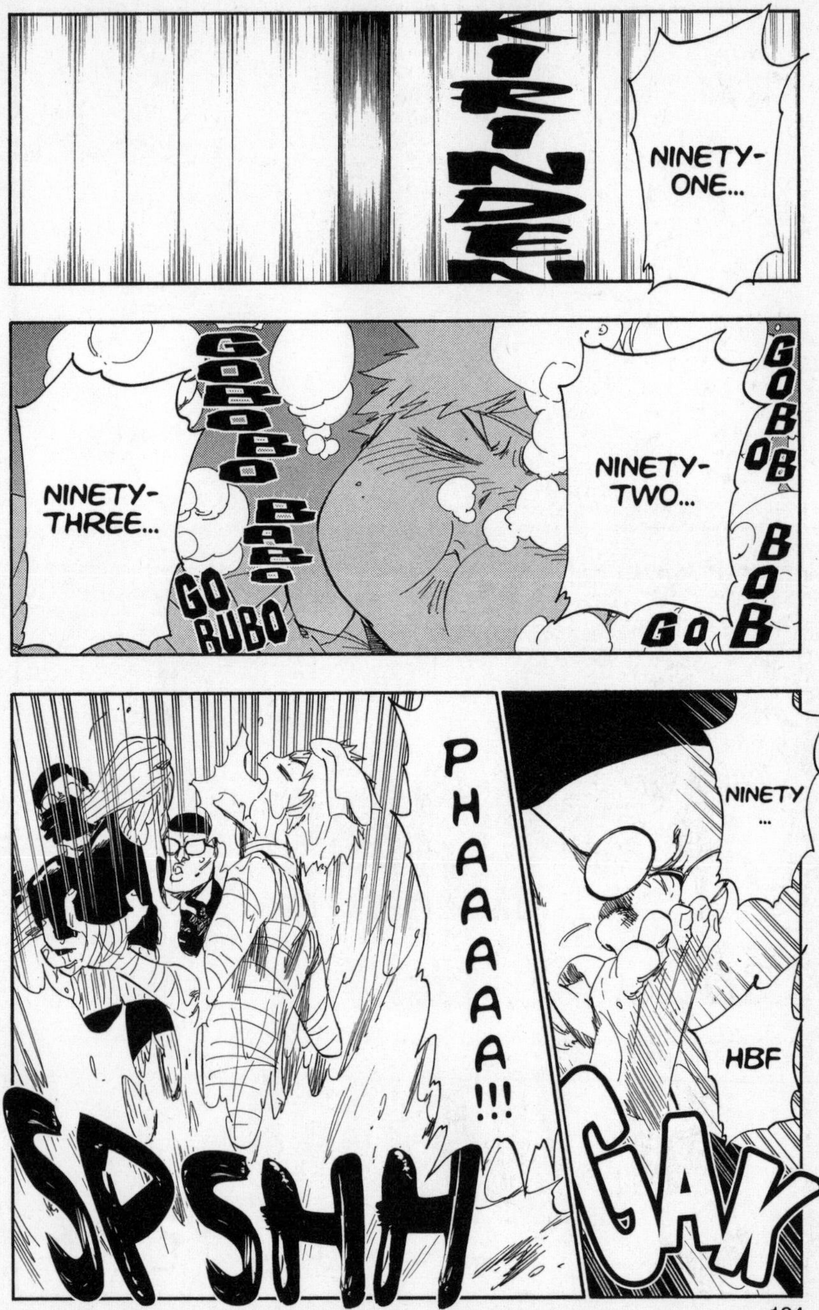
NINETY-ONE...
KIRINDEN
NINETY-TWO...
GOBOB
BOB
GO B
NINETY-THREE...
GOBOBO
BABO
GO BUBO
NINETY ...
HBF
GAK
PHAAAAAA!!!
SPSHH

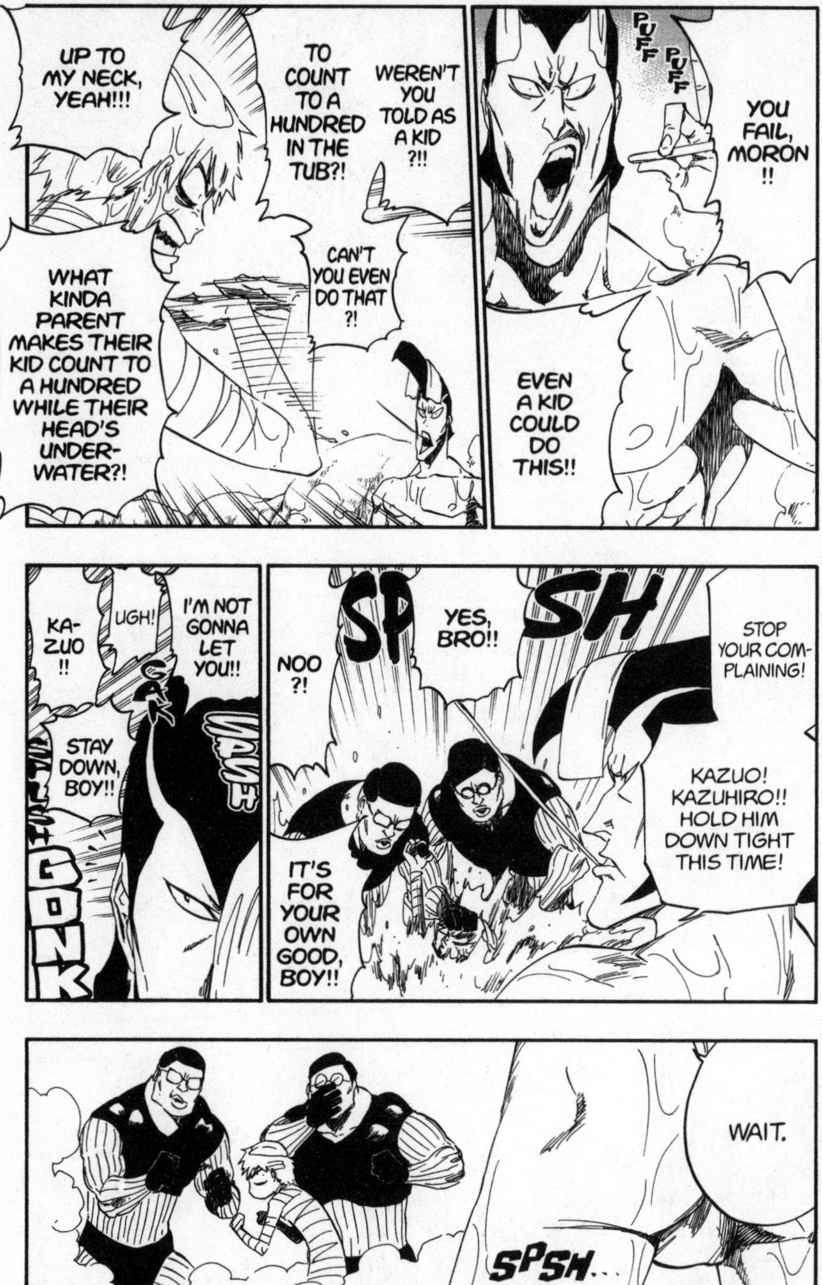
PUFF PUFF
YOU FAIL, MORON!!
EVEN A KID COULD DO THIS!!
WEREN'T YOU TOLD AS A KID?!!
TO COUNT TO A HUNDRED IN THE TUB?!
UP TO MY NECK, YEAH!!!
CAN'T YOU EVEN DO THAT?!
WHAT KINDA PARENT MAKES THEIR KID COUNT TO A HUNDRED WHILE THEIR HEAD'S UNDER-WATER?!
SH
STOP YOUR COM-PLAINING!
KAZUO! KAZUHIRO!! HOLD HIM DOWN TIGHT THIS TIME!
YES, BRO!!
SP
NOO?!
IT'S FOR YOUR OWN GOOD, BOY!!
I'M NOT GONNA LET YOU!!
UGH!
GAK
SPSH
KA-ZUO!!
STAY DOWN, BOY!!
GONK
WAIT.
SPSH...

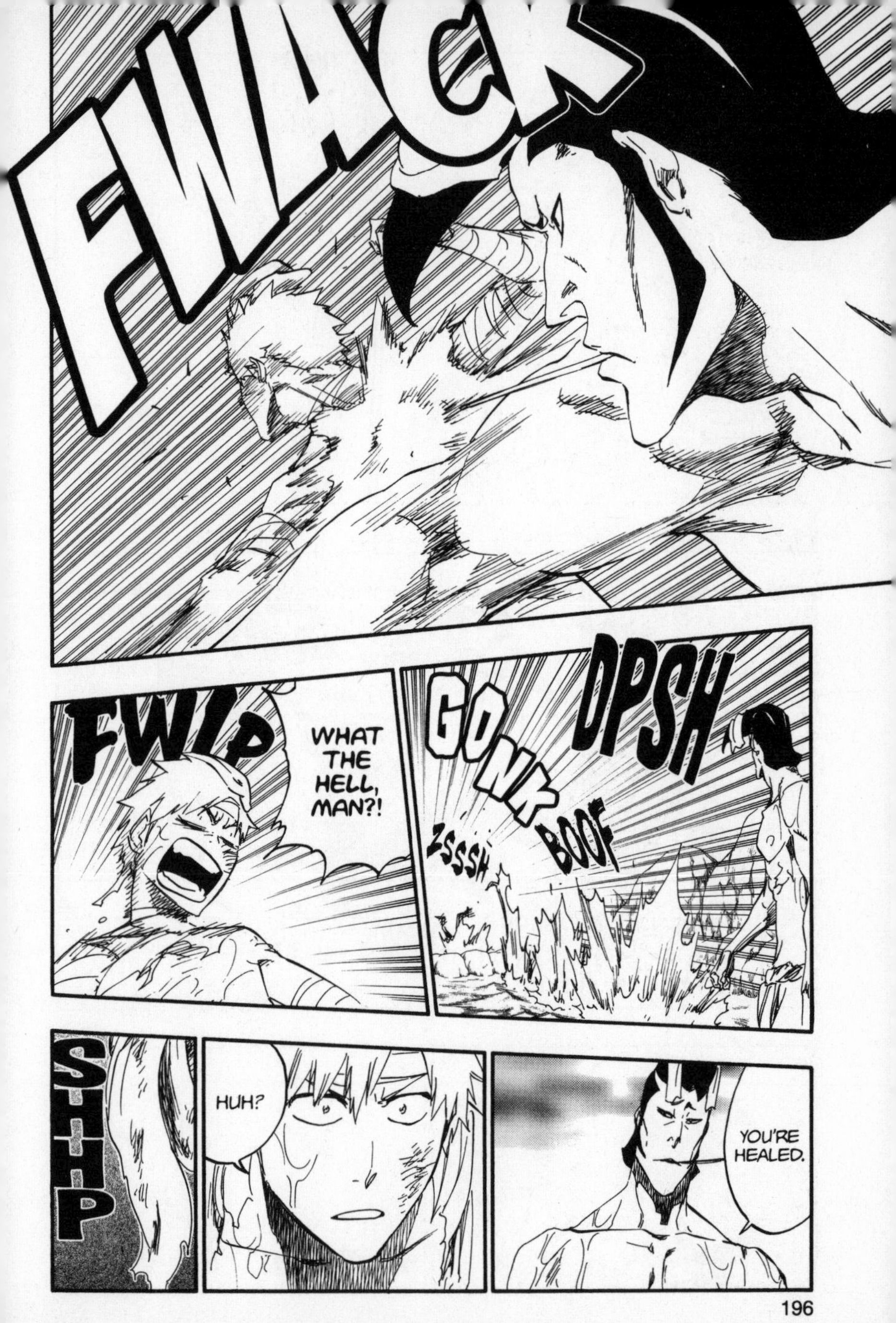
FWACK
DPSH
GONK
BOOF
ZSSSH
FWIP
WHAT THE HELL, MAN?!
YOU'RE HEALED.
HUH?
SHHP

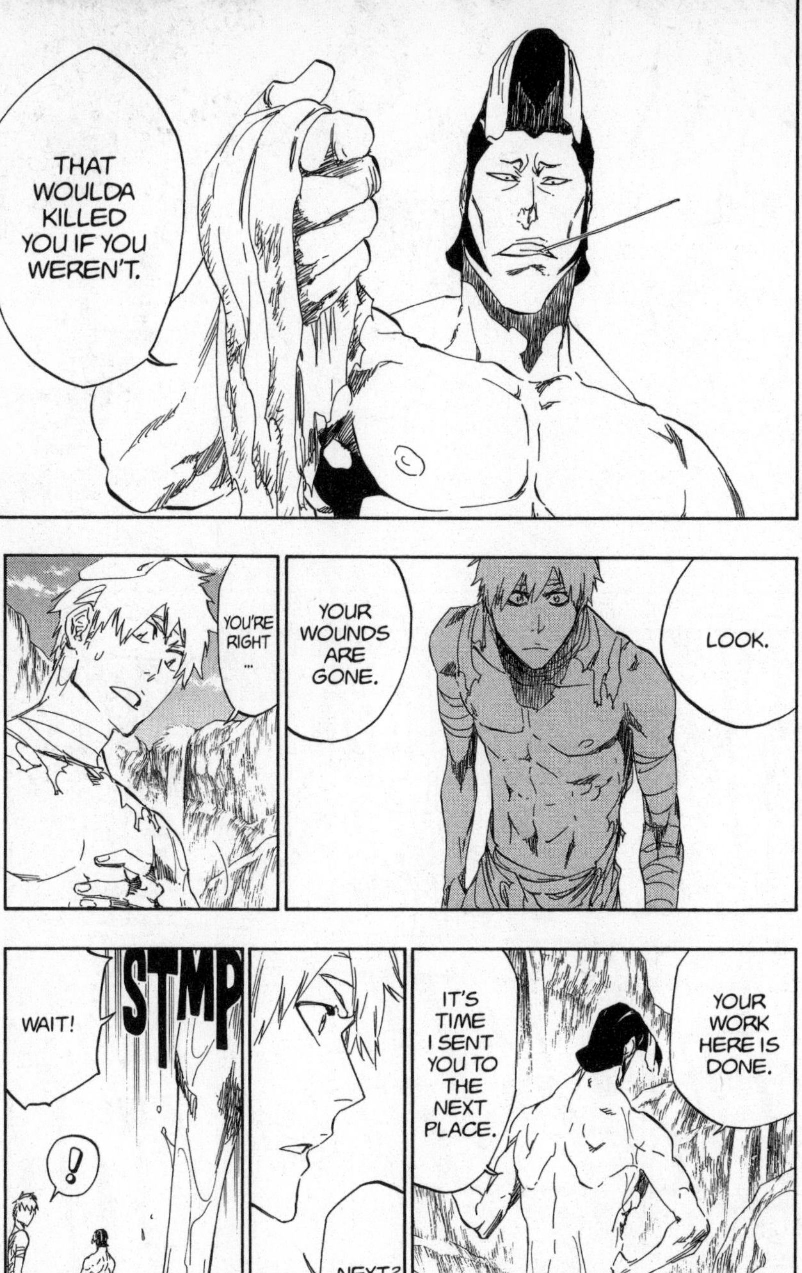
THAT WOULDA KILLED YOU IF YOU WEREN'T.
LOOK.
YOUR WOUNDS ARE GONE.
YOU'RE RIGHT ...
YOUR WORK HERE IS DONE.
IT'S TIME I SENT YOU TO THE NEXT PLACE.
NEXT?
STMP
WAIT!
!

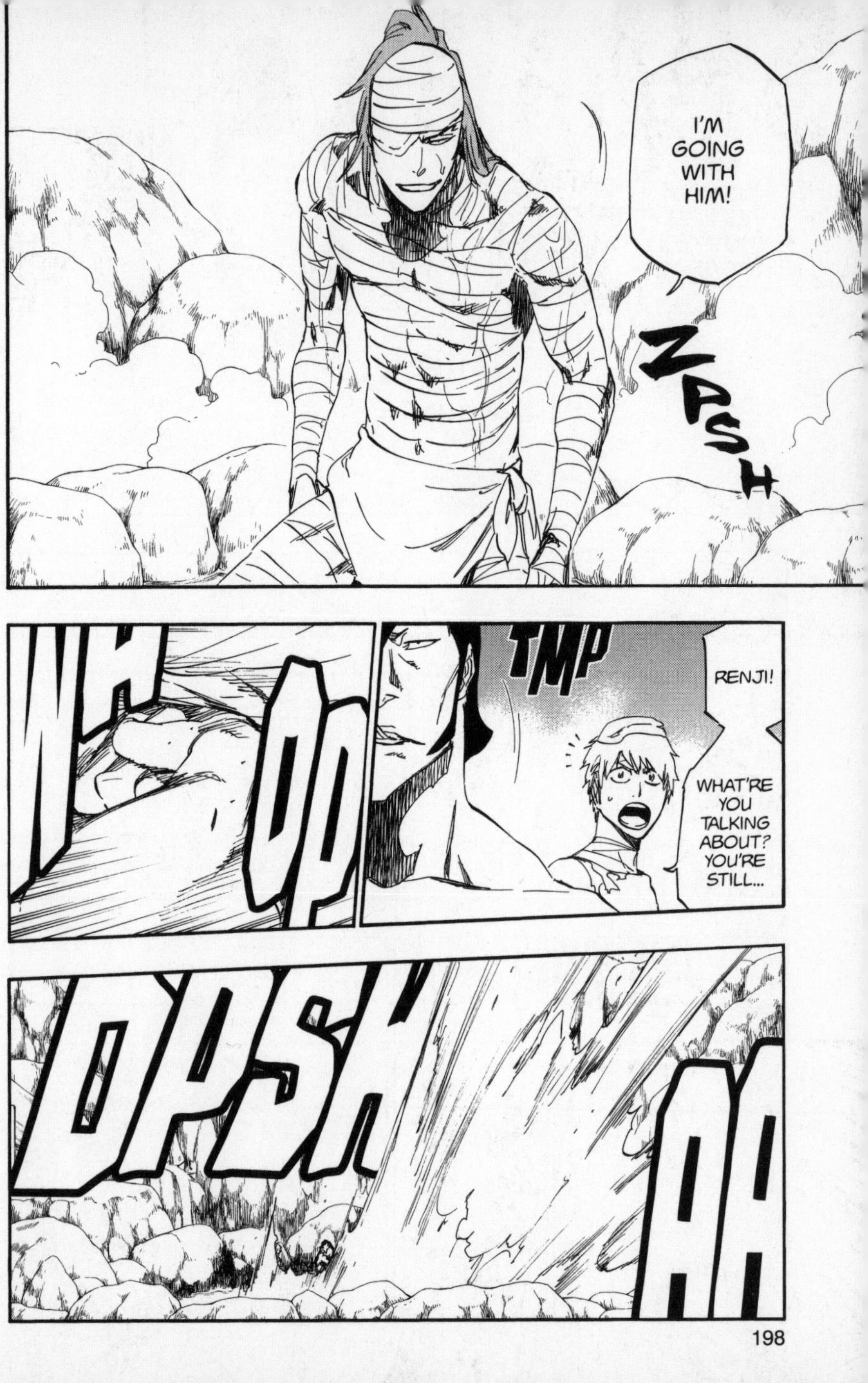
I'M GOING WITH HIM!
ZPSH
TMP
RENJI!
WHAT'RE YOU TALKING ABOUT? YOU'RE STILL...
DPSH

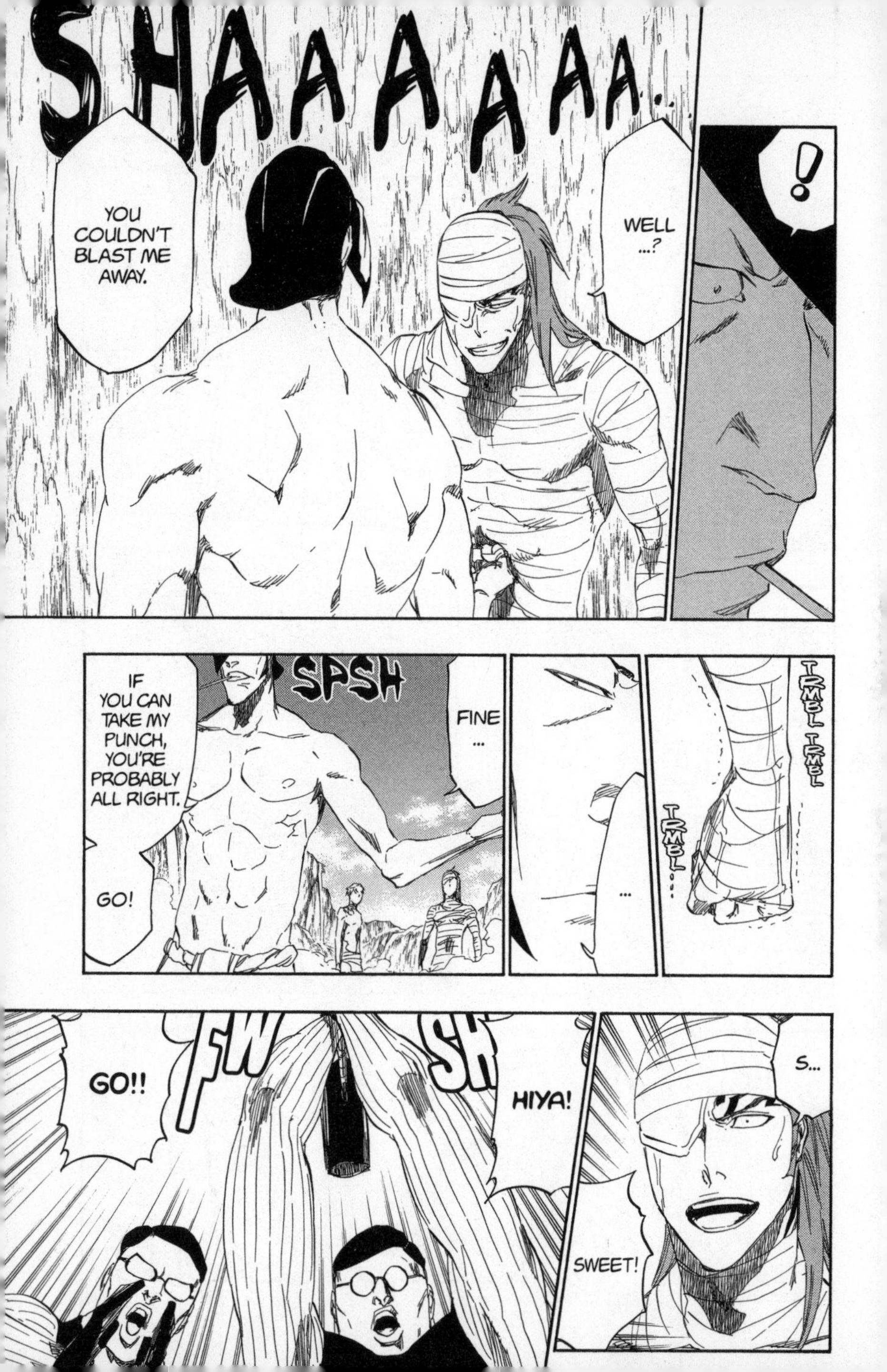
!
SHAAAAAA..
WELL ...?
YOU COULDN'T BLAST ME AWAY.
TRMBL TRMBL
TRMBL...
...
FINE ...
SPSH
IF YOU CAN TAKE MY PUNCH, YOU'RE PROBABLY ALL RIGHT.
GO!
S...
SWEET!
HIYA!
FW SH
GO!!

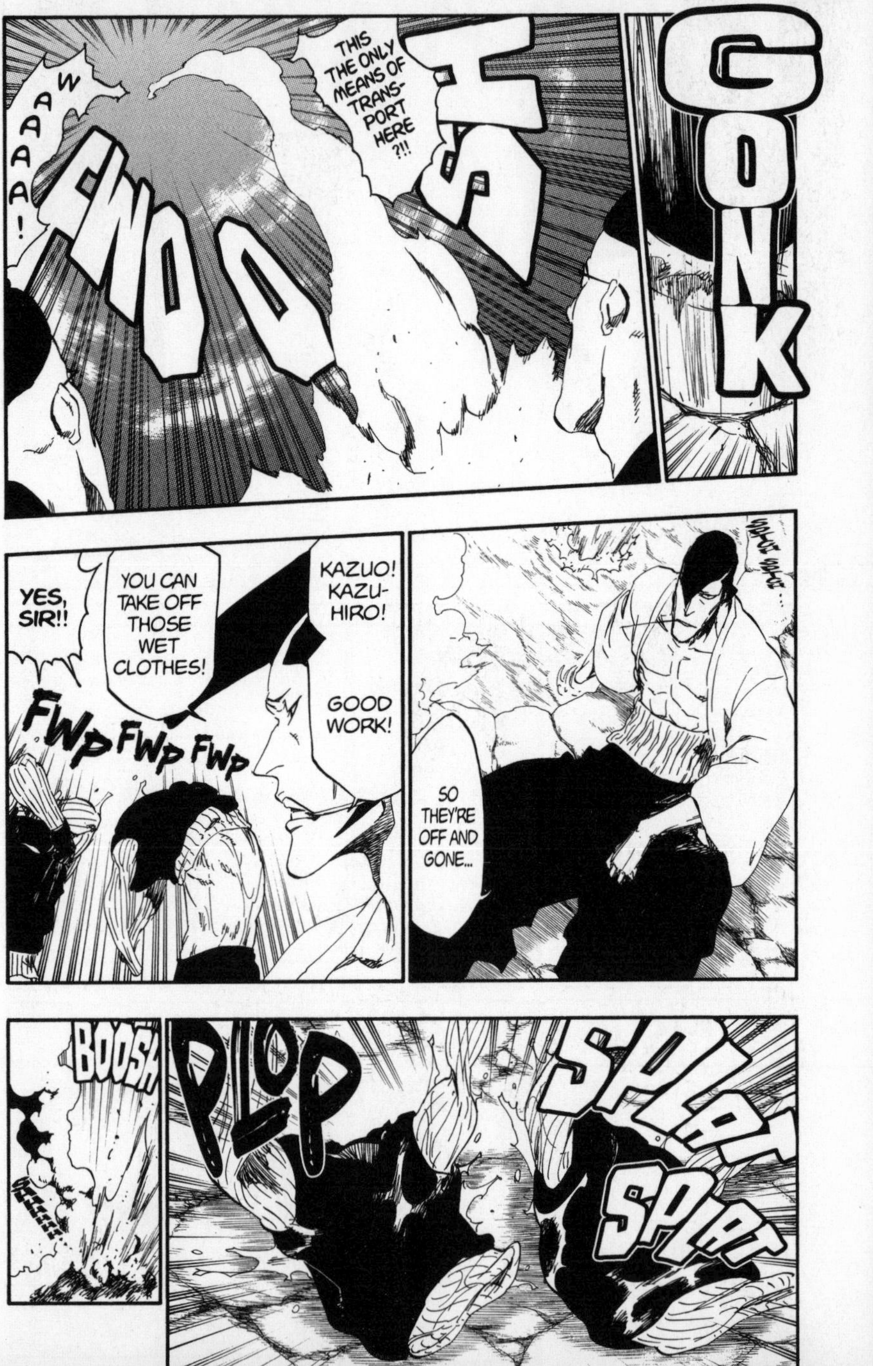
GONK
IS
THIS THE ONLY MEANS OF TRANS-PORT HERE ?!!
FWOOO
WAAAAA!
SO THEY'RE OFF AND GONE...
KAZUO! KAZU-HIRO!
GOOD WORK!
YOU CAN TAKE OFF THOSE WET CLOTHES!
YES, SIR!!
FWP FWP FWP
SPLAT
SPLAT
PLOP
BOOSH

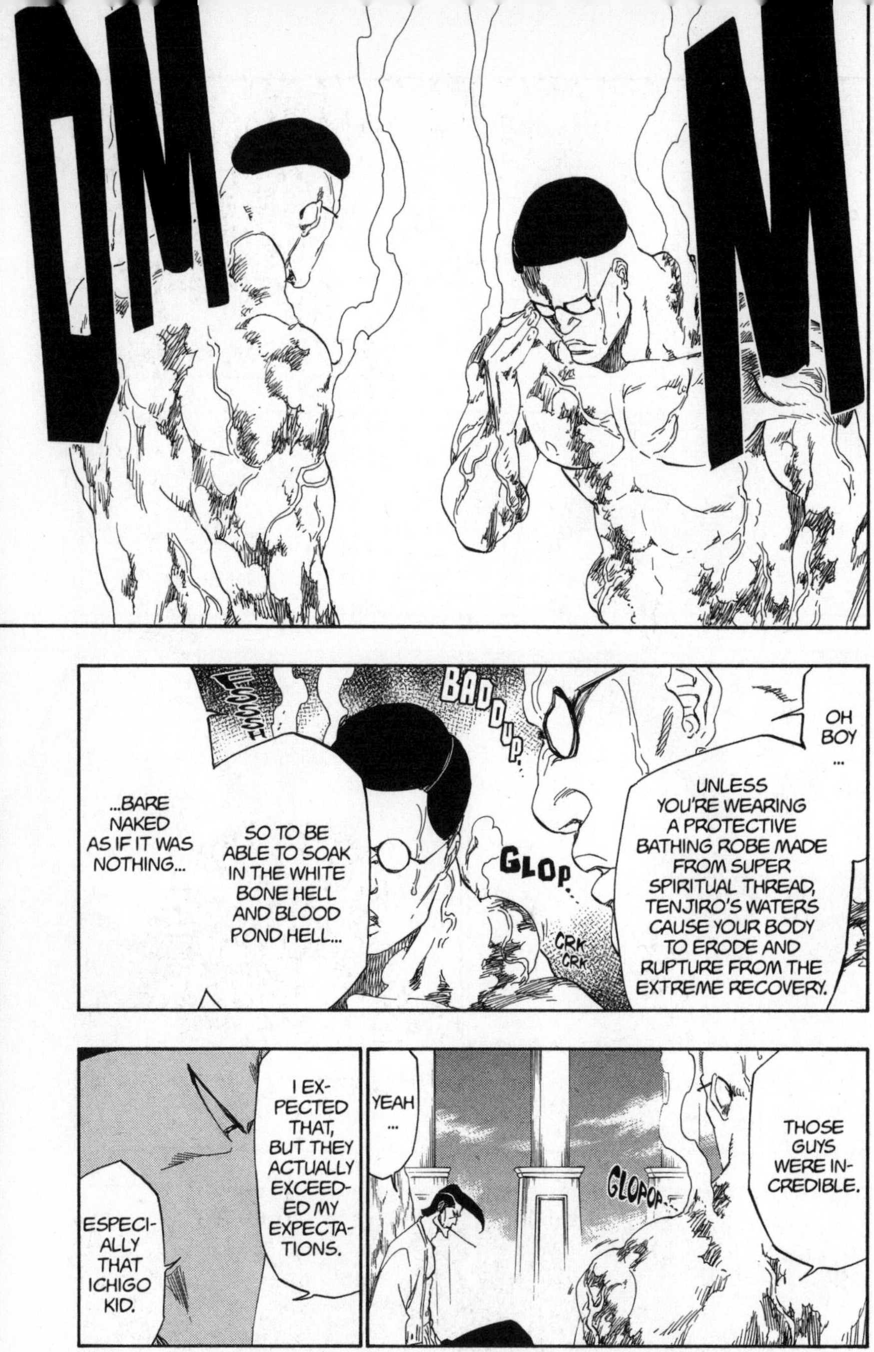
DM
M
OH BOY ...
UNLESS YOU'RE WEARING A PROTECTIVE BATHING ROBE MADE FROM SUPER SPIRITUAL THREAD, TENJIRO'S WATERS CAUSE YOUR BODY TO ERODE AND RUPTURE FROM THE EXTREME RECOVERY.
BADDUP..
GLOP...
CRK CRK
FSSSH
SO TO BE ABLE TO SOAK IN THE WHITE BONE HELL AND BLOOD POND HELL...
...BARE NAKED AS IF IT WAS NOTHING...
THOSE GUYS WERE IN-CREDIBLE.
GLOPOP...
YEAH ...
I EX-PECTED THAT, BUT THEY ACTUALLY EXCEED-ED MY EXPECTA-TIONS.
ESPECI-ALLY THAT ICHIGO KID.

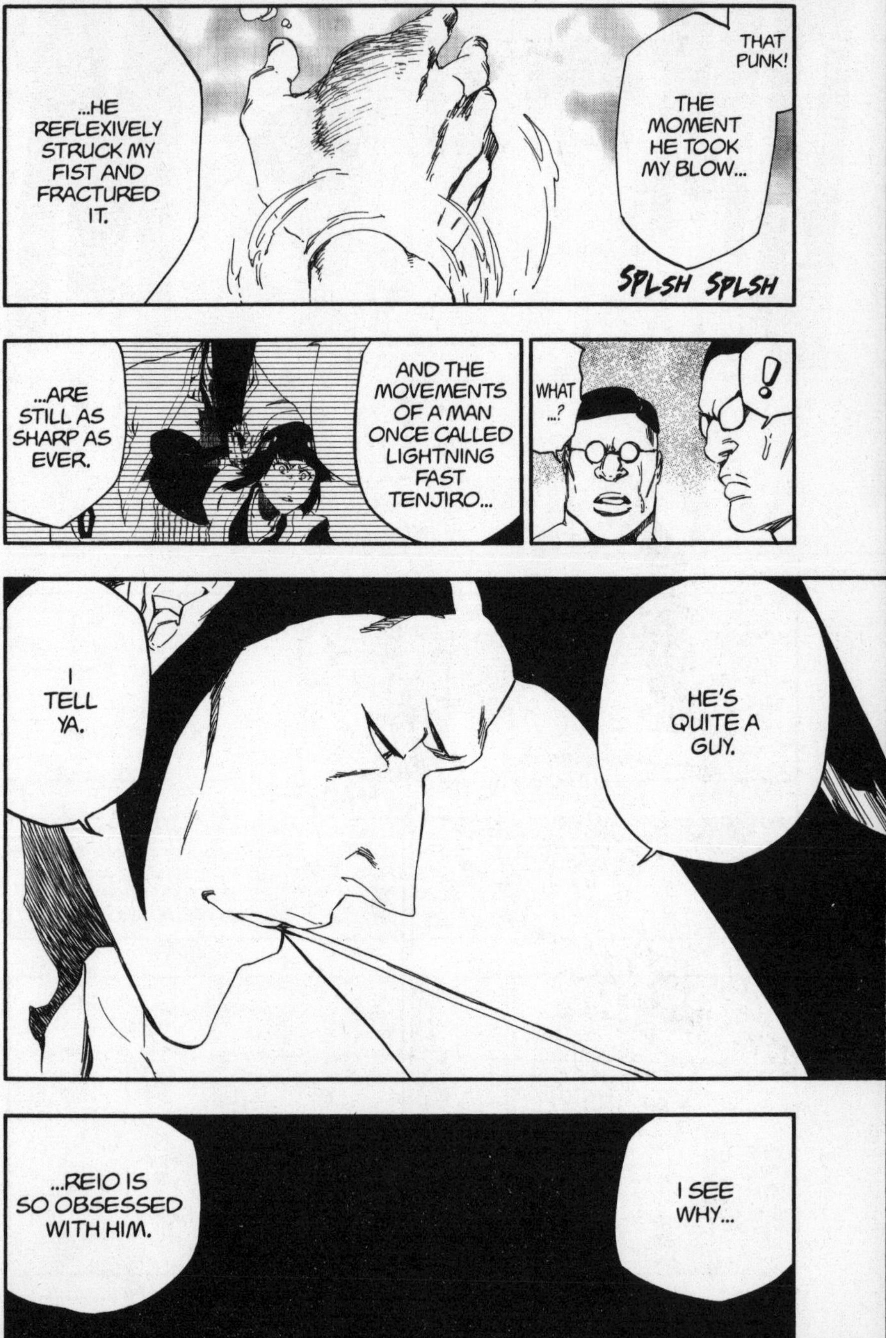
THAT PUNK!
THE MOMENT HE TOOK MY BLOW...
SPLSH SPLSH
...HE REFLEXIVELY STRUCK MY FIST AND FRACTURED IT.
!
WHAT ...?
AND THE MOVEMENTS OF A MAN ONCE CALLED LIGHTNING FAST TENJIRO...
...ARE STILL AS SHARP AS EVER.
HE'S QUITE A GUY.
I TELL YA.
I SEE WHY...
...REIO IS SO OBSESSED WITH HIM.

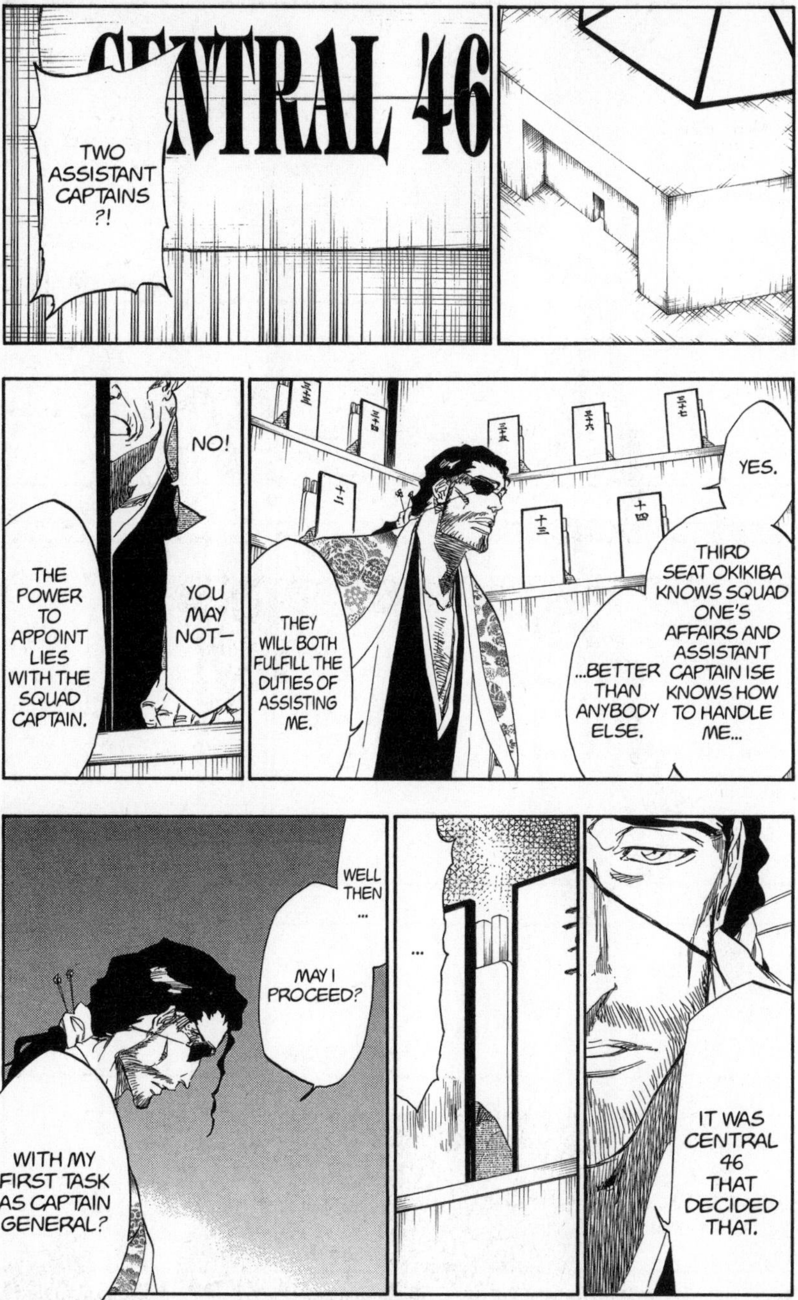
NTRAL 46
TWO ASSISTANT CAPTAINS ?!
YES.
THIRD SEAT OKIKIBA KNOWS SQUAD ONE'S AFFAIRS AND ASSISTANT CAPTAIN ISE KNOWS HOW TO HANDLE ME...
...BETTER THAN ANYBODY ELSE.
THEY WILL BOTH FULFILL THE DUTIES OF ASSISTING ME.
NO!
YOU MAY NOT—
THE POWER TO APPOINT LIES WITH THE SQUAD CAPTAIN.
IT WAS CENTRAL 46 THAT DECIDED THAT.
...
WELL THEN ...
MAY I PROCEED?
WITH MY FIRST TASK AS CAPTAIN GENERAL?

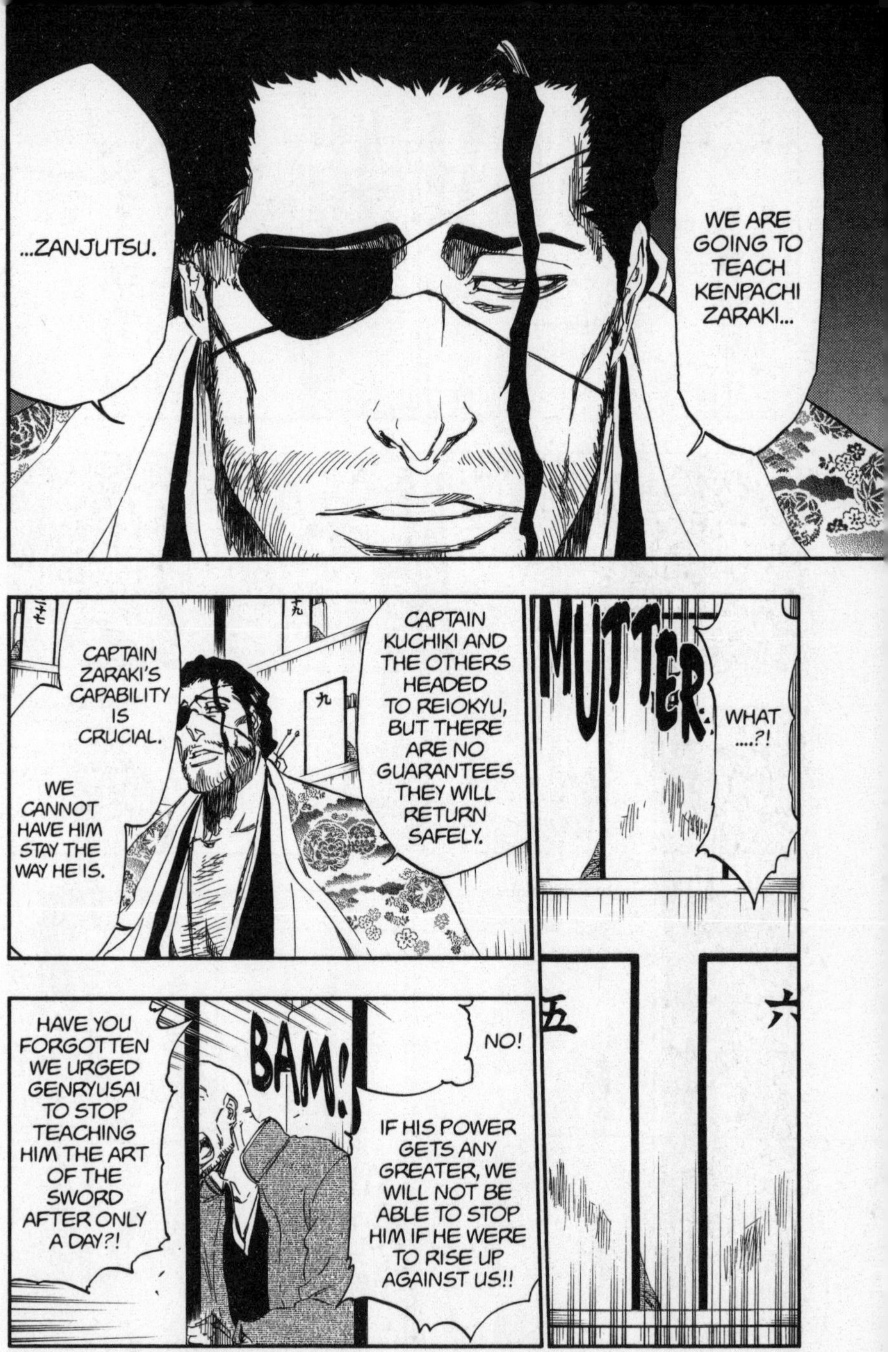
WE ARE GOING TO TEACH KENPACHI ZARAKI...
...ZANJUTSU.
MUTTER
WHAT ....?!
CAPTAIN KUCHIKI AND THE OTHERS HEADED TO REIOKYU, BUT THERE ARE NO GUARANTEES THEY WILL RETURN SAFELY.
CAPTAIN ZARAKI'S CAPABILITY IS CRUCIAL.
WE CANNOT HAVE HIM STAY THE WAY HE IS.
五
六
NO!
BAM!
IF HIS POWER GETS ANY GREATER, WE WILL NOT BE ABLE TO STOP HIM IF HE WERE TO RISE UP AGAINST US!!
HAVE YOU FORGOTTEN WE URGED GENRYUSAI TO STOP TEACHING HIM THE ART OF THE SWORD AFTER ONLY A DAY?!

READ THIS WAY

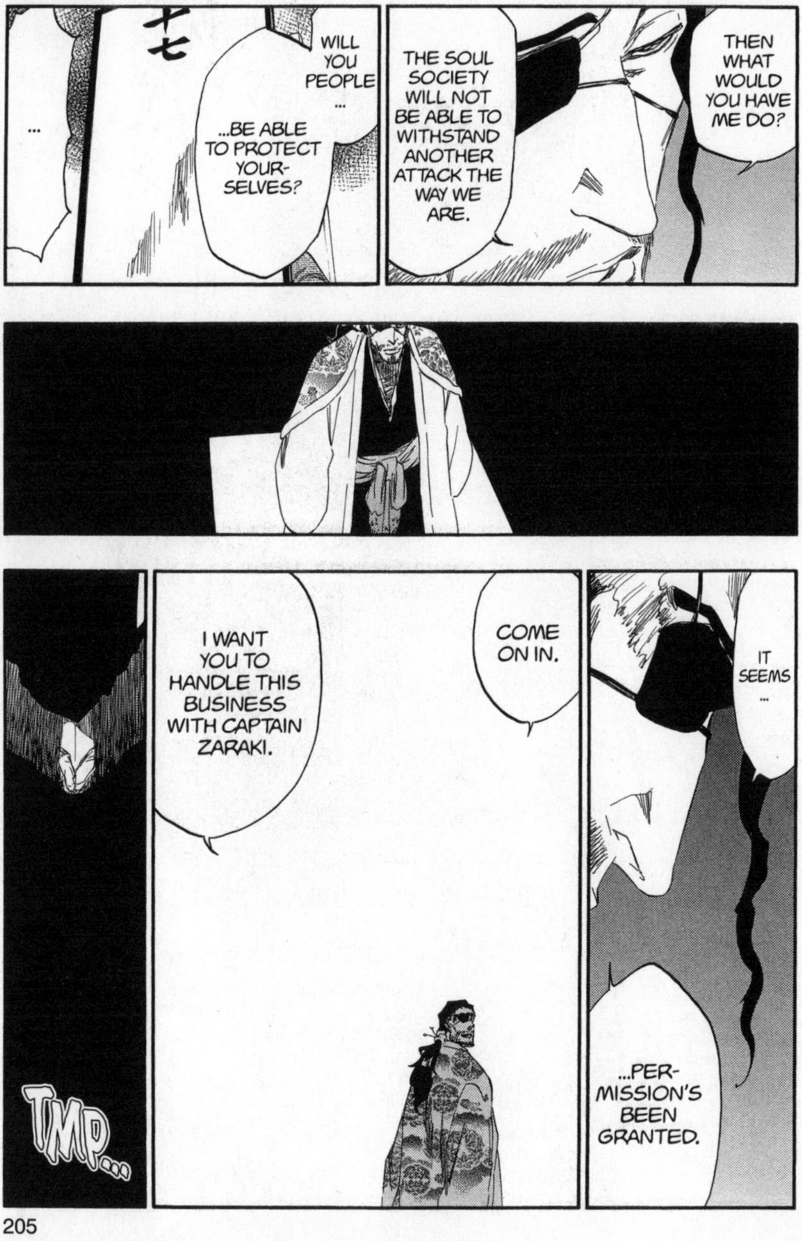
THEN WHAT WOULD YOU HAVE ME DO?
THE SOUL SOCIETY WILL NOT BE ABLE TO WITHSTAND ANOTHER ATTACK THE WAY WE ARE.
WILL YOU PEOPLE...
...BE ABLE TO PROTECT YOUR-SELVES?
...
IT SEEMS...
...PER-MISSION'S BEEN GRANTED.
COME ON IN.
I WANT YOU TO HANDLE THIS BUSINESS WITH CAPTAIN ZARAKI.
TMP...

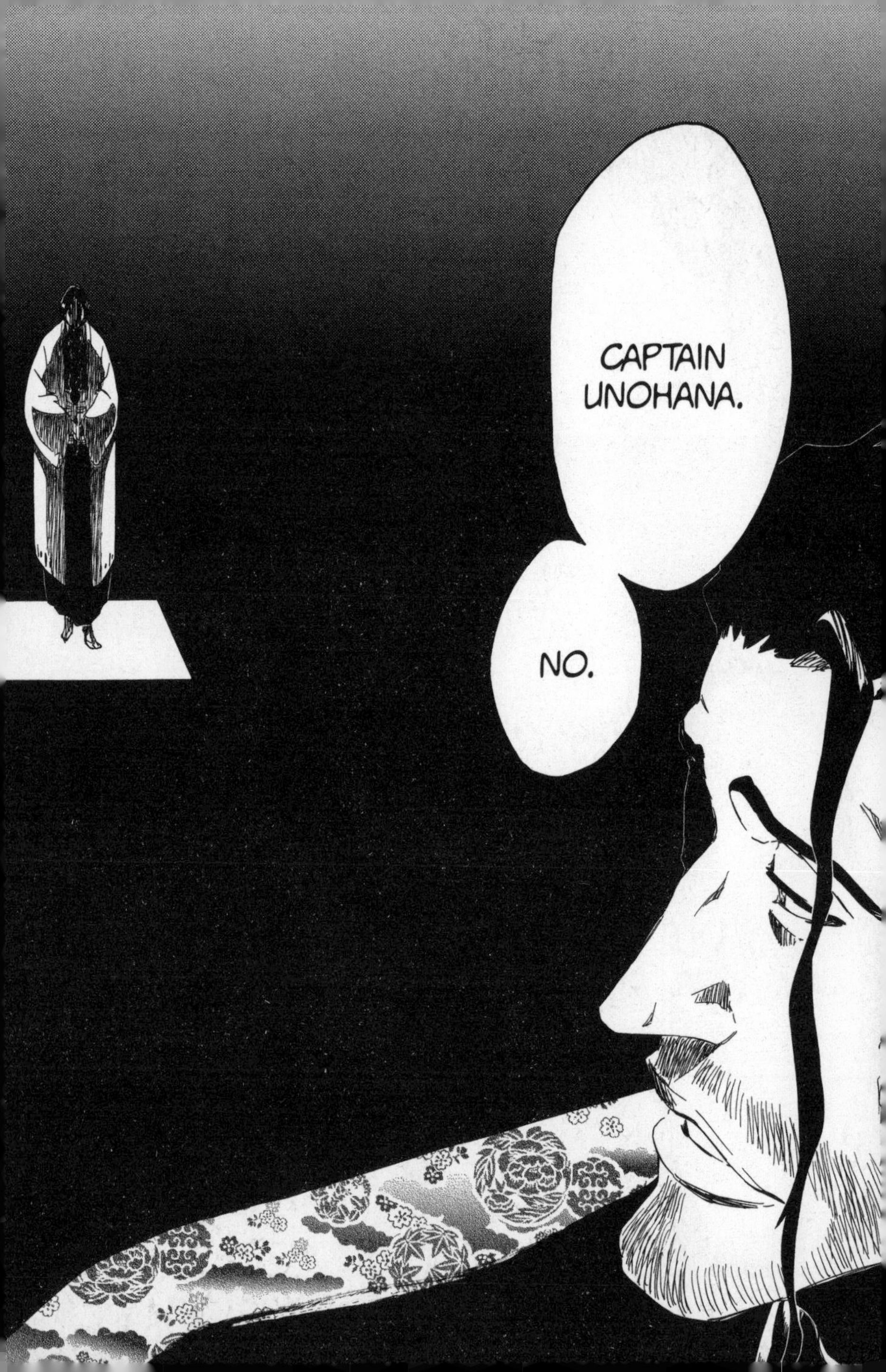
CAPTAIN UNOHANA.
NO.

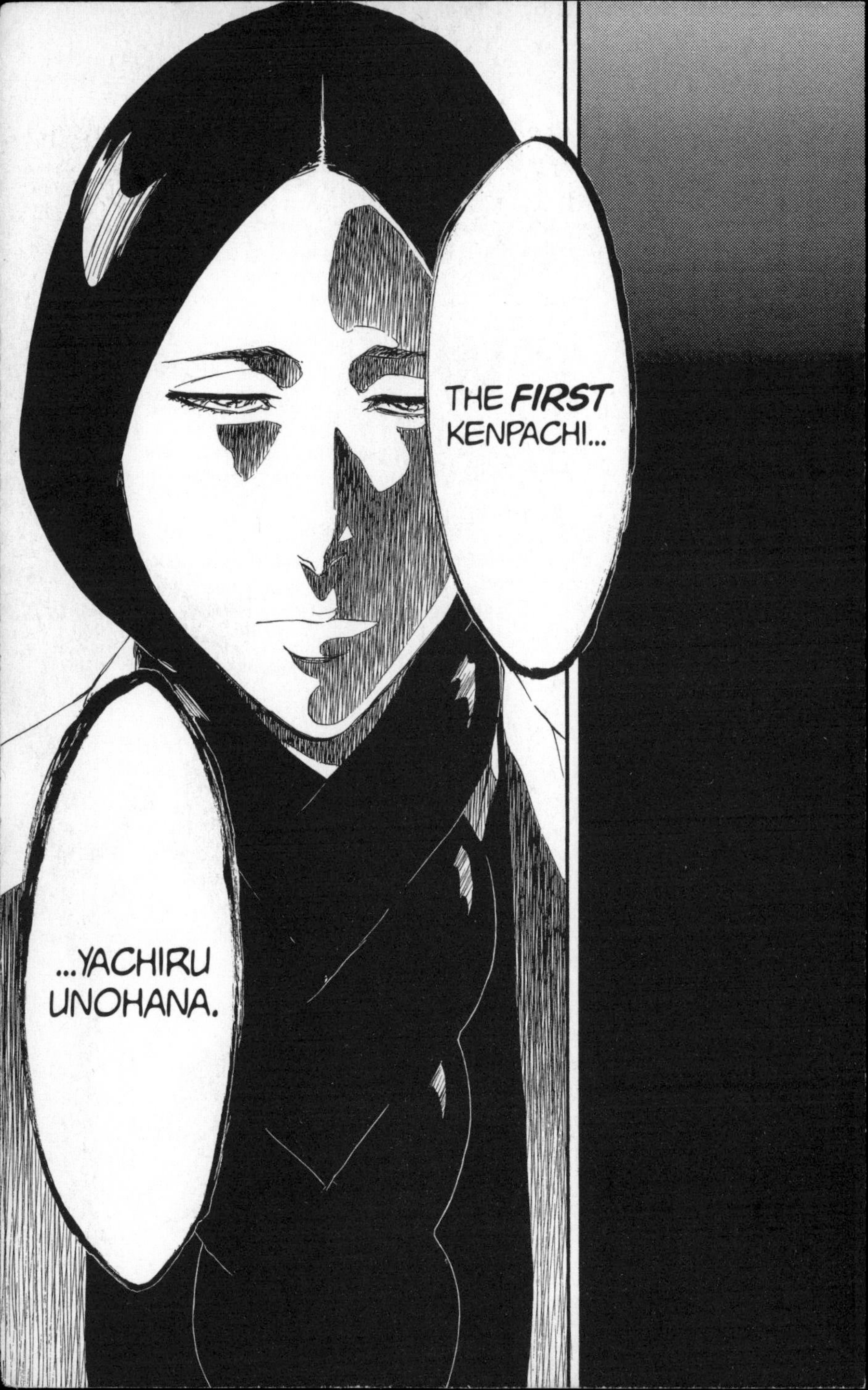
THE FIRST KENPACHI...
...YACHIRU UNOHANA.

You're Reading in the Wrong Direction!!

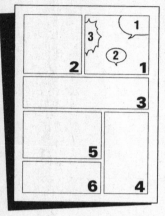

Whoops! Guess what? You're starting at the wrong end of the comic!

…It's true! In keeping with the original Japanese format, **Bleach** is meant to be read from right to left, starting in the upper-right corner.

Unlike English, which is read from left to right, Japanese is read from right to left, meaning that action, sound effects and word-balloon order are completely reversed… something which can make readers unfamiliar with Japanese feel pretty backwards themselves. For this reason, manga or Japanese comics published in the U.S. in English have sometimes been published "flopped"—that is, printed in exact reverse order, as though seen from the other side of a mirror.

By flopping pages, U.S. publishers can avoid confusing readers, but the compromise is not without its downside. For one thing, a character in a flopped manga series who once wore in the original Japanese version a T-shirt emblazoned with "M A Y" (as in "the merry month of") now wears one which reads "Y A M"! Additionally, many manga creators in Japan are themselves unhappy with the process, as some feel the mirror-imaging of their art skews their original intentions.

We are proud to bring you Tite Kubo's **Bleach** in the original unflopped format. For now, though, turn to the other side of the book and let the adventure begin…!

—Editor

◀ • • • • • •